D1507760

WAYS OF TEACHING

RONALD T. HYMAN
Rutgers University

WAYS OF TEACHING
2nd Edition

J. B. LIPPINCOTT COMPANY
New York   Hagerstown   Philadelphia   San Francisco

WAYS OF TEACHING, Second Edition

Copyright © 1974 by Ronald T. Hyman

Library of Congress Cataloging in Publication Data

Hyman, Ronald T.
  Ways of Teaching.

  Includes bibliographies.
  1. Teaching. I. Title.

LB1027.H95 1974   371.3   73–18172
ISBN 0–397–47301–X

for Suzanne

Contents

Contents

Preface

Just as the original edition of *Ways of Teaching* grew out of my own experience as a teacher and researcher, this second edition is an outgrowth of additional experience enriched and strengthened by the many welcome suggestions for improvement made by teachers and students. The aim and purpose of the book remain the same: to offer the reader a broad view of the various ways of teaching based upon a concept of the art that I believe most teachers implicitly accept.

For this edition, a chapter on behavioral objectives has been added, in addition to tape-scripts and analyses of valuative and non-valuative discussion lessons, step-by-step strategies for using various methods, and several sections designed to clarify my concept of teaching.

The organization of *Ways of Teaching* remains otherwise unchanged, except for numerous minor revisions and alterations throughout the body of the text. As in the first edition, each section is preceded by an introduction which offers a rationale for a particular method, raising the key question, "What are the arguments for using this way of teaching?" Chapters treating specific methods most commonly used follow: the Socratic dialogue, discovery, lecture, recitation, sociodrama and simulation games—each with concrete examples to demonstrate the method in use and to serve the teacher as models for reference in refining his own teaching techniques.

Additional chapters deal with three broad aspects of teaching methodology or related matters. The chapter on questioning is based on recent research into classroom verbal behavior and presents several approaches to categorizing questions.

A final chapter is devoted to the observation and evaluation of teaching and includes three illustrative instruments from recent research on direct classroom observation. The steps necessary for evaluating teaching are covered and the justification for each step is discussed.

The warm reception given the first edition of *Ways of Teaching* by teachers and students encourages me to believe they will find this revision an improvement and a more usable instrument to facilitate their study of ways of teaching. Suggestions for use in future revisions of the book will be most welcome.

Let me here thank several people for their assistance and encouragement: Suzanne Hyman, Beverly Amick, John Lake, and Bea Mayes.

RONALD T. HYMAN

New Brunswick, New Jersey
February, 1974

The *A B C*'s of Teaching

A is for Asking questions.

Asking questions is central to teaching—more so for the student than for the teacher. As a teacher, rather than asking a question, try leading your students to ask themselves what they know and how they know it.

B is for Books.

It is often more educational to write a book than to read one. Try it with your students.

C is for Curriculum.

Curriculum, put very simply, is what you want to teach. Have you considered that children are compelled by law to attend school? Is your curriculum worth it?

D is for Dialogue and Discipline problems.

Which have you had lately with your students? Try dialogue and see what happens to discipline.

E is for Exams and Evaluation.

Both need to be played down so that we can get on with E for Educating. Remember how you felt when you were constantly examined and evaluated? (See the letter *G*.)

F is for Firing line.

Firing line is a term some people frequently use when talking about classroom teaching. Since the term stems from a war perspective, keep in mind that our actions are shaped by our perspectives.

G is for Grading.

To grade someone is to judge him. To judge someone it is necessary to have both significant facts *and* criteria. Which ones do you use? Why these?

H is for Homework.

Homework is a funny thing: Students hate doing it and teachers hate checking it. Why do you assign it? Is this a valid reason?

I is for Independence and Intellectual Integrity.

Independence and intellectual integrity may not be the only elements in teaching, but they are necessary ones. Do you strive for them? In yourself? In your students?

J is for Jail.

Students often think of school as a jail. They see the teacher as jailer and themselves as prisoners. Needless to say, this is a destructive image. What can you do to eliminate it?

K is for Knowledge.

Many teachers focus on knowledge for their students. But what is knowledge? How do you know when you know something? Is this something worth knowing?

L is for Listening.

Teaching requires the teacher to listen to his students with all his powers of perception.

M is for Music.

Music offers such terms as harmony, beauty, tempo, rhythm, balance, orchestration, and style. Have you considered using these terms to view teaching?

N is for Nongraded schools.

Nongradedness allows for flexibility. Why should you place all students in a grade by age and require them to do the same things at the same time? Why keep them all together for a whole year?

O is for Observe.

Observe the advice of the ancient Hebrews: To be a wise teacher you must always remain a student.

P is for Principles.

We strive to teach principles. For example, in teaching a person to dance the waltz we teach him how to keep in time with the music —not merely to dance in a particular ballroom or to a particular Strauss piece. How do you teach principles?

Q is for Question and Query (both have the same Latin root, quaerere, *and are related to "inquiry").*

A question spurs thinking, and children are natural questioners. What are you doing to encourage your students in class to ask questions? Are the questions we ask or the answers we offer the mark of our quality?

R is for Relevance.

It may sound like a cliché by this time, but the teacher does start out with a considerable advantage if his students come to class excited and interested; they will be if they are dealing with issues which touch directly upon their lives.

S is for Student.

Our aim in teaching is to help the student to enhance his capacity for independent action. How have you helped your students to become independent?

T is for Thinking—critical, reflective thinking.

Teach a student, not what to think, but how to think. Is there anything more powerful you can teach him? How do you do this?

U is for Understanding.

We want our students to learn math and music but, more important, to understand them. To do this you have to understand the students.

V is for Values.

When teaching knowledge and skills, we teach values, implicitly and often explicitly. Which values do you teach? Which way? Which ones should you teach?

W is for Writing.

Writing is one of the basic three R's. Which other communication skills should we teach? Dancing? Photography? Playing an instrument?

X is for X the unknown.

There are many unknowns in teaching. For example, how do you precisely characterize the good teacher?

Y is left blank.

This is to demonstrate that a teacher doesn't have to know everything, despite student expectations. The sooner we come to this understanding, the better off we'll be. (Y could be for You—the teacher of whom student expectations will be enormous. Can you deliver?)

Z is for Zonked.

A teacher who has taught his lesson well will no doubt be zonked—pooped —bushed—or whatever term you use. Why do some people still think June vacation is for students only?

Reprinted with permission from the March, 1971, issue of the *Phi Delta Kappan.* Copyright March, 1971, by Phi Delta Kappa, Inc. Vol. 52, No. 7, pp. 452–453.

I *An Overview*

I Developing a Concept of Teaching

Before we can analyze teaching methodology or describe the various ways of teaching, we must first evolve a viable *concept* of teaching. The need for clarifying the word's meaning is evident to almost anyone who has engaged in conversation about it. The concept of teaching presented will not be limited to teaching performed in schools. Nor, as an alternative, shall teaching be conceived to be whatever a teacher does, though it has been defined in this manner (20:65). We propose to analyze the common usages of the word *teaching*, examine alternate (and possibly opposing) aspects and definitions of the word, and, then, suggest a usage for the purposes of this book.

(*Humpty-D umpty speaking*) "... and that shows that there are three hundred and sixty-four days when you might get unbirthday presents—"

"Certainly," said Alice.

"And only *one* for birthday presents, you know. There's glory for you!"

"I don't know what you mean by 'glory,'" Alice said.

Humpty-Dumpty smiled contemptuously. "Of course you don't— till I tell you. I meant 'there's a nice knock-down argument for you.'"

"But 'glory' doesn't mean 'a nice knock-down argument,'" Alice objected.

"When I use a word," Humpty-Dumpty said, in a rather scornful tone, "it means just what I choose it to mean—neither more nor less."

"The question is," said Alice, "whether you *can* make words mean so many different things."

"The question is," said Humpty-Dumpty, "which is to be master—that's all" (12:190).

Importance of the Question

It must be established, first, that there is a need for understanding what teaching is. Then, subsequent questions about it will not be merely semantic ones. On the contrary, answers to them will have implications both for the act of teaching and for research on teaching. First, then, there is the need of the prospective teacher to understand his chosen profession. Somewhere in his preservice preparation, the college student sets out to observe teaching as it occurs. He may do so by watching films as part of his college course, by visiting schools on a field trip, when he begins his practice teaching, or even when he looks critically at the teaching of his own college instructors. But what shall he observe? Unless he knows what teaching is, he will not know what to look for. If he sees Mr. Jones in front of the room (Usually the teacher stands there—Why?) straightening his tie, shall he call this teaching? When Mr. Jones assigns three exercises for homework, is this teaching? Obviously, not all the teacher's classroom activities should be called teaching. But, then, which ones should the prospective teacher observe?

Second, there is the need of the educational researcher to understand exactly what he is investigating. Educators perpetually investigate teaching with the ultimate goal of improving it. What is to be improved, however, must first be understood. After this, weaknesses and necessary changes must be considered. But the starting point is certainly a concept of what teaching is. Furthermore, teaching can be investigated in many different ways. And the investigatory method chosen depends largely on the concept of teaching involved. Marie Hughes, who pioneered in the assessment of teaching in the 1950s, put it this way: "There are many ways to analyze the records of actions in the classroom situation. The manner of analysis is controlled to a large degree by the definition accepted for teaching" (28:26). Thus it is clear that the empirical investigator must determine his definition of teaching *before* he begins his attempts to gather data. If he does not, he has no idea which data to gather. Definition precedes investigation.

Third, laymen and professionals spend considerable time evaluating teaching. For example, a principal is required to evaluate teachers in his school periodically. This is especially true during the first few years of a teacher's career in a particular school system. The principal must evaluate the teacher in order to be able to recommend that the school board grant or deny tenure. Clearly, the principal must know what it is he is evaluating and must have criteria for so doing. Many steps are required in an evaluation procedure, as will be shown in a later chapter. Here it is sufficient to say that the first step is the determination of exactly what is to be evaluated (3).

Fourth, the working teacher must know what teaching is because his concept of teaching guides his behavior. He can justly say to himself, "I was hired as a teacher. I shall now proceed to teach. I shall try not to engage in behavior deemed as non-teaching." For such a teacher the definition of teaching serves as a guide to his future activity. Here the emphasis is on the connection between a person's concepts and his general activity. A man's concept of *father* clearly guides the way he will relate to a teenage son. "A concept is a rule. When someone learns a concept, without exception, what he has learned is a rule, a rule of language, or more generally, a rule of behavior" (25:284).

Winch uses the example of war to illustrate the role and power of concepts in human life.

The idea of war, for instance ... was not simply invented by people who wanted to *explain* what happens when societies come into armed conflict. It is an idea which provides the criteria of what is appropriate in the behavior of members of the conflicting societies.

Because my country is at war there are certain things which I must not do. My behavior is governed, one could say, by my concept of myself as a member of a belligerent country. The concept of war belongs *essentially* to my behavior (53:127–128).

Similarly, the teacher's concept of teaching is essential to his performance as a teacher. On the basis of his concept he will determine the appropriateness of certain activities. Is he indeed *teaching* his students when he insists that honesty is the best policy? When he claims that the Allies blundered at Munich and encouraged World War II? When he demands that a student spell *though* as *t-h-o-u-g-h* one hundred times? To help answer these questions for himself, he will refer to his concept of teaching.

From these four points it is evident that the development of a concept of teaching is not trivial but central to the teacher's task. Indeed, the revered Socrates spent his days asking questions about the concepts his fellow Athenians held. John Wilson, the British educational philosopher, justifies such an approach (using *education* rather than *teaching*) in the following way:

... it would be a mistake to write off as useless all general discussion which takes its starting-point from a word like "education," however imprecise such discussion may be, and however many logical varieties of answers may be given to such general questions. For the most valuable result of such discussion is that, perhaps only half-consciously, we map out the area of meaning of a particular concept, and sketch its logical geography by contrasting it with other concepts, paying attention to borderline cases when we are in doubt, considering model cases which we know to form part of the concept's geography, and so forth. This is not merely an academic exercise, for by it—and by it alone —we come to appreciate certain salient and important features of the general landscape (52:24–25).

Level of Meaning

Teaching is what may be called an accommodating word (35). That is to say, we can use *teaching* at different levels of meaning in our daily conversation. We can even use the word differently in a single sentence. For example, "George Jones teaches at Central School, but he does not teach on Monday afternoons since at that time he attends a special class at the university." It is clear that in this example the first use of *teaching* refers to George Jones's occupation. We now know what Jones does for a living. He is a teacher and not a janitor or painter or nurse or salesman or doctor or quarterback or pilot. The second use of *teaching* in this example refers to the general enterprise of teaching, the overall cluster of activities which we associate with a teacher, such as explaining, demonstrating, questioning, attending faculty meetings, advising students, and taking attendance. But, though this sentence has two different meanings for *teach*, it is not difficult to understand, since many words in everyday language have multiple meanings.

The word *teach* has a third level of meaning, and it is this level which is of particular significance for this book. This level refers, not to the occupation or general enterprise of teaching, but to the act of teaching. This level of meaning appears in the following example: "Jones stopped talking about the World Series with the class and began teaching algebra." In this sentence it is clear that *teaching* refers to a specific cluster of activities which includes such acts as explaining, demonstrating, questioning, and motivating and which excludes such acts as patrolling the hall, chatting, taking attendance, sharpening pencils, distributing textbooks, and collecting homework papers.

This third level of meaning refers to the act of teaching, and it is to this level that we shall limit our attention in this book. This limitation is not to deny the importance of treating the dimensions of teaching which make it a significant occupation.

Nor does it deny the importance of the dimensions of teaching which lead a teacher to have a full, beneficial role as a faculty member responsible for the schooling of his students. Rather, by focusing on the interaction of teacher and student as they are engaged with some subject matter, we recognize that it is the act of teaching which is essential and without which there would be no raison d'être for faculty meetings, attendance reports, and conferences with parents. By focusing on the act of teaching rather than the occupation of teaching or the enterprise of teaching, we concentrate on the foundation of the teacher's activities.

Let us put it in a slightly different way, one that will also help us to focus in on the act of teaching (24:2–9). Let us list some activities which a teacher might do in the course of a week:

1. Questioning	11. Defining
2. Deducing	12. Attending faculty meetings
3. Motivating	13. Justifying
4. Evaluating	14. Making reports
5. Concluding	15. Chaperoning dances
6. Explaining	16. Collecting money
7. Comparing	17. Encouraging
8. Taking roll	18. Trusting
9. Testing	19. Respecting
10. Reinforcing	20. Patrolling halls

In light of the previous paragraphs, it should be clear that certain items refer to activities which the teacher does as part of his job but not when he is engaged in the act of teaching. For this reason such activities as taking roll, attending faculty meetings, making reports, collecting money, and chaperoning dances may be separated from the others and appropriately labeled *institutional acts*. The rest of the activities refer to the act of teaching but may be divided into two categories, *logical acts* and *strategic acts*. The list of twenty activities now looks like this:

Logical Acts	*Strategic Acts*	*Institutional Acts*
1. Deducing	1. Questioning	1. Chaperoning dances
2. Concluding	2. Motivating	2. Attending faculty
3. Explaining	3. Evaluating	meetings
4. Comparing	4. Testing	3. Taking roll
5. Defining	5. Reinforcing	4. Patrolling halls
6. Justifying	6. Encouraging	5. Collecting money
	7. Trusting	6. Making reports
	8. Respecting	

Logical acts in this list refer to the intellectual acts of thinking and reasoning in relation to some subject matter. Strategic acts refer to the teacher's plans and his way of directing students during teaching. Institutional acts refer to the way the teacher's job in a school is organized by those in charge. Not all acts belong precisely to one of these three categories since context and interpretation are important.

Nevertheless, further thought about these logical, strategic, and institutional acts leads us to the conclusion that it is possible to teach students without performing institutional acts whereas it is impossible to teach students without performing logical and strategic acts. It is entirely possible for a music teacher to teach his student the violin without ever attending a faculty meeting or filling out a grade report or chaperoning a dance or performing other institutional acts. On the other hand, it is impossible for that music teacher to avoid doing some logical acts and some strategic acts. If he does no logical acts or no strategic acts, it surely would be appropriate to say, "Well, whatever else it is, it isn't teaching." The logical and strategic acts are the essence of teaching, and without them there is no teaching.

In short, by concentrating on the logical and strategic acts we can keep in mind the focus of this book, the act of teaching. We shall devote our attention to understanding the act of teaching and to suggesting how a teacher might perform that act systematically, smoothly, appropriately, and with variety.

Relation to Learning

Usually a prime source of trouble people encounter when trying to arrive at a definition of teaching is determining the connection between teaching and learning (33). Specifically, must the activity result in learning in order to be called teaching? Consider these two definitions.

1. "In its generic sense, teaching is a system of actions intended to induce learning" (45:230).
2. "Teaching is what occurs when teachers by virtue of their instructional activities succeed wholly or in part in enabling pupils to learn" (19:119).

The difference between these two definitions is immediately apparent. The first requires only that teaching *intend* to induce learning, while the second requires it to *succeed*—that is, that the student learn. Which is correct? They both are if common usage is the criterion. *Teaching*, like *repairing*, among other words, can be used with a success meaning or just an intentional meaning. Which meaning the speaker intends is not always clear. (For example, "I spent the entire day repairing my lawn mower." Surely my activity was intentional. But did I succeed?) The word *teaching* is ambiguous in everyday language—we can and do use it in different ways. However, in professional use, such ambiguities must be avoided.

In this book, *teaching* shall be used in its intentional sense rather than its success sense for several reasons (40:42). Since the two strongest claims made by advocates of the success usage are not at all lost by using the intentional sense, we thus get the best of each: with the intentional sense we can still focus on the teacher's goal of learning rather than on secondary matters (e.g., class routines or furniture arrangement) and point out that the teacher is working, not with subject matter alone, but with his student's relation to subject matter. We need simply to indicate our intention in no uncertain terms so as to avoid the need for rallying the teacher to his task later on with the slogan, "If the student hasn't learned, the teacher hasn't taught" (3; 18; 23; 36).

Furthermore, by using the intentional sense we can label a teacher's activity teaching and investigate that activity without waiting to hear whether the student has indeed learned. We can study teaching on its own. This "enables us to analyze the concept of teaching without becoming entangled in the web of learning; in short to carry on investigations of teaching in its own right" (45:233). This does not mean that we can escape talking about learning. Rather, it permits us to talk about teaching by itself without confounding an already complex activity. It also allows us to delay answering some questions on learning. For example, if a student can solve seventy percent of his arithmetic problems, has he learned arithmetic? If he can solve fifty percent? Thirty percent? What constitutes learning in art? History? Literature? Is it the teacher or student who decides whether the student has learned? Shall a decision about learning be made immediately following the teaching situation? One month afterwards? One year? Ten years?

By opting for intention we can stress planning for teaching and the subsequent process of teaching along with the achievement aspect. Focusing solely on outcome narrows our perspective and eliminates ways of distinguishing preferable processes from nonpreferable ones. To make a distinction among processes is important since, in a democracy, the relationship between teacher and student in the teaching process (the relationship between government and citizen) is at least as important as the product. Indeed, the claim has been made that the process and the product are inextricably intertwined, and it is therefore impossible even to speak of process and product as two separate things. If we focus solely on the outcome, we are encouraging the notion that the end justifies the means.

The intentional sense also emphasizes that teaching is a deliberate activity. Teaching does not just happen. It is not a matter of luck or mere occurrence although in everyday language teaching can be used in a chance, or luck, sense; e.g., "I didn't realize that I did it at the time, but I guess I taught Jonathan some chemistry when he watched me work in the lab." It is not that we deny that Jonathan, in this example, learned some chemistry, but we deny that his learning was the result of teaching. To accept a luck or occurrence sense of teaching is to accept the idea that learning must come from teaching. And this is certainly not acceptable since it is evident that people do learn by a variety of means.

Manner of Teaching

In developing our concept of teaching it is most important to treat the manner in which the teacher carries on his activity. We treat manner in order to clarify what we mean by teaching, to give the teacher direction in determining how he will act, and in order not to equate teaching with "enlearning," to coin a word meaning to cause someone to learn.

The distinctive manner of teaching, as different, for example, from propagandizing and conditioning, appears in this definition offered by one educational philosopher who has written widely on teaching: "Teaching may be characterized as an activity aimed at the achievement of learning and practiced in such manner as to respect the student's intellectual integrity and capacity for independent judgment" (43:131).

Note that the author of this definition, in addition to choosing the intentional, deliberate sense of the term *teaching*, specifies that teaching requires respect for the student. The teacher needs "to respect the student's intellectual integrity and capacity for independent judgment" if his activity is to be called teaching. In this way this definition differentiates teaching from propagandizing, conditioning, and indoctrinating. These latter activities are aimed at affecting the student, but strive at all costs to avoid a genuine engagement of his judgment on underlying issues.

Another example of the significance of manner in teaching appears in the following quotation, which finds novel parallels between teaching and sexing. Teaching done with an inappropriate manner is "intellectual rape," and this leads to "mental abortion" according to this author.

The teaching act, performed when the learner is unwilling, using that learner as a means to an end, is intellectual rape. By forcing a learner mentally into a position of receiving knowledge, regardless of his attitude, the teacher is attempting to achieve normal values in a normal act but has as surely violated the person of the learner as much as the rapist has his victim. And, as in rape the sexing becomes "dirty" and distasteful, so in intellectual rape, the learning is denigrated. Little wonder that many learners attempt mental abortion at the end of such a demoralizing experience (26:190).

In short, the teacher, if his activity is to be called teaching, must act in a certain manner. Since manner is important, not every activity will count as teaching.

Relation to Allied Activities

Teaching must clearly be distinguished from a host of allied activities such as indoctrinating, drilling, conditioning, training, instructing, and propagandizing. The need for a distinction is noted in the expression, "Don't indoctrinate the student. Teach him." Clarifying the manner of teaching, as we did earlier, is helpful but not sufficient. For this reason we need a further look at the troublesome activities often confused with teaching and a schema for relating one activity to the other. To this task we now turn.

Of these activities, all of which seek to induce learning in one form or another, the one that presents the most difficulties when used in connection with teaching is *indoctrinating* (4; 7; 10; 16; 22; 27; 38; 47; 52). We are sensitive to charges of indoctrination and generally oppose indoctrinating on three counts—method, content, and ultimate aim. First, we primarily oppose it because we disapprove of *how* it is performed. Indoctrinating is performed by presenting a point of view to a student in such a way as to virtually guarantee agreement. Indoctrinating does not foster the ability to analyze issues and to draw conclusions on the basis of pertinent evidence and probable, significant consequences (38).

Second, indoctrinating is opposed because of its content. We oppose indoctrinating because it can deal with nonrational, and perhaps offensive, subject matter. For example, we oppose an activity intending to induce the learning of Naziism because of what is to be learned, no matter how that activity is performed.

If we are to avoid indoctrination, therefore, the beliefs we teach must be rational. They need not be certain in the sense of being 100 per cent proved: it may only be that the general weight of evidence is in their favor. They *may* be certain, or they may be highly probable, or probable, or just likely on the whole. What they *must* be is backed by evidence: and by "evidence", of course, we must mean publicly-accepted evidence, not simply what sectarians like to consider evidence: otherwise the truce is again broken, since we must then allow anyone to say that there is evidence for any belief whatsoever. All this stands in sharp contrast to beliefs which are held by the majority of any society, or beliefs which we think to be "good" for children, or beliefs which are traditional or beliefs which we think help to keep society together. The concept of indoctrination concerns the truth and evidence of beliefs, and our objection to it is basically that in the realm of belief we must put truth, evidence, and reality first, and other considerations second (52:28).

Third, we oppose indoctrinating because of its *aim*. This criterion suggests that, in deciding whether the teacher's activity is to be called indoctrinating, we look at his aims. If a teacher presents his students with a representative sample of material to read and even discusses the topic with them afterwards, but ultimately aims to have them agree with him because of his superior knowledge and position, then we shall call that teacher's activity indoctrinating. Indoctrinating does not treat religious, political, and moral issues as open topics in which the teacher seeks to develop students who question him. Hare describes the indoctrinator in this way:

If a teacher is willing to engage in serious and honest discussion with his pupils about moral questions, to the extent that they are able, then he is not an indoctrinator, even though he may also, because of their age, be using non-rational methods of persuasion. These methods are not, as is commonly supposed, bad in themselves; they are bad only if they are used to produce attitudes that are not open to argument. The fact that a teacher does not himself have such attitudes is the guarantee that he is not an indoctrinator (27:54).

It is on the basis of ultimate aim along with the consideration of the maturity of the pupil that we judge the teacher of young students to be indoctrinating or not. The teacher who says, "Do not steal; do not cheat" is not considered to be indoctrinating if he wishes to aid in the development of clear moral thinking in his students, and indeed does so as the students mature. The indoctrinator does not intend to encourage clear or moral thought in his students. He labels some of their thoughts as dangerous (to his purposes) a priori. He watches for signs of trouble and intervenes whenever these appear. Indoctrinating creates a perpetual job (27:69–70).

Drilling simply refers to continuous repetition where the subject learns to carry out routines and procedures without fundamentally understanding what he is doing.* *Conditioning* refers to the process through which one learns to react physically to some stimulus. Thus we speak of Pavlov conditioning his dog to salivate at the sound of a bell. Also, conditioning in no way entails desirability. The reactions it establishes may be good or bad, right or wrong. Conditioning simply leads to a certain way of behaving. Intelligence has less a role in conditioning than in drilling and less in drilling than in training. "The trained man knows what he is about, knows not only the rules of procedure but also the reasons for them, and hence knows how to adapt the rules to nonstandard conditions. The man who is merely well drilled has to make do with rules of thumb which he mechanically applies" (4:173).

Training refers to a method of shaping habits (25:286). "Training suggests the acquisition of appropriate habits of response in a limited situation" (39:99). Training involves the manifesting of intelligence, and it is this critical element that distinguishes training from drilling and conditioning. Thus we can say, "Dr. Jones is training a new surgeon at the hospital to take his place next year"; and even a trained dog or circus horse displays some intelligence in its performance.

---

* Note that general sentiment against drilling led to reform, for example, in the math curriculum.

It is this element of intelligence that leads us to speak of training mechanics, training medical technicians, training airplane pilots, and training soldiers. The preparation of prospective teachers was at one time also popularly called "teacher training." This phrase still is used in some quarters today. On the other hand, training is also used in cases where little or no intelligent behavior is implied. For example, we speak of training a horse to carry a rider, training a baby not to soil its diapers, or training a dog to heel and beg. Since training is used both in cases involving the display of considerable intelligence—e.g., training airplane pilots—and in cases involving little intelligence—e.g., training a dog to walk on its two hind legs—the thus ambiguous phrase, *teacher training*, has currently fallen into disuse by most professionals.

Instructing involves giving reasons, weighing evidence, explaining events, justifying actions taken, and drawing conclusions based on evidence. Furthermore, whereas training is concerned with the arena of habits, instructing is concerned with knowledge or understanding. "What we seek to express by the phrase *giving instruction* is precisely what we seek to omit by the word *training*." This is the way we can and do speak of instructing people, especially mature people. (Note that the generic name for teacher at the college level is instructor, whereas this is not the case at the elementary and secondary level.) Teachers of young students rely heavily on nonrational means such as drill, example, and environmental influence because their students have not matured enough to abide by reasoned thought (32).

The differentiation of teaching from its allied activities is not always clear. We need to recognize that teaching, like many abstractions, is a most complicated concept with vague boundaries. It is impossible to give absolutely precise criteria that will identify every single instance of teaching. Yet, it is possible to provide a scheme of relationships among activities so as to clarify all but the very sticky cases. The following characterization of teaching draws heavily on Green's topology of the teaching concept (25).

According to this view the central element characterizing teaching is intelligence, or the higher thinking powers associated with reason and understanding. Teaching, then, is a family of activities which essentially involves giving reasons, showing and weighing evidence, acting according to principles, drawing conclusions on relevant evidence, and justifying actions. The activities allied with teaching can be divided into two groups:

those that deal with thinking and those that deal with performing. On the basis of these notions we may construct a continuum, which includes at its extremes activities other than those of the teaching family (see Figure 1–1).

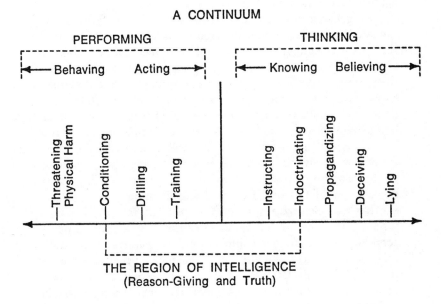

Figure 1–1*

In placing an activity on this continuum, we must first decide which side of the dividing line it belongs on and then decide on its relation to the region of intelligence. Each activity relates to the region of intelligence on the basis both of what the teacher does and of what he intends for the student to do. In this way, instructing is placed close to the center of the continuum and in the region of intelligence: the teacher, in instructing, gives reasons, weighs evidence, justifies statements, explains, and draws conclusions based on relevant evidence. He also intends for the students to do the same. Conditioning, an activity in which the teacher does not give reasons, weigh evidence, etc., is placed on the other side, further from the center. Nor does the teacher

* This figure is based on the work of Thomas F. Green and reprinted with permission from "A Topology of the Teaching Concept," *Studies in Philosophy and Education,* Vol. III, No. 4, Winter 1964–65.

expect the student being conditioned to carry on reasoning activities before reacting to the given stimuli.

The placement of these activities "is not meant to suggest that the distinctions between conditioning, training, instructing, and indoctrinating are perfectly clear and precise" (25:290). Each activity blends into its neighbor.

In general, training and instructing can be fairly readily included in, and lying and threatening as readily excluded from, the teaching family. There is some disagreement regarding the middle range of activities. As training shades into conditioning and instructing shades into indoctrinating, people begin to disagree as to whether a given case is an example of teaching. Thus certain activities are more central to the concept of teaching than others, and certain activities are borderline cases. Completely absent from the continuum are activities like counseling and advising, which are personal activities that largely involve the feelings and emotions of the people involved, as opposed to the relatively impersonal, objective, public nature of the teaching situation.

Let us *summarize* our conclusions thus far. In this book, teaching shall be treated as an intentional, deliberate family of acts (logical and strategic) aimed at inducing learning. Central to this concept of teaching are, first, a manner on the teacher's part that implies respect for the student and, second, a use of intelligence, by both teacher and student, that involves reason-giving and truth.

Teaching—Triadic and Dynamic

Up to this point we have dealt with some of the issues involved in developing a concept of teaching. Now we shall deal with the relationships and elements involved in teaching (29).

To introduce the discussion of the relationships in teaching, let us first refer to an intriguingly entitled article, "Cameras Don't Take Pictures." In it Paul Byers (11) studies "the behaviors of the *people* who are involved in photography, the photographer, the subject, and the viewer." Byers rejects the validity of the twofold, or dyadic, sender-receiver model of photography and argues for a new model that asserts that photography is a social transaction between photographer, subject, and viewer. Within this framework, the meaning of the photograph arises out of the interaction between the viewer and the picture, and the photograph itself represents an interaction between photographer and subject. This framework emphasizes the relationships in photography and further asserts that the dyadic sender-receiver model is inadequate for understanding still photography. For Byers the relationship in photography must be considered a triadic one.

This model of photography suggests several important points if we wish to use it as an analogue for investigating teaching. Teaching involves at least one teacher, at least one student, and some subject matter. Teaching is, then, *a triad of elements*; it is not dyadic. It is impossible to teach economics, for example, to no one, or to teach a student without subject matter. It is this *triad— teacher, student, subject matter*—and the relationships it creates that we must include as part of our concept of teaching.

When one of the three elements of the teaching triad is missing, the other two become disconnected and teaching cannot take place. The removal of one element destroys the relationship that exists between the other two. The nature of the teaching triad is such that it is impossible to have a teacher and student without connecting subject matter. Indeed, if the teacher intends to induce learning, it must be of something. If he does not intend to induce learning, then the relationship between the teacher and student is not a teaching relationship. It may be a purely social one where the labels *teacher* and *student* are carried over from the teaching situation.

It is equally impossible for a teaching situation to involve a student and subject matter but no teacher. The teacher may be represented by a textbook, a film, a program, or some other device; in such cases the teacher may not be present bodily, but this in no way implies the absence of any teaching element. Even in most cases where it can be said in common language, "I am teaching myself algebra," the materials used are those specifically designed for self-study, that is, designed to teach. Mitchell puts it this way:

... when we say, I teach myself, we are speaking metaphorically, and ... although there are legitimate senses in which a man can be said to question, to tell, to punish, or to encourage himself, there are certain differences in the character of these operations when compared with those directed toward another person. It is impossible, I suggest by way of example, for a man to ask himself a question using terms he has no knowledge of, or to demonstrate to himself something he has never previously done (even though such an action, doing something new, does demonstrate *something*, e.g., success, failure, possibilities, to himself). To reward, to examine, to praise oneself is significantly different from being rewarded, examined, or praised by another. On these grounds, then, I would suggest that, whereas in some senses a man *can* be said to teach himself and to engage in diverse operations in so doing, these operations are distinguishable from, and thus need to be designated as differing from the same sort of operations when they are related to another (37:166–167).

It is also impossible in teaching to have a teacher and subject matter without a student. A *teacher* interacts with subject matter in consideration of his particular students. For example, a teacher teaches different concepts, facts, and skills in history to a ten-year-old student from those he teaches to a seventeen-year-old student. At times this consideration may be minimal—as in the case of the proverbial professor who still uses the same lecture notes after twenty years of experience. Yet even those lecture notes were originally designed for a particular group of students. Further, if we claim that a teacher can write a history book without any particular group or type of student in mind, then we must say that he is not teaching history but rather writing history. On the other hand, if the teacher prepares a history *text*book, with some type or category of student in mind, we can indeed say that he is teaching. Further, the textbook writer intends for the students to learn from his book; this is often explicitly acknowledged in the prefaces of textbooks.

Perhaps more important than the idea of multiple connections among the three elements in teaching is the *dynamic quality of the triad*. This quality is implied in the triadic conception of teaching because as the relationship between teacher and student changes, as indeed it must, for life is always changing, then the teacher must continually change his relationship with the subject matter. This dynamic conception of teaching does not include the activity of that proverbial history professor who uses the same lecture notes year after year. The world of the 1970s is very different from that of the 1940s. It is apparent that the college freshman of the 1970s is quite different from the freshman of the 1940s and therefore requires a different course in world history. Time and environment change the teacher's relation with the student.

This dynamic conception of teaching also means that changes in a body of knowledge will influence the activities teachers perform. In light of Einstein's theory of relativity the physics teacher and his students perform quite different experiments in the laboratory, and these, in turn, change the relationship between teacher and student. Changes in theories and empirical data require the teacher to adjust his procedures and techniques. These, in turn, affect the teacher-student relationship. Further, if a teacher is especially interested in calculus, for example, as opposed to plane geometry, he will teach different sorts of students. That is, the teacher of calculus will teach students older both in age and mathematical knowledge than the teacher of plane geometry.

Last, as the student's relationship with the subject matter changes, the teacher element also must change. This is illustrated by the case of the prodigy in music. The teacher must quickly change his approach and demands to correspond to the rapid advances of the student. If the teacher himself cannot change appropriately, the teacher element changes: when the prodigy moves on to another teacher who can deal with his musical ability. Similarly, the teacher element changes with the retarded pupil. Different types of teachers suit different students' relationships with the subject matter at hand.

From the above it is quite clear that teaching must be viewed both as triadic and dynamic. We cannot understand the nature of teaching by looking at only one or two elements of the teaching relationship or by thinking of teaching as static. We must consider all three elements together in order to understand the interaction that occurs during teaching. We must see that the relationships are always changing. Furthermore, we must note that the interaction between any two elements influences how each of the two will react to the third one and, in turn, how all the elements will react together. This conception of teaching is represented graphically in Figure 1–2.

Each element influences and is influenced by the relationship between the other two elements. Further, the removal of any one element or the breakdown of any relationship between two elements destroys the entire teaching triad.

The recognition of the triadic and dynamic qualities of the teaching act is essential to an understanding of teaching. The points suggested here go beyond the definitions of teaching cited earlier. These points also go beyond the common but incorrect notion that the teacher must merely diagnose the student's behavior and action. The teacher must also analyze his own relationship with the subject matter as well as his student's relations with him and with the subject matter. This is necessary in order to be able to diagnose and understand the student's work.

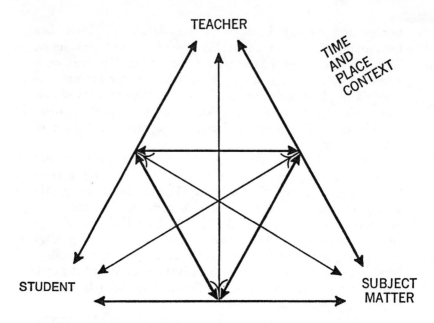

Figure 1–2: Teaching: Triadic and Dynamic

Realization of the dynamic and triadic relationships in teaching prevents a teacher from trying to use "the syllabus" as handed out by "headquarters." It is impossible to teach a syllabus as is, and, furthermore, trying to do so often ends in the creation of a static, not dynamic, relationship between teacher and subject matter. Teachers guided by a triadic dynamic concept of teaching put themselves into the teaching act not only in a dynamic relationship with the student but also in a dynamic relationship with the subject matter they teach.

In *summary*, teaching involves a triad of elements (the teacher, the student, and the subject matter), and the triad is dynamic in quality. This triad does not itself offer a prescription as to what kind of teacher-student relationship ought to be established. It does, however, require us to consider the teacher-student relationship and obtain data about it as we select methods for teaching, select observational frameworks, and gather data for evaluation.

Skills, Knowledge, and Values

When we made the point that the teacher must teach something to the student, we did not specify what that something should be.

Yet this step is necessary, for what the subject matter is affects the relationship between teacher and student as well as all other elements in the teaching triad. For example, to teach swimming is not the same as to teach philosophy, mathematics, or literature. It is necessary to treat now what the teacher teaches—not exactly the topics but, rather, the types of topics: skills, knowledge, or values.

To teach a student a *skill* such as writing, typing, piano playing, or dancing is to teach him how to do something. It is more than getting him to write or dance in a specific way at a specific time. A skill requires practice. (It is this that separates a skill from a reflex activity, such as sneezing.) A student may write the letter R under close guidance but not know how to write an R under different conditions when alone. Dancing is similar, though it should be quickly noted at this point that dancing is an example of a complex skill, as opposed to (e.g.) typing. Such skills as dancing and piano playing are not only complex because they involve great physical coordination but also because they enter the interpretive realm of aesthetics. When a teacher teaches a student how to play the piano, he teaches him to strike the keys in an acceptable way with acceptable timing. More important, he teaches the student what constitutes this acceptable way and acceptable timing. He gives reasons and explains his piano-playing techniques and expects the student to perform according to them as a result of practicing. If the teacher does not do this and his student merely hits the correct keys in imitation, without understanding what he is doing, we can say, "Yes, he played 'Mary Had a Little Lamb' but he still doesn't *know how to play* the piano." The person who *knows how to* play can do so under varying conditions and with understanding. Eventually he will not need a teacher. This is not the case with the student who plays the piano only in rote imitation and who is eternally dependent on the teacher. To know how to play a piano requires the exercise of intelligence when performing.

Besides skills, teachers teach students *knowledge* as in the following statements:

(1) The United States became independent in 1776.
(2) President Johnson followed President Kennedy.
(3) It is dark at night because we do not face the sun.
(4) 2 + 2 = 4
(5) Chef is a synonym for cook.
(6) If it rains, the street will get wet.

In other words, in addition to *teaching how to do something* teachers also *teach that something is the case:* that President Johnson followed President Kennedy; that if it rains, the street will get wet; that 2 + 2 = 4.

When Mr. Jones teaches Jonathan that Johnson followed Kennedy, he not only expects his student to learn what he is teaching, but he also is claiming it to be true. This follows from our previous points regarding the aim of teaching and the centrality of reason-giving and evidence. Sometimes, however, the teacher does teach something that can be recognized to be untrue. This may be due to a personal error, or misinformation, or a change in the overall condition of man's knowledge. For example, teachers formerly taught that the earth was flat, that the atom was the smallest particle of matter, that there were only ninety-seven elements, and that Piltdown man was the missing link. None of these "facts" was ever true; but, at the time, each was generally accepted to be true. To allow for changes over time we can say that the teacher is teaching if he and the general community—larger than a single nation or small group of nations—hold his statements to be true even though subsequent events show otherwise.

Furthermore, to *teach that*, as we shall use the phrase, means more than merely trying to get the student to state something that is correct. It is more than merely making true statements. The teacher's aim is to have the student *know that something is the case* in a strong sense of "know." That is to say, the student should be sure of his own claim and be able to support it with appropriate evidence or authoritative testimony (5:35; 41:12–13). This requirement has significant implications for the methods and the evaluation of teaching, to be treated later.

In addition to teaching *skills* (teaching how to do something) and *knowledge* (teaching that something is the case), teachers also teach students *values* (norms and attitudes). As opposed to knowledge, with which we can use the words *true* and *false*, values refer to beliefs and performances, to which the words *right* and *wrong*, *good* and *bad*, or *proper* and *improper* can be applied. Teachers teach students about such matters as honesty, friendship, politeness, citizenship, patriotism, loyalty, democracy, and kindness, to name but a few.

In regard to values, teachers can and do, for example, teach a student: (1) *that honesty is* the best policy or *that democracy* involves voting; and (2) *to be honest* or *to vote* in a democracy. In the first example the teacher intends only for the student to be able to state that honesty is the best policy or that democracy involves voting. This is the *nonactive* sense of teaching values to a student. In teaching a student to be honest or to vote in a democracy the teacher intends for the student, not only to verbalize, e.g., about honesty, but also to act, e.g., honestly. This is the *active* sense of teaching values to a student. It is important to make this distinction in teaching values, for, though each sense has its appropriate and legitimate place, the ways of evaluating them are different. If we do not keep the two uses of "to teach values" clearly in mind, we are likely to shift our uses and thereby create confusion or unintended self-deception. For example, "we may begin with an active interpretation of such nonstating sentences, shift in the process of instruction and test to a nonactive interpretation, and finally presume that we have been successful in moral instruction in the *active* sense, whereas we have actually taught and tested for knowledge as interpreted in a non-active sense" (1:473).

Moreover, *to teach a student to be* honest means, as we shall use the phrase, to teach the student to act honestly out of conviction, out of belief supported by reason and understanding. This does not imply that this is the only way a student may learn to be honest or act honestly. He may learn to be honest out of habit, i.e., by being honest over a period of time. But in learning by habit he may not be honest out of conviction or even be able to state why he is honest. To behave honestly does not imply being committed to honesty. For example, a student under the honor system may decide not to cheat on exams out of fear of expulsion from school, rather than out of commitment to honesty. There is a difference, then, between "being honest" and being honest out of commitment, for the latter implies action out of conviction, not mere honest deeds. For Mr. Jones to teach Jonathan to be honest, Jones must intend both that Jonathan act honestly and that he do so out of conviction. It is evident that just as *teach how to* and *teach that* have significant implications for method and evaluation, so does *teach to be.*

Teaching as a Language Process

"Teaching cannot occur without the use of language. Teaching is, above all, a linguistic activity" (46:342). So claims Smith in discussing the activities that constitute the anatomy of teaching. Indeed, though there may be occasional examples or specific short periods where teaching does not involve language, Smith's claim cannot be easily refuted. Research based on tape recordings of school classes shows that two-thirds of the time someone in the class is talking (21:252). In many situations the percentage is much higher, e.g., in lecture or recitation periods.

When we teach, we use language. To perform the many activities necessary to achieve the aims of teaching, the teacher needs language, whether oral or written. He uses words to communicate his ideas. He uses language: to teach the definitions, facts, explanations, interpretations, generalizations, principles, and concepts of the topic at hand; to interpret, complement, and emphasize the demonstrations of the skills he teaches; to correct, reject, accept, praise, or negate responses from the students; to encourage or prod the students in their activities; to evaluate or test the development of the students' achievement; to show respect, dignity, honesty, fairness, and equality of treatment toward his students; to express feelings of interest, hate, love, or indifference; to give directions and make assignments; to make use of maps, films, slides, tape recordings, charts, models, diagrams, and tables; and to reward, punish, admonish, blame, or approve the students' performance. In short, "the day-to-day activities are sustained almost entirely in talk, back and forth between teacher and students" (2:122).

This case for language in no way denies the presence and use of silent communication in teaching. The teacher and student are both continually sending and receiving such messages. Students, for example, raise their hands, nod their heads, smile, look drowsy, and appear puzzled. Teachers, in addition to the foregoing, point, snap fingers, and raise eyebrows. Such acts are generally understandable because they are common in our society. They are understandable even to the teacher who may reject them when they are out of place.

In teaching, then, the teacher and students continually send and receive silent messages whether these are gestures substituting for words or manifestations of feelings and cognition. Silent communication is legitimate in teaching, but the prime means of communication in teaching is through oral and written language (6:1).

Teaching and Interpersonal Relations

Teaching as it most commonly occurs involves a face-to-face relation between teacher and student. Even in those instances in which the teacher and student are not in each other's presence, as in teaching via television, or via a programmed text, or via a correspondence course, the acts of the teacher are influenced and selected on the basis of the experience gained in the usual teaching situation, which involves face-to-face contact. In this way we can say that teaching has a personal dimension.

Teaching involves a relationship between teacher and student that goes beyond the rational intellectual dimension, though this is central to it. It involves a relationship between teacher and student that goes beyond the subject matter of the teaching triad. Teaching aims at learning of a special type. The act of teaching, as opposed to (e.g.) lying or threatening, requires the teacher to treat the student as a human being, with dignity and respect, in order to encourage him to use his intelligence in supporting what he learns with appropriate evidence. This manner of teaching communicates strong interpersonal meanings to the student. We can rightly claim that this message communicated by the teaching act is as important as the subject matter the teacher teaches. This interpersonal *manner is* the *message*, to paraphrase a popular saying by Marshall McLuhan.

Thus, there is an interpersonal aspect of teaching, in which the teacher must encourage learning and must himself respect "intellectual integrity and capacity for independent judgment." The point is simply this: if the activity is to be called teaching, the teacher must respect the student, must seek to minimize anxiety and threat, and must seek to establish mutual trust. Indeed, some teachers may be warmer, or more personable, or more consistently respectful, than others. There are degrees in these matters. But to be called teaching, the activity must involve this positive interpersonal relationship to some degree that promotes learning and the development of the independence of the student. Stavsky puts it this way: "One of the main functions of teaching, then, is to reduce or control anxiety in order that the goal of the class—learning (and development)—may be reached" (48:171).

If done otherwise, the activity is not teaching. It may be labeled intimidating, telling, threatening, or "enlearning," but it is not teaching. It is the nature of teaching to involve a positive personal relationship. "To teach a person we must understand him. This is most easily accomplished by trying to see him and his world as he sees them" (8:63). And:

Teaching requires mutual confidence between student and teacher; for the activity to get anywhere, each must have trust in the general credibility and veracity of the other. I suppose each teacher has had moments of terror when this trust dies or even fails to appear. (Some teachers live with this terror.) In any honest service, both parties have an obvious and immediate recourse—termination. We need not brook the tasteless bard or baker. Since teaching cannot prosper without respect, then let it not be tried at all (34:10–11).

The teacher has a moral obligation as well to seek to develop the independence and humanity of the student. Because of the teacher's relation to the student, teaching is a moral activity. The teacher seeks to improve the student and benefit him through what and how he teaches. The teacher creates a moral tension by his action because he seeks to change what his student thinks and does. This is precisely the point in specifying that a teacher teaches skills, knowledge, and values. In his exposition of Martin Buber's ideas on teaching, A. V. Judges interprets Buber as follows:

Yet it is the kind of tension that matters. The teacher has no right to impose himself on the pupil's freedom or to proclaim his own will. He can bring the whole force of his personality into the situation—indeed he will be no convincing teacher if he fails to do so. He may display his superior skill and wisdom. He may and should love his charges, though it must be with a kind of tenderness that makes no strong personal demands. He may and should penetrate into the imaginative vision of his pupil and momentarily live his way into the pupil's role. But if he bungles, if he is a predator, if he destroys the freedom and purposiveness of the pupil's attitude to the subject matter, education ceases. And here I think I interpret Buber rightfully in stating that while the propagandist and the moralist believe, often passionately, in the virtue of their message, the true educator believes in the virtue of his pupil, sometimes within all the circumstances of failure; and that here there is a faith which the pupil must learn to shape, for it is he and not the master who will sow and reap (30:103).

Teaching is a moral activity, then, because the teacher teaches values explicitly and implicitly. He is always teaching values by the very way he relates to his students. He teaches respect by being respectful; humaneness by being humane; reasonableness by being reasonable; and truthfulness by being truthful. By being a model of an intelligent, reason-giving person and by creating an environment in which these qualities can flourish, the teacher teaches values perhaps more significantly than by what he says.

Teaching and Metaphors

If you ask a group of teachers or a group of prospective teachers to list the important things they wish to teach their students, you will quite likely find high on that list "how to think." By this expression, the teachers will mean "how to think critically" or "how to think clearly." They deserve strong praise for their choice. Yet problems generally arise when these teachers set out to teach their students "how to think." One of these problems is virtually unknown to them, and hence they generally do not overcome it. This problem involves the use of metaphors in the language of the classroom* and in the literature on education.

Metaphor is a common, everyday technique for talking about objects or events in terms appropriate to other objects or events. It is "the presentation of the facts of one sort as if they belong to another" (50:22). Most metaphors are deliberate and useful. The conscious use of metaphor in everyday language is exemplified by such statements as: clever Jonathan *is a fox*; when Rachel runs, *she's a gazelle*; and Elana really grew over the summer—is she a *weed*! It is easy to recognize the metaphors in these statements; we do not slip, become confused, and believe that Jonathan is really a fox, or Rachel is really a gazelle, or Elana is really a weed. In such statements, we know what we are saying and are continually aware that we are using metaphorical language.

However, since language is not always so simple, many metaphors go unnoticed. Here are two examples, one from the classroom and one from the educational literature. (1) The math teacher in summarizing says, "Now that Ruth has touched all the bases, we can go on." (2) An author writes, "The most effective teacher is the one who *produces* students who have learned most and who go on learning, regardless of whether he *works* with chalk and chalkboard or with the latest audio-visual techniques" (51:2) (italics mine). The sensitized reader will quickly note that in these two examples Ruth has not touched bases but performed all the steps and that teachers do not *produce* but teach students. Unsensitized teachers are not aware of such metaphors. When this occurs, confusion sets in and clear thinking goes out. The confusion, for example, between playing baseball and solving math problems, or between producing students and teaching them, can

* This section on teaching and metaphors is based on my article in *Notre Dame Journal of Education*, Volume 4, Number 1 (Spring, 1973), pp. 80–88.

lead to basic misunderstandings about math or teaching. The uncritical use of metaphors in the literature is troublesome because unaware authors influence their unsensitized readers. But it is particularly acute in the classroom, where there is a deliberate intent to teach clear thinking, because, when the teacher becomes confused, he soon leads his students into confusion.

It is doubtful that most teachers would be aware that metaphors appear in the two examples above, since the work, or manufacturing, metaphor for schooling is in common use in our country now. What is more, teachers are generally unaware that other metaphors also appear in the language of their classrooms and in the educational literature they read. Here are just three popular types of metaphors, with some of their examples in regard to teaching.

> *Horticulture metaphor*: Teachers speak about *planting* the *seed* of knowledge to watch it *grow* in the *sunshine* of the *green* classroom; about lazy students sitting like *vegetables*; about *reaping* the benefits of good discipline; about the *kindergarten* (a word meaning a "garden of children" which we use directly from the German for the type of school established by Friedrich Froebel in the 1830s to meet the educational needs of young children).
>
> *Sports metaphor*: Teachers speak about *carrying the ball* in a discussion; about *pinch hitting* for an absent classmate; about *throwing in the towel* during an argument; about *throwing* the student a *curve ball* during a test.
>
> *Military metaphor*: Teachers speak about *arming* the student with knowledge to face the future; about *battling* with the students regarding discipline; about being on the *firing line* in the classroom; about questions as an effective *weapon*; about getting the *troops* back to the classroom—the *homefront*—from the school cafeteria; about *bombing out* on an exam when unprepared.

There exist other metaphors as well—metaphors which may well have even more impact on the minds and activities of teachers than the ones cited above. Such metaphors abound when educators talk about the role of the teacher in the classroom. As the educators analyze and even prescribe the activities of the teacher, they use metaphors which influence the subsequent interaction between the teacher and his students. Metaphors appear when the educators talk about the teacher as if the teacher were a psychotherapist, a youth group leader, a jailer, a zookeeper, a tyrant, or a policeman.

That a metaphor is being employed to talk about the role of the teacher may not always be so obvious. For example, in an article dealing with the relevance of anthropology to school classrooms, the author compares the teacher with the field anthropologist, saying that each "does his job with his entire personality." Several pages later the author goes on to write, "It seems to me that many middleclass American teachers are in a 'field situation'" (9:164). Note the absence of the words "as if" in the last quote. The author is not claiming that the teacher should act *as if* he were an anthropologist in a field situation. Rather, he claims that the teacher *is* in a field situation. Without careful attention it is fairly easy to overlook the author's metaphorical language and to become confused.

The use of the word *as* rather than *as if* is often helpful in avoiding metaphorical confusion. For example, we say that the teacher functions *as* a decision-maker, *as* an explainer, and *as* an example of a mature person. We do not say that the teacher functions *as if* he were a decision-maker, or *as if* he were an explainer, or *as if* he were a mature person, for indeed he *is* precisely these things. This is what a "teacher" is. The choice of *as* rather than *as if* is correct in these cases.

Yet the use of *as* does not always preclude a potentially confusing metaphor. One recent study categorized the activities of the classroom into ten groups. Among these categories are "Teacher as Instructor" and "Teacher as Individualizer of Instruction." These two do not lead a reader into metaphorical confusion, i.e., into believing that the teacher functions as something he is not. The teacher is an "instructor" and is, or at least should be, an "individualizer" in the schoolroom. Two other categories, however, are "Teacher as Traffic Cop" and "Teacher as Tyrant" (37). These are indeed metaphors despite the use of *as* rather than *as if* in labeling the teacher's activities. These latter two categories are even more potentially confusing than usual because they appear in their context to be parallel with the former two by the very structure of the label. As sensitive metaphor-watchers we must admit that Teacher as Instructor and Teacher as Individualizer are not parallel with Teacher as Traffic Cop and Teacher as Tyrant, despite the similar format.

In short, unnoticed metaphors lead to confusion because

teachers come to believe that something is the case when it is not. Teachers are confused if they believe that the first year of public school is a *children's garden* or that they are *anthropologists in a field situation* or that they are *producing* students who work at arithmetic or that they are *traffic cops*. Moreover, a teacher who is confused about his role by accepting and believing his metaphors uncritically goes on to behave in accord with the concepts of his new images, for the concepts a person uses influence his behavior. If a teacher perceives himself as a "*sergeant* taking his troops home from the cafeteria," then he will begin to behave accordingly. As shown earlier, Winch uses the example of war to illustrate the power of a concept to influence behavior in a person's life (53).

A metaphorical concept influences teachers just as a non-metaphorical concept does. Let us return specifically to the manufacturing metaphor for special attention since it is surely the most pervasive yet unnoticed metaphor in regard to teaching. If a person sees himself *as a producer*, then he begins to behave in a manufacturing manner. Once he is in the production frame of mind, he brings in other concepts associated with that metaphor, such as efficiency, work, quality control, economy, industry, mass production, job, precise time schedules, and assembly line. The clustering of these concepts associated with the production metaphor leads to classroom behavior which reflects manufacturing behavior and which may hinder the student from developing autonomy and creativity.

This manufacturing metaphor deserves further attention, not only because it is the most pervasive of the metaphors cited, but because it is without doubt a most deadly one. Its pervasiveness reflects our society's emphasis on getting and spending, on producing and consuming. It is deadly because it subverts humane interaction. Behavior according to this metaphor leads the teacher to treat the students as inanimate objects, as things to be processed, stamped out, and finished on the conveyor-belt assembly line instead of as evolving people. It leads the teacher to think that he can and should decide what his product (the student) will become without consulting with the student.

This manufacturing metaphor strikes us with brute force in the explication of it by Ellwood Cubberley, the dean of educational historians in the early part of this century.

Every manufacturing establishment that turns out a standard product or a series or products of any kind maintains a force of efficiency experts to study methods of procedure and to measure and test the output of its works. Such men ultimately bring the manufacturing establishment large returns, by introducing improvements in processes and procedure, and in training the workmen to produce large and better output. Our schools are, in a sense, factories in which the raw products (children) are to be shaped and fashioned into products to meet the various demands of life. The specification for manufacturing comes from the demands of twentieth-century civilization, and it is the business of the school to build its pupils according to the specifications laid down. This demands good tools, specialized machinery, continuous measurement of production to see if it is according to specifications, the elimination of waste in manufacture, and a large variety in the output (17:338).

The manufacturing metaphor fosters the fragmentation of knowledge and learning processes into minute segments which cause teachers and students to lose sight of the larger subject matter context and the interpersonal context—of what and who is involved in teaching. This is the point that Alvin Toffler makes in *Future Shock* in treating the relationship between mass schooling and industrialism. According to Toffler,

... the whole idea of assembling masses of students (raw material) to be processed by teachers (workers) in a centrally located school (factory) was a stroke of industrial genius. The whole administrative hierarchy of education, as it grew up, followed the model of industrial bureaucracy. The very organization of knowledge into permanent disciplines was grounded on industrial assumptions. Children marched from place to place and sat in assigned stations. Bells rang to announce changes of time (49:400).

At this point we must ask what can be done to prevent the confusion which results when teachers insensitively use metaphors in the classroom. A simple answer is to stop using metaphors— a simple answer but an impossible venture. It is impossible to be completely literal in teaching and in talking about teaching. Much of daily-life language consists of metaphorical terms and phrases, especially for ideas relating to our feelings and values, which are invisible. Well-mannered children are *angelic*; mischievious children are *devilish*; a headache *pounds* inside; the nose *runs* from a virus; a friend is *warm* to us; a stranger is *cold* to us; pornography is *warped*; many four-letter words are *dirty*, and so forth almost ad infinitum. Since we use common language when we teach, there is no way to avoid metaphors which are so pervasive in our speech.

Furthermore, the elimination of metaphors is not only impossible but undesirable. Metaphors enrich our otherwise limited way of talking. Literal language is poor and narrow. With metaphors a person can bring new insights to a situation. An apt metaphor provides a vision and meaning that otherwise would elude us. Metaphors enlighten and broaden our views. Indeed, one of the marks of a culturally rich person is his use of metaphors to illuminate and illustrate the objects, events, people, places, and ideas he talks about.

Metaphors provide new vision even in science, which is often thought to be only literal and technical. This is brought home by Joseph J. Schwab, a biologist, in explaining the role of a concept in scientific inquiry. Schwab points out that biologists studying small aquatic animals about seventy years ago became frustrated about what to investigate in the dartings, movements, and plays of these animals. "This frustration of enquiry was resolved by appealing to the then popular view that all things, including living things, were no more than simple machines, the pattern of which was the simple one known to nineteenth-century physics. This idea of a simple machine was applied to the study of behavior by supposing that every movement through space of an animal was a response to some single, specific, stimulating factor in the environment" (44:25–26).

Biologists subsequently gave up this metaphoric concept, but the idea of a "simple machine" gave them questions to ask. Numerous other examples also exist in science. The point is that the use of metaphors has enabled scientific research to proceed. Yet, sometimes it is easy to forget those metaphors which scientists employ in theorizing and in doing research. Nevertheless, metaphors are there at critical moments in science.

Besides providing new insights and a rich source for comparisons, metaphors also serve a persuasive function. By choosing an appealing metaphor, a person can persuade others to accept his point of view. A teacher can conceive of homework as a basketball practice game, design interesting exercises for it, and thereby hope to achieve a positive attitude towards it on the part of the students. On the other hand, if the teacher thinks that doing homework is like doing the dishes after dinner, an unpleasant chore that must be done whether we like it or not, then he may well persuade the students to dislike homework. It is desirable to have metaphors in teaching because they help us in one of the main functions of language, the persuasive function (15:21–51).

The task, then, is not to strive to eliminate metaphors.

Rather, teachers and prospective teachers should first sensitize themselves to the prevalence and impact of metaphors. They should learn to recognize the various metaphors that are commonly used and in particular those that they are in the habit of using. For example, they could select a paragraph built around a metaphor like the one from Cubberley quoted earlier. They could read it and ask themselves, "What conceptions about teaching does this author hold?" As they consider the paragraph by beginning with an answer to this question, they have the opportunity to become sensitive to metaphors. Then they can easily shift to a concentration on the particular metaphors that they themselves use.

A teacher who behaves according to the prevalent manufacturing metaphor loses sight of what teaching is. By analyzing the act of teaching, the teacher will discover the essential activities of teaching and unmask metaphors employed. As mentioned earlier in our analysis of the level of meaning, we can divide the activities of teaching into three groups—the logical acts, the strategic acts, and the institutional acts. The logical group includes, among others, explaining, concluding, justifying, comparing, and defining; the strategic group includes, among others, planning, motivating, questioning, and encouraging; and the institutional group includes, among others, taking roll, collecting money, attending faculty meetings, and making reports. The logical acts relate to the element of thinking and reasoning; the strategic acts relate to the teacher's plans and his way of directing students during teaching; the institutional acts relate to the way the teacher's job in a school is organized by those in charge. Further thought on these groups shows that, whereas it is impossible to teach without performing logical and strategic acts, it is entirely possible to teach without performing institutional acts (24:2–5).

The point here is that, when teachers focus on these logical and strategic acts as necessary acts of teaching, as elements in the larger subject and interpersonal context, they can readily observe the introduction of metaphors that can potentially confuse them. It is highly improbable that under the logical or strategic group teachers would list such acts as *producing* or *planting*. By asking himself, "What logical acts do I perform?" a teacher can readily alert himself to metaphors which might otherwise slip by him. By proceeding in this way, the teacher thinks clearly, avoids confusion, and sets a proper example for his students.

The Plowden Report in England served to redirect the British in their schools (13). The British Infant Schools, popular today, gained tremendously in Britain and were copied in the United States as a result of the thrust of the Plowden Report. What is significant is to note that the Plowden Report derives much of its positive tone precisely from the metaphors it uses. The child-centered type of metaphor with such indicators as growth, harmony, discovery, and readiness pervades the Plowden Report. At the same time, the sensitive reader will note the disfavor afforded to such metaphor indicators as storing, imparting, fragmentation, and building bricks. One researcher who studied the use of metaphors in major documents on British primary education since 1905 reports empirical data to support this claim. He summarizes his characterization of the Plowden Report in part in the following way: "The picture of children as 'natural explorers' with 'boundless curiosity' and 'self-absorption' completely dominates this Report. Other types of metaphor are used un-favorably, and selective rhetorical metaphors put the child-centered view in a warm, rosy light. The section on play illustrates this very clearly: it 'seizes' their imagination, it is 'vital' to their learning, it contains the 'roots of drama', and it leads children effortlessly into the 'paths of discovery'" (14:79).

The attractiveness of the Plowden Report lies in part in its metaphors. The Plowden Report uses one type of metaphor favorably and other types unfavorably. That is to say, it speaks well of growth, for example, and ill of fragmentation in knowledge. This is a direct switch from previous documents on primary schools. Moreover, it uses metaphors much more persuasively than its predecessors (14:77).

With the Plowden Report before him as a model, the teacher would do well to seek out people who have other perspectives to help him in developing constructive metaphors. For example, people from music could help replace the destructive "teacher as producer," "teacher as sergeant," and "teacher as jailer" metaphors by refining and explicating such metaphors as the "teacher as orchestrator" and "teacher as harmonizer." The teacher could seek out our poets, as well, whose creativity lies in their talent for offering fresh insights through their choice of words. The art of the poet is in conceiving new ways of verbalizing a view of the world around us. Our poets would make a significant contribution to pedagogy if they could offer us new, positive metaphors to use in teaching.

Would not teachers benefit—and students and parents and

the entire society—if they thought of themselves as orchestrators rather than jailers? Would not everybody benefit if our students saw themselves as members of an orchestra rather than as prisoners? (The prisoner metaphor is by far the most common one students use when they talk about their lives in school.) Imagine what other constructive metaphors we could create if we set our hearts to it.

In summary, it is our task as teachers to avoid certain metaphors in order to prevent their undesirable effects, effects which can insidiously corrupt a humane activity into an inhumane one. It is our task to help create constructive metaphors. Leaders can sensitize teachers to metaphors and help them escape the trap of inappropriate thinking so as to be in a position to teach their students how to think clearly. If our teachers think clearly, conceive of teaching constructively, and then act humanely, there is hope for our students.

Summary

A person setting out to teach needs to clarify his concept of teaching because the concept he holds directly influences the activities he will engage in. In this book we will treat teaching in regard to the *act* of teaching rather than in regard to the *occupation* or *general enterprise* of teaching. We will use *teaching* to mean an intentional, deliberate family of logical and strategic acts aimed at inducing learning of skills, knowledge, and values. Teaching is a triad of elements—teacher, student, and subject matter—that is dynamic in quality. Central to it is the *manner* of teaching, requiring that the teacher respect his student. Teaching is primarily carried on through language, involves the use of intelligence, reason-giving, and truth, and requires the development of a positive interpersonal relationship so as to foster learning and the development of independence.

Teachers must be alert to the metaphors they use in thinking and talking about teaching. They would do well to avoid certain undesirable metaphors (e.g., the production metaphor and the military metaphor) and seek more positive views of teaching.

References

1. Archambault, Reginald D. "Criteria for Success in Moral Instruction." *Harvard Educational Review* 33:472–483, Fall 1963.

2. Aschner, Mary Jane. "The Language of Teaching." In *Language*

and Concepts in Education, edited by B. Othanel Smith and Robert H. Ennis, pp. 112–126. Chicago: Rand McNally, 1961.

3. Aschner, M. J. McCue. "Teaching, Learning, and Mr. Gowin." *Studies in Philosophy and Education* 2:172–202, Spring 1962.

4. Atkinson, R. F. "Instruction and Indoctrination." In *Philosophical Analysis and Education*, edited by Reginald D. Archambault, pp. 171–183. New York: Humanities Press, 1965.

5. Ayer, A. J. *The Problem of Knowledge*. Baltimore: Penguin Books, 1956.

6. Bellack, Arno A., Herbert M. Kliebard, Ronald T. Hyman, and Frank L. Smith, Jr. *The Language of the Classroom*. New York: Teachers College Press, 1966.

7. Belth, Marc. *Education as a Discipline: A Study of the Role of Models in Thinking*. Boston: Allyn and Bacon, 1965.

8. Bills, Robert E. "Believing and Behaving: Perception and Learning." In *Learning More About Learning*, edited by Alexander Frazier, pp. 55–73. Washington. D.C.: Association for Supervision and Curriculum Development, 1959.

9. Bohanan, Paul J. "Field Anthropologists and Classroom Teachers." *Social Education* 32:161–166, February 1968.

10. Butts, Robert E. "'Indoctrination With,' and 'Indoctrination Into.'" *Bucknell Review* 10:347–363, May 1962.

11. Byers, Paul. "Cameras Don't Take Pictures." *Columbia University Forum* 9:27–31, Winter 1966.

12. Carroll, Lewis. *Alice in Wonderland and Other Favorites*. New York: Pocket Books, 1951.

13. Central Advisory Council for Education (England). *Children and Their Primary Schools* (The Plowden Report). London: Her Majesty's Stationery Office, 1967.

14. Cheverst, W. J. "The Role of the Metaphor in Educational Thought: An Essay in Content Analysis." *Journal of Curriculum Studies* 4:71–82, May 1972.

15. Copi, Irving M. *Introduction to Logic*. New York: Macmillan, 1961.

16. Crittenden, Brian S. "Teaching, Educating, and Indoctrinating." *Educational Theory* 18:237–252, Summer 1968.

17. Cubberley, Ellwood P. *Public School Administration*. Boston: Houghton Mifflin Company, 1916. Cited in Herbert M. Kliebard, "Bureaucracy and Curriculum Theory," in *Freedom, Bureaucracy, and Schooling*, edited by Vernon F. Haubrich (Washington, D.C.: Association for Supervision and Curriculum Development, 1971), pp. 74–93.

18. Dewey, John. *How We Think*. Boston: D. C. Heath, 1933.

19. Eisner, Elliot W. "Instruction, Teaching, and Learning: An Attempt at Differentiation." *Elementary School Journal* 65:115–119, December 1964.

20. Fattu, N. A. "A Model of Teaching as Problem Solving." In *Theories of Instruction*, edited by James B. Macdonald and Robert R. Leeper, pp. 62–87. Washington, D.C.: Association for Supervision and Curriculum Development, 1965.

21. Flanders, Ned A. "Intent, Action, and Feedback: A Preparation for Teaching." *Journal of Teacher Education* 14:251–260, September 1963.

22. Flew, Anthony. "What Is Indoctrination?" *Studies in Philosophy and Education* 4:281–306, Spring 1966.

23. Gowin, D. B. "Teaching, Learning, and Thirdness." *Studies in Philosophy and Education* 1:87–113, August 1961.

24. Green, Thomas F. *The Activities of Teaching*. New York: McGraw-Hill, 1971.

25. Green, Thomas F. "A Topology of the Teaching Concept." *Studies in Philosophy and Education* 3:284–319, Winter 1964–65.

26. Grote, Margaret D. "Teaching and the Sex Act." *Educational Theory* 21:187–192, Spring 1971.

27. Hare, R. M. "Adolescents into Adults." In *Aims in Education: The Philosophic Approach*, edited by T. H. B. Hollins, pp. 47–70. Manchester, Eng.: Manchester University Press, 1964.

28. Hughes, Marie M. "Utah Study of the Assessment of Teaching." In *Theory and Research in Teaching*, edited by Arno A. Bellack, pp. 25–36. New York: Bureau of Publications, Teachers College, Columbia University, 1963.

29. Hyman, Ronald T. "Teaching: Triadic and Dynamic." *Educational Forum* 32:65–69, November 1967.

30. Judges, A. V. "Martin Buber." In *The Function of Teaching*, edited by A. V. Judges, pp. 89–108. London: Faber and Faber, 1959.

31. Kleine, Paul F., and Peter Pereira. "Limits of Perception: What Teacher Trainees See and Don't See in Classrooms." *School Review* 78:483–497, August 1970.

32. Kohlberg, Lawrence. "Moral Education in the Schools: A Developmental View." *School Review* 74:1–30, Spring 1966.

33. Komisar, B. Paul. "Conceptual Analysis of Teaching." *High School Journal* 50:14–21, October 1966.

34. Komisar, B. Paul. "Is Teaching Phoney?" *Teachers College Record* 70:407–411, February 1969.

35. Komisar, B. Paul. "Teaching: Act and Enterprise." *Studies in Philosophy and Education* 6:168–193, Spring 1968.

36. Komisar, B. Paul, and James E. McClellan. "The Logic of Slogans." In *Language and Concepts in Education*, edited by B. Othanel Smith and Robert H. Ennis, pp. 195–214. Chicago: Rand McNally, 1961.

37. Mitchell, Frank W. "Some Notes on the Concept of Teaching." *Journal of Teacher Education* 17:162–171, Summer 1966.

38. Moore, Willis. "Indoctrination as a Normative Conception." *Studies in Philosophy and Education* 4:396–403, Summer 1966.

39. Peters, R. S. "Education as Initiation." In *Philosophical Analysis and Education*, edited by Reginald D. Archambault, pp. 87–111. New York: Humanities Press, 1965.

40. Ryle, Gilbert. *The Concept of Mind.* New York: Barnes and Noble, 1949, pp. 309–314.

41. Scheffler, Israel. *Conditions of Knowledge: An Introduction to Epistemology and Education.* Chicago: Scott, Foresman, 1965, pp. 7–21.

42. Scheffler, Israel. *The Language of Education.* Springfield, Ill.: Charles C Thomas, 1960.

43. Scheffler, Israel. "Philosophical Models of Teaching." *Harvard Educational Review* 35:131–143, Spring 1965.

44. Schwab, Joseph J. "Structure of the Disciplines: Meanings and Significances." In *The Structure of Knowledge and the Curriculum*, edited by G. W. Ford and L. Pugno, pp. 6–30. Chicago: Rand McNally, 1964.

45. Smith, B. Othanel. "A Concept of Teaching." *Teachers College Record* 61:229–241, February 1960.

46. Smith, B. Othanel. "On the Anatomy of Teaching." *Journal of Teacher Education* 7:339–346, December 1956.

47. Snook, I. A. "The Concept of Indoctrination." *Studies in Philosophy and Education* 7:65–108, Fall 1970.

48. Stavsky, William H. "Using the Insights of Psychotherapy in Teaching." *Elementary School Journal* 58:28–35, October 1957. As reprinted in *Teaching: Vantage Points for Study*, edited by Ronald T. Hyman (Philadelphia: J. B. Lippincott, 1968), pp. 166–175.

49. Toffler, Alvin. *Future Shock.* New York: Bantam Books, 1971.

50. Turbayne, Colin Murray. *The Myth of Metaphor.* Rev. ed. Columbia, S.C.: University of South Carolina Press, 1970.

51. Vargas, Julie S. *Writing Worthwhile Behavioral Objectives.* New York: Harper and Row, 1972.

52. Wilson, John. "Education and Indoctrination." *Aims in Education: The Philosophic Approach*, edited by T. H. B. Hollins, pp. 24–46. Manchester, Eng.: Manchester University Press, 1964.

53. Winch, Peter. *The Idea of a Social Science.* New York: Humanities Press, 1959.

2 Behavioral Objectives in Teaching

People who teach believe that they can and do change their students. Whether these changes are in overt behavior or in some predisposition to alter overt behavior is an open question, but teachers do hold that teaching is beneficial, that the student can be helped and is capable of learning.

With such a belief as a basis, teachers set forth the changes they seek to effect and then establish the procedures they think will bring those changes. That is, they set their ends and then determine the means to reach them.

This approach is common in our society. Statesmen set their ends and then determine the legislation and enforcement procedures needed to achieve their policies. Doctors, generals, engineers, carpenters, and many others follow a similar pattern. With regard to curriculum, we can trace the use of this concept back centuries, but it emerged as a recognized professional method at the beginning of the twentieth century (10). Early curriculum practitioners such as Franklin Bobbitt and W. W. Charters accepted and employed it unquestioningly.

The Tyler Rationale

This means-ends, step-by-step approach to curriculum and teaching, where educators establish objectives as ends to be reached, select subject matter and a teaching method, organize the teachers and pupils, and finally evaluate their activities to see if they reached their objectives, is most notably disseminated through the work and writing of Ralph Tyler, a disciple of Bobbitt and Charters. The "Tyler rationale" was set forth in Tyler's now classic syllabus for "Education 360" at the University of Chicago, *Basic Principles of Curriculum and Instruction*. Tyler wrote his book as an attempt "to explain a rationale for viewing, analyzing, and interpreting the curriculum and instruction program of an educational institution. . . . This book outlines one way of viewing an institutional program as a functioning instrument of education" (24:1).

The Tyler rationale centers around "four fundamental questions which must be answered in developing any curriculum and plan of instruction. These are:

1. What educational purposes should the school seek to attain?
2. What educational experiences can be provided that are likely to attain these purposes?
3. How can these educational experiences be effectively organized?
4. How can we determine whether these purposes are being attained?" (24:1).

It is important to note that these questions are to be answered in the order in which they are asked. Therefore, the stating of objectives is the crucial step for Tyler. The other three responses are given in light of the objectives chosen. Tyler makes this point about objectives clearly at the beginning of his book: "These educational objectives become the criteria by which materials are selected, content is outlined, instructional procedures are developed, and tests and examinations are prepared. All aspects of the educational program are really means to accomplish basic educational purposes. Hence, if we are to study an educational program systematically and intelligently, we must first be sure as to the educational objectives aimed at" (24:3).

Though Tyler himself indicates that his rationale is but one way of viewing curriculum and teaching matters (see the first quotation from his book), the Tyler formulation has crystallized to become *the* rationale. Many students of curriculum and teaching even fail to realize that there can be other rationales (8; 12). This failure is due to the inaccessibility of other rationales and the lack of curriculums developed according to them. Many students also fail to realize that curriculum development according to a step-by-step approach began before 1949, the year Tyler first published his syllabus. Rather, in 1949 Tyler simply formally presented his interpretation of an approach which had been utilized for at least thirty years by professional curriculum theorists and practitioners. We have, then, in the Tyler rationale only one man's formulation of one approach to curriculum development, but one which has risen to the position of near dogma.

Defending and Writing Behavioral Objectives

Recently there have appeared some elaborations and defenses of the Tyler rationale as well as some criticisms of it. In particular the conflict centers around the primacy of objectives, especially specific, behavioral objectives.*

Hilda Taba (23:200), who requires as her first criterion for guiding the formulation of objectives the description of the kind of behavior expected of the student and the context to which that behavior applies, is typical of the defenders (2; 7; 9; 15; 19; 20; 21; 25). Her thought is based on that of Tyler, who says, "The most useful form for stating objectives is to express them in terms which identify both the kind of behavior to be developed in the student and the content or area of life in which this behavior is to operate" (24:46). Taba justifies her position of specifying behavior by claiming that it is "necessary in order for the objectives to serve as a platform for both curriculum development and evaluation" (23:200). The staunch defenders claim that, since planning is necessary in teaching and since evaluating is also necessary, teachers need to have guidelines. Specific behavioral objectives serve this double function. They also communicate to students and other concerned people just what the aims of the teacher are.

Therefore, precise, specific behavioral objectives are the guides by which teachers select subject matter to teach, materials to use, methods to employ, and tests by which to measure achievement. In addition, they serve as criteria for evaluating the accomplishments of teaching. For example, if the behavioral objective states that the student will announce the air temperature from a thermometer rounded off to the nearest five-degree mark, then obviously the teacher will provide a calibrated thermometer, treat the topic of heat and its measurement, decide on an appropriate teaching method, and decide when to examine the student

---

* I shall use the term *behavioral objectives* since it is best known. Some people prefer *performance objectives* or *instructional intentions*, claiming that these terms are clearer and do not carry the negative connotation often associated with *behaviorism* as an approach to understanding human activity.

on thermometer reading. At the same time, this objective offers the teacher a standard by which to evaluate the student. If the student reads the thermometer correctly, then he earns an "A" for his achievement. If not, he earns a failing mark and must proceed to restudy the topic.

Once the teacher has before him a set of such written behavioral objectives, he has a clear guide to what he has to accomplish. He knows what his student is to achieve and then can readily inform the student, his parents, and other people concerned with his achievement. He can always refer to his set of written objectives for clarification and review. Periodically he must reconsider his objectives in light of his student's success in achieving them, modify the objectives, and rewrite them as necessary.

There are several essential rules to observe in writing worthwhile specific behavioral objectives. Below are the first five; the sixth follows shortly afterward:

Rule 1. Describe the expected behavior of the *student* rather than the teacher.

Rule 2. Describe *observable behavior* in terms of an outcome verb which the student will perform (e.g., pantomime, identify, arrange, weigh, hammer).

Rule 3. Describe the *criterion* for evaluating an acceptable performance of the behavior (e.g., name at least four colors of the rainbow, hammer three nails one inch deep, run a mile in six minutes).

Rule 4. Specify *important conditions* under which the student will perform the behavior (e.g., run a mile before breakfast, kick three fieldgoals in a championship football game, solve a quadratic equation during a classroom session).

Rule 5. State only *one outcome verb* in each objective.

The following objectives are some examples that meet these writing rules:

1. The student will recite the pledge of allegiance to the flag by memory without error. He will do this in class before December 20.

2. The student will draw a bar graph to a scale of $1''$:1,000,000 votes showing the popular vote each state gave to the two recent presidential candidates. Each candidate's representation by state

must be accurate within 100,000 votes on graph paper of ten units to an inch.

3. The student will high jump over a bar four feet high at least once in three trials at the school stadium.

4. The student will compare the British and American forms of government regarding personnel in the legislative and executive branches. He will do so during an individual ten-minute oral exam in class during the week after the unit on comparative government. He will explicitly compare a minimum of three positions in each branch to pass the exam.

If the teacher writes his behavioral objectives in the above way (as advocated by some people), centering on such verbs as recite, draw, high jump, and compare, he will soon run into trouble. This is not because of the structure of his objectives but because of their level. That is to say, such objectives, precisely because of their specificity, do not give a sense of direction to the teacher for an entire year, semester, or even a unit of study. To get direction, the teacher needs more general words, such as *understanding, appreciating, thinking*, and *writing*. Direction in teaching and in any other complex activity comes from a broad perspective, a general view of things. A series of specific activities just does not add up to direction for a teacher planning for a long period of time. General verbs not only give such direction, but they also give leeway in selecting and assessing the many different activities that occur in all teaching.

Centering behavioral objectives strictly in terms of specific verbs is perhaps permissible with the simplest skills and the lowest levels of knowledge and values. But the teaching only of simple skills and low levels of knowledge and value is most rare. In the overwhelming percentage of teaching situations, the teacher builds on simple subject matter to teach complex skills, knowledge, and values. The teacher is then not concerned merely with reciting, drawing, high jumping, and comparing. Such specific actions are not ends in themselves but *examples* of still more general actions and building blocks toward complex actions. Specific actions take on meaning when seen in the context of a larger setting, when subsumed under a more general verb and taken as examples of it.

For these reasons, teachers need to write specific behavioral objectives within the context of more general activities. By listing first the general objective and then the specific objectives subsumed under it, the teacher will get direction for the long period of time as well as guidelines for the short period of time. The following set of objectives illustrates this key point:

The student will comprehend the use of graphs in presenting political science data.

1. The student will draw a bar graph to a scale of 1":1,000,000 votes showing the popular vote each state gave to the recent presidential candidates. Each candidate's representation by state must be accurate within 100,000 votes on graph paper of ten units to an inch.
2. The student will verify by computation from graphs given to him that the presidential candidate with the most popular votes has not always won the electoral college vote.

Such objectives give direction and emphasize that the teacher must concentrate on comprehension by the student. They show that *drawing* a bar graph and *verifying* by computation are but examples of comprehension of the use of graphs in presenting political science data. With objectives written in this form the teacher is not set back if the student begins to work on extrapolating from graphs dealing with congressional elections. Indeed, if the two specific objectives above are seen as manifestations of comprehension, then the teacher could even appropriately add or substitute the following specific behavioral objective to the set above.

3. The student will extrapolate from bar graph data given to him by the teacher on senatorial elections in New York State to show the greater influence of upstate New York over the New York City area. He will present his conclusions to the class in a five-minute oral report.

Obviously it is impossible to list all the many activities through which a student could demonstrate his comprehension of the use of graphs in presenting political science data. Indeed, there is no need to, once the teacher sets forth a general objective with several specific behavioral objectives subsumed under it as examples. The teacher must take care, then, that the specific objectives listed are important, representative, and indeed examples of the more general verb. This leads to another essential rule to observe in writing worthwhile specific behavior objectives.

Rule 6. Subsume sets of specific behavioral objectives under an appropriate, more general, objective (e.g., comprehend, understand, think critically, appreciate). The individual items listed should be important and representative manifestations of the general heading.

(To be added to the five rules for writing specific behavioral objectives listed earlier.)

The point here is significant. A general objective takes on meaning as it is understood through the specific objectives it subsumes as well as through its relationship with other general objectives. Just as specific objectives have meaning only within the context of a more general objective, so, too, does a general objective have meaning only within its context. It is the context that gives meaning to any objective.

In writing behavioral objectives the teacher must take care to include a variety of activities (that is, a variety from the subject matter dimensions of knowledge, skills, and values) which are relevant to the topic under study. The teacher should also be certain that the verb in the statement clearly suits the teacher's intentions and is relevant to his broader teaching aims. The teacher will need to refer to guidebooks and other people's lists of objectives for aid in determining the appropriate specific behaviors for the complex, general objectives desired. Several books devoted entirely to the writing of behavioral objectives (e.g., Gronlund and Kibler) have helpful lists of such words.

Criticisms of Behavioral Objectives

For the past few years the literature about curriculum and teaching has been strongly advocating the use of behavioral objectives. Only recently have there appeared a few equally strong voices opposing them (3; 14; 22). Yet these opponents have been able to influence some leading proponents to modify their viewpoint already (17; 18). It is worthwhile to set forth some of these influential criticisms.

The first criticism concerns the *specificity* of objectives. This criticism is made despite the rule of subsuming specific behavioral objectives under a more general verb. In practice, most people all too easily lose sight of the general, subsuming verb because, for years, curriculum workers have claimed that objectives should be stated in specific terms rather than in broad generalities if the objectives are to be helpful. Some people are now realizing that specific objectives severely restrict the curriculum and teaching. Specific objectives lead to specific elements, and the net result is a loss of the flexibility needed in a program serving a wide range of pupils varying in age, interest, and ability. Thus, though specificity in objectives may help in determining a focus, the same specificity may serve to restrict teaching in actual operation.

The second criticism concerns the stating of specific objectives in *behavioral* terms. Teaching is not merely interested in changing a student's behavior. Indeed, brainwashing, threatening, and torturing can induce behavioral changes, and if someone simply wants to induce behavioral changes, he can resort to these non-teaching approaches. Teaching, in contrast to brainwashing, attempts to induce change that is guided by reason and principle. "The widely known and accepted dogma that the aim of teaching is to change behavior is both patently false and dangerously misleading. The aim of teaching is not to change people's behavior but to transform behavior into action" (6). (Action, according to Green, the author of this quotation, entails giving reasons. In acting, a person consciously follows certain rules and has reasons for justifying what he does.)

Green's point is well taken. Teachers are interested, not only in what a student does, but in why he does it. To state merely what a student should do (for example, answer test questions on his own) is thus inadequate. An objective stated in behavioral terms without further specification of reasons is not a useful tool for curriculum and teaching development or evaluation. A teacher would rather have his students not cheat by reason of their commitment to honesty and their respect for other people than not cheat by reason of their fear of punishment. But, if all a teacher knows is that Jonathan did not cheat on his last exam, then he has insufficient data for evaluating both his own teaching efforts and Jonathan's progress in regard to cheating.

Moreover, the specification of expected behavioral changes is made with the belief that, since behavior can be observed, a behavioral objective can and will facilitate objective measurement and evaluation. In other words, overt behavior can be observed, in contrast to such activities as reflective thinking, creativity, and appreciating good music. However, we must candidly admit that presently we have no adequate way to observe and measure all the desired behavioral outcomes we already have established, let alone such desired activities as appreciating music. Some activities steadfastly remain nonmeasurable and quite resistant even to representation in terms of specific objectives.

Those who uncritically advocate behaviorally specified objectives, by their insistence on these, also seem to advocate that an objective is worthwhile only if we can observe and measure its attainment. Obviously, despite common acceptance in some quarters, it is false that only behaviorally stated objectives are valuable. J. Myron Atkin, who is involved in the teaching of science, puts it this way:

Worthwhile goals come first, not our methods for assessing progress toward these goals. Goals are derived from our needs and from our philosophies. They are not and should not be derived primarily from our measures. It borders on the irresponsible for those who exhort us to state objectives in behavioral terms to avoid the issue of determining worth. Inevitably there is an implication of worth behind any act of measurement. What the educational community poorly realizes at the moment is that behavioral goals may or may not be worthwhile. They are articulated from among the vast library of goals because they are stated relatively easily. Again, let's not asume that what we can presently measure necessarily represents our most important activity (1:30).

But even if we could adequately measure every specified behavior, we still would not automatically arrive at an evaluation. To evaluate any particular behavior we need criteria—that is, standards—with which to compare the observed measured behavior. In some fields of study, such as mathematics, there are accepted criteria for designated behaviors, and it is therefore easy to evaluate the student's work, for example, in adding, subtracting, dividing, and multiplying. However, in other fields, such as art, dance, poetry, and creative scientific research, which rely on qualitative elements that are not observable, there are no definite standards for judging the value of a performance. And it is precisely these qualitative elements, such as creativeness, understanding, critical reasoning, and insight, which most educators seek as objectives of curriculum and teaching (5).

The third criticism concerns the function of objectives. According to the Tyler rationale, teachers establish objectives prior to establishing the curriculum and teaching focus and prior to working with the students, since these objectives are to serve as guides for the teachers. Teachers operate under the belief that they know their objectives prior to teaching and can specify the outcome of teaching prior to their interaction with students. Yet it is reasonable to argue that teachers fully know their objectives only while teaching a lesson or after completing one. John Dewey claimed that "ends arise and function within action. They are not, as current theories too often imply, things lying outside activity at which the latter is directed. They are not strictly speaking ends or termini of action at all. They are terminals of deliberation, and so turning points in activity" (4:223).

In commenting on this point, Herbert M. Kliebard makes a significant contribution. What Tyler has as step number two (learning experiences) might indeed replace objectives as step number one if we accept the point that objectives emerge within the course of teaching. "If ends arise only within activity it is not clear how one can state objectives before the activity (learning experience) begins. Dewey's position, then, has important consequences not just for Tyler's process of evaluation, but for the rationale as a whole. It would mean, for example, that the starting point for a model of curriculum and instruction is not the statement of objectives but the activity (learning experience), and whatever objectives do appear will arise within that activity as a way of adding a new dimension to it" (11:268–269).

This crucial criticism of the position and function of objectives deserves restating. The same point is made cogently by James B. Macdonald in examining current myths about curriculum and instruction.

Objectives are viewed as directives in the rational approach. They are identified prior to the instruction or action and used to provide a basis for or a screen for appropriate activities.

There is another view, however, which has both scholarly and experiential referents. This view would state that our objectives are only known to us in any complete sense after the completion of our act of instruction. No matter what we thought we were attempting to do, we can only know what we wanted to accomplish after the fact. Objectives by this rationale are heuristic devices which provide initiating sequences which become altered in the flow of instruction.

In the final analysis, it could be argued, the teacher in actuality asks a fundamentally different question from "What am I trying to accomplish?" The teacher asks, "What am I going to do?" and out of the doing comes accomplishment (13:613–614).

Since teaching is a dynamic activity in which all the relationships among variables are never known and where unexpected things regularly emerge, it is impossible to specify all the outcomes ahead of time even if we cared to do so. A teacher may not only alter his objectives, but he may discover new ones to pursue during the act of teaching. What is more, the most desirable outcomes are often not those specified in advance as objectives. The most significant outcomes may be those that are not planned for nor fully anticipated when establishing objectives (4:227).

The fourth criticism concerns the effect of behavioral objectives on the act of teaching. If the teacher devotes himself steadfastly to the achievement of his stated behavioral objectives, he is apt to pay a high price for his success. Though the teacher may be evaluated as successful according to the accountability formulas held by many professionals and laymen which acknowledge only the number of behavioral objectives achieved, he may well lose sight of what "teaching" is as he proceeds. If the teacher believes that the achievement of his objectives is supreme, it is likely that he will negate what is essential in the manner of teaching. The teacher may well give up a friendly, warm, interpersonal tone in which he respects the integrity and independence of the student. In short, in order to achieve the behavioral objectives, the teacher may change his manner and hence move to nonteaching activities, such as force, threat, and intimidation. The price of achievement of objectives may be the loss of teaching—an enormously high price to pay. The value of achievement is surely questionable if achievement comes at the expense of a desirable manner. Indeed, the achievement may be self-defeating.

The fifth criticism centers on implicit values. Many of those who propose the use of behavioral objectives fail to realize that these objectives carry certain latent functions. The teacher's efforts to attain only behavioral objectives allow students to depend on him to set objectives, rather than learning to be autonomous and to set their own objectives. This is particularly important with regard to secondary and college students, who are in the stage of developing independence (16). Furthermore, when the teacher strongly sets out ahead of time to develop certain objectives, the students learn to deemphasize or disregard any unexpected outcomes or spontaneous events which may in themselves be extremely valuable. In short, though behavioral objectives have the manifest functions of facilitating measurement and evaluation and of permitting the marketing of profitable materials and machines, their latent function of restricting learning to a mode of dependence and expectedness is important enough in itself to warrant serious doubt and restricted use of them.

Suggestions for Using Behavioral Objectives

There are serious objections to the extensive use of behavioral objectives in teaching. A teacher should know the positive uses of behavioral objectives, and he should know how to write them. On the other hand, he should be alert to the serious criticisms of them because there are uncritical pressures to use them from some quarters, especially those school administrators, state departments, and zealous organizations calling for strict teacher accountability.

The teacher who uses specific behavioral objectives should do so within a framework that is flexible. He should use them in planning but must remain aware that any given specific activity of the student is but one of many manifestations possible under a general objective (see Rule 6). He should strive to remain master of his objectives and not be mastered by them, lest he slip blindly into nonteaching activities in order to achieve his objectives at any cost. He should try whenever possible to have students write their own objectives. This means that they should write their own objectives for themselves, not what they think their teachers expect them to write.

The teacher should take care to remain calm even when he sees the teaching situation moving away from his planned objective. The evolving situation may indeed be leading to a highly desirable but unplanned-for end. If the teacher panics and stops the natural movement, he may achieve a planned but less significant goal than the unexpected but highly desirable one. He may also squash the spontaneity and excitement which give life to his students and himself. The teacher will need to make on-the-spot decisions whether to pursue his stated behavioral objectives or allow the situation to evolve and unstated goals to emerge.

The teacher must also be willing to plan activities for which he is not able to state predetermined behavioral objectives or for which he has difficulty setting forth any clear specific objectives, behavioral or nonbehavioral. This procedure will serve to provide a free, unstructured situation where the teacher has the opportunity to openly move with the students' desires. It will add the needed dimensions of spontaneity and freedom from constraints. It will also serve as an antidote to a possible overreliance on predetermined specific behavioral objectives.

In summary, then, whenever the teacher uses specific behavioral objectives, he should do so knowledgeably, carefully, and flexibly. The teacher must be prepared to make many decisions about behavioral objectives on the spot, often making a professional choice by weighing the advantages and disadvantages of a predetermined objective against those of an objective that is unexpected.

References

1. Atkin, J. Myron. "Behavioral Objectives in Curriculum Design." *Science Teacher* 35:27–30, May 1968.
2. Baker, Robert L., and Richard E. Schutz, eds. *Instructional Product Development*. New York: Van Nostrand Reinhold, 1971.
3. Combs, Arthur W. *Educational Accountability: Beyond Behavioral Objectives*. Washington, D.C.: Association for Supervision and Curriculum Development, 1972.
4. Dewey, John. *Human Nature and Conduct*. New York: Henry Holt, 1922.
5. Eisner, Elliot W. "Educational Objectives: Help or Hindrance?" *School Review* 3:250–260, Autumn 1967.
6. Green, Thomas F. "Teaching, Acting, and Behaving." *Harvard Educational Review* 34:507–524, Fall 1964.
7. Gronlund, Norman E. *Stating Behavioral Objectives for Classroom Instruction*. London: Macmillan, 1970.
8. Huebner, Dwayne. "Curricular Language and Classroom Meanings." In *Language and Meaning*, edited by James B. Macdonald and Robert R. Leeper, pp. 8–26. Washington, D.C.: Association for Supervision and Curriculum Development, 1966.
9. Kibler, Robert J., Larry L. Barker, and David T. Miles. *Behavioral Objectives and Instruction*. Boston: Allyn and Bacon, 1970.
10. Kliebard, Herbert M. "The Curriculum Field in Retrospect." In *Technology and the Curriculum*, edited by Paul W. F. Witt, pp. 69–84. New York: Teachers College Press, 1968.
11. Kliebard, Herbert M. "The Tyler Rationale." *School Review* 78:259–272, February 1970.
12. Macdonald, James B. "A Curriculum Rationale." In *Contemporary Thought on Public School Curriculum*, edited by Edmund C. Short and George D. Marconnit, pp. 37–42. Dubuque, Ia.: W. C. Brown, 1968.
13. Macdonald, James B. "Myths about Instruction." *Educational Leadership* 22:571–576, 609–617, May 1965.
14. Macdonald, James B., and Bernice J. Wolfson. "A Case Against Behavioral Objectives." *Elementary School Journal* 71:119–128, December 1970.
15. Mager, Robert F. *Preparing Instructional Objectives*. Palo Alto, Calif.: Fearon Publishers, 1962.

16. Norton, David L. "The Rites of Passage from Dependence to Autonomy." *School Review* 79:19–41, November 1970.

17. Popham, James W. "Must All Objectives Be Behavioral?" *Educational Leadership* 29:605–608, April 1972.

18. Popham, James W. "Objectives, 1972." *Phi Delta Kappan* 53:432–435, March 1972.

19. Popham, James W., and Eva L. Baker. *Establishing Instructional Goals.* Englewood Cliffs, N.J.: Prentice-Hall, 1970.

20. Popham, James W., and Eva L. Baker. *Planning an Instructional Sequence.* Englewood Cliffs, N.J.: Prentice-Hall, 1970.

21. Popham, James W., and Eva L. Baker. *Systematic Instruction.* Englewood Cliffs, N.J.: Prentice-Hall, 1970.

22. Popham, W. J., and others. *Instructional Objectives.* AERA Monograph Series on Curriculum Evaluation, no. 3. Chicago: Rand McNally, 1969.

23. Taba, Hilda. *Curriculum Development: Theory and Practice.* New York: Harcourt, Brace, and World, 1962.

24. Tyler, Ralph W. *Basic Principles of Curriculum and Instruction.* Chicago: University of Chicago Press, 1949.

25. Vargas, Julie S. *Writing Worthwhile Behavioral Objectives.* New York: Harper and Row, 1972.

3 Perspectives on the Choice of Method

Ways of Teaching is based primarily on the research into teaching of the past decade and a half. It was during this time that educators, as citizens and professionals, took another hard look at teaching. Three aspects of the research that resulted are especially noteworthy for this book: (a) the emphasis on "new" methods (for example, discovery method and simulation games) that accompanied the emphasis on the "new" curriculums (for example, the new mathematics, the new physics, and the new social studies); (b) the attention paid to the verbal activity of teachers and students (Who says what to whom, and how much? Or, just what do teachers and students say to each other?); and (c) the increasing trend among analytic philosophers to investigate the concept of teaching in their professional journals and works (What do we mean when we use the word *teaching*?). It is from these most recent trends that this work takes its inspiration. The data and ideas generated as the result of research into how to teach, how to observe, and how to evaluate teaching serve as the foundation of this book.

The subject of teaching methods is accepted as a valid topic of inquiry both by philosophers (3) and pedagogical researchers. Teaching method, of course, is of utmost importance to everyone concerned with teaching. No one can teach something to someone without doing it in some particular way, and that way of teaching has significant effects on the entire teaching and learning situation. For the purpose of this book, *method* will be understood to mean a pattern or manner (which can be repeated) of treating people, objects, and events, that is directed—purposively and recognizably—toward the achievement of some goal (3:135).

A Glimpse at the Past

There is a tendency among some modern critics to claim that the concern with methods of teaching is a new phenomenon that has resulted from the growth of normal schools, departments of education, teachers' colleges, and schools of education. Such claims are false, as a look into the past quickly reveals.

In the Talmud the ancient Hebrews expressed their great concern about teaching, not by establishing specific methods to be used, but by giving advice to teachers in the form of short maxims.

Teach your tongue to say "I don't know" when you are uncertain lest you later be proven incorrect (15).

If one asks of thee a question, do not stammer but reply without hesitation. . . .

Be meek like Hillel and not irritable like Shamai, for the irritable is not fit to teach. . . .

Always teach your pupils in the shortest manner. . . .

Teach from the known to the unknown and from the simple to the complex. . . .

Use mnemonic signs as an aid to the children's memory. . . .

Make the subject of study clear by means of illuminating proofs (11:107, 128, 129).

The Talmud tells of the famous teacher Rabbah, who, "before he began to teach his pupils, was in the habit of introducing his remarks with something bright and sparkling; by this means the scholars were put in joyous mood. He then proceeded in all gravity to the subject of his discourse" (11:128). The teacher is also given a great deal of advice in the Talmud regarding his treatment of his students, his personal character traits, and the respect due him and his students.

The Sophists of ancient Greece of the fifth and fourth centuries B.C. devoted considerable effort to analyzing the activities of successful poets and speakers, in order to locate the key elements of success. For ten thousand drachmas the Sophists guaranteed that they would prepare a young man to be a success in Greek affairs of state (8). They established methods of teaching the various subjects they dealt with. Dionysius of Thrace, who lived in the second century B.C., presented the following six steps as the outline of his method of lecturing on a literary text:

1. Give the selected passages an exact reading with respect to pronunciation, punctuation, and rhetorical expression.
2. Explain the figures of speech.

3. Explain the historical and mythological references.
4. Comment on the choice of words and their etymology.
5. Point out the grammatical forms employed.
6. Estimate the literary merit of the selection (2:23).

Concern about method passed from Greece to Rome, where the teaching of rhetoric was continued. The Romans not only set forth their method for speaking effectively, but they also dealt with teaching students how to speak effectively. In fact, the Romans devoted considerable attention to establishing and discussing method. Broudy and Palmer claim that "it would be difficult to match the minuteness of analysis that went into the teaching of rhetoric in the schools of Greece and Rome" (2:24).

Nor did concern about method cease with the Romans. Under the influence of Peter Abelard, medieval teachers developed the method of disputation in lecturing.

By the time of St. Thomas Aquinas the method of logical demonstration had been perfected. Armed with the mastery of Aristotelian philosophy and the results of theological scholarship, he began with a question, reviewed the authorities, proposed the correct solution, and then systematically refuted all the objections which he thought could be brought against it (2:65).

Medieval teachers, in short, were quite aware that they followed a particular sequence of steps in disputation. Odofredus, a thirteenth-century lecturer on law at the University of Bologna, stated his method:

First, I shall give you summaries of each title before I proceed to the text; secondly, I shall give you as clear and explicit a statement as I can of the purport of each Law (included in the title); thirdly, I shall read the text with a view to correcting it; fourthly, I shall briefly repeat the contents of the Law; fifthly, I shall solve apparent contradictions, adding any general principles of Law (to be extracted from the passage), commonly called "Brocardica," and any distinctions or subtle and useful problems (questions) arising out of the Law with their solutions, as far as the Divine Providence shall enable me. And if any Law shall seem deserving, by reason of its celebrity or difficulty, of a Repetition, I shall reserve it for an evening Repetition (10:219–220).

According to Rashdall, the method outlined in this statement could be applied in any faculty of a medieval university (10:219).

In the transition from medieval times to the present, such men as Comenius, Pestalozzi, Froebel, and Herbart devoted a great deal of thought to methods of teaching as part of a more general concern with schooling. In summary, then, the interest in and concern with how to teach can be traced in a continuous line from ancient times to the present; it is not simply a twentieth-century phenomenon.

Common Points Among Methods

To gain a clearer concept of method, it is helpful to abstract several elements common to different teaching methods. Broudy and Palmer suggest seven common steps or phases in teaching (2:9):

1. *Preparation for instruction*—what the teacher does before he confronts the student. This includes gathering materials, making a lesson plan, reviewing notes, and predicting possible student responses to his actions.

2. *Motivation*—what the teacher does to capture the attention of the student. This does not include the use of "gimmicks" that capture the student's attention temporarily.

3. *Presentation of the learning task*—what the teacher offers to the student—what the student is to learn. This is the essence of the teaching act, and it is in the specification of this step that the various teaching methods differ.

4. *Inducement of the trial response*—what the teacher does or asks the student to do in order to determine whether the student has learned the material or task presented.

5. *Correction of the trial response*—what the teacher does in order to correct the response of the student. If the trial response shows that the student has learned the material or task, then this step is unnecessary. (It is usually necessary.)

6. *Fixation of response*—what the teacher does to assure that the student retains what he has learned.

7. *Test response and evaluation*—what the teacher does to determine how well the student has learned the task presented.

The seven steps of Broudy and Palmer clearly resemble the five Formal Steps of Instruction formulated from the ideas of Herbart by his disciples. The Herbartians, in establishing their "universal" method, took "Herbart's description of the way the mind works in organizing a subject as a whole and converted it into a method of instruction which requires that children, in the acquisition of knowledge, move in lockstep fashion through five steps in learning" (16:10).

The five Herbartian steps are as follows (9:288):

1. *Preparation*—in which the teacher readies the students for what they are about to learn. The teacher calls to mind previously acquired knowledge and experiences related to the new material.

2. *Presentation*—in which the teacher transmits the new knowledge to the students in the form of a clear succession of particulars.

3. *Comparison and abstraction*—in which the student, or (less desirably) the teacher, examines the new particulars carefully for similarities among them.

4. *Generalization*—in which a general principle or rule is formulated from the data in steps 2 and 3.

5. *Application*—in which the generalizations reached are put to use. According to the Herbartians, knowledge is not knowledge until it is put to use.

A third set of common steps, based on Jackson (6), divides teaching into three general categories. The first step is labeled *preactive* (6:12). For the teacher, this step includes such activities as preparing lesson plans, arranging furniture to suit intended groupings of students, mimeographing charts or diagrams to hand out to students, etc. The second step is labeled *interactive*. This step includes those activities that the teacher participates in with the students (6:12), such as making statements of fact and explanation, asking questions, and reacting to the responses. The third step is labeled *postactive*. For the teacher, this step includes such activities as grading homework assignments and tests and thinking about the consequences of the various parts of the lesson.

In this schema the first and third steps blend together, as the postactive considerations of the teacher lead him to particular preactive activities. That is to say, in light of the scores on the tests, which he reviews in the postactive step, the teacher prepares his next lesson in a particular way. (See Figure 3–1.)

It is this cyclical idea that leads to the fourth and fifth sets of common steps or features. The fourth set is offered by Strasser (14), who bases his model primarily on the research of Smith, but also considers the work of Taba, Gallagher and Aschner, and Suchman.* Strasser's model is an elaboration of Smith's earlier

* See the author's book of readings for reports on this research: Ronald T. Hyman, ed., *Teaching: Vantage Points for Study* (Philadelphia: J. B. Lippincott, 1974).

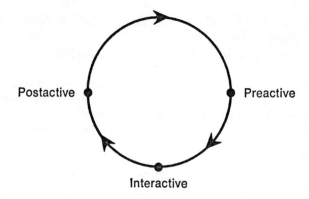

Figure 3–1: The Teaching Action Cycle

schema, in which the flow of teaching is depicted as involving perception, diagnosis, and action by both the teacher and the student. That is, *perception* by the teacher of the student's activity; *diagnosis* by the teacher of the student's state of interest, readiness, knowledge, made by inference; *reaction* of the teacher as the result of his diagnosis; *perception* by the student, etc. (12:235).

Smith puts it this way in a later elaboration of this idea:

Everyone knows that the teacher not only influences student behavior but that he is also influenced by student behavior. The teacher is constantly observing the student and modifying his own behavior in terms of his observations. The teacher perceives the student's behavior. He diagnoses what he perceives, that is to say, he decides upon the meaning of the observed student behavior. For example, he may decide that the student has made a grammatical error, that he is emotionally upset, or that he has made an error in reasoning, a mistake in fact, or misread a passage; or the teacher may note that the student has made an appropriate or unusual response. Finally, the teacher responds to what he has perceived in terms of his diagnosis. We may therefore say that instructional behavior consists of a chain of three links—observing, diagnosing, acting (13:296).

Strasser is intrigued by three ideas in particular: (1) the teacher as influencing the student; (2) the teacher as influenced by the student; and (3) the teacher as "behaver, observer, and diagnoser" (14:66). From these three notions Strasser derives four steps:

1. *Teacher planning*—in terms of what the teacher knows of the learner, the curriculum, the situation.

2. *Teacher behavior, initiatory*—to create a focus for thinking and working: what the teacher does to get things started.

3. *Teacher observation, interpretation, and diagnosis of learner behavior*—in terms of the situation, knowledge of prior experiences of

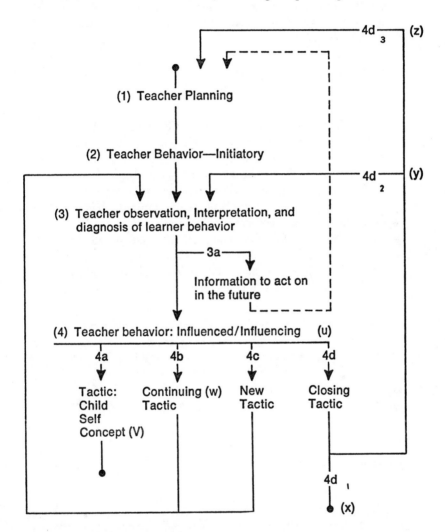

Figure 3–2: A Conceptual Model of Instruction*

* The figure, *A Conceptual Model of Instruction*, by Ben Strasser, is reprinted with permission from the *Journal of Teacher Education* 18:67, Spring 1967 (letters U–Z were added to the chart by the present author, for further clarification, based on Strasser's discussion of the chart [14:68]).

the learner, prior observations of learners' behavior, enhancement of child's self-concept, the curriculum (affective, cognitive, and action dimensions).

4. *Teacher behavior, influenced/influencing*—influenced by the observations, interpretations, and diagnosis of learner behavior, and influencing to the degree that teacher behavior stimulates further learner behavior (14:66).

Strasser uses these four steps to develop a diagram to show the flow of teaching. (See Figure 3–2.)

(U) There are four possibilities at this point.

(V) This is an example of a side tactic: "an exception to the development of the lesson strategy is teacher behavior designed to enhance immediately a child's concept" (14:68).

(W) This continuing tactic comes from previous work.

(X) This position, $4d_1$, indicates something which is not to be considered again, i.e., something closed off.

(Y) This type of closing tactic sets the stage directly for work next time, as in, "Tomorrow we'll pick up where we left off."

(Z) This type of closing tactic implies that it provides information which the teacher will consider in planning the next lesson.

The heart of the model in Figure 3–2 is the tactical loop, which is similar to Smith's teaching cycle and the Teaching Action Cycle shown in Figure 3–1. The tactical loop is depicted as:

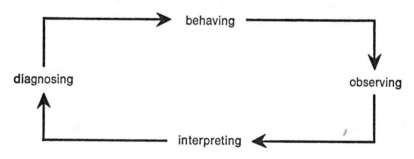

Figure 3–3: Tactical Element Loop*

* The figure, *Tactical Element Loop*, by Ben Strasser, is reprinted with permission from the *Journal of Teacher Education* 18:69, Spring 1967.

The fifth set of common steps also builds on the cyclical element. This flow model of teaching (5) stems from the research of the author and colleagues on the language of the classroom (1). In developing concepts with which to analyze verbal discourse of teaching, researchers took the view that the language of the classroom was a kind of *language game*. This idea derives from the Austro-British analytic philosopher Wittgenstein, who used the metaphor of language games "to point up the fact that linguistic activities assume different forms and structures according to the functions they come to serve in different contexts" (1:3). The researchers, for the purposes of the project, defined the main language game of the classroom as the overall teacher-student verbal discourse during a unit of study on economic trade. This language game might include such subgames as debating the advantages of common markets by two teams of students, viewing

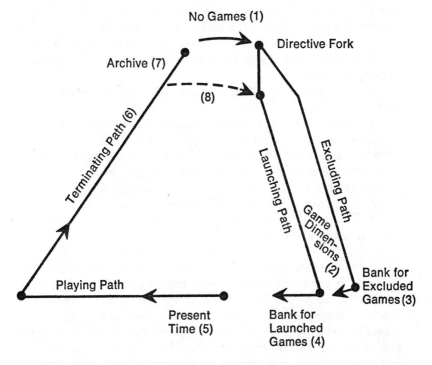

Figure 3–4: Flow Model of Teaching*

* The figure, *Flow Model of Teaching*, is reprinted with permission of the author and the California Association of Secondary School Administrators, from the *Journal of Secondary Education* 42:105, March 1967.

a film on foreign investments, and discussing United States–Canadian trade.

In this context the general steps of the flow model of teaching become (5): no-game state; launching a game or subgame or excluding another game or particular subgame; playing the game; terminating the game; recording (i.e., remembering) the game. These steps are then related as shown in Figure 3–4. Note the cyclical element here also.

1. The no-game state ends when the teacher or a student moves the lesson into activity or when activity begins automatically. This latter condition occurs when a game leaves the bank for launched games (see point 4), since its proper time has arrived.

2. The dimensions of a game or subgame are agent (who is to participate in the game); time (specifying beginning point and duration); topic; activity (test, film, talk) and/or method (lecture, dialogue, debate); thinking process to be emphasized.

3. An excluded game or subgame may be moved to the bank for launched games if it is so directed and if a new time dimension is assigned to it.

4. Both present and future games and subgames are stored here.

5. Launched games moved to this point at appropriate times.

6. A game or subgame may terminate: (A) when its assigned time has expired (e.g., an hour exam), or (B) when a speaker halts it by saying, for example, "Now we'll stop this debate," or (C) when a new game or subgame replaces the ongoing one.

7. All played games enter the archive.

8. The no-game state is bypassed when the terminating game is replaced with a new one.

This enumeration of the common features in teaching methods, as presented in the five sets above, offers a framework for comparing the various methods that will be discussed in later chapters. It may well be that two methods, for example, differ in regard to three steps in Broudy and Palmer's list of steps but are similar in regard to the other four. These five sets are not presented as the only ones possible, nor necessarily as the best. Rather, they represent five possible ways of listing the common points in teaching methods. The reader is asked to keep them in mind as he reads the following chapters.

Criteria for Method Selection

At some point the teacher must decide which method he will use in a given situation. This decision is seldom made by the student. Nor is it frequently made cooperatively by teacher and student. The teacher is responsible for guiding the student, and thus it is he who determines the appropriate method for doing so. If the student takes part in making the decision on method, it is generally because the teacher has permitted or encouraged him to do so.

In order to decide which method is appropriate, the teacher needs criteria. By referring to these criteria the teacher, in effect, considers the students, the situation, and himself, while drawing on his understanding of the various methods. His decision is a judgment arrived at by weighing various factors involved. In treating the lecture and the discussion methods, Oliver Loud, a professor of physical science, puts it this way:

It seems very clear to me that these two procedures [presenting lectures and conducting discussions] have very different consequences surely for all but the exceptional student. Which procedure to employ—during a particular course meeting or, as the more frequently scheduled experience during a course—should, then, be decided not by default, for conventional or trivial, extra-pedagogic reasons, but in terms of the consequences sought (7:30).

The following set of criteria for selection of method is offered at this point to serve as a guide for the reader in later chapters. If any one criterion seems trite or superfluous, the teacher should consider it as simply a reminder of some factor he might otherwise have forgotten.

The teaching method should:

1. Suit the teacher's abilities, knowledge of subject matter, and interests. That is, the teacher should draw on his strengths; he should be comfortable in what he does. This does not mean that he should not try new methods. It does mean that he should continually develop those methods which he finds compatible with his abilities and inclinations. "Methods, like the clothes we wear, must fit the people we are" (4:372).

2. Suit the student's abilities—verbal and psychomotor. That is, if the students are unable to deliver long prepared statements on their viewpoints, it would be unwise to choose a method that requires them to do so.

3. Suit the type of teaching aimed at: teaching how to . . . (skill-oriented), teaching that . . . (knowledge-oriented), or teaching to be . . . (value-oriented). If the teacher wants to teach writing, then he should provide the student with opportunities to write.

4. Suit the time and place context of the teaching situation. For example, if it is 2 P.M. on a Friday afternoon, and the class is comprised of tenth-graders who have a sophomore prom that evening, it would be unwise to choose a method that requires the students to sit quietly and attentively for fifty minutes. A method that involves student participation or comparatively free movement for the students would probably be better suited to the students' mood.

5. Suit the subject matter at hand. For example, to teach the students the effects that oxygen has on metals, it would seem inappropriate to set up a debate on the issue. Demonstrations or laboratory exercises would be more to the point. Similarly, the methods appropriate for teaching archaeology will differ from those for teaching mathematics.

6. Suit the number of students being taught. For example, it hardly seems appropriate to employ a discussion method in a session where 115 students are present.

7. Suit the interests and experience of the students. For example, if most of the previous lessons have been conducted according to the discussion method, it might prove worthwhile to employ the lecture method. Students often are eager to listen to a carefully reasoned lecture in a class in which a discussion or inquiry method has generally been used. Variety in methods is advantageous.

8. Suit the student's relationship with the subject matter. For example, for an introductory class in biology, the teacher would do well to choose a method that will familiarize the students with fundamental terms and skills.

9. Suit the teacher's relationship with the student. For example, if the teacher has not yet established mutual trust, the method selected should lead to such trust.

In other words, in deciding which method is appropriate to a particular lesson or series of lessons, the teacher must consider the following aspects of his teaching situation: the context of the teaching situation (time and place); the number, ability, interests, and previous experience of the students; the nature of the subject matter; the teacher's own abilities and inclinations; and what he wishes to emphasize in his teaching—skills, knowledge, or values.

The teacher must also consider, in reference to his method, the time requirements of the method; the demands the method will make on him and his students; the materials required in using the method; the results that the method brings.

This chapter has presented a general analysis of method, and some criteria have been set forth for method selection. The ensuing chapters will consist in a treatment of the various teaching methods. The rationales underlying these methods will be discussed; examples of the methods will be given; and analyses of the examples will serve as a basis for examining the methods. In addition, the appropriate organization of teachers and students for the purposes of employing these methods will be outlined. The final section will treat questioning and the observation and evaluation of teaching.

References

1. Bellack, Arno A., Herbert M. Kliebard, Ronald T. Hyman, and Frank L. Smith, Jr. *The Language of the Classroom.* New York: Teachers College Press, 1966.

2. Broudy, Harry S., and John R. Palmer. *Exemplars of Teaching Method.* Chicago: Rand McNally, 1965.

3. Buchler, Justus. *The Concept of Method.* New York: Columbia University Press, 1961.

4. Combs, Arthur W. "The Personal Approach to Teaching." *Educational Leadership* 21:369–377, 399, March 1964.

5. Hyman, Ronald T. "The Language of the Classroom: Implications for Supervisors and Teachers." *Journal of Secondary Education* 42:106–113, March 1967.

6. Jackson, Philip W. "The Way Teaching Is." *The Way Teaching Is,* pp. 7–27. Washington, D.C.: National Education Association, 1966.

7. Loud, Oliver S. "Lecture and Discussion in General Education." *Journal of General Education* 8:30–33, October 1954.

8. Maurrou, H. I. *A History of Education in Antiquity.* Translated by George Lamb. London: Sheed and Ward, 1956.

9. McMurry, Charles A., and Frank M. McMurry. *The Method of the Recitation.* New York: Macmillan, 1926.

10. Rashdall, Hastings. *The Universities of Europe in the Middle Ages.* Oxford, Eng.: Clarendon Press, 1895.

11. Rosenberg, Meyer J. "The Historical Development of Hebrew Education from Ancient Times to 135 C.E." Master's thesis, Rutgers University, 1927.

12. Smith, B. Othanel. "A Concept of Teaching." *Teachers College Record* 61:229–241, February 1960.

13. Smith, B. Othanel. "A Conceptual Analysis of Instructional Behavior." *Journal of Teacher Education* 14:294–298, September 1963.

14. Strasser, Ben. "A Conceptual Model of Instruction." *Journal of Teacher Education* 18:63–74, Spring 1967.

15. Talmud: Berachot 4:71.

16. Thayer, V. T. *The Passing of the Recitation.* Boston: D. C. Heath, 1928.

2 *The Discussion Method*

4 Introduction to the Discussion Method

These chapters will treat the discussion method of teaching, which includes both the Socratic dialogue and the discovery methods, as used in the social sciences, natural sciences, and humanities. It is interesting to note at the outset that educators who defend the Socratic method of teaching usually support the discovery method as well and that often the two methods are not differentiated. The underlying justification for these methods, elements of the methods, and the organizational techniques involved will now be examined. In the three chapters that follow, techniques for employing the methods will be discussed.

Underlying Justifications

Those who support the discussion method of teaching are guided by a point of view that includes many interrelated features. The first of these involves the position that knowledge arises within the person, rather than from external sources. According to this view, knowledge is not transmitted by the teacher to the student. Either knowledge already lies within man, since it derives from an immortal soul (or God), or knowledge is generated by man through his own efforts, by building on what he already knows.

Some who hold this view (including Socrates and Augustine) claim that there is an immortal soul or God that is the source of knowledge. Socrates, in the *Meno*, claims that knowledge arises when man awakens that which he already knows, which before lies dormant in his immortal soul (21:III, 35). As Broudy and Palmer describe it:

Everything in the educational scheme depended on the existence of absolute models of the virtues that could be discerned by human beings. Socrates reasoned that inasmuch as absolutes of any kind (ideal forms) could not be found in the world of space and time, then if known at all, they were not learned, but innate. As to why we did not know these from birth, Socrates conjectured that they were forgotten each time the soul was reincarnated in a different body. Hence teaching did not convey these fundamental notions to their learner; it merely prodded him into reminiscing or remembering what he already knew in a previous life but had forgotten (1:35–36).

Augustine holds that man gains knowledge through his own internal activity and by inner illumination from God. In order to arrive at knowledge, an individual must consult his inner experience, and this derives from God (26:151–159).

In his analysis of the concept "teaching," Augustine arrives at the conclusion that teaching consists in the teacher's use of language to prompt the student to his own activity of learning, and that learning involves the student's seeing, by divine illumination, that the statements he learns are true. This analysis of "teaching" depends upon the existence of God, the source of inner illumination. It would be nonsensical were there no such source, for it would amount to the assertion that teaching which does occur consists in something which does not (22:143).

Yet it is not necessary to believe in God or an immortal soul in order to hold the view that knowledge arises within man. Indeed, few who support the discovery method today do agree with the theory of innate ideas. Most hold the view that knowledge comes about as the individual builds on his existing knowledge through the processes of reasoning and deliberating. That is to say, man generates knowledge himself through "deliberation, argument, judgment, appraisal of reasons *pro* and *con*, weighing of evidence, appeal to principles, and decision making" (27:138).

Dewey states that ideas occur in the mind and are capable of development there through stimulation. "Given a fertile suggestion occurring in an experienced, well-informed mind, that mind is capable of elaborating it until there results an idea that is quite different from the one with which the mind started" (10:111).

Whether one holds that God or an immortal soul is the source of knowledge or that man derives his knowledge through his own activity, knowledge is seen as something arising within man. Knowledge, in this view, does not arise from the reception and storage of bits of information from an outside source.

This view that knowledge comes from within is in contrast to one in which knowledge is conceived of as the result of impressions from external stimuli that the brain receives and assimilates. The *from within* view holds that what the student needs to know and can know derives from his own intellectual effort of relating new data to his current structure of knowledge. This means that the student puts things together for himself. "The learner must construct his own conceptual schemata with which to process and/or organize whatever information he receives" (37:311).

Proponents of this viewpoint also contend that the teacher does not communicate knowledge, but rather prods the student's memory, stimulates the knowledge he already has, or creates a situation that encourages the student to find relationships among ideas. According to this view, the teacher either does not have the knowledge himself, or, if he does, cannot transfer it to the student in such a way as to constitute knowledge. According to Taba, "teaching is directed to enabling the learner to establish a relationship between his existing schemata and the new phenomena and to remake or extend the schemata to accommodate new facts and events" (37:311).

This role of the teacher is likened by Socrates to that of a midwife.

Socrates: Such are the midwives, whose work is a very important one, but not so important as mine; for women do not bring into the world at one time real children, and at another time idols which are with difficulty distinguished from them; if they did, then the discernment of the true and false birth would be the crowning achievement of the art of midwifery—you would think that?

Theaetetus: Yes, I certainly should.

Socrates: Well, my art of midwifery is in most respects like theirs; but the difference lies in this—that I attend men and not women, and I practise on their souls when they are in labor, and not on their bodies; and the triumph of my art is in examining whether the thought which the mind of the young man is bringing to the birth is a false idol or a noble and true creation. And like the midwives, I am barren, and the reproach which is often made against me, that I ask questions of others and have not the wit to answer them myself, is very just; the reason is, that the god compels me to be a midwife, but forbids me to bring forth. And therefore I am not myself wise, nor have I anything which is the invention or offspring of my own soul, but the way is this:—Some of those who converse with me, at first appear to be absolutely dull, yet afterwards, as our acquaintance ripens, if the god is gracious to them, they all of them make astonishing progress; and this not only in their own opinion but in that of others. There is clear proof that they have never learned anything of me, but they have acquired and discovered many noble things of themselves, although the god and I help to deliver them (21:IV, 329–330).*

Teacher as Enabler

Based on this analogy of the midwife in the *Theaetetus*, Socratic teaching is often called maieutic teaching. This notion was held not only by the ancients; John Dewey, who inspired many contemporary ideas on the role of the teacher, had the following to say:

The educational moral I am chiefly concerned to draw is not . . . that teachers would find their own work less of a grind and strain if school conditions favored learning in the sense of discovery and not in that of storing away what others pour into them; nor that it would be possible to give even children and youth the delights of personal intellectual productiveness—true and important as are these things. It is that no thought, no idea, can possibly be conveyed as an idea from one person to another. When it is told, it is, to the one to whom it is told, another given fact, not an idea. The communication may stimulate the other person to realize the question for himself and to think out a like idea, or it may smother his intellectual interest and suppress his dawning effort at thought. But what he *directly* gets cannot be an idea. Only by wrestling with the conditions of the problem at first hand, seeking and finding his own way out, does he think. When the parent or teacher has provided the conditions which stimulate thinking and has taken a sympathetic attitude toward the activities of the learner by entering into a common or conjoint experience, all has been done which a second party can do to instigate learning. The rest lies with the one directly concerned. If he cannot devise his own solution (not of course in isolation, but in correspondence with the teacher and other pupils) and find his own way out he will not learn, not even if he can recite some correct answer with one hundred per cent accuracy. We can and do supply ready-made "ideas" by the thousand; we do not usually take much pains to see that the one learning engages in significant situations where his own activities generate, support, and clinch ideas— that is, perceived meanings or connections. This does not mean that the teacher is to stand off and look on; the alternative to furnishing ready-made subject matter and listening to the accuracy with which it is

* From *Works of Plato: Theaetetus*, Vol. IV, trans. by Benjamin Jowett. Tudor Publishing Company: New York. Reprinted with permission of publisher.

reproduced is not quiescence, but participation, sharing, in an activity. In such shared activity, the teacher is a learner, and the learner is, without knowing it, a teacher—and upon the whole, the less consciousness there is, on either side, of either giving or receiving instruction, the better (9:159–160).*

The teacher, as enabler, challenges the student to find things out for himself (39). He leads the student to generalizations and inferences regarding the subject matter under study (12:27). The teacher prompts the student. He, in effect, says to the student, "If you wish to know, you must exert your own intellectual effort. You must work with the data from experience yourself. Through your own inquiry will come knowledge." Knowledge comes about as the student comprehends the relationships among experiences, that is, understands the basic underlying principles of a particular field of study. This act of comprehending, or grasping generalizations, is sometimes called insight, sometimes inquiry, and sometimes discovery (28).

The act of discovery occurs at the point in the learner's efforts at which he grasps the organizing principle imbedded in a concrete instance or in a series of instances and can therefore transform this information: the learner can see the relationship of the facts before him, he can understand the causes of the phenomenon, and he can relate what he sees to his prior knowledge.[†] This point in the learner's efforts is also referred to as the moment of insight (27:311).

It (i.e., knowledge) can, at most, be stimulated or prompted by what the teacher does, and if it indeed occurs, it goes beyond what is thus done. Vision defines and organizes particular experiences, and points up their significance. It is vision, or insight into meaning, which makes the crucial difference between simply storing and reproducing learned sentences, on the one hand, and understanding their basis and application, on the other (25:135).

The teacher was observed to encourage children to catch hold of ideas and 'run with them' beyond what is, as yet, known for sure (3:205).

* From *Democracy and Education*, by John Dewey, © 1916, 1944. Reprinted by permission of The Macmillan Company (Paperback Ed., 1961).

† Taba gives two citations at this point. Gertrude Hendrix, "Learning by Discovery," *Mathematics Teacher* 54 (May 1961), pp. 290–299; Allen Newell, S. C. Shaw, and Herbert A. Simon, "Elements of a Theory of Human Problem-Solving" (Santa Monica, Calif.: Rand Corporation, 1957). (See also references 13 and 19.)

I shall operate on the assumption that discovery, whether by a schoolboy going it on his own or by a scientist cultivating the growing edge of his field, is in its essence a matter of rearranging or transforming evidence in such a way that one is enabled to go beyond the evidence so reassembled to new insights. It may well be that an additional fact or

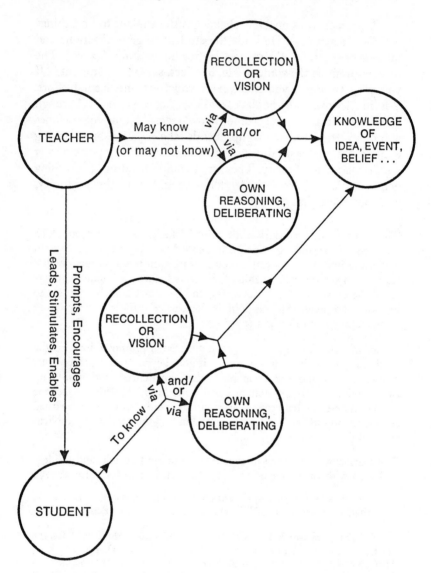

Figure 4–1

shred of evidence makes this larger transformation possible. But it is often not even dependent on new information (4:82–83).

These ideas are depicted graphically in Figure 4–1.

Teaching also leads the student to independence if it provides him with a way of gaining knowledge on his own. Teaching, then, must aim at producing "intellectual potency" in the student, to use Bruner's term (4:83). The discussion method accomplishes just this. Through discussion the student not only gains knowledge but—and this is more important—he learns how to acquire knowledge autonomously (42). He learns the techniques for discovering, i.e., the heuristics of discovery. The student can therefore be free since he knows how to generate knowledge himself (16; 17). He is not dependent on external sources. Thus, through the discussion method the teacher works with the student on two levels simultaneously: he teaches him to grasp the principles of the subject matter at hand, and he teaches him a way of grasping and generating such principles without the aid of a teacher.

This notion is connected to the idea that an individual must expand and deepen his knowledge all through his life. He must do so early in formal school situations where teachers are present to guide him. Indeed, the raison d'être of schools is precisely to facilitate the student's effort in this task. But, since a person spends most of his time away from his teachers even during the years he attends school, he must be able to further his knowledge on his own, and to acquire knowledge when teachers are not around to teach him. Discussion in this way serves both the purpose of schooling and the purpose of preparing for life after schooling is completed (41).

Bruner states this point in terms of a hypothesis to be tested, in the following manner:

Emphasis on discovery in learning has precisely the effect on the learner of leading him to be a constructionist, to organize what he is encountering in a manner not only designed to discover regularity and relatedness, but also to avoid the kind of information drift that fails to keep account of the uses to which information might have to be put. Emphasis on discovery, indeed, helps the child to learn the varieties of problem solving, of transforming information for better use, helps him to learn how to go about the very task of learning (4:87).

These notions of autonomy and lifelong pursuit of knowledge are closely linked with another concept, namely, democracy. Although most of the current proponents of the discovery method draw support for their thinking from cognitive psychologists, e.g., Piaget and Bruner, they might also look for support to American philosophy. Brown investigated the relationship between the teacher's belief in Dewey's experimentalist philosophy and actual classroom practices. He found that

teachers who conceived knowledge as a vital and inseparable part of the active process of inquiry held educational beliefs and used classroom practices that were distinctly different from those of teachers who conceived knowledge as something to be acquired for its own sake. . . . Teachers who saw knowledge as inquiring were thorough-going experimentalists who provided situations that were inclined to be open and free, emphasizing participation of the pupils as initiators as well as reactors. Teachers who saw knowledge as acquiring were decidedly non-experimental, providing somewhat restricted or tightly controlled situations in which pupils participated primarily as respondents to plans and purposes impinging upon them from without (2:12).

That is to say, those who hold to a philosophy of experimentalism—Dewey's philosophy—support the discussion method. As this excerpt from Brown makes clear, the use of this method of discussion and inquiry entails that the teacher be democratic in his dealings with his students and therefore tends to prepare the student for the action required of a citizen in a democracy. Indeed, early supporters of the inquiry method claimed that it was the method required for preparation for citizenship (14; 15; 23). Further, the teacher using the inquiry method is himself being democratic in his dealings with his students.

This is not meant to imply that only experimentalists support inquiry. Nor is it valid to say that the use of the discovery method is the sum and substance of the experimentalist's ideas about teaching in the public schools. Rather, those who do hold to this philosophical system also tend to support inquiry as an essentially democratic method. Clearly, in short, the inquiry method has for some time been closely and rightly identified with Dewey's notions about democracy.

A student becomes capable of autonomous inquiry only over a rather long period of time. He does not suddenly become autonomous after being dependent on external sources. To achieve intellectual potency and autonomy, the student must actively participate with the teacher in teaching. (Active participation, here, does not indicate only oral activity, for it is surely possible to be active intellectually yet passive physically.) This participation obviously requires that the teacher be, not a dispenser, but an enabler, facilitator, adviser, guide. This requirement, in turn, is related to the idea that a student learns to be autonomous by practicing, by noting his errors, and by practicing again with his mistakes corrected. The discussion method does tend to evoke in the student active engagement in the teaching process (29:72).

The combination of active participation and intellectual potency yields another feature of the discussion method. The quality rather than the quantity of the knowledge gained by a student is critical in teaching (33). The discussion method of teaching yields high quality, in that the student actively involved "will retain his new knowledge more completely than he would retain a system of facts and ideas imposed upon him from the outside" (12:28).

The discussion method emphasizes the qualitative aspect of teaching in that it aims at establishing something (18). Buchler claims that a student can assimilate more of the subject matter when he has helped to establish the "product," than when he has simply received what is transmitted by the teacher (6:8). This goes beyond the idea of better retention. Discussion is intellectually productive because it leads to a high degree of retention *and* assimilation.

Learning by discovery may, then, still be considered the chief mode for intellectual productivity and autonomy. When an individual has developed an organizing scheme for his own cognitive activity, he is presumably in a position to harvest a greater amount of knowledge as well as to become increasingly autonomous and independent of all forms of authority. He is better equipped to move into unknown areas, to gather data, and to abstract from these ideas and concepts. A person who can transform what Bruner [*] calls 'episodic information' into systematic knowledge is in control of organizing ideas and thereby increases his intellectual power. Further, when the learner relies on his own cognitive processes, when he is aware of the relationship of the learning tasks to his own experience, and when he has developed an attitude of search and an expectation or a set to learn under his own steam, he is in a position to continue these processes on his own (37:313).

Another reason for choosing the discussion method applies perhaps more to the discovery method than to Socratic dialogue. A physics teacher, for example, will consider physics not only as a

---

* At this point, Taba cites Jerome S. Bruner, *On Knowing* (Cambridge: Harvard University Press, 1962). (See also reference 4.)

body of knowledge to be learned, but as one division of a general body of science, which is continually changing. According to Schwab, science is "a fluid enquiry, utilizing changing concepts, producing continuous reorganization and revision of its knowledge" (31:24). Given this understanding of science the teacher can no longer present physics as a set of preestablished, irrevocable conclusions. In accordance with this concept of physics or other sciences or bodies of knowledge, the teacher may choose the discovery (or enquiry) method.

Intrinsic Reward

Another argument for the discussion method involves the view that, ultimately, gaining knowledge is its own reward. That is to say, the teacher in his attempt to lead the student to independence must stress the point that the student should not seek extrinsic rewards for learning. Extrinsic rewards influence the student to keep at least one eye on the "gold star chart," and this will cause him to lose his focus. The student, in working only toward some extrinsic reward, whether it is a gold star, a teacher's approving smile, a high mark, or even a college scholarship, tends to conform to other people's expectations of him. In contrast, by accepting the notion that knowledge is its own reward, the student frees himself from others' expectations of him, and also frees himself from his immediate school situation. He can then set his own goals and standards and can learn at his own pace. The intrinsic reward, itself, serves also as the student's motivation—it leads him as well as praises him (4:87–88).

People who hold this view assert that teaching by the discussion method helps make the act of learning a rewarding experience. That is, "discovery and the sense of confidence it provides is the proper reward for learning" (4:123–124). Indeed this is the view of the Panel on Educational Research and Development of the President's Science Advisory Committee. "Curriculum units can be designed that are self-contained and self-demonstrating, enabling children to discover things for themselves" (20:32). In commenting on this suggestion Strodbeck says, "The Committee believes that such approaches will keep student interest high primarily because of the intrinsic stimulation of the materials and secondarily by avoidance of the ill effects of passive listening" (34:95).

These people claim that three elements characteristic of the discussion method—active participation, exploration, and the gaining of knowledge that leads to mastery—fulfill a basic human need. This need has been depicted by R. W. White in the following manner: Every animal, including the human animal, is inwardly motivated to be competent in handling his environment. An animal does not need to have external stimuli in order to explore. To be competent is intrinsically rewarding because "it satisfies an intrinsic need to deal with the environment" (40:317). Bruner hypothesizes that "to the degree that one is able to approach learning as a task of discovering something rather than 'learning about' it, to that degree there will be a tendency for the child to work with the autonomy of self-reward or, more properly, be rewarded by discovery itself" (4:88).

The notion that there is a *drive* in students to resolve problems is the basis of much contemporary curriculum work (35; 38). It underpins, for instance, the entire Inquiry Training research project started at the University of Illinois. As a part of this project, physics demonstrations with an element of perplexity for students are presented, with the intention of sparking the postulated drive. After the demonstrations, students seek to explain the cause of the perplexing situation. In this way the demonstration itself triggers the student's drive. "Our technique is predicated on the belief that the drive to 'find out why' can surpass in sustained motivational power almost any other classroom incentive" (36:438).

Though it is perhaps implied in several places above, another feature of the discussion method now deserves explicit treatment. Along with independence through intellectual power, the student should develop the feeling that he can work alone. He should be able to rely on himself, confident that he can continue on his own. Suchman, in defense and justification of the method of inquiry, states that from the research on this topic there emerges the conclusion that a "reinforcing sense of power and self-confidence comes from successful autonomous discovery" (35:151).

Another argument in support of the discussion method concerns the need for a positive interpersonal relationship between student and teacher. To establish this relationship, it is necessary for the teacher and student to interact in such a way as to create and maintain mutual trust and respect. Such interaction occurs when the teacher and student engage in exchanges that seek to establish satisfactory generalizations, conclusions, or solutions. That is, when people work together on a common issue, a positive interpersonal relationship is quite likely to result.

Schwab, a leading advocate of the inquiry method for teaching biology, asserts that discussion creates the opportunity for the teacher and student to meet face to face as individual to individual (25). Such face-to-face encounters can strongly promote positive interpersonal relationships. Discussion "affords a situation in which the teacher can establish more effective interpersonal relations and use them more frequently with many more students in a given learning period than most teaching methods permit" (29:72).

The teacher constantly needs feedback from the students in order to assess the effectiveness of his teaching. He can easily get this feedback when he uses the discussion method, because of the frequent exchanges among the participants.

The flow of talk in a discussion is represented in Figure 4-2.

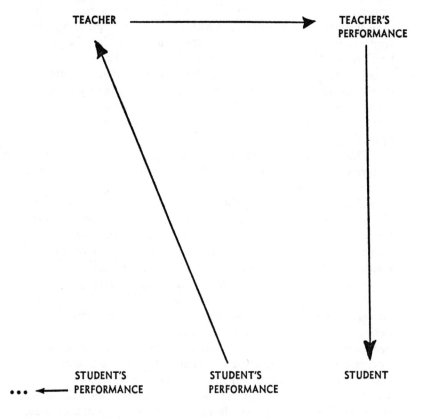

Figure 4-2

For discussion is the form of human communication in which the essence of communication is maximized. The conveying of information is followed by behavior which is itself information—information of what meanings were conveyed and what behaviors were evoked by the first conveying. This second relay of information then modifies the communication—behavior of the first speaker—the teacher. He can adjust his second communication so as to convey or change the effect of his first communication. In the same way, communications by the student evoke feedback from the teacher which informs the student of the consequences of his first communication and thus teaches him how to modify his further behavior and later communications. Thus the teacher and the students become cooperative and communicating pursuers of a common problem (29:70–71).

The impetus to seek knowledge, to arrive at new ideas from data at hand, comes from puzzlement or doubt.

... the origin of thinking is some perplexity, confusion, or doubt. Thinking is not a case of spontaneous combustion; it does not occur on 'general principles.' There is something that occasions and evokes it. General appeals to a child (or to a grown-up) to think, irrespective of the existence in his own experience of some difficulty that troubles him and disturbs his equilibrium, are as futile as advice to lift himself by his own boot-straps (10:15).

Dewey's point is an example of a modern idea with ancient roots. Socrates relies on such perplexity in his teaching, as the following interchange with Meno about the slave boy he had questioned, and thus taught, shows:

Socrates: But do you suppose that he would ever have inquired or learned what he fancied that he knew and did not know, until he had fallen into perplexity under the idea that he did not know, and had desired to know?
Meno: I think not, Socrates.
Socrates: Then he was the better for the torpedo's touch?
Meno: I think that he was (21:III, 32).

Even those people who hold that perplexity is not the sole impetus to thought do hold that it is greatly significant in inspiring thought.

The impetus for seeking knowledge is created by questions. Indeed, Dewey goes so far as to say that thinking which is inquiry —i.e., thinking that strives to come up with something new or something already known but seen in a new light—is questioning

(10:265). The question is the prod to thought. Also in the *Meno*, Socrates continues with the significant statement that the slave boy's further development of the issue will derive from Socrates' forthcoming questions (21:III, 32). The role of the teacher as stimulator is to ask questions. However, it takes great skill to ask the right questions—those that will lead the student to knowledge. The teacher must understand very well both the student and the problem under consideration.

A last viewpoint related to the discussion method is the belief that through discussion the student comes to understand a topic with a special clarity and vividness that would not be possible by most other means. By talking aloud, by presenting his ideas to someone else, and by listening to himself as he reacts to another person's ideas, an individual clarifies his own position. Writing, too, is an external presentation of one's thoughts so that a person can hear and see himself. For this reason writing has been likened to discussion; both can provide the incentive to clarify and comprehend. (Note the increase in the trend toward student term papers at the same time as the growth of interest in the discussion method of teaching.) Bruner states:

My colleague, Roman Jakobson, assures me that there is a Russian proverb to the effect that one understands only after one has discussed. There are doubtless many ways in which a human being can serve as a vicar of the culture, helping a child to understand its points of view and the nature of its knowledge. But I dare say that few are so potentially powerful as participating in dialogue. Professor Jan Smedslund, at Oslo, has recently remarked that even in the domains of formal reasoning, logic, and mathematics, the social context of discussion can be shown to be crucial (5:90).

Elements of the Discussion Method

The elements of the discovery method are directly or indirectly derived from elements outlined by Dewey. In analyzing the "complete act of reflective activity," Dewey (8:106–107) outlined five modes of thought that occur between man's situation before reflection ("a perplexed, troubled, or confused situation at the beginning") and man's situation after reflection ("a cleared-up, resolved situation at the close").

In between, as states of thinking, are (1) *suggestions*, in which the mind leaps forward to a possible solution; (2) an intellectualization of the difficulty or perplexity that has been *felt* (directly experienced) into a *problem* to be solved, a question for which the answer must be sought; (3) the use of one suggestion after another as a leading idea, or *hypothesis*, to initiate and guide observation and other operations in collection of factual material; (4) the mental elaboration of the idea or supposition as an idea or supposition (*reasoning*, in the sense in which reasoning is a part, not the whole, of inference); and (5) testing the hypothesis by overt or imaginative action (8:107).

It must be noted that Dewey commented about this statement that: there is no set order in the five phases; there is nothing sacred about having five phases; there are subphases within each phase; in practice two phases may telescope into one; some phases may be passed over hurriedly; and "the burden of reaching a conclusion may fall mainly on a single phase, which will then require a seemingly disproportionate development." In short, Dewey did not ascribe an orthodoxy to the five phases (as other people who followed him did). He was wise enough to conclude his treatment of the phases by saying, "No set rules can be laid down on such matters. The way they are managed depends upon the intellectual tact and sensitiveness of the individual" (8:115–116).

Since Dewey wrote *How We Think*, many variations of these five phases have been suggested. Some authors have reduced the five steps to three, while others have increased them to nine (24:256). Some authors prefer such popular labels as "the steps of the scientific method," "the general pattern of scientific research" (8:433), "the main steps in disciplined thought" (32:40), or "steps in a mode of inquiry for the social studies" (11:16). Some authors suggest variations in Dewey's list depending on whether the problem is valuative or nonvaluative (7:317). In any case, the similarity between these variations and Dewey's five phases of reflective thought is evident.

Educators have been concerned with these five phases and have presented many variations because they recognize the benefit to both teacher and student of following a paradigm of some sort. The value lies in offering a way of conducting discovery, a way of knowing what to do, a way of benefiting from successes, a way of avoiding certain error.

Teaching people how to do things just *is* teaching them methods or *modi operandi*. . . . A method is a learnable way of doing something, where the word 'way' connotes more than mere rote or routine. . . . We should think of the inculcation of methods rather as training the pupils to avoid specified muddles, blockages, sidetracks, and thin ice by training them to recognize these for what they are. Enabling them to avoid troubles, disasters, nuisances, and wasted effort is helping them to move where they want to move. Road signs are not, for the most part, impediments to the flow of traffic. They are preventatives of impediments to the flow of traffic (25:114–116).

Though these five phases can be applied to the lecture and recitation methods, they are more generally associated with the discovery method of teaching. This is so because the discovery method requires continued, active participation by both the teacher and the student. These phases provide a guide for the teacher and the student who are working together on a problem. Also, because the discovery method involves complex interaction among the participants, there is more interest in providing a *modus operandi*.

These five phases do not constitute a "method of teaching," as the phrase has been used in this book. They are not teaching steps but rather stages of thought applicable to many activities, including teaching. The teacher and students may use these stages as a guide, but the steps are not unique to teaching.

The outlines of several sets of variations on Dewey's steps are presented below. This will provide the reader with a wider range for choosing guidelines to follow, or a basis for working out his own guidelines.

Variation 1   The General Pattern of Scientific Research (8:433–451)
1. A problem is discerned
2. Preliminary hypotheses
3. Collecting additional relevant facts
4. Formulating the hypotheses (to explain the facts encountered)
5. Deducing testable consequences
6. Testing the consequences
7. Practical application.

Variation 2   The Main Steps in Disciplined Thought (32:40–42)
1. Identification of the issue or problem
2. Gathering, organizing, and evaluating relevant data
3. Analysis of the issue or problem
4. Formulating and testing hypotheses
5. Drawing warranted conclusions
6. Testing conclusions.

Variation 3   Phases in Judgment in Policy-making (23:102–110)*
   1. Clarification of common purpose—the projection of a desired state of affairs
   2. The survey and assessment of the existing state of affairs
   3. Suiting the ideas employed to the claims of the situation as a "whole"
   4. The fusion of the ideal and the existent in a program of action.

Variation 4   Steps in a Mode of Inquiry for the Social Studies (11:16–17)
   1. Recognizing a problem from data
   2. Formulating hypotheses
      a. Asking analytical questions
      b. Stating hypotheses
      c. Remaining aware of the tentative nature of hypotheses
   3. Recognizing the logical implications of hypotheses
   4. Gathering data
      a. Deciding what data will be needed
      b. Selecting or rejecting sources
   5. Analyzing, evaluating, and interpreting data
      a. Selecting relevant data
      b. Evaluating sources
         (1) Determining the frame of reference of an author

---

* Smith, Stanley, and Shores have modified this variation into three phases of thought: "(1) the formulation, through mutual interpersonal persuasion, of a concerted idea of the state of affairs the students desire to have established in the future with respect to that aspect of society which the problem embraces; (2) an exploration of existing conditions and their connection with the ends projected and desired, and (3) the charting of a plan of action leading through existing conditions to the projected state of affairs" (31:376–377).

Burton, Kimball, and Wing have modified the variation into five phases: (1) points of conflict are located and defined; (2) contrasting normative positions are openly stated and examined; (3) the historic origins of the norms and the factual conditions related to these norms are analyzed; (4) "a new policy is formulated if the norms can be reconstructed sufficiently to reduce the conflict, if not eliminate it" (7:318); and (5) new policy or program is put into operation and the consequences observed and judged by the extent to which they uphold a fundamental philosophy—the democratic values (7:311–334).

(2) Determining the accuracy of statements of fact
  c. Interpreting the data
6. Evaluating the hypotheses in light of the data
  a. Modifying the hypothesis, if necessary
    (1) Rejecting a logical implication unsupported by data
    (2) Restating the hypothesis
  b. Stating a generalization.

In some quarters the emphasis on these phases of reflective thought or the emphasis on scientific method, however it is referred to, has served to obscure a significant point, namely, that it is not enough for the teacher to be aware of or to follow these steps.

The teacher and especially the student need some schema to help them assess a policy decision, for example, made while following these five phases. The teacher must know what constitutes a reasonable justification of a policy decision in order to guide the student toward a rational approach to problems. This is the very point of this book made in its presentation of the schema for valuative discovery and nonvaluative discovery in the following chapters.

Organizing Teachers and Students for Discussion

There is the obvious need to organize teachers and students in such a way as to facilitate discussion. Just as it is virtually impossible to lecture to one student, so too is it virtually impossible to conduct a Socratic dialogue or discovery session with 200 students. Discussion requires considerable interchange among participants, and too large a group prohibits it. For teaching, the maximum number of students for even a skilled teacher is somewhere around thirty. Beyond this number it is quite easy for an intended discussion to slip into a lecture punctuated with occasional student contributions. The optimum number is perhaps in the range of twelve to twenty, for below this there may well be a lack of diversity among students and a paucity of knowledge to be pooled.

These numbers are offered tentatively since there is no easy formula for calculating just how many students are needed for a discussion. The optimum number of students in the class and the optimum number of participants vary with the topic, the level of knowledge of the teacher and students, the reasoning ability of the students, the skill of the teacher in leading a discussion, the interest of the class, and the diversity of beliefs and preparation.

The desirable degree of participation in discussion varies with the particular subject, the extent and nature of the background reading, the ability of students to discern what is going on, the psychological readiness of students, and a host of other factors. Since participating can mean raising questions as well as expressing viewpoints, a large number of participants is a fact which, taken by itself, signifies nothing (6:12).

To facilitate the exchange of ideas, it is wise to arrange the chairs in a circle or horseshoe. Such face-to-face situations promote the exchange of ideas and the building up of mutual trust. Also, the participants should be close enough to each other to be able to interact without raising their voices or squinting to see. Such physical arrangements are essential in creating an atmosphere where teaching by the discussion method can take place.

If the teacher plans to conduct the discussion along the lines suggested by the Illinois Studies in Inquiry Training, then it would be most helpful to arrange for a room that facilitates tape-recording. A tape recording—video or even the inexpensive audio—is most helpful in conducting the critique session following a discussion or Socratic dialogue. Some schools have rooms designed for recording class sessions, and these should be utilized whenever possible.

Similarly, if the discussion centers on the use of various pieces of laboratory equipment or maps, then the appropriate room and materials will facilitate the interaction among teacher and students. Obviously the seats and materials should be so arranged as to allow all parties clear and unobstructed view of the demonstrations and props. If the teacher wishes to have the students handle the materials, he would be wise to have several sets of materials. This will also allow for ease in switching back and forth from discussion among small groups to discussion involving the entire class.

It is wise to arrange for students and teacher to have easy access to library and laboratory references. With such an arrangement the teacher will more readily be able to halt a discussion and send the students off to gather necessary data. Easy switching from discussion to small-group or independent study will make the subsequent exchanges among participants more meaningful. Such movement will concretely demonstrate to the students that a discussion continually requires further data if it is to be fruitful.

This movement from large to small groups or individual study promotes the ends sought in the use of the discovery method. To further facilitate this movement it is helpful to have other teachers available when the discussion involves specialized topics. When students move into individual areas, one teacher may not be able to handle all the numerous fine points. A teacher who knows that he can draw on colleagues will be willing to encourage specialized, independent work. This use of more than one teacher will in the long run benefit the students' discussions, for they will be able to bring more to class sessions.

In short, just as the teacher must be flexible in conducting a discussion, so too must teachers and students be organized for discussion in a flexible way. The discussion method depends on flexibility and fluidity for its utility, and to hamstring it with poor physical arrangements and poor scheduling is an error.

References

1. Broudy, Harry S., and John R. Palmer. *Exemplars of Teaching Method*. Chicago: Rand McNally, 1965.

2. Brown, Bob Burton. "Acquisition versus Inquiry." *Elementary School Journal* 64:11–17, October 1963.

3. Brown, Bob Burton. *The Experimental Mind in Education*. New York: Harper and Row, 1968.

4. Bruner, Jerome S. *On Knowing*. Cambridge: Harvard University Press, 1962.

5. Bruner, Jerome S. "Culture, Politics, and Pedagogy." *Saturday Review* 51:69–72, 80–90, May 18, 1968.

6. Buchler, Justus. "What Is a Discussion?" *Journal of General Education* 8:7–17, October 1954.

7. Burton, William H., Roland B. Kimball, and Richard L. Wing. *Education for Effective Thinking*. New York: Appleton-Century-Crofts, 1960.

8. Copi, Irving M. *Introduction to Logic*. 2d ed. New York: Macmillan, 1961.

9. Dewey, John. *Democracy and Education*. New York: Macmillan, 1916. Paperback ed., 1961.

10. Dewey, John. *How We Think: A Restatement of the Relation of Reflective Thinking to the Educative Process*. Boston: D. C. Heath, 1933.

11. Fenton, Edwin. *The New Social Studies*. New York: Holt, Rinehart, and Winston, 1967.

12. Friedlander, Bernard Z. "A Psychologist's Second Thoughts on Concepts, Curiosity, and Discovery in Teaching and Learning." *Harvard Educational Review* 35:18–38, Winter 1965.

13. Hendrix, Gertrude. "Learning by Discovery." *Mathematics Teacher* 54:290–299, May 1961.

14. Hook, Sidney. *Education for Modern Man: A New Perspective*. New York: Alfred A. Knopf, 1963.

15. Hullfish, H. Gordon, and Philip G. Smith. *Reflective Thinking: The Method of Education*. New York: Dodd, Mead, 1961.

16. Kersh, Bert Y. "Learning by Discovery: What Is Learned?" *Arithmetic Teacher* 11:226–232, April 1964.

17. Kersh, Bert Y. "The Motivating Effect of Learning by Directed Discovery." *Journal of Educational Psychology* 53:65–71, April 1962.

18. Loud, Oliver S. "Lecture and Discussion in General Education." *Journal of General Education* 8:30–33, October 1954.

19. Newell, Allen, J. C. Shaw, and Herbert A. Simon. "Elements of a Theory of Human Problem-Solving." Santa Monica, Calif.: Rand Corporation, 1957.

20. Panel on Educational Research and Development, The President's Science Advisory Committee. *Innovation and Experiment in Education*. Washington, D.C.: U.S. Government Printing Office, 1964.

21. Plato. *Works*. Translated by Benjamin Jowett. 4 vols. New York: Tudor Publishing Company.

22. Price, Kingsley. *Education and Philosophical Thought*. Boston: Allyn and Bacon, 1962.

23. Raup, R. Bruce, and others. *The Improvement of Practical Intelligence*. New York: Bureau of Publications, Teachers College, Columbia University, 1962.

24. Russell, David H. *Children's Thinking*. Boston: Ginn and Company, 1956.

25. Ryle, Gilbert. "Teaching and Training." In *The Concept of Education*, edited by R. S. Peters, pp. 105–119. New York: Humanities Press, 1967.

26. St. Augustine. "The Teacher." In *Education and Philosophical Thought*, edited by Kingsley Price, pp. 145–159. Boston: Allyn and Bacon, 1962.

27. Scheffler, Israel. "Philosophical Models of Teaching." *Harvard Educational Review* 35:131–143, Spring 1965.

28. Schwab, Joseph J. "Teaching and Learning as Inquiry and the Contribution of Television." In *Inquiry: Implications for Televised Instruction*, edited by Wilma McBride, pp. 13–22. Washington, D.C.: National Education Association, 1966.

29. Schwab, Joseph J. "The Teaching of Science as Enquiry." In

The Teaching of Science, lectures by Joseph J. Schwab and Paul F. Brandwein. Cambridge: Harvard University Press, 1962.

30. Schwab, J. J., and Evelyn Klinckmann. "Discussion in the Teaching of BSCS Biology." In *Biology Teachers' Handbook*, Joseph J. Schwab, Supervisor, Biological Science Curriculum Study of the American Institute of Biological Sciences. New York: John Wiley, 1963. Reprinted in *Teaching: Vantage Points for Study*, edited by Ronald T. Hyman (Philadelpha: J. B. Lippincott, 1968), pp. 458–465.

31. Smith, B. Othanel, William O. Stanley, and J. Harlan Shores. *Fundamentals of Curriculum Development*. New York: Harcourt, Brace, and World, 1957.

32. Starr, Isidore. "The Nature of Critical Thinking and Its Application in the Social Studies." In *Skill Development in Social Studies*, Thirty-third Yearbook of the National Council for the Social Studies, edited by Helen McCracken Carpenter, pp. 35–52. Washington, D.C.: National Council for the Social Studies, 1963.

33. Steinberg, Erwin R., and others. "The Inductive Teaching of English." *English Journal* 55:139–157, February 1966.

34. Strodbeck, Fred L. "The Hidden Curriculum in the Middle-Class Home." In *Learning and the Educational Process*, edited by J. D. Krumboltz, pp. 91–112. Chicago: Rand McNally, 1965.

35. Suchman, J. Richard. "Inquiry Training: Building Skills for Autonomous Discovery." *Merrill-Palmer Quarterly of Behavior and Development* 7:147–169, March 1963.

36. Suchman, J. Richard. "Inquiry Training in the Elementary School." *The Science Teacher* 27:42–47, November 1960. Reprinted in *Teaching: Vantage Points for Study*, edited by Ronald T. Hyman (Philadelphia: J. B. Lippincott, 1968), pp. 434–441.

37. Taba, Hilda. "Learning by Discovery: Psychological and Educational Rationale." *Elementary School Journal* 63:308–316, March 1963.

38. Thelen, Herbert A. *The Concept, Characteristics, and Use of Discovery Materials in Teaching*. Professional Reprints in Education, no. 8822. Columbus, Ohio: Charles E. Merrill, n.d.

39. Vavoulis, Alexander. "Lecture vs. Discussion." *Improving College and University Teaching* 12:185–189, Summer 1964.

40. White, R. W. "Motivation Reconsidered: The Concept of Competence." *Psychological Review* 66:297–333, September 1959.

41. Wittrock, M. C. "The Learning by Discovery Hypothesis." In *Learning by Discovery: A Critical Appraisal*, edited by Lee S. Shulman and Evan R. Keislar, pp. 33–75. Chicago: Rand McNally, 1966.

42. Worthen, Blaine R. "A Study of Discovery and Expository Presentation: Implications for Teaching." *Journal of Teacher Education* 19:223–242, Summer 1968.

5 The Socratic Method: Dialogue as Direct Teaching

What, then, should a teacher do in order to teach by the Socratic method? There is no doubt that many teachers do try to teach like Socrates. They do so although they do not accept the Socratic notion that "there is no teaching, only recollecting" (6:35). As was pointed out earlier, very few educators hold the theory of recollection today. Also, many teachers know little more about the Socratic method than that it involves questioning by a "Socrates" (6:35). It seems that many teachers are familiar with the term *Socratic method* without knowing what it is that constitutes the method.

Examples and Analysis

It is possible to extract from the writing of Plato certain essentials of the Socratic method and to utilize these techniques in teaching, without necessarily subscribing to Socrates' belief in innate ideas. It is

... important to realize that the dialogic model of Plato contains not only directions for methods of education, but also a series of beliefs about the nature of man, the meaning and function of soul, and the operation of reminiscence. In Plato, the method of educating is bound to the beliefs which are part of the entire model. But the *model form* need not be limited to these beliefs. The form functions with any content of belief ... (1:189).

Therefore the teacher does not have to accept the idea that "there is no teaching, only recollecting; learning is remembering" in order to employ the Socratic method in teaching.

It is possible instead, for example, to contend that, in learning by the Socratic method, the student is motivated by the teacher's questions to reason rather than to recollect. Indeed this is what Oliver and Shaver (11:287) and Bode (2:216) hold when they treat the Socratic method. Before exploring teaching by the Socratic method, however, a descriptive analysis of the method itself should be set forth.

Meno

There is no better source of information on the Socratic method than Socrates himself. A selection from Plato's writings—in which Socrates gives a clear demonstration of his method—will now be presented. This is the popular section from the *Meno* and should be read carefully.*

Socrates: . . . In that confiding, I will gladly inquire with you into the nature of virtue.

Meno: Yes, Socrates; but what do you mean by saying that we do not learn, and that what we call learning is only a process of recollection? Can you teach me how this is?

Socrates: I told you, Meno, just now that you were a rogue, and now you ask whether I can teach you, when I am saying that there is no teaching, but only recollection; and thus you imagine that you will expose me in a contradiction.

Meno: Indeed, Socrates, I protest that I had no such intention. I only asked the question from habit; but if you can prove to me that what you say is true, I wish that you would.

Socrates: It will be no easy matter, but I am willing to do my best for you. Suppose that you call one of your numerous attendants, whichever you like, that I may demonstrate on him.

Meno: Certainly. Come hither, boy.

Socrates: He is Greek, and speaks Greek, does he not?

Meno: Yes, indeed; he was born in the house.

Socrates: Attend now, and observe whether he learns of me or only remembers.

Meno: I will.

* This section of *The Dialogues of Plato: The Meno,* translated by Benjamin Jowett, is reprinted by permission of The Clarendon Press: Oxford, 4th Edition (Vol. I) 1953. (Diagrams do not appear in the original Greek text. The author has modified the diagram which appears in this 1953 edition, added others, and inserted letter markings in the dialogue (such as [AB]) to aid the reader.)

Socrates: Tell me, boy, do you know that a figure like this is a square?

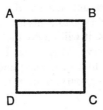

Boy: I do.
Socrates: And you know that a square figure has these four lines equal?
Boy: Certainly.
Socrates: And these lines which I have drawn through the middle of the square are also equal?

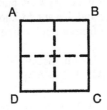

Boy: Yes.
Socrates: A square may be of any size?
Boy: Certainly.
Socrates: And if one side of the figure be two feet long [AB] and the other side two feet [AD], how much will the whole be? Let me explain: if in one direction the space was two feet long, and in the other direction one foot, the whole space would be two feet taken once?
Boy: Yes.
Socrates: But since this side is also two feet, there are twice two feet?
Boy: There are.
Socrates: Then the square is twice two feet?
Boy: Yes.
Socrates: And how many are twice two feet? count and tell me.
Boy: Four, Socrates.
Socrates: And might there not be another figure twice as large as this, but of the same kind, and having like this all the lines equal?

Boy: Yes.

Socrates: And how many feet will that be?

Boy: Eight feet.

Socrates: And now try and tell me the length of the line which forms the side of that double square: this is two feet—what will that be?

Boy: Clearly, Socrates, it will be double.

Socrates: Do you observe, Meno, that I am not teaching the boy anything, but only asking him questions; and now he fancies that he knows how long a line is necessary in order to produce a figure of eight square feet; does he not?

Meno: Yes.

Socrates: And does he really know?

Meno: Certainly not.

Socrates: He fancies that because the square is double, the line is double?

Meno: True.

Socrates: Now see him being brought step by step to recollect in regular order. (*To the boy.*) Tell me, boy, do you assert that a double space comes from a double line? Remember that I am not speaking of an oblong, but of a figure equal every way, and twice the size of this— that is to say of eight feet; and I want to know whether you still say that a double square comes from a double line?

Boy: Yes.

Socrates: But does not this line become doubled if we add another such line here [add BE to AB; BE = AB]?

Boy: Certainly.

Socrates: And four such lines, you say, will make a space containing eight feet?

Boy: Yes.

Socrates: Let us describe such a figure: Would you not say that this is the figure of eight feet?

Boy: Yes.

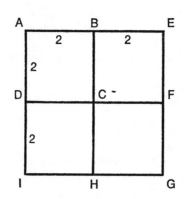

Socrates: And are there not these four divisions in the figure, each of which is equal to the figure of four feet?

Boy: True.

Socrates: And is not that four times four?

Boy: Certainly.

Socrates: And four times is not double?

Boy: No, indeed.

Socrates: But how much?

Boy: Four times as much.

Socrates: Therefore the double line, boy, has given a space, not twice, but four times as much.

Boy: True.

Socrates: Four times four are sixteen—are they not?

Boy: Yes.

Socrates: What line would give you a space of eight feet—for that gives a fourfold space, of sixteen feet, does it not? [AE yields a square of 16 feet.]

Boy: Yes.

Socrates: And the space of four feet is made from this half line? [AB yields a square of 4 feet.]

Boy: Yes.

Socrates: Good; and is not a space of eight feet twice the size of this [ABCD], and half the size of the other [AEGI]?

Boy: Certainly.

Socrates: Such a space, then, will be made out of a line greater than this one [AB], and less than that one [AE]?

Boy: Yes; I think so.

Socrates: Very good; I like to hear you say what you think. And now tell me, is not this a line of two feet [AB] and that [AE] of four?

Boy: Yes.

Socrates: Then the line which forms the side of the eight foot space ought to be more than this line of two feet [AB] and less than the other of four feet [AE]?

Boy: It ought.

Socrates: Try and see if you can tell me how much it will be.

Boy: Three feet.

Socrates: Then if we add a half to this line of two, that will be the line of three. Here are two [AB] and there is one [BJ]; and on the other side, here are two also [AD] and there is one [DL] and that makes the figure of which you speak?

Boy: Yes.

Socrates: But if there are three feet this way [AJ] and three feet that way [AL], the whole space will be three times three feet?

Boy: That is evident.

Socrates: And how much are three times three feet?

Boy: Nine.

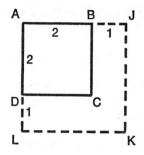

Socrates: And what was to be the number of feet in the doubled square?

Boy: Eight.

Socrates: Then the eight foot space is not made out of a line of three feet?

Boy: No.

Socrates: But from what line?—tell me exactly; and if you would rather not reckon, try and show me the line.

Boy: Indeed, Socrates, I do not know.

Socrates: Do you see, Meno, what advances he has made in his power of recollection? He did not know at first, and he does not know now, what is the side of a figure of eight: but then he thought that he knew, and answered confidently as if he knew, and felt no difficulty; now he feels a difficulty, and neither knows nor fancies that he knows.

Meno: True.

Socrates: Is he not better off in knowing his ignorance?

Meno: I think that he is.

Socrates: If we have made him doubt, and given him the 'torpedo's shock', have we done him any harm?

Meno: I think not.

Socrates: We have certainly, as would seem, assisted him in some degree to the discovery of the truth; and now he will wish to remedy his ignorance, but then he would have been ready to tell all the world again and again that the double space should have a double side.

Meno: True.

Socrates: But do you suppose that he would ever have started to inquire into or to learn what he fancied that he knew, though he was really ignorant of it, until he had fallen into perplexity under the idea that he did not know, and had desired to know?

Meno: I think not, Socrates.

Socrates: Then he was the better for the torpedo's touch?

Meno: I think so.

Socrates: Mark now the further development. I shall only ask him, and not teach him, and he shall share the inquiry with me: and do you watch and see if you find me telling or explaining anything to him, instead of eliciting his opinion. Tell me, boy, is not this a square of four feet which I have drawn?

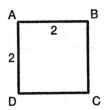

Boy: Yes.
Socrates: And now I add another square equal to the former one?

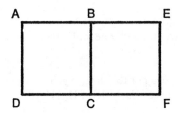

Boy: Yes.
Socrates: And a third, which is equal to either of them?

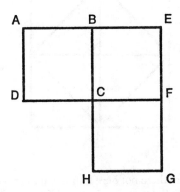

Boy: Yes.
Socrates: Suppose that we fill up the vacant corner?
Boy: Very good.
Socrates: Here, then, there are four equal spaces?
Boy: Yes.

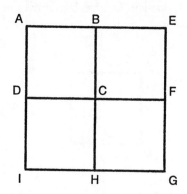

Socrates: And how many times larger is this space [AEGI] than this other [ABCD]?

Boy: Four times.

Socrates: But we wanted one only twice as large, as you will remember.

Boy: True.

Socrates: Now, does not this line, reaching from corner to corner, bisect each of these spaces [DB, BF, FH, HD]?

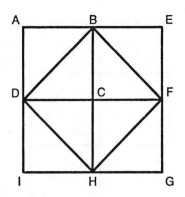

Boy: Yes.

Socrates: And are there not here four equal lines which contain this space? [DB = BF = FH = HD; they contain space DBFH.]

Boy: There are.

Socrates: Look and see how much this space is.

Boy: I do not understand.

Socrates: Has not each interior [line] cut off half of the four spaces?

Boy: Yes.

Socrates: And how many such spaces are there in this section [DBFH]?

Boy: Four.

Socrates: And how many in this [ABCD]?

Boy: Two.

Socrates: And four is how many times two?

Boy: Twice [that is, DBFH is twice as big as ABCD].

Socrates: So that this space [DBFH] is of how many feet?

Boy: Of eight feet.

Socrates: And from what line do you get this figure?

Boy: From this [DB].

Socrates: That is, from the line which extends from corner to corner of the figure of four feet?

Boy: Yes.

Socrates: And that is the line which the learned call the diagonal. And if this is the proper name, then you, Meno's slave, are prepared to affirm that the double space [DBFH] is the square of the diagonal?

Boy: Certainly, Socrates.

Socrates: What do you say of him, Meno? Were not all these answers given out of his own head?

Meno: Yes, they were all his own.

Socrates: And yet, as we were just now saying, he did not know?

Meno: True.

Socrates: But still he had in him those notions of his—had he not?

Meno: Yes.

Socrates: Then he who does not know may still have true notions of that which he does not know?

Meno: Apparently.

Socrates: And at present these notions have just been stirred up in him, as in a dream; but if he were frequently asked the same questions, in different forms, he would know as accurately as anyone at last?

Meno: I dare say.

Socrates: Without anyone teaching him he will recover his knowledge for himself, if he is merely asked questions?

Meno: Yes.

Socrates: And this spontaneous recovery of knowledge in him is recollection?

Meno: True.

Socrates: And this knowledge which he now has must he not either have acquired at some time, or else possessed always?

Meno: Yes.

Socrates: But if he always possessed this knowledge he would always have known; or if he has acquired the knowledge he could not have acquired it in this life, unless he has been taught geometry. And he may be made to do the same with all geometry and every other branch of knowledge; has anyone ever taught him all this? You must know about him, if, as you say, he was born and bred in your house.

Meno: And I am certain that no one ever did teach him.

Socrates: And yet he has these notions?

Meno: The fact, Socrates, is undeniable.

Socrates: But if he did not acquire them in this life, then he must have had and learned them at some other time?

Meno: Clearly he must.

Socrates: Which must have been the time when he was not a man?

Meno: Yes.

Socrates: And if there are always to be true notions in him, both while he is and while he is not a man, which only need to be awakened into knowledge by putting questions to him, his soul must remain always possessed of this knowledge; for he must always either be or not be a man.

Meno: Obviously.

Socrates: And if the truth of all things always exists in the soul, then the soul is immortal. Wherefore be of good cheer, and try to discover by recollection what you do not now know, or rather what you do not remember.

Meno: I feel, somehow, that I like what you are saying.

Socrates: And I too like what I am saying. Some things I have said of which I am not altogether confident. But that we shall be better and braver and less helpless if we think that we ought to inquire than we should have been if we thought that there was no knowing and no duty to seek to know what we do not know;—that is a belief for which I am ready to fight, in word and deed, to the utmost of my power.

Meno: There again, Socrates, your words seem to me excellent.

Socrates: Then, as we are agreed that a man should inquire about that which he does not know, shall you and I make an effort to inquire together into the nature of virtue? . . .

What points is Socrates trying to make to Meno in this demonstration? The first critical point is that Socrates is demonstrating to Meno what he considers to be the essentials of the Socratic method. The student in this episode is Meno and not the boy (3:245; 1:188). The boy is, in one sense, an audiovisual pedagogical prop. The point of the entire episode is that Socrates is deliberately teaching something to Meno through this demonstration; and, to be sure that Meno understands his strategy, he interrupts the demonstration several times to explicate it.

Even though Socrates, because of his belief in innate ideas, denies that he is teaching the boy, he is in effect teaching Meno. Socrates is teaching Meno a skill; namely, the Socratic method. Every teacher would do well to emulate three qualities Socrates manifests in this demonstration: Socrates is clear about his objectives (10); he knows why he is doing what he is doing; and he chooses a technique to suit his objectives.

Socrates claims that he is demonstrating the method whereby memory is stimulated. He claims that there is no teaching, but only recollecting. It is for this reason that Socrates states to Meno that he is only asking questions and not teaching, i.e., not telling the boy the geometric principle involved in the episode. For Socrates, the way to stimulate the memory is to ask questions, since these elicit responses which lead to the end in mind. Through questioning, a person recalls the knowledge possessed by his immortal soul.

However, even if one does not accept Socrates' notion that there is only recollecting, but rather claims that by reasoning and deliberating the student can go beyond the data at hand, it is clear that questioning is an effective technique for stimulating the student to think about issues. The crux of the matter, whether the result be recollection or reasoning, is in the questions Socrates asks.

This leads to another point. The questions are, for Socrates, a means by which he can carry out his overall strategy. This must be kept in mind, for if we focus on the individual questions, we will miss the general strategy. This is why Socrates interrupts the chain of questioning several times: he wants Meno to focus on the strategy. "The most delightful parts of the dialogue are those exchanges in which Meno becomes increasingly conscious of the way in which he [Socrates] has been arguing, and of the limitations of his arguments" (1:188).

Socrates, through his questions, (1) gets the boy to make an initial proposition, (2) leads him to doubt that proposition, (3) leads him to admit that he does not know the proposition to be true, and (4) leads him to formulate a correct proposition. This is the strategy. The second step is no doubt the most important one.

Socrates justifies this strategy in his remarks to Meno. He claims that the boy would never have inquired into or learned what he thought he knew (though he was really ignorant of it), until he had fallen into perplexity. Doubt, uncertainty, puzzlement, and perplexity are the motivating forces for inquiry. "The point is that inquiry does not start unless there is a problem. And the presence of a problem means that the traditional beliefs are in question" (9:16).

Therefore, Socrates does not correct the boy when he makes the initial false statement that a double line doubles the area of the square. The boy at this point thinks he knows, though he is wrong. But, for Socrates, it is perplexity, and not merely being wrong, that stimulates a person to inquire. With this in mind, Socrates does not correct the boy but rather constructs a square according to the boy's initial answer. When the double line does not yield the double area and when a line one and one-half times as long does not yield the double area either, Socrates triumphantly gets the boy to admit, "I do not know." For Socrates this admission is the critical point. Now—and only now—does Socrates begin to lead the boy to the correct answer to his original question: "And now try and tell me the length of the line which forms the side of the double square."

Another very important point is that the Socratic method involves the notion that we clarify our thoughts by testing them against alternatives. The job of the teacher is to bring counter-instances before the student for his consideration. The centrality of this point to the Socratic method cannot be overemphasized. "The fundamental educational principle—that ideas must be confronted with alternative ideas—is at work here. When ideas are exposed to one another they are refined, their limitations are recognized, and their deeper meanings grasped" (1:187). This is illustrated in the episode when Socrates introduces the square based on a line three feet in length. It is better illustrated in other dialogues in which Socrates is not demonstrating but performing his method.

Euthyphro

For further illustration of this aspect of the Socratic method and for other characteristics not readily seen in the slave-boy episode, a selection from another dialogue, the *Euthyphro*, is presented below.* In this dialogue Euthyphro and Socrates meet, each with a legal matter on his mind. Out of piety Euthyphro is prosecuting his own father for neglecting an accused murderer who had been put into his care. (The accused man died from cold and hunger before a messenger could bring instructions on what was to be done with him.) Socrates is awaiting his own trial for impiety. He is convinced that he must know about piety before the

---

* Much of the discussion of the *Euthyphro* below is based on the work of James Jordan (7).

trial begins and seeks such knowledge from Euthyphro, who claims to have "exact knowledge of all these matters."*

Socrates: I know that, dear friend; and that is the reason why I desire to be your disciple. For I observe that no one, not even Meletus, appears to notice you; but his sharp eyes have found me out at once, and he has indicted me for impiety. And therefore, I adjure you to tell me the nature of piety and impiety, which you said that you knew so well, and of murder, and the rest of them. What are they? Is not piety in every action always the same? and impiety, again, is not that always the opposite of piety, and also the same with itself, having, as impiety, one notion which includes whatever is impious?

Euthyphro: To be sure, Socrates.

Socrates: And what is piety, and what is impiety?

Euthyphro: Piety is doing as I am doing; that is to say, prosecuting any one who is guilty of murder, sacrilege, or of any other similar crime—whether he be your father or mother, or some other person, that makes no difference—and not prosecuting them is impiety. And please to consider, Socrates, what a notable proof I will give you of the truth of what I am saying, which I have already given to others:—of the truth, I mean, of the principle that the impious, whoever he may be, ought not to go unpunished. For do not men regard Zeus as the best and most righteous of the gods?—and even they admit that he bound his father [Cronos] because he wickedly devoured his sons, and that he too had punished his own father [Uranus] for a similar reason, in a nameless manner. And yet when I proceed against my father, they are angry with me. This is their inconsistent way of talking when the gods are concerned, and when I am concerned.

Socrates: May not this be the reason, Euthyphro, why I am charged with impiety—that I cannot away [agree] with these stories about the gods? and therefore I suppose that people think me wrong. But, as you who are well informed about them approve of them, I cannot do better than assent to your superior wisdom. For what else can I say, confessing as I do, that I know nothing of them. I wish you would tell me whether you really believe that they are true?

Euthyphro: Yes, Socrates; and things more wonderful still, of which the world is in ignorance.

Socrates: And do you really believe that the gods fought with one another, and had dire quarrels, battles, and the like, as the poets say, and as you may see represented in the works of great artists? The temples are full of them; and notably the robe of Athene, which is

* From the *Works of Plato: Vol. III, Euthyphro*, trans. by Benjamin Jowett. Tudor Publishing Company, New York. Reprinted with permission of publisher.

carried up to the Acropolis at the great Panathenaea, is embroidered with them. Are all these tales of the gods true, Euthyphro?

Euthyphro: Yes, Socrates; and, as I was saying, I can tell you, if you would like to hear them, many other things about the gods which would quite amaze you.

Socrates: I dare say; and you shall tell me them at some other time when I have leisure. But just at present I would rather hear from you a more precise answer, which you have not as yet given, my friend, to the question, What is "piety?" In reply, you only say that piety is, doing as you do, charging your father with murder?

Euthyphro: And that is true, Socrates.

Socrates: I dare say, Euthyphro, but there are many other pious acts.

Euthyphro: There are.

Socrates: Remember that I did not ask you to give me two or three examples of piety, but to explain the general idea which makes all pious things to be pious. Do you not recollect that there was one idea which made the impious impious, and the pious pious?

Euthyphro: I remember.

Socrates: Tell me what this is, and then I shall have a standard to which I may look, and by which I may measure the nature of actions, whether yours or anyone's else, and say that this action is pious, and that impious?

Euthyphro: I will tell you, if you like.

Socrates: I should very much like that.

Euthyphro: Piety, then, is that which is dear to the gods and impiety is that which is not dear to them.

Socrates: Very good, Euthyphro; you have now given me just the sort of answer which I wanted. But whether it is true or not I cannot as yet tell, although I make no doubt that you will prove the truth of your words.

Euthyphro: Of course.

Socrates: Come, then, and let us examine what we are saying. That thing or person which is dear to the gods is pious, and that thing or person which is hateful to the gods is impious. Was not that said?

Euthyphro: Yes, that was said.

Socrates: And that seems to have been very well said too?

Euthyphro: Yes, Socrates, I think that; it was certainly said.

Socrates: And further, Euthyphro, the gods were admitted to have enmities and hatreds and differences—that was also said?

Euthyphro: Yes, that was said.

Socrates: And what sort of difference creates enmity and anger? Suppose for example that you and I, my good friend, differ about a number; do differences of this sort make us enemies and set us at variance with one another? Do we not go at once to calculation, and end them by a sum?

Euthyphro: True.

Socrates: Or suppose that we differ about magnitudes, do we not quickly put an end to that difference by measuring?

Euthyphro: That is true.

Socrates: And we end a controversy about heavy and light by resorting to a weighing-machine?

Euthyphro: To be sure.

Socrates: But what differences are those which, because they cannot be thus decided, make us angry and set us at enmity with one another? I dare say the answer does not occur to you at the moment, and therefore I will suggest that this happens when the matters of difference are the just and unjust, good and evil, honorable and dishonorable. Are not these the points about which, when differing, we quarrel, when we do quarrel, as you and I and all men experience?

Euthyphro: Yes, Socrates, that is the nature of the differences about which we quarrel.

Socrates: And the quarrels of the gods, noble Euthyphro, when they occur, are of a like nature?

Euthyphro: They are.

Socrates: They have differences of opinion, as you say, about good and evil, just and unjust, honorable and dishonorable: there would have been no quarrels among them, if there had been no such differences— would there now?

Euthyphro: You are quite right.

Socrates: Does not every man love that which he deems noble and just and good, and hate the opposite of them?

Euthyphro: Very true.

Socrates: But then, as you say, people regard the same things, some as just and others as unjust; and they dispute about this, and there arise wars and fightings among them.

Euthyphro: Yes, that is true.

Socrates: Then the same things, as appears, are hated by the gods and loved by the gods, and are both hateful and dear to them?

Euthyphro: True.

Socrates: Then upon this view the same things, Euthyphro, will be pious and also impious?

Euthyphro: That, I suppose, is true.

Socrates: Then, my friend, I remark with surprise that you have not answered what I asked. For I certainly did not ask what was that which is at once pious and impious: and that which is loved by the gods appears also to be hated by them. And therefore, Euthyphro, in thus chastising your father you may very likely be doing what is agreeable to Zeus but disagreeable to Cronos or Uranus, and what is acceptable to Hephaestus but unacceptable to Here, and there may be other gods who have similar differences of opinion (12:III, 70–74).

This gambit effectively destroys Euthyphro's definition of piety. The dialogue next proceeds with another definition that the two men analyze and test. The dialogue ends without an agreement on a definition of piety since Euthyphro has not been able to maintain a position—even a modified one—against the counter-instances raised by Socrates.

Analysis

From these two dialogues, the *Meno* and the *Euthyphro*, it is clear that a critical tactic in the Socratic strategy is to seek continual clarification of a proposition or definition by testing it with alternative, conflicting possibilities. Socrates holds the view that "we make mistakes only because we do not collect together all of the acts which are like each other, and we confuse them with acts which do not really belong to the same class" (1:188).

Another point about the Socratic method is that Socrates employed his method among friends rather than mere disputants (1:186). Further, he questioned adults who had had experience in the world (7:103). The *Meno* is not an exception if we remember that the slave boy episode is peripheral. The main theme of the dialogue is whether virtue can be taught, and Socrates engages Meno, not the young boy, in this major inquiry. It is important for the teacher to note this dependency on life experience. In asking Meno about virtue and Euthyphro about piety Socrates asked them to draw upon their own experience. He sought no higher authority than the participants themselves. Socrates

got them to think about what they already knew, i.e., their own definitions and the relationship between these and instances covered by their experience. He certainly asked them to rely upon no authority for definitions other than themselves and no authority for the legitimate connections between ideas other than their own rational sense. The arbiter of dispute was what appealed to the inquirer's sense of rationality. There was no higher court and no authority other than this. Each man was granted to have a sense for what is rational, and Socrates never urged that one listen to him rather than to rationality (7:103).

Socrates is quite aware of this factor. In demonstrating with the slave boy he deliberately chooses not to continue to inquire into virtue or any other moral issue. Socrates realizes that the boy is not suited for such an inquiry since his life experiences do not permit it. (Note the warning.) Rather, Socrates chooses to raise a mathematical issue, one which he feels the boy can handle.

And, aware of the need for experience as a starting point even in the demonstration, Socrates, through his early questioning, establishes first that the boy has a basis for proceeding. That is, the slave boy is a Greek, speaks Greek, and knows that the figure in question is a square. Only after he has established this does Socrates proceed.

The Socratic method also can lead to the discomfort of the one being questioned. For example, at the end of the dialogue, Euthyphro leaves Socrates in a huff, saying, "Another time, Socrates; for I am in a hurry and must go now." In the *Meno*, Anytus, a friend who participated for a while in the dialogue, is described as "exasperated" from his encounter with Socrates. Socrates succeeded quite well in arousing the anger of his fellows because he revealed their ignorance and inconsistency of thought. Needless to say, if this method can be unsettling to adults, it can also cause young people to feel harassed, angry, and devastated. "Anyone who has used this questioning in class—even with graduate students—knows the havoc it spreads among the ego" (3:245).

Socrates, at least to some extent, is aware of this possibility in his demonstration with the boy. This is one reason why the demonstration is short and why Socrates eases the tension several times by talking with Meno. Socrates takes pain not to humiliate or even frustrate the boy in front of his master. On the contrary, it is the boy who reaches the right conclusion, which Socrates is then willing to accept. He has not exposed the boy and then allowed him to remain exposed as he did with Euthyphro.

In choosing to do this, Socrates, in effect, chose not to make other critical points to Meno in the demonstration. This limitation is indeed characteristic of this demonstration and any demonstration. In highlighting certain elements in order to make a point, a person gives up the opportunity to make others. He thus gains and loses through the same demonstration. This process is clear only when we carefully compare the slave boy episode with the *Euthyphro*. What Socrates lost in the *Meno* demonstration is a significant point that must now be made explicit.

Socrates, as evidenced in the complete *Meno* and in the *Euthyphro*, is concerned with seeking the moral truths, such as "what is virtue" or "what is piety." It is for this reason that Socrates claimed that he did not have wisdom and that he was seeking it with Meno and Euthyphro. But he was willing to admit that he did know the true answer to the mathematical question of the slave boy episode. Therefore, for Socrates, moral issues are not the same as mathematical ones. Indeed, giving a definition of piety or virtue is not the same as stating a proposition in geometry. Furthermore, tracing the logical implications of a definition of piety is quite different from tracing the logical implications of a proposition in mathematics. Witness the fact that Socrates and Meno, after their entire dialogue, still have to inquire further into the nature of virtue, while in a relatively short time the slave boy reached the truth about the length of the line that yields a double area.

The slave boy episode is not necessarily typical of the Socratic method for two major reasons: first, the episode does not deal with moral issues, and second, it does give the impression that Socrates, because of his method, has succeeded in reaching correct answers. "How can it represent his method when even in the dialogue in which it occurs it is peripheral to his central concern, used only as a demonstration, not to push the main inquiry? To think of the slave incident as typical Socratic method is much like thinking of Death Valley as typical of the United States" (7:98).

Socrates misleads Meno in this episode in several ways. He gives the impression that he is demonstrating his overall method and that this method can lead to quick success. In spite of Socrates' claims that he was mainly interested in demonstrating how a person recollects (regardless of subject matter), the slave boy episode is misleading. Socrates is not noted as a mathematics teacher who got speedy results, and it is not correct to think that Socrates was primarily engaged in investigating mathematical issues.

Moreover, whereas in the *Euthyphro* both Socrates and Euthyphro are concerned initially with the issue of piety, in the slave boy episode Socrates himself creates the issue. The length of the line that doubles the area is not something the boy himself cares about. This, too, may be one reason why Socrates led the boy quickly to a correct answer. Socrates may have been able to show him the way out of perplexity because Socrates had caused the perplexity. Socrates believes that, if perplexity is raised about an issue important and relevant to a person, he will definitely seek further knowledge on his own. But it is misleading to think that a student will seek further knowledge about *any* perplexing issue. On the contrary, many educators hold that only when the student generates the issue himself, or when the issue pertains to his personal condition, will he inquire further once perplexity has been raised.

For these reasons it is false to use this small illustrative episode from the *Meno* as typical of Socrates' dialogues. But on the positive side, Socrates, in this one demonstration, is able to spotlight two essential characteristics of his method: the need to raise perplexity in order to stimulate the desire to inquire, and the sharpening of ideas through consideration of counterinstances. Socrates, in order to make these two crucial points, pays the price of misleading Meno on several other accounts.

Socrates chose an issue in mathematics for the boy because he knew that with it he could quickly and effectively demonstrate two additional points. First, he demonstrates how, through astute questioning, the boy can be led to deduce the Pythagorean theorem (as it is called today) from what he already knows. The episode is indeed an effective demonstration of "how to teach a deductive system of relations" (4:38). Second, he demonstrates that in working with other people we must be sure to start with what the student already knows and move on from there. This, too, is significant, however trite it might appear.

The *Euthyphro* is, however, a more typical Socratic dialogue. James Jordan aptly analyzes the first part of that dialogue, excerpted earlier, and clearly explicates the genius of Socrates.

Let us pause a moment to examine what Socrates is up to. Clearly he is not conveying information to Euthyphro. He seems to be concerned to elicit a definition from Euthyphro that can be used to judge individual instances of piety or impiety. There is no suggestion from Socrates of what the definition may be, though he points out to Euthyphro that citing examples is not what he meant by defining. He wants to know what all acts of piety have in common. Once he elicits a proper definition from Euthyphro, he can begin to test the definition. But first he must attempt to capture the defining characteristic of piety. What is a definition that enables one to recognize acts of piety and impiety? Neither Socrates nor Euthyphro thinks the request improper nor is there any disagreement over whether or not there is such a thing as a defining characteristic. They are working within the framework of common agreements, and Socrates is trying to discover whether the way Euthyphro thinks of piety is true. If Euthyphro gives an adequate definition of piety, it will cover all the instances of piety that Socrates or anybody else can think up. If Socrates can construct from the definition a possible example of piety that Euthyphro does not want to admit, then Socrates can force Euthyphro to acknowledge that the standard by which he recognizes an instance of piety is not the same as that set forth in his definition and, therefore, his definition must be modified. If his definition must be modified, then Euthyphro must admit that he has not given a definition which shows he knows what piety is. Obviously the teaching principle involved in this rather complicated process is not a very simple one.

Let us return to the dialogue. Socrates gets Euthyphro to agree that the gods, like men, disagree over what things are good and evil. From this admission he proceeds, "Then the same things are hated by the gods and loved by the gods, and are both hateful and dear to them?" Euthyphro admits that this is true, and Socrates answers, "And upon this view the same things, Euthyphro, will be pious and impious?" This question obviously destroys Euthyphro's definition of piety, for if piety is what the gods love and some gods love one thing and other gods hate the same thing, then the same thing is both pious and impious (7:99–100).

As both the *Euthyphro* and the *Meno* close, it is quite evident that Socrates did not succeed in coming to correct or acceptable answers regarding the nature of piety or virtue. He and his friends admit this. If Socrates is satisfied, it is only because he has inquired and will continue to inquire into fundamental moral issues. But he has no correct answers. He has not succeeded in attaining them through his method.

The farthest thing from what one can be taught by the Socratic method is a set of correct responses. The Socratic method is simply not useful when the proper answers to questions are already known. The method itself is a way of exploring the kinds of answers that can be given to questions and perhaps a way of weeding out bad answers and moving toward good ones (7:103).

Typically then, to reiterate, Socrates uses his method to treat moral (policy) issues and to inquire into issues for which he does not already have the correct answers.

To avoid being misled by Socrates himself, the reader should now consider one of Socrates' statements to Meno. After the slave boy episode is completed, Socrates says to Meno, "And he may be made to do the same with all geometry and every other branch of knowledge." Socrates uses mathematics in the demonstration and then claims that what is characteristic of it is characteristic of all fields of study. However, mathematics deals with a set of relationships from which implications can be drawn apart from experience. "Mathematical truths are not dependent on experience, though an awareness of them may be suggested by experience" (13:3). (For example, if $A + B = C$, and $B + C = D$, and $5A = D$, then it must be that B is twice as large as A. We know of this relation, independent of our sense data, as a result of the first three relations already established.) Unless this is noted, the impact of the dialogue is lost. "It is implicit in the employment of the dialogue that understanding of meanings is a purely verbal and conceptual matter, and that once this is clear, all action will necessarily be bound by that knowledge. This latter implication is probably one of the unique elements of the dialogue as a model" (1:187).

Those who do not accept Socrates' view of innate ideas will note that this characteristic of mathematics does not hold for such fields as literature, sociology, and history. That is to say, since relations within these fields are not based only on an interior logic, independent of sense data, it is not possible to start with only a proposition, as Socrates suggests, and then deduce from it a set of true relations. Therefore, it is not valid for Socrates to say that one could follow the same technique with all geometry and every other branch of knowledge. What is more, Socrates himself admits in the selection from the *Euthyphro* quoted above that there is a difference among subject fields. Note that Socrates says that the disagreements among men regarding calculations and measurement of weight have different effects and resolutions from disagreements regarding ethical matters. The Socratic method for deducing relations is best used in fields of study that deal with symbols independent of sense experience.

The Socratic method is a slow and complicated one. It is slow because, as Socrates shows, the questions must move from one small point to the next, always eliciting responses before advancing. It is slow because it allows one to go up blind alleys. It is slow because it allows, or rather encourages, the student to trace the consequences of his thoughts, so that he detects his own errors (8:81).

Socrates at all times, in the *Euthyphro* and in the complete *Meno*, is virtually asking his readers to emulate him. He is teaching (if the word may be used despite his disclaimer) his readers or disciples to be like Socrates; he is teaching the art of the dialogue. Socrates is asking his students to inquire after the truth—the truth that is not yet clear but can become clear if the students exert intellectual effort. Socrates, by his very method, is demonstrating that discussion can be fruitful; it is productive because man has the intellectual power to search for the truth (7:103). Man can put his intellect to work through the Socratic method.

Recapitulated below are the points made thus far in the analysis of the Socratic method.

1. Socrates was clear about his objective; he knew why he did what he did, and he chose his technique to suit his objective.

2. Socrates, in the slave boy episode in the *Meno*, was demonstrating his method to Meno, not to the boy.

3. Socrates' method involved a strategy consisting of four basic parts: (a) he got his companion or student to state an initial proposition; (b) he led the student to doubt; (c) he got the student to admit that he didn't know the way out of the perplexity; and (d) he guided the student in the pursuit of truth about the issue.

4. The Socratic method involves the notion that perplexity serves as the motivation for further inquiry.

5. The Socratic method involves the notion that people clarify their thoughts by testing them against alternatives.

6. Socrates used his method among friends (not disputants) who were adults with a great deal of experience of the world.

7. The Socratic method leads to the discomfiture of the respondent.

8. Socrates typically used his method for inquiring into moral issues for which he did not already have correct answers.

9. Socrates' dialogues did not typically end in the establishment of a set of correct answers.

10. Socrates claimed that the method used to arrive at truths of geometry could be applied to all branches of knowledge. Those who do not accept the notion of innate ideas will reject this claim.

11. The Socratic method is slow and complicated.

12. Socrates held that through this method man could utilize his rational powers to inquire into issues that perplexed him.

Teaching Techniques

In spite of its slowness and complexity and in spite of some obvious negative features, the Socratic method can be effectively employed by today's teachers. This method requires much more skill than the recitation method, since the teacher must be constantly alert and has no way of knowing ahead of time what responses his student will give. Furthermore, timing is most important. Nevertheless, the teacher can learn to use this method. The starting point is an understanding of the features described in the previous section.

It is true that Socrates claimed that the Socratic method was not a teaching method but rather a method of philosophical inquiry, a way of seeking wisdom. The contemporary educator

Jordan (7) also makes this claim. But even if the claim is granted, it is still possible for the essentials of Socrates' method to serve as the basis of an effective teaching method (15:384). That is to say, the four-part strategy of Socrates (in which the teacher leads his student from an initial statement, which is then doubted, to pursuit of truth about an issue), the use of perplexity as a motivation for inquiry, and the notion that we clarify our thoughts by testing them against counterinstances are all eminently suitable as the foundation for a Socratic teaching method.

The question is, then, what to modify in the Socratic method in order to convert it into a teaching method. Modifications are necessary in light of the havoc the method can cause when it is used without modification. In their study of styles of classroom discourse Oliver and Shaver found that a Socratic approach can arouse a high level of affective reaction in students—frustration, agitation, and tension (11:290). Modifications are especially necessary for teachers working with young students.

First, the teacher must take care not to humiliate, devastate, beat down, or even discourage his students with the sharpness of his questioning. This is absolutely essential. If he is not careful, the teacher will destroy the relationship of trust and respect necessary for teaching. (It was precisely the anger aroused by Socrates as he exposed the ignorance of his fellows that led to his death.) Snygg cites this very aspect of the Socratic method as his objection to Socrates: "Dozens of generations have admired Socrates, but from what I have read, the victims of his dialogues usually felt beaten but unconvinced" (14:26–27). The teacher's job may or may not be to "convince" the students, but certainly it is not to beat them down. The teacher must remember this at all times when he is using the Socratic method.

There are several ways in which the teacher may reduce and even remove the tension and anger that can result from Socratic questioning. The first and simplest way is to keep the dialogue short. In the beginning, ten to fifteen minutes would be an appropriate time span. This may well be enough time for the teacher to lead the student to doubt without putting the student under much pressure. Also, the teacher may talk with several students at the same time on the same issue. In this way no one student will feel the brunt of the teacher's questions. The danger here, of course, is that, in eliminating the negative aspect, it is likely the teacher will lose the positive aspect of arousing perplexity. If a student feels that the questions are pertinent to someone else but not to himself, he may not feel doubtful about the original statement. The teacher will have to decide when to stay with one student and when to shift to another. Even with some shifting, however, the Socratic method does require the teacher to focus on one student for a longer time than he would have to in the recitation method, for example. "Socratic teaching demands relatively long interchanges between student and teacher. The student cannot be led into an evaluative or definitional inconsistency in one or two statements. The teacher must first establish what the student's position is, suggest exceptions through analogies or contradictory evidence, and counter the student's defense" (11:289).

A second way of reducing tension is to employ humor. This is the age-old technique of comic relief. The use of humor is necessary in order to maintain a climate of friendliness rather than disputation. It is all too easy for the student to feel badgered and denigrated unless the teacher is reassuring. Pleasant humor is a most effective means of reassuring the student, and the arousing of perplexity offers good opportunity to inject humor into the dialogue.

A third way of reducing tension is to shift the student's attention away from his perplexity or self-contradiction. The teacher can direct the student's attention to a critical view of the definition, facts, or beliefs that have led him to his present position. This technique will permit the student to see more clearly the issue at hand. The teacher can thus lead the student to an understanding of how the perplexity came about. The teacher can show that when, for example, the student said, "A is related to B," the teacher countered, "But B is also related to C when we change locations." This analysis of the discourse may be difficult at first for the student to follow; nevertheless, after several times he will be able to. This technique can be an effective way of reducing the sting of the questioning, as well as a means of teaching the process of dialogue discourse. This is virtually teaching on a double level. Oliver and Shaver used this technique in their experimental curriculum project.

We have attempted to teach this two-level consciousness to the student by bringing the argument to a halt after a period of frustration and asking the student to apply the analytic concepts to this particular argument. If the student is unable to do so, the teacher "explains" the argument in terms of the analytic concepts. ("I am attacking your value by the use of this analogy. You could counter the analogy with one of your own, qualify your position and make the analogy less relevant, or find some important difference between the situation in the analogy and the situation in the case, which also makes the analogy less relevant") (11:289).

The teacher may find that an effective way to work on this double level is to tape-record the dialogue and then allow the students to analyze it. This procedure will obviate the usual statement, "But I didn't say that, so why did you ask me about it?" This procedure will also allow the students to analyze their own dialogues without initial help from their classmates and teacher. Later the teacher can go over the dialogue with the various students. In effect this closely resembles the demonstration and asides in the *Meno* that Socrates obviously thought were beneficial. Finally, a tape recording will also allow the dialogue to return to a particular point. From there the teacher and the student can proceed in other directions, if they desire.

Another way of reducing the tension is simply to proceed very slowly. The teacher ought not to rush; if the student is not hurried, much tension will be obviated. The student will feel more relaxed and will be more likely to follow the flow of the dialogue. If so, he can help reduce his own tension as he moves along. He can remove frustration arising from contradiction by eliminating contradictions through careful thought.

A second necessary modification involves the outcome of the dialogue. The teacher should attempt to lead the student to a new position, however temporary it might be. He should not leave the student high and dry. This may not be possible in the very beginning since the dialogue may be very short. But after several attempts the teacher will no doubt be able to lengthen the dialogue in order to be able to arrive at a new position. The student may not be satisfied with his position, but at least he will not feel devastated or irreparably exposed. With a new position the student will not leave with a sense of emptiness, as did Socrates' fellows. He will maintain his drive to inquire that was first sparked by the perplexity aroused. In short, the student may have a position but still realize that he must further clarify it.

With these considerations in mind, the teacher can begin to use the Socratic method. With practice and reflection he can improve his ability to ask the questions that lead to perplexity, to perceive the clues that indicate tension, and to analyze the flow of the dialogue with the students.

While using the Socratic method, the teacher should keep several other points in mind as well. The Socratic method requires that the teacher prepare himself thoroughly. To do so he must carefully think through the issue in question so that he will be able to advance instances counter to the possible positions a student might take. This will sharpen his grasp of the issue but will not provide ready-made counters since the actual dialogue is unpredictable. Without adequate preparation the teaching situation can easily turn into a meandering bull session of little value. Dearing, who has great respect for the Socratic method, goes so far as to say ". . . when it is the excuse for structureless maundering or puffy pontification, the pseudo-Socrates would far better serve the cause of education by preparing his lectures or sending the students out of earshot into the library" (5:66).

Moreover, the teacher must recognize that the Socratic method exhausts the teacher as well as the student, although this might not be readily apparent to the inexperienced. The method is exhausting because it requires the teacher to be on the alert at all times: he must constantly assess both the student's cognitive progress and his affective reactions. It requires great patience, intellectual power, and sheer physical stamina (5:66). It requires total involvement without the support of prepared statements.

Thus, for reasons affecting the teacher as well as the student, the teacher must not constantly use the Socratic method. He must mix the Socratic method with other methods. He must balance it with other, less demanding, techniques. In no way, however, does this qualification imply rejection of the method. The method can yield exciting results and deserves to be used.

The teacher must also keep in mind that the Socratic method is designed to be used in moral-legal issues where there is no easy set of correct answers. There might never be such a set. In any case it is for this reason that Oliver and Shaver found the Socratic method so compatible with their experimental curriculum project, which dealt with case studies in public controversy. They employed a jurisprudential framework within which the students were asked to take positions on public issues such as private property versus equal opportunity in civil rights cases. However, an attempt to use this method in areas where the teacher already knows the correct answer or could easily get it would result in a loss of impact.

In dealing with normative issues, such as piety, virtue, private property, monopolies, population control, or atomic war, the teacher must assess the student's readiness carefully. The teacher, even in a high school or a college, cannot make the assumptions that Socrates did about his fellows. The teacher must realize that students may lack the life experiences requisite to engaging in dialogue. Students may also be unqualified or even unwilling to rely solely on themselves as authorities. Nor will all students have sufficient cognitive maturity to be able to follow or fully participate in complex, rational, logical dialogue. This consideration is a further reason for mixing the Socratic method with other methods.

Finally, in light of the fact that the Socratic method requires relatively long interchanges between teacher and student, the teacher must plan for the involvement of the onlookers if he is in a class situation. If not, long interchanges will generate boredom that might result in disruption by some students. The teacher can involve a number of students by conducting a dialogue with several students at the same time or even with the class as a unit. Or he may choose to employ the Socratic method during those sessions in which students are scheduled for individual or small-group work. He may also involve onlookers by asking them to analyze the flow of the dialogue afterwards.

The next method to be considered will be another approach to learning through discussion—the discovery method.

References

1. Belth, Marc. *Education as a Discipline*. Boston: Allyn and Bacon, 1965.

2. Bode, Boyd H. *Modern Educational Theories*. New York: Macmillan, 1927.

3. Broudy, Harry S. "Socrates and the Teaching Machine." *Phi Delta Kappan* 44:243–246, March 1963.

4. Broudy, Harry S., and John R. Palmer. *Exemplars of Teaching Method*. Chicago: Rand McNally, 1965.

5. Dearing, Bruce. "Three Myths about the College Teacher." *Saturday Review* 47:65–67, January 18, 1964.

6. Hyman, Ronald T., and Arthur G. Krespach. "Perspectives on Teaching." *Research Bulletin* (New Jersey School Development Council) 12:32–39, Spring 1968.

7. Jordan, James A. "Socratic Teaching?" *Harvard Educational Review* 33:96–104, Winter 1963.

8. Kant, Immanuel. *Education*. Ann Arbor, Mich.: University of Michigan Press, 1960.

9. Northrop, F. S. C. *The Logic of the Sciences and the Humanities*. New York: Meridian Books, 1959.

10. "Not from Teaching But from Questioning." *The Carnegie Corporation of New York Quarterly* 9:1–5, October 1961. Reprinted in *Vital Issues in American Education*, edited by Alice and Lester D. Crow (New York: Bantam, 1964), pp. 253–260.

11. Oliver, Donald W., and James P. Shaver. *Teaching Public Issues in the High School*. Boston: Houghton Mifflin, 1966.

12. Plato. *Works*. Translated by Benjamin Jowett. 4 vols. New York: Tudor Publishing Company.

13. Scheffler, Israel. *Conditions of Knowledge: An Introduction to Epistemology and Education*. Chicago: Scott, Foresman, 1965.

14. Snygg, Donald. "The Cognitive Field Theory: New Understandings About the Person." In *Influences in Curriculum Change*, edited by Glenys G. Unruh and Robert R. Leeper, pp. 21–27. Washington, D.C.: Association for Supervision and Curriculum Development, 1968.

15. Stolurow, Lawrence M., and Kenneth R. Pahel. "Is Programed Instruction Socratic?" *Harvard Educational Review* 33:383–385, Summer 1963.

6 Discovery Through Discussion: Values and Feelings

The reader no doubt realizes that the Socratic dialogue is not the only way for the teacher to deal with normative issues. It is therefore appropriate that this chapter treat another method for dealing with issues involving values (moral values or personal preferences) and social policies. (*Policies* is used to refer to courses that *ought* to be taken and hence involve value choices.) The terms *valuative discovery* or *valuative inquiry* will be used to refer to inquiry that centers on valuative matters including social matters (What should American foreign policy toward China be?), morals (What is justice?), evaluations (Is *King Lear* Shakespeare's best play?), or feelings (How do you feel when people discriminate against you?).

Discovery Sessions: Examples and Analyses

Two examples of a valuative discussion, presented below, will serve as a springboard for treating the valuative discovery method and will aid in drawing distinctions between this method and the Socratic method.

Example 1: Young Adolescents Focusing on a Public Policy Issue

Teacher: All right, now, let's take a look at the topic you read about yesterday in class and at home last night. I'm wondering, Jonathan, if you'd start us off by commenting on the very question in the title—let's see, I'll check to be exact, "Should Teenage Lawbreakers Be Jailed?" That is, should young criminals be put behind bars?

Jonathan: Well, I'm not so sure I agree with the whole article, but I guess I do agree. Yeah, I guess I think they should be jailed.

Teacher: Okay. Charles?

Charles: I'm with Jonathan—it seems to me that kids who break the law should be punished.

Teacher: Well, we've got two separate thoughts here which are similar. We seem to be—Ruth?

Ruth: I just want to say that I disagree, and I want to know why the two of them say that.

Teacher: Okay. Jonathan, back to you, then.

Jonathan: Well—uh, the law is the law, and if kids who break it are punished, then they'll learn to obey the law—that's why. (NOISE—At this point there's clatter, and several hands go up.)

Teacher: Okay, okay, now—since Jonathan has given us his reason, let's talk to this point to see if it's true.

Rachel: I don't agree with Jonathan. I think that sometimes when you punish people they just do more of the same thing, since they get madder and madder. Then look what happens.

Teacher: Linda?

Linda: I read some place that 85 percent of the men in jail are repeaters. So it seems that jailing juvenile delinquents doesn't help at all—'cause if it did so many of them wouldn't be put back.

Jonathan: Well, I think she's wrong. Anyway, we're talking about juvenile delinquents, not men.

Charles: Look, I know that when I got caught sneaking into the football game last month, and Mr. Jensen found out and punished me, I didn't try it again. And I'm a juvenile. So you can't say that punishment doesn't work. I'll bet you've all been punished sometime, and then you didn't try that stuff again. And I'm sure it works with a lot of us juvenile delinquents, too. So what Linda says is just not so.

Teacher: Before we go further, maybe it would help to quickly clear up what we mean by *juvenile delinquent*. Linda, you used it first, so go ahead.

Linda: Well, according to our article, a juvenile delinquent is someone—in most states it's under eighteen—who gets his name into the police books—someone who commits a crime. That's what I meant when I said that juvenile delinquents aren't cured by being jailed.

Teacher: Okay. For the time being, then, let's all stick with this notion, or else we'll never get anyplace. Let's keep to this legal definition—someone under eighteen who has a police record. Now if we use it this way, then Charles can't claim he's a juvenile delinquent and. . . .

Charles: Well, it's still true—I got punished, and I didn't do it again, and that's the way it is for most of us teenagers, whether we're Linda's delinquents or not.

Teacher: Suzanne, you seem quite eager to comment, so go ahead.

Suzanne: Well, I wanted to say before, that when we studied English history, Mr. Herold said that putting people to death in the public square for picking pockets didn't seem to stop other people any.

Jonathan: That's the same thing Linda said, and it's not true. She's talking about adults, and we're supposed to be talking about teenagers—and teenagers are different, that's all. Besides, she didn't prove it.

Teacher: I think it's time to examine closely the position so far. Jonathan says we should punish, that is, jail, juvenile delinquents so they'll learn to obey the law. Linda and Suzanne claim that that won't work, and Charles claims it will. Now, it seems to me that we'll get hung up here on this argument between Charles and the two girls unless we have some way of deciding who's right. But we'll come back to that in a minute. Let's see if any others of you want to offer any other reason for jailing delinquents. Terry?

Terry: Yes, I think that you have to put 'em away, but I don't mean jail, 'cause that's too much, but I mean like a special school or something—'cause like—well, we just can't let people get away with things—like if a kid steals a car one week, and he gets away with it, then everyone who knows about it will say to themselves, "Gee, maybe I can steal a car." And then, boy, we're in a mess. You've gotta teach people a lesson, but I just think jail is too much.

Elana: Well, Terry's just saying what Jonathan said before, only he's changing from jail to some kind of school. I don't think that that's going to help much. But I want to say that we've got to fit the punishment to the crime, and sending every delinquent to jail doesn't make much sense. We don't send every adult to jail.

Teacher: That's a very good point. Elana is suggesting that somehow we can't treat every crime alike, and that some crimes are worse than others, and. . . .

Elana: Like murder is awful, but speeding isn't.

Teacher: Let me finish my sentence—Elana is suggesting, it seems to me, that we recognize that not all crimes are alike and that we punish according to the crime. Jonathan, will you speak to this point, please.

Jonathan: I guess I agree with her there, so maybe we ought to jail only the worst ones, like murder, stealing cars, robbery, and stuff like that. But for the little things, like shoplifting and making too much noise at night in the streets, we ought to fine the kid or make him do some good deed for a bad one—something like that, maybe.

Arnold: I was thinking that, if we start saying that this crime is different from that crime, then we've got to also say that this juvenile delinquent is different from that one. Like, if one kid steals a buck or so to buy a guitar, that's not the same as some poor kid stealing so he can buy his lunch at school.

Paul: Anyone who steals to buy his lunch at our cafeteria deserves whatever he gets. Wow!

(NOISE—Laughter.)

Teacher: Okay, okay. The example might not be so good, but the point is important. Is it necessary to consider the delinquent, his background and such, before deciding on how to punish him?

Ruth: Yes, it is—I said before that I disagreed with Jonathan, and that's why—it seems to me that we just can't go around putting everyone in jail for everything. Sometimes you have to allow for a J.D. coming from a bad home—so he's not to blame.

Charles: Wait a minute, Ruth. You can't do that, 'cause then every J.D.'ll say, "I'm not to blame," like that guy in *West Side Story* who says he comes from a bad home. Boy, then you're really in trouble, 'cause no one's to blame. If a poor kid steals, what are you going to do—put his old man in jail? Who's to blame?

Paul: I think Chuckie is right—if someone does something wrong, like kill a cop, you've got to blame him. If you don't, just because his father was a crook, then, well, you're setting a bad example for everyone.

Teacher: Now, Arnold's suggestion that we consider who the juvenile delinquent is and what his background is has led us to a point where we have to examine whether we want to treat everyone alike who commits the same crime. Is it fair if we do? Is it fair if we don't? Elana?

Elana: I don't know about that—I haven't thought about that before, so I don't know. What do you think, Mr. Lincoln? Tell us your opinion.

Teacher: I'll be glad to comment personally later. First, I think it would be wise to ask ourselves what would happen if we jailed every juvenile lawbreaker? Jonathan and Charles claim that a J.D. will learn not to commit crimes from this. Is there anything else that probably would happen?

Arnold: In the article we read, it did say that people who go to jail often learn more about crime, because they're with experts who are always swapping tales. They called it "hardening the criminals." So putting J.D.'s in jail might only teach 'em to be worse J.D.'s when they get out in several months.

Gloria: Also, if you put kids in jail, you might not only harden the J.D., but you give him a bad mark on his name and harden other people against him. Then even if he wants to go straight, he can't, because other people won't give him a chance. So you might lose in the long run.

Teacher: Before we close, let's look at it the other way. Let's go to the other extreme. What would happen if we never jailed a juvenile delinquent?

Elmer: Are you asking what would happen if we never punished a J.D., or if we never *jailed* a J.D.?

Teacher: I asked about never jailing a J.D., but you can reply to either or both, if you wish.

Elmer: Well, it seems to me, never punishing is foolish. So, then, if we never jailed, we'd have to find other ways of punishing, like fines or special schools where a J.D. can learn to be better.

Delores: If we never jailed a J.D., I think the result wouldn't be any different unless we changed other things, too. For instance, if you sent him to a school, you'd have to make sure he didn't get hardened there just like he'd get hardened in jail. Also, that going to a special school wouldn't be a black mark. Otherwise special schools or fines and stuff have all the same effect as jails. So it's just not eliminating jail. Personally, I think we ought to warn everybody first—that would be one way of a J.D. not getting a black mark against his name right away, and he'd have another chance. Gee, I didn't think I thought that before—but I guess I do, don't I? I guess I think I do.

Teacher: Before our time runs out, let me return to a critical point raised earlier that we sort of dropped. Jonathan said that jailing juvenile delinquents would teach them to obey the law. It is important that we all remember that neither Jonathan nor Linda, who disagreed with him, gave facts to convince us that what they said was so. And when I didn't give my own personal opinion before to Elana about whether we ought to consider what type of delinquent we are dealing with before we jail him, it was this critical point I had in mind. What I mean is that we, in our class, don't know yet how much and what kind of effect jailing has on the different types of criminals—especially J.D.'s, as you call them. We need more facts. Do J.D.'s really get hardened in jail? What I'm saying is that it seems to me that we need to get more evidence about jailing and juvenile delinquents, and then we can discuss it better. Right now, we have to "return to the drawing boards" as our friend back there, Arnold, usually says. So, that's where we all have to go—back to the drawing boards for more information about jailing. Okay, any suggestions on how and where? . . .

Features of Valuative Discovery as Shown in Example 1

The preceding discussion reveals several features of the valuative discovery method. These are enumerated below. (Obviously the discussion on juvenile delinquency will continue in subsequent sessions, but this fragment is itself sufficiently illustrative.)

1. This teacher clearly recognizes that the topic "Should Teenage Lawbreakers Be Jailed?" is a policy issue and hence open-ended. That is, this teacher is aware that valuative issues are not factual, although they clearly involve facts. There is no single correct answer to the question posed. Various people will have different answers to this question. Each person must respond on his own unless he is willing to accept somebody else's response. But then he still has the task of deciding who that "somebody else" will be, and this decision also involves a valuative judgment, i.e., he prefers that Jones rather than Smith respond for him.

The recognition that valuative questions are essentially different from factual questions (e.g., Can hydrogen be mixed with oxygen to produce water? Is Brazil larger in size and population than the United States?) is absolutely necessary. Awareness of this difference leads the teacher in the session above to encourage students other than Jonathan, the first respondent, to offer their views. If the teacher had considered the question to be factual, the entire discussion would have focused on whether Jonathan was right or wrong. The teacher would most likely have said at some point, "Jonathan, you're correct (or dead wrong) about jailing teenagers." Rather, in the discussion we hear such words (or their classroom synonyms) as *disagree* and *agree* in regard to Jonathan's reply.

Furthermore, the students recognize that this is a valuative question. They sense this from the way their teacher reacts, as well as from previous experience. In any case, they, too, do not say, "Jonathan is wrong," in reaction to his reply. Note that when

Jonathan accuses Linda of being wrong, it is in regard to an empirical statement not a valuative one. This recognition by teacher and student that the question is valuative permits the discussion to proceed as it does. Without it there would be chaos.

2. The teacher above has structured the discussion quite clearly. There is no doubt about what the class is to discuss. This teacher has clarified the question posed in the article by rephrasing it. He has also, quite early in the discussion, sought a definition of the term *juvenile delinquent*. These steps eliminate any haggling over what the topic is and what the term means. (It is interesting to note that the group accepts a legal definition rather than a psychological or ethical one.) As a result, the discussion never bogs down but proceeds from the initial question. There is a need for clarification of the topic and key terms in every discussion. According to Passmore, this clarification is the first stage in the pattern of a good discussion. "The members of the group must know what they are supposed to be talking about, and must all be talking about the same thing. Often enough, these conditions are not fulfilled, unless there is a preliminary clarification of the problem" (15:12). The teacher usually does the clarifying, as in the situation above, though occasionally a student can do it.

Students' Defense of Position

3. The teacher above recognizes that in valuative discovery participants must defend the viewpoints they offer. Indeed, the discussion itself begins and thereafter hinges on the defense of the opinion offered. The justification of the opinion is crucial; it is this process that promotes meaningful discussion. Dewey aptly put it this way:

One of the most important factors in preventing an aimless and discursive recitation [*] consists in making it necessary for every

---

* Dewey, in Chapter 18 of *How We Think*, alternates between the terms *recitation* and *discussion*. From the context it is clear that his *recitation* is different from the *recitation* to be treated in Chapter 9. Rather, it is synonymous with *discussion* as that term is being used here. Dewey opens his chapter by showing that he disapproves of the old recitation method. However, he also says that when students and teacher are in closest contact in order to perform reflective thinking, he will call that type of lesson—which he advocates—recitation. Thus, while he recognizes the usual sense of the word *recitation*, Dewey utilizes the term in presenting his new method. To avoid the semantic confusion that Dewey's style causes, two separate words have been used above for the two methods. Dewey's use of *recitation* is synonymous with *discussion* as it is used in this book.

student to follow up and justify the suggestions he offers. He should be held responsible for working out mentally every suggested principle so as to show what he means by it, how it bears upon the facts at hand, and how the facts bear upon it (5:271).

This demand for (and examination of) the justification of any viewpoint offered to the class accounts in large measure for the attentiveness of the students. Because the students must be reasonable themselves and must also assess the reasonableness of their classmates, they are involved in "complex problem types of thought" (1:169). Bloom's research reports that students in discussions engage in eight times as much of this type of thought as students in lectures. Indeed, this high incidence of complex forms of thought is one very strong reason for teaching via the discussion method.

In regard to his research on thinking during discussion, Bloom says:

The discussion typically centers on the attack on problems. In such attacks the major task for the student is to find relationships between what is said and the problem which has been posed. It is, thus, not the following or comprehending which is important but the evaluation, finding answers or solutions, and synthesizing which are significant in the discussions.

This hypothesis is, in part, supported by the data on thoughts we have classified as problem-solving in nature. The thoughts in which the student applies the ideas being considered are approximately the same for the discussions and lectures. But the thoughts in which the student attempts to answer a problem or question raised, or to synthesize and integrate the ideas being considered by relating a specific to some abstraction, by reconciling conflicting points, or by relating the ideas being considered to the general problem which has been posed, are quite different, being only 1 percent in the lecture as compared with 8 percent in the discussion. While the average (8 percent) for this most complex type of problem-solving represents a relatively small proportion of the thoughts reported, all the discussions, with one exception, involve more of this type of thinking than any of the lectures (1:168).

In the illustrative discussion the teacher did not ask Jonathan immediately for a defense of his position. He could have done so but chose rather to encourage other people to participate. By carefully summarizing after Charles spoke, the teacher successfully prompted another student to request a defense from Jonathan and

Charles. This technique was employed so that the discourse among the students would continue. Since a student (Ruth) asked for a justification, the discussion became a class matter.

Wisely the teacher requested Jonathan to respond to Ruth. He thereby acknowledged that the request was legitimate. Note that the teacher chose Jonathan rather than Charles because there is no doubt that Jonathan had not given a justification. However, there was doubt about Charles. Was Charles justifying jailing or simply rephrasing his position when he said, "Kids who break the law should be punished"?

Smith and Meux (16:161; 12:12; 4; 13) state that as a result of their team's research on classroom language they distinguish several logical elements in valuative discourse: (1) something such as an object, statement, expression, event, action, or state of affairs to be evaluated; (2) a value term such as good, unjust, false, desirable to be applied to the value object; (3) a criterion or generalization by which it is judged whether the value term applies to the value object; (4) evidence about the value object which connects it to the criterion or generalization and thereby supports its use in evaluation; and (5) the value judgment which arises from the interaction of the first four elements.

Figure 6–1 shows these five elements and the interrelationships among them. The figure shows that on the basis of the four outer elements the person makes a value judgment about the value object. The upper horizontal shows the application of the value term to the value object. The lower horizontal line shows that both evidence and a criterion must be present in relation to the value object. The dotted line shows that the evidence must relate directly to the given value object and the criterion. The vertical line shows that the evidence and criteria support the value judgment, which is like a conclusion in an argument.

At this point and according to this schema it is possible to

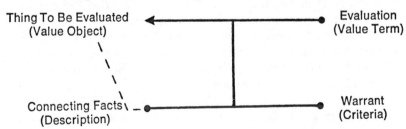

Figure 6–1

show that Ruth's request for justification was not only legitimate but also necessary. Jonathan's remarks after his response to Ruth may be diagrammed as follows (Figure 6–2). It is important to note that the teacher in the illustration has analyzed the discourse in this fashion, for his subsequent questions stem from this type of analysis.

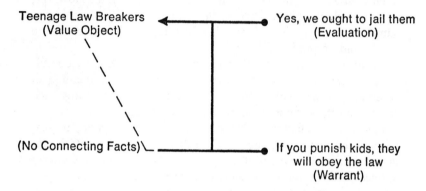

Figure 6–2

4. The teacher has correctly called class attention to the critical point: whether the reason (or justification or criterion) Jonathan gives is valid. Jonathan has not offered evidence to back up his statement. His justification, or criterion, however, is a generalization from many separate cases. This general statement can be analyzed in terms of being correct or incorrect in the ensuing discussion. To do this, evidence must be offered. This is the heart of the discussion. Passmore claims that "discussion does not even begin, properly speaking, until we are out of the region of preference. No *assertion* has been made, as I am using the word, until a statement of fact has been proposed for the consideration of the group" (15:14). The teacher in the sample discussion is clearly aware of this.

Seen in this light, the teacher's strategy is quite obvious and quite correct: the decision to jail teenage lawbreakers hinges on the notion that jailing them will cause them to obey the law in the future. If it can be shown that jailing will not result in obeying the law, then there will be no reason to jail the lawbreakers. As the discussion proceeds, two students seriously call into question Jonathan's warrant, though Charles supports it by a personal instance. (How supportive is a personal instance?) The teacher soon realizes that the validity of Jonathan's statement is in doubt. More important, he realizes that the students simply do not have sufficient evidence to either accept or reject it.

Rather than allow the discussion then to bog down in uninformed dispute about the generalization, the teacher attempts to elicit other criteria. That is, there may be more than one justification of the decision to jail juvenile delinquents. By seeking additional criteria, the teacher clearly demonstrates that he is following the flow of the discourse and is trying to prevent a bottleneck. Note, however, that the teacher does not treat Terry's criterion as he treated Jonathan's. But note also that it was the teacher's request for further criteria that led to Elana's significant contribution regarding differentiation among crimes and delinquents.

Teacher's Clarification of Points

5. At several points, the teacher rephrases the statements of the students in such a way as to sharpen and clarify the point being made. For example, the teacher senses that Elana has introduced a pivotal point into the discussion. He takes the opportunity to rephrase her point but wisely gives her the credit even though his own statement differs slightly from hers.

Sharpening or enlarging comments by restating them is a particularly effective technique for the teacher to employ. First, it offers him an excellent opportunity to praise significant contributions and thus to encourage subsequent participation. Second, it affords the teacher a springboard for properly introducing ideas that he believes will aid the discussion. This is not the only way a teacher may legitimately participate and contribute his thoughts on the topic, but it is an effective way for him to participate unobtrusively. It is a way for him to participate without monopolizing the session and without making his remarks carry special weight because he is the teacher. Also, this technique serves to advance the discussion, especially if the teacher asks a student to comment on the point he has clarified and rephrased.

The teacher who uses this technique must be careful lest he overuse it. The effectiveness of the technique decreases with constant use, because it then appears to the students that the teacher monopolizes the discussions. The teacher must somehow strike a balance between leading the flow of ideas and determining the flow of ideas, for this should be, after all, primarily a discussion in which the students can express their ideas.

The teacher must not abdicate as leader or remain silent. The students expect him to lead the discussion. The teacher must be careful to participate at critical points, for the great benefit to the student comes from reflecting on his classmates' ideas. It is obviously for this reason that the teacher in the illustration chose to delay his response to Elana in spite of her specific request. The temptation to respond was probably great, but the fact that he did not do so is to his credit. To give his own personal judgment at this early point in the discussion would have lessened the students' motivation to arrive at their own decision unbiased by the teacher's opinion.

The teacher can legitimately offer his own decision on a policy issue to the students. To do so he must set forth his warrants and supporting data. Then he must allow for open questioning about his decision, his warrants, and his connecting facts. He can legitimately advance his own judgments, for he is demonstrating how a reasonable adult citizen comes to a decision on policy matters. In fact, he even has an obligation to offer his own view-point for this reason.

The practical problem of the teacher is to preserve a balance between so little showing and telling as to fail to stimulate reflection and so much as to choke thought. Provided the student is genuinely engaged upon a topic, and provided the teacher is willing to give the student a good deal of leeway as to what he assimilates and retains (not requiring rigidly that everything be grasped or reproduced), there is comparatively little danger that one who is himself enthusiastic will communicate too much concerning a topic. If a genuine community spirit pervades the group, if the atmosphere is that of free communication in a developing exchange of experiences and suggestions, it is absurd to debar the teacher from the privilege and responsibility freely granted to the young, that of con-tributing his share. The only warning is that the teacher should not forestall the contributions of pupils, but should enter especially at the critical junctures where the experience of pupils is too limited to supply just the material needed (5:270).

Nevertheless, the teacher chose not to accede to the student's request at this point because of timing. Students can and will reflect on issues if the teacher does not squelch them. This is clearly exemplified by Jonathan in his reaction to Elana's point. Jonathan modified his view so that only teenagers who commit the worst crimes should be jailed. Delores reacts similarly, and even expresses to the class that only now does she realize what her viewpoint is. (The reader might find it helpful here to amend Figure 6–2 to show that new viewpoints were established.)

Indeed, a major point in support of the discussion method is that students are stimulated to reflect when they are confronted by questions and contrary viewpoints. The point of a discussion is to establish a product (position) through reflection. This process is what makes a discussion worthwhile, for the establishment of something concrete is fundamental to the deepening of the student's power of thought and ability to assimilate ideas (2:9). This involvement in the establishment of a product is what accounts for the fact that students participating in discussion classes have only 7.5 percent tangential thoughts, compared with 18.8 percent for students in lecture classes, in Bloom's research (1:166). "Thus, the evidence presented here strongly confirms the hypothesis that the lecture is much less successful than the discussion method in holding the student's thoughts actively to the immediate situation. Irrelevant and passive thoughts occur twice as frequently in lectures as in discussions" (1:167).

6. The teacher handled the humor injected by Paul in an excellent manner. He accepted it, realizing that it helped relieve some of the tension that is everpresent in a discussion where there is conflict on viewpoints. The teacher, in his reaction to the humor, tactfully turned the previous two remarks into "important" contributions, since they related to a significant point in the discussion. He thus used the humor to advance the inquiry.

7. In this illustrative discussion the teacher chose a middle course in regard to presenting data. First, he had assigned an article on the topic as common reading; this provided some initial familiarity and basic information. "The good discussion leader begins his questioning with references to materials and ideas with which the students have some familiarity" (10:24). A question based on the article was enough to get the discussion off the ground. Once it was started, the teacher then pointed out the kinds of further information the students should gather. Thus, the teacher was able to give direction to the students in a way that was pertinent, for they themselves then saw what they lacked. The teacher fully realized that discussion is possible only if "the

members of the group have information to throw into a common pool. That is a limitation upon discussion from the very start. Most of that information has to be acquired not by discussion, but by reading, by listening, or by looking" (15:60). From the points raised by the students it became clear that the assigned article was not sufficient to cope with the questions raised in the class session. The students, as intimated by the teacher, had to look to additional sources.

This teacher's decision about reading material marks a middle position between two possible extremes. The teacher could have simply raised the question without having his class prepare in some fashion. This would have put a greater burden on himself as resource person. Also, the possibility that the discussion might have degenerated into a mere bull session would have been great. It is in reference to such situations that Walton states, "There are times when one succinct, well-organized lecture or exposition is worth more than 100 discussions by the students" (18:162).

On the other hand, the teacher could have had the students read, listen, and consider the topic of juvenile delinquency for several days or even weeks before opening a discussion. Obviously there are times when a teacher might use this approach. However, the teacher in this case no doubt felt he could not have held the students' interest and enthusiasm. Also, much of the students' work might have been forced since they might not have seen the pertinence of the topic or the direction of their discussion.

Considered in this light, it becomes clear why the teacher used his summary at the end to raise further questions. In effect, he is attempting to give direction to the students' future investigations on the topic. Note, too, that his questions are geared toward encouraging the students to continue searching. The questions are specific and are phrased in such a way as to tempt the student to respond to them. These questions well suit the notion that we need relevant facts about an issue in order to come to grips with it.

As a general rule, the researcher would do well to state as fully and as positively as he can what his hunch really is and why. It is only then that he is in a position to undertake, with any rigor, a design for the con-vergence of evidence. It is easy to uncover facts, including correlations. But until the facts converge on something—some idea which is part of a pattern of meaning—the facts are not evidence of anything. It is only when they gain evidential status that we may properly call them data, not before (11:127).

When these students will later read at home or in the library, listen to radio or watch television, or talk to their friends, they will have questions to guide them. They will have direction for their individual efforts, and these, in turn, will tie in with their future classroom work. Judging from the last line of the excerpt, the group did talk about where to go and how to answer the questions raised.

8. The teacher, at three points, summarized the discussion and tied the various parts together. In this way he gave a focus to the discussion and aided students who were less able to follow the flow of ideas. Summaries—several internal ones and a final one—are essential. As used in this illustration, they serve as a springboard for advancing. They may also be used "to check needless repetition, to get the discussion back to the problem, or to record points of agreement and disagreement" (6:286).

If the class is unaccustomed to discussions, the teacher will, no doubt, be responsible for summarizing, since this requires careful listening and experience in following the flow of a complex issue. Students may find summarizing difficult to do since they are involved in the issue at hand and cannot plot the flow of ideas. However, if certain members of a class show the ability to summarize and point out key elements of the discussion, the teacher would do well to appoint them to this role. The technique of using student summarizers will further involve the whole class in the discussion and will give selected students an opportunity to participate in a varied way. Then, summaries can be given either at the teacher's or students' discretion. In any case it is generally most helpful to briefly note the main points of the summary on the chalkboard in order to have a reference point for the ensuing section of the discussion.

9. The teacher advanced the discussion by directing the students to the probable consequences of two opposite policies. He asked them to consider the probable consequences, first, of jailing delinquents and, then, of not jailing them. Questions about probable consequences are essential in a valuative discovery discussion, and the teacher must ask such questions himself if the students do not raise them. Note from the responses of these students how each of the teacher's questions on probable consequences brought new and critical points to bear on the main question.

Once the student has considered the probable consequences of jailing or not jailing delinquents, for example, he must still decide which set of consequences he prefers. That is to say, estimating the consequences is not sufficient and does not automatically yield a decision. Rather, the student must then choose his policy in full awareness of what will most likely result. Consideration of the probable consequences of a policy is necessary for a rational decision.

It is for this reason that students need as much relevant data on the topic in question as they can gather. By examining the facts about jailing and not jailing juvenile delinquents, the students can better establish probable consequences. This is why authoritative data are needed; the lack of relevant data can easily spell disaster for the discussion. Thus, contrary to what is accepted in some quarters, the teacher must carefully prepare for a discussion. He must be a resource person and must guide his students to relevant data.

10. The teacher, it seems clear, is not antagonizing or threatening the students with his questions. There is a climate of acceptance of ideas by both teacher and students. The students seem to accept the questions as prods to further thought and as the teacher's method of advancing their thinking on the topic. They do not take the questions as personal challenges, as ways of exposing their ignorance, or as methods of catching them in embarrassing contradictions. In this way the teacher's actions are significantly different from Socrates' dealings with Euthyphro. It is this difference in particular which must be kept in mind when comparing Socratic dialogue with the valuative discovery method.

This technique of encouraging the students is the most important way a teacher can support inquiry, according to Suchman (17:70). In accepting the students' remarks and welcoming their contributions to the discussion, the teacher helps to motivate future inquiry. That is to say, well-conducted inquiry produces further inquiry. "If the teacher encourages the pupil to think and inquire autonomously, in the long run the structure of knowledge and meaning he acquires will be far deeper and more functional than that gained through more prescriptive teaching" (17:70).

11. The teacher has involved enough students in the discussion to permit a free and continuous interchange (9). There is a need in discussion for diversity among the participants to assure a diversity of thought. The reflections of the various students should be expressed verbally to the class; the teacher must facilitate the exchange of ideas among students. Further, with a diversity of participants, students do not feel compelled to participate. The

student should express his views from a desire to do so, rather than from an obligation to keep the discourse going. Since it is necessary to have diversity among students, it is possible for a discussion group to be too small (2:12), contrary to a common myth.

In regard to this point about student participation, the teacher must be careful not to assume that a student who sits quietly during a particular session is not wrestling with the issue. The teacher must not equate physical passivity with intellectual passivity. A critical listener is virtually essential to a good discussion. The silent but noticeably present listener helps keep speakers on the right track by his watchful eye.

In summary, the items below, based on the lesson "Should Teenage Lawbreakers Be Jailed?" outline steps to follow in teaching a *valuative discovery lesson focused on taking a stand.* These steps are, then, a strategy to follow in other, similar discussions. These steps coordinate with the valuative model presented earlier in Figure 6-1.

1. Present and clarify the valuative issue.

2. Have students take a stand—a first tentative stand.

3. Have students assemble facts and establish criteria.

4. Clarify and define key terms.

5. Have students assess truth and relevance of facts (i.e., determine what facts will count as *evidence*).

6. Have students defend criteria.

7. Have students examine alternative positions and probable consequences of all positions presented.

8. Have students take a stand—a *second* tentative stand, based on a reassessment of the first one and amounting to a firmer decision.

9. Have students test the valuative principle implied in the stand taken.

10. Summarize, halt discussion, and launch into new, related activity.

Mix in among these steps when appropriate: rephrasings of statements, humor, clarifications, and summaries. Conduct the discovery lesson in a positive atmosphere in which many students can be involved in a nonthreatening way.

Example 2: Eight- and Nine-year-olds Focusing on Feelings and Proposed Action

Teacher: What I'd like to do today is read you a short story and then talk to you about it. OK, here goes.

"Sharon Nelson loved to play outdoors. She roller-skated, rode her bike, jumped rope, played tag, played hopscotch, and, best of all, played baseball. Whenever the kids in her neighborhood got a ball game together, Sharon always played with them. They all knew that she was the best second baseman of all the nine- and ten-year-old kids.

"No wonder, then, that when the tryouts came for the midget league, Sharon appeared with her own bat and glove. The coaches were all quite impressed with her ability to hit and throw. That's why Coach Cooper was so happy he could choose Sharon to play on his team, the Flames.

"When the midget league season began in April, Sharon was the starting second baseman. In the opening game she hit a single and a triple in five times at bat to lead the Flames in beating the Giants, 3–2. After the game the coach of the Giants told Coach Cooper that he would protest the game because, according to the midget league rules, girls are not allowed to play. He said that the rule says, 'The Midget League of Mayville is open to boys age 8–12.' 'Besides,' said the coach, 'since baseball is known as a boys' sport, it's not fair that Sharon should take some guy's place.'

"And so, because of the rule, Sharon did not play baseball in the midget league."

Well, that's it. I hope you all understood it. [Pause—as teacher surveys the heads nodding vertically.] Mark, would you please take a few seconds to briefly tell some of the important points of the story.

Mark: Well, she wanted to play on the baseball team because she was a great second baseman. The Flames said she could play. She hit a triple and single, and she was the starting second baseman. And, and after the game, the coach protested the game that girls aren't allowed to play from age 9 to, I think, 11. And so she couldn't play.

Corinne: 8 to 12.

Teacher: OK. Fine. Let me ask you another question. How do you think Sharon felt? Betty?

Betty: She felt bad—not "bad" but disappointed.

Matthew: Depressed.

Betty: Disappointed, depressed, let down—and she felt that boys think that girls aren't good.

Shirley: Yeah, equal rights.

Corinne: Yeah, now maybe some girls are better than boys.

Robert: Most of the guys may not want girls to play baseball, but that doesn't mean all of the girls.

Jean: I bet you that they were just jealous and the coach was jealous, otherwise he wouldn't have brought it up because his team was losing.

Betty: Yeah, some people have too much confidence, and when they lose, they really can't stand to lose, so they try to pick at something to protest and pick about. And he found something on the other team. He should have done it before.

Mark: Yeah, why didn't he do it before the game when he knew she was picked.

Teacher: Well, what do you think Sharon could do now?

Betty: Just because she's a girl doesn't mean she shouldn't play baseball, so she could protest.

Teacher: So she could protest.

Corinne: Yeah, I would.

Teacher: What else could she do?

Ann: She could do nothing.

Matthew: She could start a league of her own and not let any boys play.

Teacher: OK. She could start her own league, she could protest, and she could not do anything. Anything else?

George: Go to the mayor of Mayville and talk to him.

Mark: She could go to the head of the midget league and talk it over with him.

Teacher: OK. Now these are things she *could* do. What do you think Sharon *should* do?

Robert: She should go to the head of the midget league and tell him that just because she's a girl doesn't mean she's not allowed to play baseball. She's better than some of the boys.

Matthew: I think she should go talk to the two coaches to see if they can work something out.

Corinne: She should go across the field with a sign saying, "Equal rights for girls!"

Teacher: There we go again with "equal rights."
You think women are equal to men. In what ways are women and men equal? What facts do you have that women and men are equal?

Ann: Like, you know, actors; famous women actors.

Rosemarie: Like Eleanor Roosevelt, she's a famous woman; she's a good example. She's famous like her husband.

Andrew: Men work and women work.

Betty: When I was in the hospital, there were some women doctors—there even was a woman surgeon.

Matthew: Can I tell this joke: There was a man and his son who got into a car accident. So they took them to the hospital in the ambulance. When they got the boy to the operating room, the doctor said, "But I can't operate—that's my son." How can that be?

Joe: The doctor was his mother.

Matthew: You shouldn't have told, Joe, you knew the answer. Foo!

Teacher: Sorry, Matthew. But are there any other ways that men and women are equal?

Robert: When we went on our trip to the West, we went into this gas station. And this woman in boots and hot pants came up to my dad and said "What do you want?" and my dad said, "Fill 'er up."

Alice: Men and women both vote.

Joe: I heard on the news there's even a woman umpire in the major leagues.

Matthew: Yeah and there's even a woman rabbi now. One now, then there'll be two and three and so on.

Teacher: OK. You've mentioned several ways they're equal: work, doctors, gas station workers, famous people like the Roosevelts, actors, umpire, and rabbi. Now Matthew suggested before that Sharon should go talk to the two coaches. What should Sharon do or what would you do if the coaches agree that midget league should be for boys only?

Corinne: I wouldn't walk away. I'd still try to talk it over.

Matthew: I guess I'd finally walk away and start my own team.

Teacher: Any other things Sharon should do or you would do? [Pause—silence.]
OK. Then let me ask you this. Do you think girls *should* play in the midget league?

Betty: Yes, I think midget league should be a freer thing so anyone who wants to join can join. So she's a girl, so what? Like blacks and whites, girls and boys, so what? Equal rights.

Robert: Like Mary Lake on my block; she's better than most of

the boys I know. She'd be really good on a midget league team; she's good at baseball.
And football.
And basketball.

Teacher: Has Mary been in a similar situation?

Robert: No, she just never tried out because she knew of the same rule here.

Teacher: How would she feel if she made the team and then wasn't allowed to play like Sharon.

Debbie: She'd sock everyone in sight.

Robert: She would go bam to anyone who wouldn't let her play.

Debbie: She'd be in a grouchy mood for ten days.

Teacher: So, do you all think that a girl should be allowed to play in midget league.

Students: Yeah. [Lots of voices together.]

Teacher: What reasons do you give for allowing her into the midget league?

Corinne: Equal rights!

Teacher: Any other reasons?

Betty: Because of women's lib has come out and all that. She *should* be allowed to play.

John: But not everyone agrees with woman's lib.

Betty: Tough luck on them!

Teacher: So we've got girls equal to boys and women's lib. Any other reasons?

Ruth: There shouldn't really even be a special reason for it. It's like saying, why should boys be able to play. There shouldn't really be a particular reason.

Mark: It should count only if you can hit and field. That's all; doesn't matter if you're a boy or girl.

Corinne: Like in Junior Chef. There are boys in there. They don't say cooking is only for girls. Whoever wants to cook.

Teacher: You're saying that just like Junior Chef is for girls and boys so midget league should also be for boys and girls.

Corinne: Right.

Matthew: But maybe Junior Chef isn't like midget league.

Corinne: Oh, yes it is!

Teacher: Let me sum it all up here for today. We heard a story about Sharon Nelson who couldn't play in the midget league. You said she felt disappointed and let down, but she could talk to the coaches or the mayor or even start her own girl midget league. Then you said that she *should* go talk to the coaches, and someone even said that she should protest. You gave some examples of how men and women are equal, like voting and doctors. Finally, you all agreed that girls should play in the midget league for several reasons—midget league should be freer, it should be like Junior Chef, equal rights, and even no need really for a reason. Let's leave it here. Till the next time would you please talk with your friends to see who doesn't want girls in the midget league. Find out why. Maybe we can even invite him here to talk it over with you since he believes differently. Happy hunting!

Features of Valuative Discovery as Shown in Example 2

The analysis of Example 2 will build on the features set forth in the analysis of Example 1. No attempt will be made to repeat all the features of valuative discovery that were cited in the preceding analysis. Instead, those additional features will be emphasized that are peculiar to this example.

1. The teacher here recognizes that the story about Sharon Nelson involves feelings as well as a policy decision. The teacher obviously has a strategy for conducting a discussion involving feelings and policy. That is to say, the teacher knows what procedures to follow and also knows the simple value model presented earlier (see Figure 6–1). Since these are young students (eight- and nine-year-olds), the teacher began by asking a student to recount briefly the story so as to be sure that the students know the essential facts of the situation. Only then did he move to the next step, to ask about Sharon's feelings. His question asks the students to infer how Sharon felt.

The teacher realized that soon the students would be expressing their own personal feelings about girls playing in the midget league. Because he believed that it would be easier for them to do this if they first were able to talk about someone else's feelings, he began by asking the students to make inferences about Sharon. This is an important and interesting strategic step. Sometimes students will not be eager or willing to state their own feelings but will be willing to talk about someone else's feelings. The teacher must accept this situation and realize that, even if the students do not explicitly state their own feelings, he can treat the matter of feelings significantly via these inferences of others' feelings. With this request to infer Sharon's feelings, the teacher not only brought feelings out onto the floor for comment, but also facilitated the later expression of feelings by the students.

2. The teacher then pursued alternative solutions by asking the students to suggest things "Sharon could do now." This is a necessary step in that it emphasizes the idea of multiple possibilities rather than a single, determined path. The students now have the opportunity to explore probable consequences of several probable actions.

From here the teacher moves to the preferred one of these alternative actions. The difference between "could do" and "should do" is significant, and the students pick up the shift in emphasis. Three different preferred actions come out rather than just one before the teacher personally comes back into the discussion. When he does, the teacher sets out to clarify the meaning of the term *equal rights*, which seems to be central and recurrent.

This step of clarification is not a formal, pre-established step which must occur at a certain spot. It is rather one that this teacher shifts to because he notices something occurring during the course of the discussion. The teacher sets out to clarify the term *equal rights* by asking for ways in which women are equal to men. As they offer examples of equality, the students concretize the notion of equal rights.

The teacher ends the clarification step and shifts to exploring the probable consequences of one suggested, preferred solution. He does not explore the probable consequences of all the alternatives or all the preferences. He chooses to explore (perhaps because of time limitations) only one suggestion. After treating this point, the teacher shifts to a significantly different step.

3. Now the teacher pursues with the students the issue of policy: Should girls play in the midget league? With this question the teacher leaves the issue of feelings and enters the domain of policy. Obviously he feels that it is not enough to discuss Sharon's feelings and possible avenues of action. The teacher shifts now to the more general issue regarding policy.

4. The teacher picks up the point offered by Robert that Sharon Nelson is "like Mary Lake on my block." The teacher has not yet asked for any parallel situations which the students know firsthand. When Robert offers one, however, the teacher is most alert and sensitive to the need for parallels. So he explores it a bit. The teacher probably was awaiting an analogy, since students often offer one spontaneously. For this reason, he noticed Robert's

analogy quickly and played it up briefly. The teacher recognizes the power of an analogy in thinking through an issue. If someone had not offered an analogy, the teacher may have had to ask for one, since parallel situations are very important in valuative discussions. It is with this in mind that the teacher also quickly picks up Corinne's analogy of Junior Chef a bit later and rephrases it for clarity.

5. Next the teacher asks the students to support their policy decision with good reasons. At this point the teacher is following the same model held by the teacher in the previous discussion, "Should Teenage Lawbreakers Be Jailed?" Once again the teacher elicits multiple responses before leaving the policy issue.

6. With his time nearly finished, the teacher uses his last few seconds of the class period to perform three important steps in one utterance; he summarizes the day's discussion, he halts that discussion, and he launches the students into some new activity. He obviously seeks some carry-over until the next lesson and will use this lesson as a springboard into the next one. In this way he gives the students something to do and also gives himself a starting point for his next lesson.

Although there are a few other features of this discussion to comment on, it is appropriate to leave them for the reader himself to note and to summarize now the steps involved in a *valuative lesson focused on feelings and proposed action*. The following steps, based on an analysis of this lesson, are a suggested strategy for conducting such a valuative discussion. There is flexibility in these steps, but what follows is a good procedure in general.

1. Present the valuative episode.
2. Have student restate the essence of the story. This is especially important for young students so as to check comprehension.
3. Have students infer feelings.
4. Have students offer alternative possible actions.
5. Have students offer their preferred action. That is, ask students which of the alternative actions they prefer.
6. Probe with students the probable consequences of the solutions offered.
7. Explore parallel situations. Have students offer situations from their own lives which are similar to the one in the valuative episode. This step is good here but could come at any point in the

discussion. It is perfectly all right for parallels to arise in several spots, too.

8. Have students take a stand on the policy issue involved in the valuative episode.

9. Have students justify their policy stands.

10. Summarize, halt discussion, launch into new, related activity.

Mix in among these steps when appropriate: rephrasings of statements, humor, clarifications, and summaries. Conduct the discovery lesson in a positive atmosphere in which many students can be involved in a nonthreatening way.

Other Valuative Discussions

The two examples presented above, dealing with juvenile delinquency and midget league baseball, are illustrative of but two types of valuative discovery. The lesson centering on "Should teenage lawbreakers be jailed?" is illustrative of valuative discovery regarding public policy controversy. That is, the students focus on taking a stand regarding a public issue. The lesson centering on Sharon Nelson's attempt to play baseball in the midget league is illustrative of valuative discovery emphasizing feelings and attitudes. That is, the students focus on inferring feelings experienced by someone else, suggest possible courses of action for that person, and seek parallel situations in their own lives. In that lesson the students also took a stand on membership in midget league, but that is not the focus of the lesson.

There are two other types of valuative discovery. One type focuses on value analysis. That is, the students examine a case where values are involved and search out the values held by the people involved. The lesson revolves around locating and understanding the values in the sample situation. The other type of valuative discovery focuses on value conflict. That is, the students who hold conflicting values seek to resolve their conflict. The lesson revolves around locating the points of disagreement leading to conflict and reexamining values held so as to remove or reduce the conflict raised by different facts and value preferences.

These four types of valuative discovery are obviously all interrelated. The differences among them are mainly matters of emphasis rather than matters of uniqueness. There are overlaps, for example, in that people who engage in value analysis express their own feelings as well as value positions. Also, in any given lesson the teacher and students may combine two types of valuative discovery, as did the teacher in the sample lesson concerned with midget league baseball when he combined attention to feelings with attention to policy. Nevertheless, it is possible to list four types of valuative discovery with different emphases:

1. Value analysis
2. Taking a stand on a public issue
3. Resolution of value conflict
4. Expression of feelings and attitudes

Other Characteristics of the Method

The reader who carefully reviewed the illustrative discussions no doubt realizes that the teacher failed to do certain things that are desirable in leading a discussion. The reader is indeed correct, but in any one discussion it is difficult to do all the desirable things that might be done. A single class session is, no doubt, too short a time in which to complete a thorough discussion of juvenile delinquency. Therefore, any one-session discussion might better be viewed as only a part of a larger discovery discussion. Treated below are some of the more salient items that are desirable in a discussion but that were not included in these illustrations. What else might the teacher do in ensuing sessions with the students?

1. The teacher would do well to deepen and broaden the students' knowledge of the problem of juvenile delinquency and mixed sports. These students need more knowledge if they are to come to a reasonable position on their own. To ask the students to make a value judgment without a stronger foundation of facts and criteria employed by others is to place them in an unreasonable position.

This tack, of course, must be preceded by, or at least accompanied by, an analysis of the problem. Only through analysis of the problem will it be possible to determine which facts to search for and which facts are relevant. As the students analyze the problem and come to understand it better, they have clearer guidelines in their search for evidence. As they gather evidence, they sharpen their analysis of the problem. This interaction is necessary in inquiry. "It is the problem and its characteristics as revealed by analysis which guides one first to the relevant facts and then, once the relevant facts are known, to the relevant hypotheses" (14:17).

The first teacher could have suggested further readings, from which students could gain further facts and reasons for their positions on teenage lawbreakers. The teacher could also arrange for films or tape recordings that would bring the students, through additional senses, closer to situations and people connected with juvenile delinquency. (There is no need to detail here the merits of audiovisual devices in promoting understanding of a topic.) The teachers could bring the students into even closer contact with the delinquency problem and mixed sports. They might arrange for classroom interviews with officials who deal directly with these issues, or they might arrange for a field visit to appropriate places and people. The use of firsthand sources, whether printed, visual, or aural, is necessary for the students to arrive at their decisions.

2. The teachers would do well to examine the course of events and policies that have led up to current policies on teenage lawbreakers and midget league for boys only. They would do well to solicit answers to such questions as, "When did juvenile delinquency first become an issue of public concern? How did we treat juvenile delinquency then? What changes, if any, have occurred in our treatment of J.D.'s? What reasons were offered in the past for treating J.D.'s as they were treated then?" When was the midget league officially organized? How did we regard women and girls in our society then? What reasons were given for excluding girls then? In a valuative discussion this approach puts the topic into perspective. Wolf, in examining how to deal with conflict crises involving policy issues, claims that this approach is essential. In his words it is necessary "to give the history of the conflict or to state what was done prior to the crisis" (19:119). In any valuative discussion, whether it involves a crisis topic or not, the treatment of past conditions and reasons for policy ought to be explored. These factors provide information about the topic that is most helpful in intelligently supporting our own decision (3:317).

3. The teacher would do well to examine the assumptions implicit in the students' remarks. For example, the teacher would do well to examine Charles's statement that "kids who break the law should be punished" or Paul's statement that you must blame someone if he does wrong. This teacher might ask, "What assumptions is Paul making?" Or, "What lies behind Charles's belief that kids who break the law should be punished?" Or, "Why did Charles give us that reason, do you suppose?"

This aspect of a discussion is what Goldmark calls Level III of an inquiry. Level I here would refer to the agreement that teenage criminals should be jailed. This is the basic judgment. Level II would refer to the reasons for the judgment—such as, "Kids who break the law should be punished" and "If they are punished, they'll learn to obey the law." Accordingly, "Why did Jonathan give that reason?" is a Level III question, since it solicits the reasoning behind people's criteria or the reason for giving a reason (7:8).

If the teacher were to ask such Level III questions regarding Jonathan's and Charles's contributions, the answers might well shed new light on the topic. The teacher might make it clear, for example, that the students believe that a person should suffer because he did wrong, or that the students believe that the fear of future suffering will deter people from breaking the law. Once such beliefs were out in the open, the teacher might well point out that punishment is but one method of treating lawbreakers. Such Level III questioning would help the students to broaden their understanding of the topic and their own approach to it. Surely it would help them to think of the various possibilities involved.

4. The teachers would do well to lead the students further in testing out the values implied in the stand they have taken. Each time a person takes a stand on a public issue, he implies a value principle. If a person decides to jail teenage lawbreakers, for example, the person implies that imprisonment for a crime is a desirable punishment. If a person decides to stand for mixed sports, then he implies that boys and girls should not have separate activities determined by gender. The teacher and students would do well to examine whether they would be willing to accept these principles in regard to similar lawbreaking, sports, and general youth cases. Or, they can test out the acceptability of the principle by asking if it is subsumed as a special case of an even more general value. They can also test out the principle by engaging in a role-playing situation where, for example, the student holding for imprisonment takes the role of the person to be punished or a relative of that person. As the student takes the role of the affected person, he can test to what extent he still accepts the implied principle in the stand he has taken. Whether he uses the similar-case test, the subsumption test, or the role-exchange test, it is important for the student to reexamine the values he holds as manifested in the stands he takes.

5. The teacher would do well to examine the truth of the statements put forth by the students. For example, Linda claims

that 85 percent of the men in jail are repeaters. Note that no one challenged Linda. Everyone simply accepted her statement as true, though she did not cite any reference at all. The source of her information remains unknown and unverified. How do we know that Linda's figure of 85 percent is true? Is Linda's source authoritative? Who qualifies as an expert on this topic? Is Suzanne's source better than Linda's? (Suzanne's source of information about pickpockets is Mr. Herold—obviously, from the context, a teacher in the school and known to the class.)

Through this type of questioning, students will become sensitive to the need for backing up their statements with authoritative references. The demand for acceptable and appropriate evidence is partly what lies behind Jonathan's assertion that Suzanne did not prove her point. The teacher who follows this line of questioning thus has an excellent opportunity for treating the canons of acceptable evidence, i.e., he can help show his students how facts and explanations can be verified and what constitutes authoritative data.

Once students are sensitive to the need for authoritative information, they will expect each other to use statements from accepted experts and to supply references for the sources of the information they cite. This is necessary if a discussion is to be more than a bull session in which students try to persuade rather than enlighten each other. Not all statements are equally valuable. Without acceptable and reliable information, the discussion is bound to be fruitless. In a discussion involving the seriousness of jailing teenagers, the teacher would do well to point out that policy decisions must rest on facts from sources more authoritative than "I read it someplace."

6. The first teacher would do well to point out the conclusions the discussants have reached. He could do this himself in his summaries, or he could ask one of his students to state the conclusions that can be drawn from the discussion. It is necessary for the students to acknowledge these conclusions clearly, since they must at some point weigh them. At some point in the first discussion, for example, the students would need to recognize the probable consequences of jailing and not jailing teenage delinquents and then decide if they desire these consequences. "This final weighing of conclusions, this transition from statements of facts to a decision of policy, serves at once as summary and as moral of the whole discussion" (15:20). For this reason, as conclusions and decisions are reached, it is wise for the teacher to

list these on the chalkboard so that they will be available to everybody.

The individual students do not have to agree on which policy to adopt, since they may give different weights to the various conclusions. Nor should any student be absolutely sure of his position at the end of the discussion, as agreement and certainty about policy are not the objectives of a discussion. Rather, the most important objective is the awareness, careful examination, and weighing of the facts, criteria, and consequences connected with a policy issue, in order to take a reasoned position. Through such discussions, it is hoped that students will come to recognize (a) the need for evidence, (b) the criteria available for justifying a policy, and (c) the assumptions underlying various policy decisions. The teacher who leads the discussion should be concerned with the "quality of the evidence and reasoning" (6:287). Passmore states this point quite well: ". . . the quality of a group will be judged, not by the assurance of its final conclusion, but, more often, by the extent of the gaps it has discovered in its knowledge. Not the extent of agreement, but the growth of understanding, is the test of the value of a discussion" (15:21).

7. The second teacher would do well to examine the pros and cons of each of the alternative actions the students offer for Sharon Nelson. When the teacher has the opportunity, he should take each alternative separately and list with the students the probable positive and probable negative features for each. This procedure is necessary in order to make the choice of a preferred action more meaningful. Students will be able to recognize what makes the best solution best when they can analyze the pros and cons of each alternative presented.

References

1. Bloom, B. S. "Thought-Processes in Lectures and Discussions." *Journal of General Education* 7:160–169, April 1953.

2. Buchler, Justus. "What Is a Discussion?" *Journal of General Education* 8:7–17, October 1954.

3. Burton, William H., Roland B. Kimball, and Richard L. Wing. *Education for Effective Thinking.* New York: Appleton-Century-Crofts, 1960.

4. Chadwick, James, and Milton Meux. "Procedures for Values Education." In *Values Education*, edited by Lawrence E. Metcalf, pp. 75–119. Washington, D.C.: National Council for the Social Studies, 1971.

5. Dewey, John. *How We Think: A Restatement of the Relation of Reflective Thinking to the Educative Process*. Boston: D. C. Heath, 1933.

6. Ewbank, Henry Lee, and J. Jeffrey Aver. *Discussion and Debate*. New York: Appleton-Century-Crofts, 1951.

7. Goldmark, Bernice. "'Critical Thinking': Deliberate Method." *Social Education* 30:329–334, May 1966.

8. Goldmark, Bernice. *Social Studies: A Method of Inquiry*. Belmont, Calif.: Wadsworth Publishing, 1968.

9. Gross, Richard E., and Frederick J. McDonald. "The Problem-Solving Approach." *Phi Delta Kappan* 39:259–265, March 1958.

10. Hatch, Winslow R. *Approach to Teaching*. Washington, D.C.: U.S. Department of Health, Education, and Welfare, 1966.

11. Hullfish, H. Gordon, and Philip G. Smith. *Reflective Thinking: The Method of Education*. New York: Dodd, Mead, 1961.

12. Meux, Milton. "The Evaluating Operation in the Classroom." In *Theory and Research in Teaching*, edited by Arno A. Bellack, pp. 11–24. New York: Bureau of Publications, Teachers College, Columbia University, 1963.

13. Meux, Milton. "A Model of Evaluative Operations in the Classroom." *High School Journal* 51:39–45, October 1967.

14. Northrop, F. S. C. *The Logic of the Sciences and the Humanities*. New York: Meridian Books, 1959.

15. Passmore, John. *Talking Things Over*. Melbourne, Australia: Melbourne University Press, 1963.

16. Smith, B. Othanel, and others. *A Study of the Strategies of Teaching*. Cooperative Research Project 1640, U.S. Department of Health, Education, and Welfare. Office of Education. Urbana, Ill.: Bureau of Educational Research, College of Education, University of Illinois, 1967.

17. Suchman, J. Richard. "In Pursuit of Meaning." *The Instructor* 75:32, 70, September 1965.

18. Walton, John. *Toward Better Teaching in the Secondary Schools*. Boston: Allyn and Bacon, 1966.

19. Wolf, Frank E. "Conflict Episode Analysis." *Social Education* 23:118–120, March 1959.

7 Discovery Through Discussion: Concepts and Content

The reader might well ask if the discovery method applies to issues that do not involve valuative judgments. Specifically, do the elements of the discovery method which are exemplified in valuative discussion—and which distinguish the discovery method from the lecture method, recitation method, and Socratic dialogue—hold for nonvaluative issues as well?

Discovery method certainly does apply to topics that do not involve policy decisions. It applies, as witnessed in the "new" curriculum projects, to issues in such fields as history, biology, mathematics, and literature, which do not require decisions on policies. For example, the discovery method is quite appropriate for dealing with such questions as: (1) What trends exist in adult literacy in the countries of Africa and Asia? (2) What will be the status of the radio and the automobile in the year 2025? (3) In looking at the voting data county by county from the last presidential election, what do you conclude about the strength of the Republican and Democratic parties? (4) What are the causes of today's inflation? (5) How and when was the Grand Canyon formed? (6) Why (and how) has Shakespeare influenced subsequent English playwrights? In contrast to the question about jailing teenagers in the previous chapter, none of these questions require the student to arrive at a decision—involving his personal values—as to what action ought to be taken. To answer these six questions, the student must rather employ facts, concepts, and generalizations. He will most likely arrive at these by using pertinent documents, equipment (laboratory or audiovisual), and other relevant aids. He will be involved in explaining, not evaluating, as well as observing, generalizing, categorizing, inferring, concluding, and predicting.

The Discovery Techniques: A Comparison

At the outset, even before giving any examples, it is possible to state that in general the techniques used in employing the discovery method involving concepts and content (nonvaluative) are the same as those for the discovery method involving issues on value (valuative), in spite of the difference between the two types of subject matter. That is to say, valuative discovery techniques, such as clear structuring, sufficient involvement of participants, provision of relevant materials (books, equipment, artifacts), shaping and rephrasing of student contributions, nonthreatening questioning, use of humor, and summarizing, all equally apply to nonvaluative discussions.

Other extremely important elements of the valuative discovery method are the need for analysis of perplexing questions, development of possible answers (i.e., hypotheses), consideration of probable consequences of an answer, the need for relevant data, and arrival at a carefully weighed conclusion. These, too, are relevant to nonvaluative discovery (11).

Two examples of a nonvaluative lesson, one with a mixed class of twenty-four eight- and nine-year-olds and one with adults, will serve as vehicles for clarifying and understanding the similarities and the differences between valuative and nonvaluative discovery. The elementary school example will be given first and then the adult example. In these transcripts, only the spelling has been corrected. The reader should carefully note the significant high levels of thinking in both classes as elicited by a simple technique of using coins in a novel way for teaching.

Example 1

The elementary school students grouped themselves four or five to a table. Each group took five coins (an Indian-head penny, a buffalo nickel, a "Mercury" dime, a Washington quarter, and a Franklin half-dollar) from a plate of coins distributed to the entire class.

Teacher: Each group has five coins. Here's what you have to do now. Look at the five coins. Each person should ask himself, "What do I see?" and together ask yourselves, "What do we see? What do we observe about these coins?" Write down on your sheets of paper what you see for each coin. Please look at all five coins.

(The students talked and wrote in their small groups for the next twenty minutes. The teacher circulated among the groups during this time. He facilitated their task, but he did not answer any questions about the coins. For example,

Student: What do you call this thing on the back of the dime?
Teacher: Call it whatever you want. If you can't give it a name, then describe it with words you already know. Just write down what you see.

The teacher helped some students spell some words correctly (e.g., *Indian, George, Benjamin,* and *buffalo*) when they asked him. He helped students in sharing the coins at their table. Once again, he did not offer help in observing in order to allow the students the opportunity to observe and write on their own.)

Teacher: Now, look at your papers to see what you've written for each coin. On your paper write some sentences that fit all the coins in general. In other words, ask yourself, "What can I say in general about all five coins from what I see?"

(Again the students talked and wrote. After about five minutes the teacher asked for their attention.)

Teacher: You now have two lists: the first on what you see; the second on some general things for all the coins. I'd like you now to try just one more thing. Look at both lists and ask yourselves, "What can we say about the people who made these coins? Just like the way I dress and the way I wear my hair tells you lots of things about me, these coins tell you things about the people who made these coins and the country they live in. Write down some sentences about these people and their country based on your two lists.

(Once again the students talked and wrote. After about five minutes most of the students finished.)

Teacher: OK now. Let's take a look at what you've done up till now. First, let's list what you see.
Judy: I see the liberty bell.
Ned: A bald eagle.
Corinne: Benjamin Franklin.
Allen: The flying God.
Diane: That's Mercury.
Steven: An Indian man with a feather hat.
Andrew: George Washington on front, an eagle on the back.

Judy: Dates, 1906, 1969, 1944, 1951, 1930 for the penny, quarter, dime, half-dollar, and nickel.

Debbie: A buffalo.

Mathew: A wreath and three arrows.

Peter: The words, "In God We Trust."

Robert: A tree and a telephone pole.

Ann: I see a tree and a pole for a vine to grow up.

David: A bell with a crack.

Ross: E pluribus unum.

Cathy: Liberty on the tops of all of them.

Robert: A shield on the copper penny.

John: A bull.

Ellen: A person with a wing on her head.

Karen: An ax and a lady.

Michael: "One cent," "five cents," and "dime" on them.

Teacher: Fine. That makes a nice long list for us, and I've written them on the board, as you can see, just as you said them. Now, will someone please give us one sentence that he wrote about all the coins in general.

Judy: All the coins are metal.

Teacher: Fine. Anyone else?

Karen: They are all round.

Michael: All say "In God We Trust."

David: No they don't. The Indian head coin doesn't have that on it.

Michael: Most have "In God We Trust"; all except the Indian penny have it.

Teacher: Judy?

Judy: All have human creatures on them, they all have dates, and they are all change.

David: They all have their value on them, and they're all worth something.

Robert: They come from the United States, and they all have presidents.

John: Oh no they don't! There was no Indian president. George Washington was the first president, and there has not ever been an Indian president after him.

Teacher: Yes, that's so. Well, we have several of these general things on the board now, too. Why do you think these people made the coins out of metal.

Allen: Because they're hard so if you bite one you won't mess it up.

Judy: 'Cause metal is hard and you can't destroy then or rip them.

Robert: What else could you make them out of?

Allen: Wood and—

Robert: Yeah, that's right. My Aunt says she has a wooden nickel.

Teacher: Why do you think these people put an eagle and the liberty bell on their coins?

Karen: The eagle because it's our emblem and the liberty bell so they could remember what happened to it.

Teacher: Karen, say more about both of those, please.

Karen: Well, the eagle stands for our country; that's what an emblem is, and the liberty bell, well it cracked and they wanted to remember that.

David: See, they got freedom and so they rang the bell. Then it cracked and they wanted to remember how happy they were.

Karen: Yeah, that's what I wanted to say.

Teacher: Fine. Let me now ask you to do one more thing before we stop today. You have made two lists—one on what you see on the coins and the second on what you can say about all of the coins. Now let's make a third list. Will someone give us one sentence about what these coins tell us about the people and country who made these coins—one that he wrote or one that he can think of now?

Michael: There're lots of Indians there.

Corinne: No, you can't say that. There aren't lots of Indians here.

Teacher: Now, if Michael can't say that, what can we say about these people?

Peter: They have creative artists there. Because you can tell the way they 'graved the coins the people puff out on the coins. They must be creative artists to do that.

Judy: Not all of them are creative artists.

Teacher: Yes, and Peter just said that there are some. He did not say that they all were creative artists, and he did tell us why he said so. That's fine. Now we have something from each of the three lists you made. Well, class, it's time to stop today. We've got lots more still to talk about. We just began. I'd like to look at your papers. Till tomorrow would you please think of some other things we can say about these people. Also, would you—

John: Could we start a coin collection? These coins are interesting.

Steven: Yeah, I never knew there were two kinds of half-dollars. I've got one with President Kennedy on it at home. But I thought that that was the only kind.

Teacher: Well, that sounds like a good idea. Time now for your music teacher. We'll continue on the coins tomorrow to see about starting a collection and possible other things we can learn about the people who made these coins.

Example 2

The thirty adult students sat at six tables, five to a table. The teacher distributed five coins to each table, an Indian-head penny, a buffalo nickel, a "Mercury" dime, a Washington quarter, and a Franklin half-dollar.

Teacher: Each table has a set of five coins. In class you'll have the remaining half an hour or so to work with these coins. Observe the coins carefully and take notes. Talk among yourselves about the coins. Then each person should work on his own during the week to prepare a page or two about the people who minted these coins based on the observations you made.

(Each group talked and wrote for a long time. The teacher circulated among the groups to listen to their conversation but did not comment on the coins in regard to description or meaning. Near the end of the session one group raised a question.)

Bruce: We think we need more time observing the coins. Can we borrow these during the week if we wish to have them for further study?

Teacher: Yes, you sure may. They are available for you to use if you wish. Some may not need the coins and may wish to use only their notes. Others may wish to observe the coins further. Just let me know. The idea was to get you started today in small groups and to let you finish up writing by yourself for the next time.

(At the next meeting of the class.)

Teacher: I have here a copy of Ms. Suel's paper. I'd like her to read it to you. Afterward would you please comment on her points and/or ask her some questions. We'll use her paper as a springboard for our discussion.

Ms. Suel: I am presenting five American coins: a 1902 cent, a 1937 five-cent coin, a 1944 dime, a 1959 quarter, and a 1948 half-dollar. In this paper, especially in the table which follows, the coins are typed by value because in terms of function this is their most significant attribute. These coins, as opposed to those of other times, have an assigned, stipulated value rather than a value determined by the preciousness of their metal or the amount of their metal.

In terms of their use the only important facts about these coins are their country of origin (i.e., the United States) and their monetary value (i.e., one cent, five cents, one dime, quarter dollar, and half dollar). However, other characteristics may be of more importance because they yield data from which ideas may be induced about our society.

I will discuss these coins on three levels: (1) specific and general observations, (2) empirical inferences, and (3) cultural inferences and reflections. They are in ascending order of importance and emphasis.

These American coins are round and die cast of metal, mostly silver. All state their value and country of origin in English and have a numerical date dating from the birth of Christ. They all have an obvious obverse and reverse side with a human head in relief on the obverse sides and a variety of designs on the reverse side. Specific observations appear in the accompanying table.

From these observations one can infer the following: The United States is a large country which mints great numbers of coins. This is shown by the three mint marks (San Francisco, Denver, and plain (i.e., without a mint mark signifies the mint in Philadelphia). The society is a highly technological one since it can and does produce coins of different metals in different sizes with highly detailed and finely wrought images and lettering. Witness the designer's mark on several coins and the feathers on Mercury's wings on the dime.

We may also infer that English is at least the dominant language of the country and that the metric system is used for coins. In addition, Americans appear to hold that the bigger something is in size and weight the more valuable it is. This is shown by the fact that even though the value of the coins is stipulative, with but one exception, size and weight correlate one hundred per cent with value. Moreover, silver is obviously more valuable than copper since only the lowest value coin is minted from copper.

On the level of cultural inferences and reflections I submit the following: These coins reflect a Protestant conservative mercantile ethos economically and an aggressive, nationalistic ethos politically, both wrapped in a cloak of classical antiquity for legitimacy and ballast.

The conservative character of the society is evidenced by the coins' designs. The coins are all very similar and extremely symmetrical in design (e.g., note the position of the word "liberty" on the dime and the quarter). To say that the designs of the coins are aesthetically timid is to put it mildly. The feel of the coins is heavy, weighty, and solid as opposed to that of aluminum coins of some countries. The mercantile aspect is practically verbalized for us by the appearance of Mercury, Roman god of commerce, on the dime.

The number of coins for different values indicates a large economy based on trade. The wealth of detail on the coins shows them to be of great importance to the society. Indeed they are so important that they have been specially and carefully designed.

All of the more recent coins bear the inscription "In God We Trust." Thus, there is obviously a powerful group in the society which considers public declarations of faith in a god to be of great importance. Also, each coin has a date on it from which we see (1) that this is largely a Christian country and (2) that time is of great importance to Americans because the date upon the coin serves no function except to proclaim itself.

We see a strong, aggressive central government as witnessed by the phrase "E Pluribus Unum" and the symbol of the eagle, the king of predatory birds who has a strong territorial instinct. The word "liberty" appears prominently on all the coins and a relief of the liberty bell appears on one. Hence, liberty is also an important value to Americans.

We see the cloak of classical antiquity in the motto in Latin, the classical style of the heads in relief on the coins, the previously mentioned appearance of Mercury on the dime, and the fasces on the reverse side of the dime.

In addition to the inferences above, I want to conclude by commenting on the startling appearance of the Indian on two of the coins. On the 1902 penny the Indian is really a Caucasian with a feather headdress. On the later nickel, at last we do get a real Indian.

Some of the darkest pages of our national history deal with our treatment of the Indian, and yet we proudly use him as a symbol on our coins. Over his head we print the word "liberty." This is truly ironic in the light of what happened to the liberty of the Indians. Furthermore, it bespeaks a staggering lack of sensitivity and self-awareness that as late as 1937 we could put the Indian and the Buffalo, two creatures we have nearly rendered extinct, on a coin as symbols of our picturesque past.

Country of Origin U.S.A.

	1 cent	5 cents	dime	quarter dollar	half dollar
Apparent metal	copper	silver	silver	silver	silver
Shape	round	round	round	round	round
Diameter	18 mm.	20 mm.	17 mm.	23 mm.	30 mm.
Weight	3.1 gm.	4.9 gm.	2.5 gm.	6.2 gm.	12.3 gm.
Thickness	1.2 mm.	2 mm.	1 mm.	1.5 mm.	2 mm.
Edging	plain	plain	milled	milled	milled
Die cast	yes	yes	yes	yes	yes
Mint mark	none*	S(an Francisco)	D(enver)	none*	none*
Date	1902	1937	1944	1959	1948
Language	English	English	English	English	English
Designer's mark	none	under date†	right of neck	trunca- tion of neck	truncation of shoulder†
Picture (obverse)	Indian head	Indian head	Mercury head	George Wash- ington head	Benjamin Franklin head
Picture (reverse)	Laurel wreath and U.S. shield	Buffalo	Fasces and olive branch	Perched eagle and olive branch	Liberty Bell and perched eagle
Style of head (on obverse)	Classical, statue- like	Realistic	Classical, statue- like	Classical, statue- like	Classical, statue- like
Head faces	left	right	left	left	right
Lettering	All capital letters. Simple bold style on all five coins.				

Inscriptions

"In God We Trust"	no	no	yes	yes	yes
Latin: "E Pluribus Unum"	no	yes	yes	yes	yes

*none = Philadelphia
†These marks are not decipherable

"United States of America"	yes	yes	yes	yes	yes
"Liberty"	no	yes	yes	yes	yes
Value	"ONE CENT"	"FIVE CENTS"	"ONE DIME"	"QUARTER DOLLAR"	"HALF DOLLAR"

Teacher: Mr. Burns?

Mr. Burns: Ms. Suel has some fine points, but she overstepped herself a bit. Let me state that Mercury is not on the dime even though it's called a Mercury head dime. It's not, it's just an error; it's just supposed to be a woman representing Liberty like on lots of other old American coins. I happen to be a coin collector. People just think it's Mercury because of the wings and the design on the back of the dime. That's all.

Ms. Suel: Sure does remind me of Mercury. Well, there goes the God of Commerce bit. I'll yield only that.

Ms. Robinson: Some of what you call "cultural inferences" seem shaky to me. Like, that we have a big economy. How did you get that?

Ms. Suel: I said that there is a "large economy based on trade." I said that because there are five coins here; probably the country has more but we don't know for sure from these coins. And there are three mints. So not only do we see five types of coins, but there must be a lot of them if there are three mints. So there must be a lot of trade if they need so many coins.

Ms. Hill: I agree with what you said. But I wrote something you missed completely. If you look at these coins, it's obvious that this is a male chauvinist society. Not one woman is on these coins.

Mr. Voorhees: Wait a minute! That's going too far. No way can you say that from these coins.

Mr. Shiff: Name one woman in this country that you could put on a coin that's equal to guys like Washington, Franklin, Jefferson, and Lincoln. Name one.

Ms. Hill: Eleanor Roosevelt or Jane Addams or

Mr. Shiff: Come on, now!

Ms. Weber: That's just the point—the women have been kept down for so long that they haven't been able to achieve high status in government; so they don't get on the coins or decide who goes on the coins.

Mr. Voorhees: I don't want to argue that point with you. All

I said was that you can't say it based on just these five coins. That's all.

(The discussion continued for another forty minutes. The class discussed the points related to a conservative mercantile ethos, strong central government, and the place of the Indian in American society. The session ended with a decision to investigate the role of symbols in American life in further discussions.)

Analysis

The two above examples of nonvaluative discovery manifest several excellent features of teaching via the discovery method. These are enumerated and treated below. An attempt will be made to treat the two examples by building on the points already made in regard to valuative discovery, which are obviously closely related to nonvaluative discovery. The reader should now recall the features of valuative discovery treated earlier (see p. 119) as well as the summary of similar essentials listed just prior to the two examples on coins.

Analysis of Example 1

1. The teacher clearly recognizes that it is essential in nonvaluative discovery to work with concrete data, especially firsthand data. By using artifacts that are common to almost every society, the teacher encouraged the students to draw on their own everyday experience; in the present case they are led to examine coins in a new way, as artifacts of a society that give clues to the nature of that society. The teacher began with a fundamental step—observing. The students generated their own data by observing the material they had. They observed the coins and noted their observations on paper in order to have a record of their activities as well as a way of organizing their data. The students later used these observations in making their second list of generalizations and their third list of inferences.

The students were free to observe without restrictions set by the teacher. The students freely accepted the challenge. The teacher accepted the many different items the students offered and listed them on the board. In doing this, he established a sufficient list for the making of generalizations later and also provided each student the opportunity to see what other people observed. It also allowed one student, Diane, to identify the "flying god" observed by Allen as Mercury. This further gave a clue to the teacher about the knowledge the students had.

This tactic of eliciting many responses before moving to another task serves as an indirect way of showing each student that there is much to observe on the coins when taken as cultural artifacts. As the students together saw the list, they realized what else each person could have seen had he been more complete. It is a way of helping students sharpen the ability to observe and is for this reason, too, an important procedure in nonvaluative discovery teaching.

2. The teacher is clearly alert to the various cognitive tasks involved in the lesson. He next asked the students to form generalizations on their own based on their own observations. By starting with the less complex task of observing, the teacher was able to move to the task of generalizing, which here means relating concepts used and discovered when dealing with the coins. The students eagerly accepted this challenge, too, because of the clarity and openness of the questions. Also, the students were willing to do this generalizing task because they themselves had generated the set of observations from which to generalize. This is most important because there is built-in motivation for the students to continue inquiring.

The teacher also listed on the chalkboard the generalizations offered by the students. Again, this tactic of eliciting, accepting, and listing served the purpose of showing the students that there are many possible generalizations based on the observation of the coins and also what some of them are. It also allowed the one student to correct an invalid generalization. This occurred when David corrected Michael in regard to the inscription "In God We Trust" and when John corrected Robert in regard to the presidents. If the group had not shared their generalizations with each other, these significant instances of student-to-student interaction would not have occurred. Michael was quite willing to accept David's rejection of his statement and then corrected himself. This type of interaction also occurred when John corrected Robert's generalization that all the coins have a president on them.

Such interaction is peer teaching and is valuable in all methods of teaching, for students are often more influenced by their classmates than by their teacher. Peer teaching gets students involved with each other, allowing them to realize that they need not always be dependent on the teacher.

It is important to recognize that via this procedure the teacher easily led the students to generalize. The situation set up by the teacher encouraged and facilitated the task of the students. The teacher knows that generalizations are cognitively more complex than observations. Therefore, he led them into generalizing carefully and warmly. Because generalizing involves relating the concepts used in observing the coins (e.g., metal, Indian, human being), it is considered more complex than just observing. In recognition of this rise in cognitive level, the teacher established the activity so that the generalizing phase was preceded by a simpler successful activity. The transition was smooth and profitable.

3. The teacher recognizes that the process of inferring is involved in this lesson and is more complex than generalizing. For this reason he carefully separated this cognitive task from observing and generalizing and strategically led the students to it. The teacher prepared the students for inferring by having them prepare the two lists of observations and generalizations on their own first. The students not only had generated the observations and generalizations on their own but also had sufficient material from which to make the inferences.

Once the students had prepared their first two lists, the teacher asked the students to infer about the people and their country in a simple way. He did not use difficult, technical language and did not even use the word *infer*. He just asked in a straightforward way which these eight- and nine-year-olds could understand, "What can we say about the people who make these coins?" He used an analogy about personal appearance to help communicate the meaning of his question. Obviously, he took these pains because he is aware of the complexity and abstractness involved in this third step of his lesson. By talking simply and by using an analogy which even young students understand, the teacher was able to convey his intent to his students.

When he requested some of the students' inferences later on, the teacher used the tactic of eliciting and listing many responses again. The very first one presented by Michael turned out to be incorrect. However, the openness of the situation led Corinne to reject Michael's inferences. (Note that Corinne's objection is based on her knowledge of reality rather than on whether there is sufficient available data to support the inference.) The teacher then simply accepted Corinne's statement and asked again for some inferences. He did not focus on Michael's statement because there was no need to focus on an incorrect response and because Corinne had dealt with it. He moved on to a positive response. The teacher is most alert to the cognitive complexity here and is obviously trying hard to provide a successful experience. "Discovery of generalizations and inferring is essentially a creative, productive, and innovative process ..." (23:38). It is for this reason that he stepped in quickly after Judy spoke in order to support and praise Peter for offering an acceptable inference, obviously a difficult task for these young students to perform.

4. When the teacher ends the lesson, he is aware that there are many ways open to him and the class in the future. Therefore, he is most willing to accept the suggestion made by John and seconded by Steven. He realized that the coins had captivated the interest of these boys and probably the other students as well, since many youngsters today have not seen some of the everyday coins adults know well, such as the buffalo nickel and the "Mercury" head dime. The teacher accepted the students' enthusiasm, for he had generated it and knew that the students would surely continue observing, generalizing, and inferring if they started a coin collection. He knew that with motivation high the students would have an excellent opportunity to learn about the people of the United States. This leads to the next point.

5. The teacher realizes that, in generalizing and in inferring, students are often also involved in explaining. When he asks the students why the coins are made from metal, why there is a liberty bell (on the Franklin half-dollar), and why there is an eagle (on the Washington quarter), the teacher is asking the students to perform yet another cognitive task. In leading the discussion following the preparation of the three lists, the teacher asks for these three explanations before going on to the students' inferences. He clearly praises Karen's explanation, completed and clarified with the help of David, who stepped in when Karen was having trouble. Later we also see that Peter offers an inference and proceeds to explain it. The teacher is aware of this, because he even points out to the class that Peter explained his inference in addition to offering it. He praises Peter accordingly.

Explaining is a logical process essential in nonvaluative discovery. Whenever students go beyond the facts at hand (i.e., here the correct observations made about these coins), they will quickly be involved in explaining. Students explain when they defend their generalizations and inferences. The explanations constitute a key subject matter the teacher teaches his students in nonvaluative discovery in addition to the cognitive tasks of observing, generalizing, and inferring.

Explaining appears as a key element in Example 2, in which the adult class performs a similar activity with these coins. Because explanations are central to nonvaluative discovery, more attention to them follows the analysis of Example 2.

6. The teacher facilitates the involvement of each student by setting up individual tasks within each small group. Each student wrote out his own observations, generalizations, and inferences. However, each student discussed the coins with his classmates. This procedure served several purposes. (1) It provided an opportunity for students to interact with their peers in a legitimate way. The coins were interesting and evoked student comments, as the teacher knew they would. The small-group organization permitted the students to discuss the coins with each other. It utilized a natural inclination to talk socially as an integral part of the lesson. (2) It provided a smooth way for those students unsure of themselves and the assignment to get going. The students were able to see what their peers were doing and received both encouragement and clarification from them. (3) It provided an opportunity for the teacher to offer individual help but in manageable numbers. The teacher had only five groups and so was able to circulate among them easily.

Analysis of Example 2

7. The teacher recognizes that these adults are cognitively developed and do not require the slow, separate steps used with the young elementary students. In light of this recognition the teacher simply directs the students to observe and infer. His confidence is borne out by Ms. Suel's paper, which goes beyond his request. The choice of Ms. Suel's paper as a springboard is a key element here. Ms. Suel, in writing "about the people who minted these coins based on the observations," noted her observations, her generalizations, her inferences, and her personal reflections. The teacher's confidence is borne out in the discussion of Ms. Suel's paper, a discussion which centers on the validity of the students' inferences.

8. The teacher shifts his role in working with adults. He was less directive in getting the students going and absent from the partial discussion presented following Ms. Suel's paper. The teacher did not need to join in since he had set up the assignment so

well and had chosen a paper packed with provocative statements. The first person to react, Mr. Burns, was the only one to challenge the facts in Ms. Suel's paper. The others reacted to inferences either by Ms. Suel or another student. The students themselves picked up the centrality of the inferences made and their validity. Witness Mr. Voorhees' reaction to Ms. Hill's inferences concerning male chauvinism.

Ms. Robinson asks Ms. Suel to explain her inferences regarding a big economy. Ms. Suel's response is an explanation of how she arrived at her statement. From the context of the discussion it appears that this explanation satisfied Ms. Robinson since she offers no further protest. Because the students are asking for explanations, offering explanations, and challenging the validity of the inferences, there is no need for the teacher to enter the discussion here. Because the students are going well and are on the correct path, the teacher did not enter the discussion to redirect or refocus it. He may have done so later on, but we cannot tell from just this portion of the lesson available here.

9. The teacher realizes that even adults need a spur to a cognitively complex assignment. The teacher used part of the class session to start off the assignment. He also grouped the students six to a table for the same reasons enumerated in point 6 above, dealing with the elementary school students. By discussing the assignment in groups, the students were able to clarify it and get going as the teacher offered individual help when needed. Each student then had the opportunity to complete his assignment on his own at his own convenience and pace. Since the class met but once a week, the teacher was thus able to begin immediately with a finished paper by one of the students. Thus, this approach accomplished several things simultaneously: clarification, kickoff, peer interaction, individual help, and motivation for independent extra-class thinking.

10. The teacher and the students realize the potency of the topics raised by these five coins. The class decided, according to the notation at the end of the typescript, to pursue the general point of symbolism in the U.S.A. so as to relate the many ideas together. Obviously, there are other topics worthy of discussion, too. However, the teacher and students allowed the discussion first to revolve around the points immediately raised by Ms. Suel's paper and then to proceed to the topic of general concern, symbolism. As evidenced by this lively excerpt, motivation for future discussion of symbolism in American life will be high.

Other Characteristics of the Method

Though these two examples are offered as good illustrations of teaching through nonvaluative discovery, the careful reader no doubt realizes that the teachers here have failed to do certain things in these discussions. Even though these two examples manifest many good features, it is difficult to do, in one discussion, all the desirable things that might be done. A single class session is, no doubt, too short a time in which to complete a thorough discussion of these five coins. Therefore, any one-session discussion might better be viewed as only part of a larger discovery discussion. Treated below are some of the more salient items that are desirable in a nonvaluative discussion but were not included in these illustrations. What else might the teacher do in ensuing sessions with the students?

1. The teacher would do well to point out several of the inaccuracies in observing by the elementary school students. The teacher chose to accept all the items offered by the students. He listed them on the chalkboard without comment. However, some students may believe that Allen and Diane are correct in saying that the face on the dime is the "flying god" Mercury. Indeed, Mr. Burns in the adult class is correct that the face on the dime is not Mercury, as popularly believed, but a representation of Liberty with wings crowning her cap to symbolize liberty of thought. Similarly, some students may believe that the reverse of the dime shows a telephone pole as offered by Robert. Rather, this side of the dime shows a representation of Roman fasces, the symbol of authority in ancient Rome.

Unless the teacher takes time in future lessons to correct the errors offered, he will, in effect, be teaching untrue items about the coins. Worse yet, he will be teaching those students who simply saw, for example, the face of a lady on the dime that their ability to observe is lacking, whereas, in reality, they were closer to the coin designer's intent. By going over the items listed by the students on their papers, the teacher is teaching the students the all-important skill of observing. Indeed, constant review, correction, and sensitizing students by pointing out additional items are key ways of teaching how to observe.

2. The teacher would do well to clarify the meaning of "observe." In the opening directions the teacher used the expressions, "What do I see?", "What do we see?", and "What do we observe about the coins?" To avoid having the students restrict

"observe" to mean "see" rather than the broader "perceive through all the senses," the teacher should point out that people can observe through hearing, tasting, smelling, touching, and seeing. Perhaps, these young students in Example 1 thought they were to note items perceived through their sight only.

3. The teacher would do well to deepen and broaden the students' knowledge about the coins and the people who minted them. It seems reasonable to assume that, in both classes, the teachers will lead their students in further study introduced by this activity with coins. Yet, the teacher would do well to direct the students into individual study and/or small-group projects related to such topics as "The Role of the Indian in U.S. Life," "Art and Coins," "Different Metals for Different Coins for Different Countries," "Symbols We Live With," and "Design for a New Coin System for the U.S." Obviously, there are many, many more topics that could lead the students to a deeper understanding of both the coins and the people, while at the same time improving their skills of observing, generalizing, inferring, and explaining.

4. The teacher would do well to establish a framework for observing coins with the students so that they can improve their future observing. For example, the elementary students did not observe the difference in edging on the five coins as did Ms. Suel. With a set of questions as framework for observing, the student would be able to observe things previously unnoticed. More important, the teacher will be teaching the students the vital process of observing. That is, he will be teaching how to observe. (See Chapter 15 on observing for a rationale on the need to provide a framework.) When the students use guidelines for observing, they will improve, sharpen, and increase their specific observations. They will add to their observations, whether noted individually or offered collectively.

5. The teacher would do well to explicitly teach the tasks of generalizing, inferring, and explaining, which are also involved in nonvaluative discovery. These, along with observing, are process skills essential to becoming an independent person. The teacher should go over the generalizations, inferences, and explanations made by the students to check for accuracy and possibility for clarification. The teacher should raise these points in class with the students. By utilizing class participation, the teacher can receive excellent help from the students themselves, as when Corinne rejected Michael's inference about many Indians living in the U.S.A. Also, the teacher can point out that a valid inference

depends upon accurate observing. Some of the strength of Ms. Suel's inference about the commercial ethos of the U.S.A. disappeared when Mr. Burns pointed out that the face on the dime is not Mercury, god of commerce, but Liberty. Ms. Suel recognized this quickly and was willing to yield on all points built on the "observation" that Mercury was represented on the dime.

6. Because the task of explaining is perhaps the most complex, pervasive, and yet common one to nonvaluative discovery, a special section devoted to it follows this section of the chapter.

Explanation

Though the discovery methods have many similarities, there is a broad area in which they differ. It is in the types of questions posed in nonvaluative discovery that the key difference between valuative and nonvaluative discussion lies. Just as the teacher ought to use some scheme for evaluation when leading his class in a valuative discussion, so he ought to use some scheme for explanation when leading the nonvaluative discussion.

In contrast to valuative discovery, nonvaluative discovery focuses on agreement about definitions, facts, or explanations. For example, in the six nonvaluative questions posed at the beginning of this chapter, the student who responds must offer an explanation for the fourth and sixth questions and a fact in the form of a date, in addition to the explanation, for the fifth question. That is, in saying why there is inflation today, why and how Shakespeare influenced subsequent English writers, and how the Grand Canyon was formed, the student offers explanations. In telling when the Grand Canyon was formed, the student gives a fact which he arrives at through an investigation involving measurement of some sort. The responses to the first, second, and third questions will also be facts. That is, we will verify the answers with criteria appropriate to nonvaluative, empirical matters. (See the section on empirical questions in Chapter 14.) Fact-stating and the offering of explanations are similar in that both involve reliance on evidence, but explaining is the more complex of the two in that it involves relating facts either to each other or to a generalization or a function.

The questions raised by teachers and students in classroom discovery are similar to these nonvaluative ones. The prevalence of nonvaluative questions can be seen in the changing curriculum reform projects (12). Since the new projects call for the discovery method, it is all the more necessary for teachers involved with them to know the techniques of the discovery method as well as the schemas for explanation (to be presented below).

This book will deal with the subject of explanations because most discovery projects involve explanations, as they go beyond the statement of facts. Also, teacher and student groups have identified explaining as one of the key cognitive tasks for a teacher in an ideal teacher-student relationship (14). Moreover, an explanation schema is related to a request for a cause or function in the same way that an evaluation schema is related to a request for a policy justification and value preference.

An explanation is an answer to the question, "Why?" (13: 245; 18:15). The explanations involved in such a question as, "Explain the meaning of the term *onomatopoeia*" will not be considered. The use of *explain* in the sentence above is equivalent to *define* in the sense of "define a particular term." Rather explanations will be considered in the context of such questions as: "Explain why robins fly south in the winter"; "Explain what caused World War II"; "Explain how the Grand Canyon was formed"; "Explain why former President Johnson decided not to seek the presidency in 1968"; and "Explain why 7 times 3 equals 21."

For the sake of simplicity, the three main types of explanation will now be considered, with diagrammatic schemas that can guide the teacher in leading a discussion (7; 18; 19; 22; 24).

Generalization-Specific Instance

In this type of explanation there are several basic parts: a generalization of some kind which may be a rule, a norm, or an empirical (scientific) law; a situation or event to be explained; evidence showing that the situation is a specific instance of the generalization; and the conclusion that follows and thus explains the situation. That is to say, we explain a situation by offering evidence that this situation is a specific instance of some generalization. Three examples follow; the first uses an empirical generalization, the second a nonempirical generalization (nonempirical here refers to such areas as logic, grammar, games, and mathematics, where the generalization is established by agreement rather than from sense experiences), and the third an empirical generalization based on probability.

A. Empirical:

Question: Why is Jonathan's room bright?

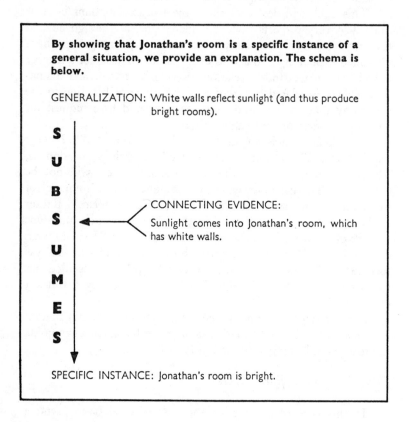

By showing that Jonathan's room is a specific instance of a general situation, we provide an explanation. The schema is below.

GENERALIZATION: White walls reflect sunlight (and thus produce bright rooms).

SUBSUMES

CONNECTING EVIDENCE:

Sunlight comes into Jonathan's room, which has white walls.

SPECIFIC INSTANCE: Jonathan's room is bright.

Response: Since white walls reflect sunlight and sunlight is hitting Jonathan's white walls, Jonathan's room is bright.

B. Nonempirical:

Question: Why do we write *teams'* and not *team's* in the following sentence? "Mr. George Stevens, the basketball and baseball teams' coach, became athletic director of the entire college."

Response: Since we use *s'* to show the possessive plural, and Mr. Stevens is the coach of both teams; it's correct to write *teams'*.

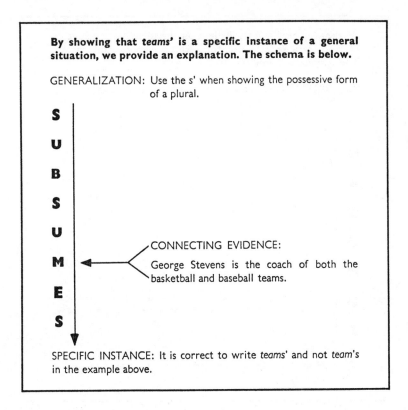

By showing that *teams'* is a specific instance of a general situation, we provide an explanation. The schema is below.

GENERALIZATION: Use the s' when showing the possessive form of a plural.

S
U
B
S
U
M   CONNECTING EVIDENCE:
          George Stevens is the coach of both the basketball and baseball teams.
E
S

SPECIFIC INSTANCE: It is correct to write *teams'* and not *team's* in the example above.

C. Probabilistic:

Question: Why was the turnpike jammed up yesterday at noon?

Response: Since, in other than rush hours, traffic jams are usually the result of a collision, and since there was an accident on the turnpike in the late morning, the jam on the New Jersey Turnpike at noon was probably the result of a collision.

Purpose or Function

In this type of explanation there are several basic parts: a purpose, function, intention, or desire by an agent; a particular situation to be explained; evidence that the action accomplished is consonant with the purpose of the agent; and (in the case of human activity) evidence that the agent's character is consonant with the purpose. That is to say, we explain a situation by connecting it with a (reasonable) purpose or function and by showing evidence that the action has achieved its purpose. A functional

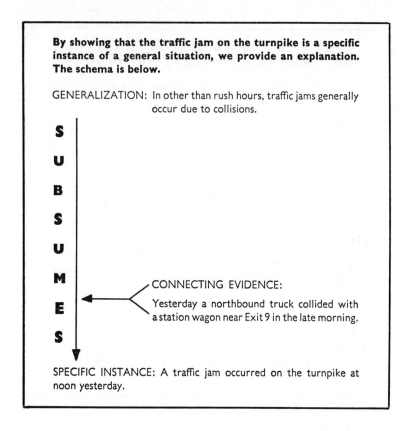

By showing that the traffic jam on the turnpike is a specific instance of a general situation, we provide an explanation. The schema is below.

GENERALIZATION: In other than rush hours, traffic jams generally occur due to collisions.

S
U
B
S
U
M
E
S

CONNECTING EVIDENCE:

Yesterday a northbound truck collided with a station wagon near Exit 9 in the late morning.

SPECIFIC INSTANCE: A traffic jam occurred on the turnpike at noon yesterday.

explanation may be offered for the occurrence of a particular situation at a particular time or for the existence of a particular situation in a system for however long the system may exist. Functional explanations characteristically employ phrases like *in order to* and *for the sake of* and then refer to some future situation or state. Two examples follow, the first from biology and the second from politics.

A. Biology:

Question: Why do we have a heart that beats?

Response: In order to pump vital blood to nourish the body, we have a heart that beats. The heart accomplishes that function by sending reoxygenated blood from the lungs to all parts of the body.

By showing that the heart is a specific instance of a body organ serving a purpose, we provide an explanation. The schema is below.

PURPOSE: In order to accomplish the vital function of pumping blood to nourish the body.

S ↑ A

U   C

P   H

P   I ◄――― CONNECTING EVIDENCE:

1. When the heart stops, men die. Therefore, we cannot do without a functioning heart.

O   E

2. The heart can be temporarily replaced by a mechanical pump during surgery; however, the heart's function--pumping blood--must be continued.

R   V

T   E

3. The body needs reoxygenated blood, and it gets it from the lungs via the heart as center of the circulatory system.

S   S

SPECIFIC INSTANCE: Human beings have hearts that beat.

B. Politics:

Question: Give one interpretation of why Lyndon B. Johnson chose not to run for the presidency in 1968.

Response: In order to hasten peace in Vietnam, President Johnson decided to retire. Soon after this decision peace talks were arranged, his sincerity grew, and the country became united. Also, the President had talked about peace talks earlier.

Sequential, Genetic, or Chronological

In this type of explanation there is a series of events that results in the situation or event to be explained. That is to say, an event is explained by listing chronologically some of those steps relevant to and necessary for its occurrence. This type of explana-

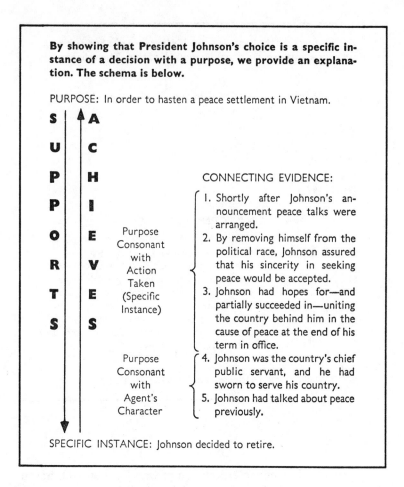

By showing that President Johnson's choice is a specific instance of a decision with a purpose, we provide an explanation. The schema is below.

PURPOSE: In order to hasten a peace settlement in Vietnam.

S · A

U · C

P · H

P · I — CONNECTING EVIDENCE:

O · E — Purpose Consonant with Action Taken (Specific Instance)

R · V

T · E

S · S

1. Shortly after Johnson's announcement peace talks were arranged.
2. By removing himself from the political race, Johnson assured that his sincerity in seeking peace would be accepted.
3. Johnson had hopes for—and partially succeeded in—uniting the country behind him in the cause of peace at the end of his term in office.

Purpose Consonant with Agent's Character

4. Johnson was the country's chief public servant, and he had sworn to serve his country.
5. Johnson had talked about peace previously.

SPECIFIC INSTANCE: Johnson decided to retire.

tion applies to human history as well as to historical geology and biology.

Geology:

Question: Explain how the present Mare Imbrium area of the moon was formed.

Response: The present Mare Imbrium came about because a meteorite struck the moon's surface forming the crater. Small craters formed on top of the older Mare Imbrium. Some material filled up the existing craters and buried others. Newer craters formed, such as Eratosthenes, and finally the ray craters, Copernicus and Aristillus, formed.

By listing the events that have led up to the present formation of Mare Imbrium, we provide an explanation. The schema is below.

A SERIES OF EVENTS: (based on hypothesis derived from information about the impact of meteorites and suppositions from this hypothesis).

L E A D S T O

I. A huge meteorite struck the moon's surface, and the impact formed the Mare Imbrium crater.

2. Small craters, such as Plato, Sinus Iridum, and Archimedes, were formed on top of the huge, older Mare Imbrium.

3. Some material of unknown nature and origin filled some of the existing craters and probably completely buried others. This formed the present floors of Mare Imbrium, Plato, Sinus, Iridum, and Archimedes.

4. More and newer craters were formed on this new surface. These craters probably include Eratosthenes, Timocharis, and Autolycus.

5. The ray craters Copernicus and Aristillus were then formed. These are the most recent in the Mare Imbrium area.

SPECIFIC INSTANCE: The present formation of the Mare Imbrium area of the moon.

Uses of Explanation Schemata

The teacher who keeps these three types of explanations and their schemata in mind, as well as the many other previous points about the discussion method, will obviously be in position to direct a nonvaluative discovery involving an explanation of some perplexing situation. The teacher will be able to understand where the specific contributions of the various students fit into the total picture of the explanation offered. He will be able to schematize the flow of discourse and lead the students to an answer.

The teacher who keeps these types of explanations and their schemata in mind will also be able to eliminate two sources of confusion and lack of understanding in a classroom. First, he will be able to avoid trouble arising from an incomplete explanation. It is quite common for students to offer elliptical explanations (16:153).

For example, let us return to the first explanation schema presented earlier. Either of the following two sequences or both might occur in a teaching situation.

Sequence 1

Question: Why is Jonathan's room bright?
Response: Because white walls reflect sunlight.

Sequence 2

Question: Why is Jonathan's room bright?
Response: Because sunlight is hitting his white walls.

That is to say, in the first sequence the response gives the generalization but not the connecting evidence. In the second sequence the response gives the connecting evidence but not the generalization. Both of these responses are explanations, albeit elliptical ones in contrast to the complete one offered earlier with the schema. To understand each of these two sequences here, the listener must fill in the gaps per the schema shown. When he does so, he will accept each response here as a correct one.

In either case there will probably be students in class who fail to understand the explanation because they cannot supply the missing parts. They cannot make the leap that other students can. For these students the explanation in either of these two responses is inadequate and leads to confusion. Therefore, the teacher would do well to elicit the missing parts of the schema. At times he might simply supply it himself in order to have a complete explanation.

If the explanation is elliptical, the teacher may use the direct tactic of asking for the missing parts of the schema. Or, he may use the indirect tack of asking the students to comment on the completeness of the explanation offered. Through this, the students may discover on their own which parts need to be supplied in order to complete the explanation. This is similar to the Level III questioning treated in the chapter on valuative discovery. This indirect tack also has the advantage of leading the students, not only to an explanation, but toward an understanding of what constitutes an explanation.

The critical point is that only when the students understand all the parts of the explanation being offered can the teacher and students discuss the acceptability of that explanation. Is the generalization relevant to the specific instance? Is the connecting evidence pertinent? Is the connecting evidence true? Is the sequence of events correct? Is the conclusion drawn compatible with established knowledge? (9:428). Is the purpose consonant with the performer's character? Unless the various parts of the explanation are explicitly before the students, it is difficult to discuss the acceptability of the explanation—and such discussion is at the heart of teaching by the discovery method.

Second, with these schemata in mind the teacher will be able to assess the pertinence of a student's contribution according to the particular type of explanation being sought. For example, the teacher may ask, "Why is Jonathan's room bright?" and expect a generalization–specific instance type of explanation. One student may offer the fact that the walls of Jonathan's room are white. The teacher will obviously admit this into the schema. A second student may say, "Because he likes a bright room." This student is seeking to establish a purpose-functional explanation rather than the expected type. The student, for whatever reason, does not understand which type of explanation the teacher expects. Only when the teacher realizes this can he deal with the student's statement appropriately. To this second student the teacher needs to point out that the statement is not wrong but unsuitable to the type of explanation being sought. Obviously, the teacher must make clear to the student which type of explanation is expected. Unless the teacher does so the student may not be able to follow the discussion and eventually may lose interest in trying.

Also, the teacher hopefully will be able to clarify his questions when posing a problem that calls for an explanation. If he expects an explanation involving a generalization and a specific instance, he would do well to state so. This will not only obviate undesired responses but will sharpen the focus of the students. The teacher may even choose an approach in which he asks the students which type of explanation they choose to establish for a particular question. This level of questioning will sensitize the students to the various types of explanations and the appropriateness of different types to different situations. The usefulness of this tack is not to be minimized.

Problems and Modifications of the Method

We have thus far been treating underlying justifications, similarity between valuative and nonvaluative inquiry, illustrations of students observing, generalizing, and inferring the three main types of explanation, and the use of explanation schemas. Two major problems involved in employing the nonvaluative discovery method will now be considered.

If the teacher already knows the answer to such a question as, "Explain how the Grand Canyon was formed," is it proper to call the ensuing discussion *discovery* or *inquiry*? Is the teacher inquiring? Are the students inquiring or discovering if the teacher asks exactly the right question in order to elicit exactly the right response? Are the students actually inquiring if the teacher has provided them with exactly the right equipment, the right artifacts, and the right procedures to follow in the laboratory? (Many times in the "new" curriculum projects the teacher just happens to have the right equipment handy during a particular lesson.) Is it discovery if the students arrive at exactly the evidence and explanation the teacher has led them to through his questions, demonstrations, and laboratory experiments? If the students are inevitably successful because of the teacher's close guidance, will they later be able to inquire on their own when they do not have a teacher pointing the way for them? If the students have fail-safe direction, do they get the sense of groping, exploring, and occasional failure that comes to the individual inquiring on his own?

Note that it is within the treatment of nonvaluative discovery that these questions are raised. There are correct answers to most nonvaluative questions, and the teacher may know them before his discussion with his students. However, there are no such correct answers to policy issues, and, therefore, these questions could not be appropriately raised for valuative discovery.

Bob Burton Brown replies that the *guided* or *structured* discovery most common in today's reform projects is but a mockery of the inquiry set forth and defended by early exponents of the method.

When inquiry is made but a means to the acquisition of a certain predetermined body of knowledge, it ceases to be free, open, experimental inquiry. "Inquiry" is mockery when it is controlled from the outside to produce answers already settled upon, or desired and demanded by those who run the educational enterprise. If we insist that learners acquire, above all, a predetermined set of answers, concepts, and generalizations, then we have to give up our pious lip service to the glories of open inquiry (8:14).

Guided versus Open Inquiry

In light of the above questions and the scathing comment by Brown, it is obvious that we must quickly distinguish between "guided" inquiry and "free, open experimental" inquiry (17: 1). There is no doubt that most of the points advanced about leading discovery as well as the case advanced for the underlying justification of the discovery method do not distinguish between these types of discovery. But now we must ask to what extent guided discovery is indeed a mockery. Is guided discovery simply a slight variation of the lecture and recitation methods of acquiring knowledge external to the student? Can we still claim the advantages for guided discovery that Brown claims belong to free, open, experimental inquiry? Is guided inquiry a deception of the student, as the teacher must often play dumb? Is guided inquiry necessarily a guessing game wherein the student simply guesses what the teacher has in mind? Is guided discovery a deception of the student, since he is manipulated into a position?

To the extent that guided discovery remains the sole discovery inquiry that a teacher and his students engage in, it is indeed a mockery of the rationale supporting the discovery method. When guided inquiry is used as a means for subtly getting the student to acquire what the teacher predetermines, it is indeed a mockery.

On the other hand, to the extent that guided discovery serves as a precursor of free, open, experimental inquiry, it is supported by the rationale previously presented. If, indeed, the teacher uses guided inquiry to teach the skills, knowledge, and values needed to conduct open inquiry, and if indeed the teacher does lead the students into open inquiry, then guided discovery can be called a teaching method. To do this the teacher must make it clear at the outset what his intentions are. He must "level" with the students about having just the right equipment available on certain days. The students will well appreciate this if indeed the time arrives when they are on their own and must search out their own equipment. In short, guided discovery can be legitimately called a discovery teaching method if the teacher has the larger intention of providing for open, individual inquiry. Even more than this, guided discovery may be considered an essential part of a teacher's long-range program, for without, it is doubtful that students could handle the great number of demands that arise in free, open, experimental inquiry (1). In this sense, guided discovery is not only justified but also necessary.

Modifying Guided Discovery

In guided discovery, the teacher, not the student, generally selects the problems and the class materials. Generally he takes a direct role by asking questions that will lead the students to the desired explanation. This situation can be modified in several ways in the evolution from guided to open discovery.

First, the teacher might well encourage the students to study a problem they find perplexing. He can do this by simply asking for suggestions. Naturally, many suggestions will have to be restated or simplified to suit the level of the teacher and the students. Or, the teacher can offer a wide range of alternative problems through reading material and demonstrations. A period of exploration time could be set aside in which the class could search for issues students find perplexing and intriguing.

Second, the teacher might well select for investigation a question to which he and his students do not already know the answer (although he might have an incomplete explanation before he starts the inquiry). Thus, the teacher can set up the situation so that he himself learns along with the students (15:318).

Third, the teacher can take a somewhat inactive role in questioning the students (whether or not he knows the explanation for the problem being studied). Rather than ask the right question at precisely the right time, the teacher can request further student contributions or further individual and small-group study. He might also allow the students to sense the need for sharper inquiry. The teacher might also use the tactic of asking the students why they seem to be drifting, i.e., question them, not about the problem itself, but about their approach to it.

Fourth, the teacher might structure the discussion so that the students will ask him questions, which he will then answer. Furthermore, the students, in order to gather the data they need for the explanation, may be told to ask only questions that elicit a yes or no response. This technique quickly teaches the students about the need for careful questioning and sharp analysis of the answers obtained. This technique is essentially the approach developed by Suchman in the University of Illinois science project entitled the Illinois Studies in Inquiry Training (20; 21). With preparation, direction, and practice the students will be able both to ask the appropriate questions and to utilize the evidence received in resolving the problem before them.

This technique will be treated further, as it requires more of the teacher than meets the eye, especially at the beginning. Also, the strategy it establishes pertains as well to other forms of guided discovery and open discovery. Presented below is an outline of the practical application of the technique, as developed in the Illinois Studies (20; 21).

(A) The students witness (in film) a physics demonstration of a perplexing phenomenon slated to provoke the question, "Why?" For example, they see a brass ball that fits through a brass ring at room temperature. "The ball is then heated and placed on the opening of the ring which is held in a horizontal position. It does not slip through at once but is held in place by the ring. After some time has passed the ball drops through" (21:434). The students are then perplexed and wish to explain why this situation with the ball occurs.

(B) The students are presented with a plan to direct them in their questioning. This plan consists of three stages. In Stage One the students seek to identify, verify, and measure the importance of various aspects of the problem. They attempt to identify the elements involved, the properties of these elements, conditions pertaining to them, and events (i.e., the changes) occurring in some connection with them. In Stage Two the students attempt to identify the conditions necessary for these events to occur. In Stage Three the students seek to formulate and test relationships among the variables in the overall situation.

(C) The students attempt to construct an explanation by questioning the teacher along the lines of his three-stage plan of attack. In addition to asking questions slated to help them identify the problem, the students may ask experimental questions that would help them understand the invariable elements within the situation and that would also enable them to test hypotheses. These, too, are yes and no questions. The students may not ask the teacher to make inferences for them from the data. That is, they may not ask, "Does the heat affect the ball?" If the student does ask such a question, the teacher should request him to rephrase it so that it will not test the teacher's understanding of the data. The point of all this is to shift the responsibility of problem-solving to the student, ensuring that he makes the inferences himself from the empirical data he obtains.

(D) The teacher follows the discovery session with a critique period. Here, with tape recordings made during the study, or simply by drawing on their own memories, the teacher and students review the effectiveness of the questions asked. They discuss their weaknesses and possible ways of improving their ability to inquire. They also discuss their successes and the ways they can continue to succeed. This critique period is crucial, for here the teacher integrates the entire procedure. "The critique is indispensable; when it is eliminated, morale slips and inquiry becomes progressively worse" (21:440).

These four modifications of the guided-discovery method are offered as possible means by which a teacher can move toward free, open, experimental inquiry. These suggestions are not offered as panaceas or stopping points. Though the fourth technique, as developed by Suchman, has rightly attained some popularity because of its strengths, the reader should note that it has certain weaknesses, too. Its obvious strength is that it gets the students to ask questions; but, on the other hand, the students must rely on the teacher for their yes or no answers. This means that the teacher who has selected the demonstration already knows the correct explanation for the perplexing problem. In contrast, there is no one to give the student a yes or no answer in open inquiry, and this is a crucial aspect of the method. Perhaps, though the Suchman method is geared toward training the students to become independent, they may actually become more dependent on the teacher. But this in no way detracts from the advantage of giving the students practice in asking questions based on the sensible three-stage program of attack. Therefore, the teacher would do well to use all four variations, and others he may develop himself.

Burdens of Discovery

Another problem concerning nonvaluative discovery pertains to both guided discovery and free, open, experimental discovery. It centers on three principal objections to the discovery method: (1) The discovery method considerably increases the time and cost of teaching. (2) The discovery method puts a great burden on the student in that it requires him to be his own critic. (3) It is increasingly unnecessary for a person who has reached cognitive maturity (i.e., the abstract stage of cognitive development, as described by Piaget) to depend on prior personal concrete-empirical evidence in order to understand the relationships and generalizations the teacher is discussing.

The first objection, in focusing on the time/cost factors of teaching, states that the discovery method is too slow and expensive in terms of effort expended by the teacher and students. Hence, students learning within a situation limited by time and finances will not be able to delve into many areas of study. In short, they will learn fewer facts and principles simply because they will not have studied them. For those people concerned with increasing the students' store of knowledge, the time/cost objection is significant (2; 3; 4; 5; 6).

The second objection focuses on the burden placed upon the student. Indeed the discovery method requires that the student correct his own mistakes. Many students cannot do this well. Nor can many teachers adequately identify and analyze their students' errors, for they get quickly confused with the fact in the course of inquiry. Thus, many errors go uncorrected and become the sources of later confusion. Moreover, in requiring a student to be self-critical we detract from his spontaneous efforts to explore the topic at hand freely. For those people concerned with correctness and free creative exploration, this objection is significant. For them the discovery method exacts too high a price (11).

The third objection focuses on the need for the discovery method. For those who raise this objection, the discovery method is defensible for young pupils on the elementary level or older students confronting a new subject matter area. In both situations, concrete props are required. But mature, seasoned students can "form most new concepts and learn most new propositions by directly grasping higher order relationships between abstractions" (6:94). Thus, the discovery method, according to this claim, is simply unnecessary much of the time for adolescent and adult students (2; 3; 4; 5; 6).

Though not easily dismissed, these three objections can be met. First, no one, not even the staunchest supporter of the discovery method, advocates using it as the sole method of teaching. It is most important that the teacher employ the discovery method along with, rather than to the exclusion of, other methods. This is basically the caution these objections call for, because not even the staunchest critic of the discovery method advocates eliminating it completely—even with adolescent and adult students. Those who object, in all fairness, advocate not an elimination but a deemphasis as the student gets older. It is the teacher's job to balance the methods used.

Second, the time/cost objection applies primarily to school situations where a certain quantity of knowledge is to be learned within a given time. This objection is often offered by those concerned with covering great amounts of subject matter. But surely not all teaching situations are so constrained by time and cost. And even where this is a problem, such a situation is often self-imposed and not necessarily unchangeable. Further, even though there may be a valid time/cost constraint, other factors deemed more important, such as student interest and the belief that knowledge comes from within, may suggest the utilization of the discovery method. For many teaching situations, then, the objection to increased time and cost of teaching does not loom large.

Third, the objection centering on the student as his own critic also turns out to be answered by proper timing and emphasis. Surely, if the teacher wishes to lead the student to independence, then at some time he must begin to put the student on his own. The wise teacher will, no doubt, do so gradually. It is up to the teacher to balance a student's self-criticism with external help in order to enable the student to correct his errors justifiably and at the same time sustain his individual work level.

The important points regarding the nonvaluative discovery method may be summarized as follows:

1. The technique of the discovery method as illustrated and examined in Chapter 6 applies equally well to nonvaluative discovery as evidenced in the two illustrations on coins, focusing on observing, generalizing, and inferring.

2. Nonvaluative discussion usually involves explanation.

3. It is most helpful for the teacher to keep in mind the three types and schemata of explaining: (a) generalization–specific instance; (b) purpose or function; and (c) sequential, genetic, or chronological.

4. The teacher can often eliminate confusion among the students by avoiding elliptical explanations and by not mixing elements from different types of explanations.

5. It is helpful to distinguish between guided, structured discovery and free, open, experimental discovery. The former may be considered as one step in the teachers' attempt to involve the students in the latter.

6. Four modifications of the usual guided discovery may be employed as a means of moving toward open discovery: (a) the student may select his own problem to work on; (b) the teacher may choose questions to which he does not already know the answers; (c) the teacher may take a fairly inactive role in the discussions; and (d) the teacher may set up a procedure in which the students must ask the questions.

7. The discovery method should be employed along with other methods of teaching.

References

1. Atkin, J. Myron, and Robert Karplus. "Discovery or Invention?" *The Science Teacher* 29:45–51, September 1962.

2. Ausubel, David P. "Implications of Preadolescent and Early Adolescent Cognitive Development for Secondary School Teaching." *High School Journal* 45:268–275, April 1962.

3. Ausubel, David P. "In Defense of Verbal Learning." *Educational Theory* 11:15–25, January 1961.

4. Ausubel, David P. "Learning by Discovery." *Educational Leadership* 20:113–117, November 1962.

5. Ausubel, David P. "Learning by Discovery: Rationale and Mystique." *Bulletin of the National Association of Secondary School Principals* 45:18–58, December 1961.

6. Ausubel, David P. "Some Psychological and Educational Limitations of Learning by Discovery." *New York State Mathematics Teachers Journal* 13:90–108, June 1963.

7. Brodbeck, May. "Logic and Scientific Method in Research on Teaching." *Handbook of Research on Teaching*, edited by N. L. Gage, pp. 44–93. Chicago: Rand McNally, 1963.

8. Brown, Bob Burton. "Acquisition versus Inquiry." *Elementary School Journal* 64:11–17, October 1963.

9. Copi, Irving M. *Introduction to Logic.* New York: Macmillan, 1961.

10. Dewey, John. *How We Think: A Restatement of the Relation of Reflective Thinking to the Educative Process.* Boston: D. C. Heath, 1933.

11. Friedlander, Bernard Z. "A Psychologist's Second Thoughts on Concepts, Curiosity, and Discovery in Teaching and Learning." *Harvard Educational Review* 35:18–38, Winter 1965.

12. Goodlad, John I. *The Changing School Curriculum.* New York: Fund for the Advancement of Education, 1966.

13. Hempel, Carl G. *Aspects of Scientific Explanation and Other Essays in the Philosophy of Science.* New York: Free Press, 1965.

14. Hyman, Ronald T. "The Concept of an Ideal Teacher-Student Relationship: A Comparison and Critique." In *Teaching: Vantage Points for Study*, edited by Ronald T. Hyman, pp. 175–185. Philadelphia: J. B. Lippincott, 1968.

15. Hyman, Ronald T. "The Name of the Game Is Teaching." *Media and Methods* 4:10–12, April 1968. Reprinted in *Teaching: Vantage Points for Study*, edited by Ronald T. Hyman (Philadelphia: J. B. Lippincott, 1968), pp. 315–319.

16. Meux, Milton, and B. Othanel Smith. "Logical Dimensions of

Teaching Behavior." In *Contemporary Research on Teacher Effectiveness*, edited by Bruce J. Biddle and William J. Ellena, pp. 127–164. New York: Holt, Rinehart, and Winston, 1964.

17. Morine, Greta. "Discovery Modes: A Criterion for Teaching." *Theory Into Practice* 8:25–30, February 1969.

18. Nagel, Ernest. *The Structure of Science: Problems in the Logic of Scientific Explanation*. New York: Harcourt, Brace, and World, 1961.

19. Smith, B. Othanel, and others. *A Study of the Strategies of Teaching*. Cooperative Research Project 1640, U.S. Department of Health, Education, and Welfare. Office of Education. Urbana, Ill.: Bureau of Educational Research, College of Education, University of Illinois, 1967.

20. Suchman, J. Richard. *The Elementary School Training Program in Scientific Inquiry*. Urbana, Ill.: College of Education, University of Illinois, 1962.

21. Suchman, J. Richard. "Inquiry Training in the Elementary School." *The Science Teacher* 27:42–47, November 1960. Reprinted in *Teaching: Vantage Points for Study*, edited by Ronald T. Hyman (Philadelphia: J. B. Lippincott, 1968), pp. 434–441.

22. Swift, Leonard F. "Explanation." In *Language and Concepts in Education*, edited by B. Othanel Smith and Robert H. Ennis, pp. 179–194. Chicago: Rand McNally, 1961.

23. Taba, Hilda. "Implementing Thinking as an Objective in Social Studies." In *Effective Thinking in the Social Studies*, Thirty-seventh Yearbook of the National Council for the Social Studies, edited by Jean Fair and Fannie R. Shaftel, pp. 25–49. Washington, D.C.: National Council for the Social Studies, 1967.

24. Toulmin, Stephen E. *The Uses of Argument*. Cambridge: Cambridge University Press, 1958.

3 Recitation and Lecture: A Reappraisal

8 Introduction to Recitation and Lecture

Lecture and recitation are perhaps the two oldest methods employed by teachers working with groups of students. They are traditional methods and, in addition, stem from a similar view of teaching. In any era of reform and reconsideration of teaching, traditional methods bear the brunt of sharp negative criticism. However, it is precisely in an era of reform that what is valuable in traditional practices should be preserved and given careful reexamination and reformulation. These two methods require respecification of rationale and a new consideration. In this way it is possible to build upon tradition. This, indeed, is the intent of the following two chapters.

It is essential for the teacher who uses the lecture and recitation methods to keep in mind that, though these methods are in common use, their negative image is of long standing. Samuel Johnson, the famous writer and lexicographer, is quoted by his biographer, James Boswell, as saying in 1766,

People have now-a-days got a strange opinion that everything should be taught by lectures. Now, I cannot see that lectures can do so much good as reading the books from which the lectures are taken. I know nothing that can be best taught by lectures, except where experiments are to be shewn. You may teach chymistry by lectures.—You might teach making of shoes by lectures (5:337).

The teacher, in coping with this image, must explore and keep in mind the underlying justifications of these methods. This will aid him in recognizing the nature of the activity he is performing. Hopefully he will then be able to cope with the limitations of the methods and will be able to utilize their strengths to his best advantage.

Underlying Justifications

Those who support the lecture and recitation methods of conducting a class are guided by a view of teaching that has several special features. The *first* of these features involves the concept that what the student needs to know, do, or believe and can know, do, or believe is external to him. The knowledge, for example, that a student needs to possess and can come to possess is actually held by someone else (the teacher) who can transmit it to the student. Knowledge lies outside of the student, not within him. When someone communicates knowledge to the student, the student's mind receives it, assimilates it, and stores it along with other knowledge previously gained. The mind is seen as a never-full receptacle that continually receives, sorts, and interrelates externally generated stimuli. This view of teaching depicts the mind, according to Scheffler, "essentially as sifting and sorting the external impressions to which it is receptive" (8:132).

Second, teaching is viewed as the activity that brings about the accumulation of the knowledge that is to be utilized by the student as he performs his life's activities. Man is born without knowledge and begins to accumulate it immediately upon birth. Teaching fosters that accumulation of knowledge by giving the student direction and seeing to it that he receives and stores the appropriate knowledge. "The desired end result of teaching is an accumulation in the learner of the basic elements fed in from without, organized and processed in standard ways, but, in any event, not generated by the learner himself" (8:132).

The *third* important feature is the idea that the *teacher* has the knowledge to give the student or can easily acquire it when necessary or can readily guide the student to some book or film or the like that contains it. This gives the teacher status with the students, for he has what they do not have but need to have. Thus, the teacher serves as the external source of stimuli for the student. The teacher can, furthermore, direct the process of accumulation through considered, deliberate selection and timing of inputs. This earns the teacher further status.

Moreover, and critical to the entire process of teaching, there is the *fourth* idea—that the teacher can transmit his knowledge to the student. The teacher tells what he knows, and the student receives and learns. Teaching is essentially the dispensing of knowledge and thus ideally leads to the eventual elimination of the mystery surrounding the knowledge the teacher has amassed. This concept of teaching and the teacher is illustrated in the diagram below:

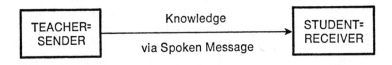

Figure 8–1

The skill of the teacher thus amounts to being able to transmit knowledge—usually by means of verbal communication—so that the student not only receives it but accumulates it. The diagram is amplified to become:

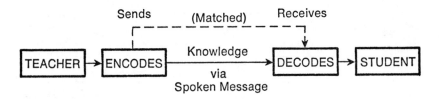

Figure 8–2

Of course the teacher assumes, or takes steps to assure: that what he sends is received and decoded by the student; that what he sends, not less, reaches the student; that what he sends arrives with no changes that would confuse or distort; that he can encode, or translate, his knowledge into language that is meaningful to the student; that the student can and does decode the message in such a way as to learn it.

This feeding in of external stimuli further involves the idea that there is congruence and validity in what the student decodes. It must be assumed, for example, that the impressions of an event that the student receives from the teacher are valid and correspond to the event itself; that the student can learn about the event from the stimuli he receives. This is illustrated in Figure 8–3, p. 192.

Note that in Figure 8–3 the teacher tells the statements about the event in such a way as to suit the student's ability to perceive. The teacher selects the appropriate levels of words, speed, and other controls (6) in order to assure that the student will be able to comprehend the statement about the event.

Fifth, this view of teaching acknowledges that the reception by the student may be either rote reception or meaningful reception (1). The failure to make the distinction between rote reception and meaningful reception is one factor that has led to misunderstanding and the subsequent repudiation of the lecture and recitation methods. "Few pedagogic devices in our time have been repudiated more unequivocally by educational theorists than the method of verbal instruction. It is fashionable in many quarters to characterize verbal learning as parrotlike recitation and rote memorization of isolated facts, and dismiss it disdainfully as an archaic remnant of discredited educational tradition" (1:15).

Stressing the distinction between rote reception and meaningful reception, many have argued that disapproval of the recitation

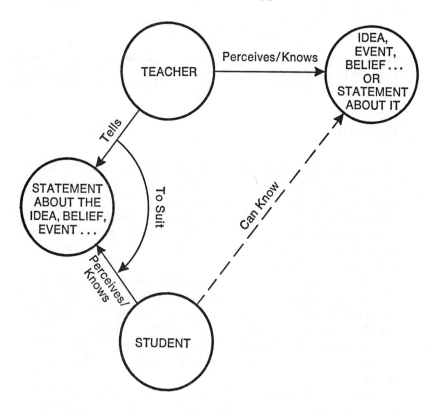

Figure 8–3

and lecture methods arises from an abuse of these methods rather than from their nature. Ausubel claims that "the weaknesses attributed to the method of verbal instruction do not inhere in the method itself" (1:16). Various techniques for having students absorb lectures and recitations in a meaningful way rather than by rote will be treated later on. The point here is simply that, according to those who acknowledge the value of lectures and recitations, the communication of knowledge via verbal exposition can be meaningful to the student. This view is in direct opposition to the view of many of those who discredit the recitation and lecture methods.

Sixth—and this is a very significant feature of the recitation and lecture methods—this view of teaching is entirely consistent with and supportive of the anthropological concept of culture. That is to say, man can communicate the knowledge he has acquired to his offspring. A man's children can benefit from their father's learning provided he can relate it to them. This ability to transmit knowledge is one essential characteristic that sets man off from the lower animals.

...perhaps the most unique attribute of human culture, which distinguishes it from every other kind of social organization in the animal kingdom, is precisely the fact that the accumulated discoveries of millennia can be transmitted to each succeeding generation in the course of childhood and youth, and need not be discovered anew by each generation. This miracle of culture is made possible only because it is so much less time-consuming to communicate and explain an idea meaningfully to others than to require them to re-discover it by themselves (4:91).

Seventh, the lecture and recitation methods of teaching are consistent with the concept of the school as agent for transmission of knowledge to students. According to this view, teaching school should concern itself with communicating to the student the skills, knowledge, and values of his culture, so that he can employ these in his life. The student "is primarily engaged in an effort to learn the same basic subject matter . . . which the scientist had learned in his days. . . . Most of the student's time should be taken up with appropriate expository learning" (3:38–39).

Eighth, this view of teaching, moreover, accommodates and encourages efficiency in gaining knowledge. This notion is closely related to the concept of culture mentioned earlier. Teaching by means of lectures is simply an efficient way of teaching a large number of students. This indeed has always been a matter of consideration for teachers, especially teachers in schools. But today, when school enrollment is growing yearly, due to a combination of factors—including increased population—the issue of efficiency is important. Efficiency must be considered in terms of time and cost (2:117). It costs less to teach, via a lecture, a group of 100 students in a single room than it does to teach via some other method that involves small groups in many sessions in many rooms. There are certain experiences "that are too expensive to repeat for subgroups of the course" (7:31). Time and cost efficiency is also gained in the recitation method. The teacher utilizes a common textbook for communicating the desired knowledge, and the students study their textbooks at home in their free time. This decreases the time required by the teacher for transmitting the desired knowledge.

Ninth, students often are happy when they are considered part of a large group made up of their friends and acquaintances. They want to have the same experiences as their classmates, and they want to share those experiences. They want to experience just what their fellows experience, and they want to know just what their fellows know. They feel secure sitting with a large group, and this sense of security and satisfaction promotes learning. Thus, the lecture and recitation methods can be, and often are, justified in terms of satisfying social needs of the student.

Furthermore, during the question-and-answer interplay which may be a part of a lecture but is especially important during the recitation session, the student learns from his classmates. This is not to be denigrated or minimized, for there are many students who benefit greatly from this aspect of the lecture and recitation methods.

Organizing for Recitation and Lectures

It is clear that in order to employ these two methods, recitation and lecture, the teacher and students need an organizational plan. Although it may seem entirely possible for a teacher to lecture to one student, or to conduct a recitation with a hundred students, the characteristics of these methods in fact set certain limitations on the number of participants and the size of the classroom. Furthermore, since individual teachers differ in skill, knowledge, voice quality, and personality, as do students, there are obviously no absolute figures one can offer. For example, some teachers can project a personal touch in a lecture to 200 students, while others can only reach fifty students, at most, in this manner. Nevertheless it is possible to talk in general terms.

RECITATION.   Because the recitation method depends on personal feedback, it is unwise to have more than twenty-five to forty students in a session. Obviously, the fewer the students, the more feedback the teacher receives from each one. It is for this reason that it is undesirable to have a large-group recitation. With a large group, there is less of an opportunity for each student to recite, nor can the teacher devote much time to individual student responses. Also, as the group becomes larger, personal contact is difficult to maintain.

The recitation is best conducted in a small room, with students seated in a horseshoe or circle arrangement. This helps reduce the threatening aspect of the situation—informality and face-to-face contact are promoted. Further, the students tend to learn more from each other.

Finally, the teacher can lessen or avoid the potential dangers of the method if he does not conduct recitation sessions daily. He might schedule two recitation sessions a week; even better, he might schedule no formal recitation sessions at all, but rather conduct them as the situation demands. This will help to create a feeling of flexibility and freedom in the classroom. The recitation method is most productive when used sparingly and in combination with other teaching methods.

LECTURE.   The minimum number of students for a lecture class is about fifteen to twenty. With less than this number it is difficult for the teacher to lecture, since the small number of students discourages him from presenting a formal address. Small groups invite, rather, an informal relationship, where one person does not talk *to* the others. On the other hand, if the number of students is too high, the lecturer becomes so distant as to virtually eliminate the interpersonal relationship between teacher and student. The teacher becomes merely an impersonal speaker. The upper limit on students is perhaps several hundred. However, the number drops considerably as the age of the students decreases. This is due to the reduced attention span of younger pupils and the increased probability that they will lose the lecture flow in a very large group.

The number of students can remain high if the teacher chooses not to have a question-and-answer period or a critique period in conjunction with the lecture. He may decide this because he has scheduled separate critiques by small groups (twelve to twenty-two students) soon after the session. This is common when there is some type of multi-teacher approach, perhaps a professor and graduate assistants, or a secondary school situation where a "co-operating" teacher has student teachers or several senior teachers working with him.

If the lecturer knows that there will be small-group sessions that will encourage an exchange of opinion and information regarding the lecture, he can bypass the many interruptions that could sidetrack him. This in no way implies that he ought to eliminate student participation in the lecture. Rather, arranging for a critique period after the session allows the lecturer more freedom in his prepared remarks and in his replies to questions. He knows that the students will soon deal intensively with the various points. Such small-group sessions are highly desirable and are strongly recommended.

Without small groups and without the opportunity for questions, it would seem quite reasonable for the lecturer to film, televise, or videotape his lecture. In fact, with the abundant availability of advanced electronic techniques, many educators advocate the elimination of the live lecture. However, such technological devices, in spite of the fact that they offer the distinct advantages of efficiency and possible reuse, entail certain problems that deserve careful consideration.

The television or film lecture commonly 1) eliminates the feedback the lecturer might get from his students as he lectures, since he cannot see their faces, respond to their questions, or sense the classroom atmosphere; 2) eliminates the question-and-answer or critique periods, where the student could solicit elaboration, expansion, and clarification of points raised in the lecture; 3) eliminates the feeling of a close contact between the student and the teacher—that is, the student may rightly feel that he is but one student, and an unidentified one at that, among hundreds or thousands of students whom the lecturer does not know and who do not know the lecturer; and 4) eliminates the dynamic quality of a teacher who is grappling with an issue, who is willing to change his mind in mid-lecture, and who is willing to speculate in anticipation of student questions—for these electronic devices encourage a polished, flawless presentation (in that it will be preserved). Further, once the lecture is recorded in this way, the temptation to use it again and again arises. If this happens, then a static rather than a dynamic situation evolves. Teaching, to be effective, must involve a dynamic relationship among the elements of the teacher-student-subject matter triad.

For these reasons, television or film lectures, if used at all, should frequently be revised and, further, should be conducted in combination with other techniques, such as a telephone hookup that allows students viewing a live televised lecture to interact with the teacher. Such a device is a way of avoiding some of the disadvantages of a televised lecture and at the same time having the advantages of a lecture that might otherwise be unavailable.

On the other hand, a live lecturer needs a minimum of equipment. First, if the room is large, he needs a microphone in order to assure that every student will hear him. Second, he needs a chalkboard for noting and sketching important examples. (If the room is large, it would be better to use an overhead or opaque projector, which has greater visibility than the chalkboard. In addition, the desired diagrams can be prepared ahead of time by the lecturer himself, purchased, or used directly from another source such as a book or journal.) Third, the lecturer would be wise to have a good supply of such props as wall maps, scale models, wall charts, and globes. All of these serve to enrich the lecture.

References

1. Ausubel, David P. "In Defense of Verbal Learning." *Educational Theory* 11:15–25, January 1961.

2. Ausubel, David P. "Learning by Discovery." *Educational Leadership* 20:113–117, November 1962.

3. Ausubel, David P. "Learning by Discovery: Rationale and Mystique." *Bulletin of the National Association of Secondary School Principals* 45:18–58, December 1961.

4. Ausubel, David P. "Some Psychological and Educational Limitations of Learning by Discovery." *New York State Mathematics Teachers Journal* 13:90–108, June 1963.

5. Boswell, James. *The Life of Samuel Johnson, L.L.D.* Oxford ed., vol. 1. London: Henry Frowde, 1904.

6. Gerbner, George. "A Theory of Communication and Its Implications for Teaching." In *The Nature of Teaching*, edited by Louise M. Berman, pp. 33–47. Milwaukee: University of Wisconsin-Milwaukee, 1963. Reprinted in *Teaching: Vantage Points for Study*,

edited by Ronald T. Hyman (Philadelphia: J. B. Lippincott, 1968), pp. 18–31.

7. Loud, Oliver S. "Lecture and Discussion in General Education." *Journal of General Education* 8:30–33, October 1954.

8. Scheffler, Israel. "Philosophical Models of Teaching." *Harvard Educational Review* 35:131–143, Spring 1965.

9 Recitation as Interaction

The recitation method, in some variation or another, is quite commonly used by teachers working with young students. Many teachers conduct daily periods in which students recite lessons based on their homework. Yet, perhaps recitation is the method most in need of revitalization. It is an abused method. The recitation can be transformed into a respectable teaching method by the use of techniques based on careful consideration of its rationale.

Example and Analysis

What should a teacher do in order to teach via the recitation method? First, he will have to rescue the method from its generally unpopular image. For many people recitation has come to symbolize the dull, routine activity that was the source of their aversion to school (3:133). "Going to school meant reciting from a textbook, and learning was identified with reproducing for the teacher what the book contained" (7:15). The common recitation may be characterized as a question-and-answer session in which the teacher asks questions and the students provide set answers based on a textbook or a previous short presentation by the teacher. The recitation method is certainly overused in that many teachers employ it almost exclusively.

By using the recitation method, the teacher checks, or tests, whether his students have learned the assigned material (8). Since this method often involves little more than a rehash of material presented in the textbook, many people do not consider recitation a valid teaching method. The following illustration—admitted as an extreme case even by Page (6) who reports it—is an excerpt from a recitation lesson conducted in the 1840s. Similar situations, no doubt, exist today.

I may further illustrate this *drawing-out* process, by describing an occurrence, which, in company with a friend and fellow-laborer, I once witnessed. A teacher, whose school we visited, called upon the class in Colburn's First Lessons. They rose, and in single file marched to the usual place, with their books in hand, and stood erect. It was a very good-looking class.

"Where do you begin?" said the teacher, taking the book.

Pupils: On the 80th page, 3rd question.

Teacher: Read it, Charles.

Charles: (Reads.) "A man being asked how many sheep he had, said that he had them in two pastures; in one pasture he had eight; that three-fourths of these were just one-third of what he had in the other. How many were there in the other?"

Teacher: Well, Charles, you must first get one-fourth of eight, must you not?

Charles: Yes, sir.

Teacher: Well, one-fourth of eight is two, isn't it?

Charles: Yes, sir; one-fourth of eight is two.

Teacher: Well, then, three-fourths will be three times two, won't it?

Charles: Yes sir.

Teacher: Well, three times two are six, eh?

Charles: Yes, sir.

Teacher: Very well. (A pause.) Now the book says that this six is just one-third of what he had in the other pasture, don't it?

Charles: Yes, sir.

Teacher: Then if six is one-third, three-thirds will be—three times six, won't it?

Charles: Yes, sir.

Teacher: And three times six are—eighteen, ain't it?

Charles: Yes, sir!

Teacher: Then he had eighteen sheep in the other pasture, had he?

Charles: Yes, sir!

Teacher: Next, take the next one.

At this point I interposed, and asked the teacher if he would request Charles to go through it alone. "Oh, yes," said the teacher, "Charles, you may do it again." Charles again read the question, and—looked up. "Well," said the teacher, "You must first get one-fourth of eight, mustn't you?" "Yes, sir." "And one-fourth of eight is two, isn't it?" "Yes, sir." And so the process went on as before till the final eighteen sheep were *drawn out* as before. The teacher now looked round, with an air which seemed to say, "Now I suppose you are satisfied."

"Shall *I* ask Charles to do it again?" said I. The teacher assented. Charles again read the question, and again—looked up. I waited, and he waited;—but the teacher could *not* wait. "Why, Charles," said he,

impatiently; "you want one-fourth of eight, don't you?" "Yes, sir,"
said Charles, promptly; and I thought best not to insist further at this
time upon a repetition of "*yes, sir,*" and the class were allowed to proceed
in their own way.

This is, indeed, an extreme case, and yet it is but a fair sample of
that teacher's method of stupefying minds (6:81–83).

The recitation depicted above hardly constitutes a teaching
method at all; the teaching has degenerated rather into a threatening inquisitional activity. It causes dependency on the teacher,
rote learning, and uncritical regurgitation of answers. In effect,
it leaves the students with the notion that there is a single correct
answer for most questions. This method is not to be confused
with the discussion method treated in the previous chapters. Page,
in commenting on this poor illustration of a recitation, claims that
such "extraction at recitation, aside from the waste of time by
both parties, and the waste of strength by the teacher, has a direct
tendency to make the scholar miserably superficial" (6:83).

In describing recitation, Thayer claims that this popular
method found what at one time was a nearly universal acclaim
because of three ideas.

These three conceptions of education as the acquisition of knowledge
from books, education as a process of writing impressions upon the
mind, and education as an individualistic and selective process which
operates primarily by elimination, were three of the most important
principles which determined the character of teaching one hundred
years ago. They justified a procedure which was characterized by
assignments in daily installments, identical demands upon all pupils,
identification of ground covered with genuine learning, and docility
and passivity in reproducing for the teacher the information contained
in the book (7:27).

The recitation is thus clearly allied to the lecture in that the
students are expected to learn knowledge which is presented to
them from an outside source. Dewey points this out quite well
and with two interesting metaphors.

The recitation exhibits, more definitely than anything else in the school
system, the domination of the ideal of amassing information without a
purpose for it, because information would help master a difficulty, and
without judgment in selection of what is pertinent. It is hardly an
exaggeration to say that too often the pupil is treated as if he were a
phonographic record on which is impressed a set of words that are to be

literally reproduced when the recitation or examination presses the proper lever. Or, varying the metaphor, the mind of the pupil is treated as if it were a cistern into which information is conducted by one set of pipes that mechanically pour it in, while the recitation is the pump that brings out the material again through another set of pipes. Then the skill of the teacher is rated by his or her ability in managing the two pipe-lines of flow inward and outward (2:261).

Techniques for the Recitation

It is in this light that the brief suggestions that follow are aimed at transforming the recitation back into a teaching method, as it once, no doubt, was intended.

1. Because of the general negative impressions students already have (or quickly get, once involved in the recitation method) and because of the inherent dangers of the method, the teacher should emphasize to the students the greatest natural strength of this method, namely, that the teacher can quickly get direct feedback from the students, and that the teacher can give prompt responses to the students' remarks. Whereas in the lecture method the teacher relies mainly on facial expressions and the responses of a few students, the teacher in the recitation method can and should rely on many direct verbal responses to questions.*

However, though the teacher's intent is clear to him, he must be especially careful to make this intent known to the student. The teacher must make it patently clear, both in words and action, that he uses the recitation method for purposes of feedback and commentary—elaboration and expansion of ideas—rather than to judge or bludgeon the students. This must be established because the recitation method has great potential for creating a threatening situation for the student. Threat is inherent because the teacher is checking on the students' learning. The student is, after all, being asked to produce on demand proof that he knows certain things. Even if the teacher praises correct responses, the situation is obviously unpleasant for the student and for the teacher, too. The student feels, and probably knows from past experience, that he will generally not be rewarded for correct answers, and will probably, in fact, be reprimanded for answering incorrectly. Herein lies the threat. Indeed, any situation is threatening where someone is constantly being evaluated, especially by a superior.

* In this way, the recitation method lends itself to the communication feedback loop depicted in Figure 10–2, p. 218.

Surely, this potential for threat is one significant reason why a number of educators have attacked the recitation method. It is difficult, if not impossible, to establish mutual trust and to encourage independent thought when a superior with the power of reward and punishment is sitting in constant judgment. It is for this reason that the teacher must concentrate on the fact that he is using the recitation method to teach his student. To do this the teacher must focus on diagnosis and commentary. This does not imply the elimination of evaluation, for surely the student needs to be encouraged and praised for his achievements. He even needs to be reprimanded at times for poor performances. But the correction of a wrong answer does not have to imply or be accompanied by emotional rejection and humiliation. The student can surely come to understand this if the focus of the class is on feedback for diagnosis and commentary.

Below are several suggestions on how to use the recitation method. The first two are contrary to suggestions commonly offered.

1. It is not crucial whether the teacher asks a question and then designates the student who is to respond or first designates the student and then asks his question. The significance of the teacher's action lies in the tone and purpose of his question. The respondent must not feel that the question is being used to attack him. Indeed, the reason usually given for designating the student after the question is asked is precisely to keep everyone on the hook, or, putting it more euphemistically, to keep the students interested. "Call on pupils after, not before, the question is posed. Calling the name of a pupil to answer the question before it is posed is an invitation for the rest of the class to slacken their interest. If they will not be called upon, why should they listen?" (1:40). (Any number of other texts could be cited as well.) No wonder there is threat. The students sit waiting for the axe to fall, waiting to relax their interest once someone else is called upon, as if interest is aroused and retained only if the individual himself must answer the question. In any case, the tone of the citation above is quite clear. The person who follows such advice as given in that quotation resembles more an inquisitor than a teacher.

It is also undesirable to use questions as a weapon to keep students attentive. The teacher must not be saying by his actions, "If you don't pay attention, I'll ask you a question. So you'd better be attentive or at least look attentive." In short, the teacher must not harass the students, even if this means not calling upon every student in every lesson. No one, especially students, can pay attention all the time. The teacher should not seek to embarrass or humiliate the student because his attention has strayed.

The teacher hopes to get feedback in using a questioning technique; if a student is inattentive, that in itself is feedback. The teacher learns that the student, for whatever combination of reasons, is more interested in something else or at least not interested in what the teacher and his classmates are doing at that moment. Rather than threaten him with a question, the teacher might well consider the possibility of shifting the entire activity, or requesting the student to be attentive, or simply leaving the student alone for the moment.

An opposite approach is taken in the quotation below. The tone is clear. What seems a generous gesture is quickly withdrawn.

Call upon the inattentive student. Do not repeat the question for him. Go on to another student, or have a student repeat the question.

Distribute questions widely among volunteers and nonvolunteers. It is generally desirable to start with volunteers and to involve the non-volunteers after the lesson has developed momentum. The non-volunteer should not be made to feel harassed, but he must understand that a response is expected, if not to the particular question, perhaps to a following one. Thus, when the nonvolunteer fails to respond the teacher might move on quickly to the next pupil, with a casual reminder to the nonvolunteer that he will soon be called upon again. Do not fail to follow through on this promise (1:40).

2. Because of the potential for monotony, boredom, and meaninglessness in the recitation method, the teacher should take steps to make the recitation more than a mere regurgitation of previously learned material. (The recitation is often boring for bright students since they have already learned the assigned material. It is often meaningless to the student who finds it difficult to read the textbook on his own at home.) The recitation can afford the teacher the oppurtunity to modify, expand, elaborate, and comment on his students' responses. Through it, he will be able to relate and synthesize the various points raised by his students. Further, if the teacher seizes upon this opportunity, he can conduct his recitation on the principle of guiding his students from the known to the unknown.

This was the intention of Herbart's disciples, who crystallized his ideas into the five Formal Steps of Instruction: preparation, presentation, comparison and abstraction, generalization, and application (5:288). But the emphasis on the techniques of the teacher and rigid adherence to the order of the steps by teachers who followed these principles merely strengthened the already existing evils of the common recitation. Thus the Herbartian method of teaching soon, and easily, became associated with the recitation as depicted by Thayer and Dewey earlier. Indeed some people mistakenly equate the recitation method with the five steps of the Herbartians.

The teacher should remember which students make which points; this should then serve as a springboard for forming a general picture of the various student responses. The teacher should seek to tie the lesson with previous ones. He should try to redirect the efforts of various students, or even an entire class, in light of the particular answers given. The students will benefit by adding to their store of knowledge, rather than just reviewing or summarizing what they already know.

The act of adding to already acquired knowledge is one significant benefit of a recitation lesson. A second benefit is that students crystallize and reinforce their learning when they speak to others. "The act of oral repetition can serve as a means of reinforcement of learning of what the students may remember only very vaguely from previous experience" (4:362). A third benefit arises from the fact that students get to hear their classmates recite. This is peer learning and is not to be discounted. Students often understand a point that first seemed ambiguous if they hear their friends explain it. Students, by listening to their peers, get a firmer idea of what is expected of them. The fourth benefit of the recitation method stems from the fact that the teacher, through his questions, is able to demonstrate what should be learned and remembered. The teacher's questions should therefore focus on what he considers important in the broad area covered by the textbook. This leads to another suggestion.

3. The teacher should carefully select, organize, and frame his questions with the purpose of demonstrating the chronological, logical, or conceptual connections among the expected answers. The questions in a recitation can lead to more than unconnected facts; they can go beyond the level of unrelated facts stemming from answers to such questions as: Who? What? Where? What kind? How many? This is not to say that answers to such questions are unnecessary. Rather, by asking such questions in a particular order the teacher can lead the students to a comprehension of

connections. Without doing this, it is questionable whether the isolated questions add up to teaching and whether the isolated facts elicited leave the student with a knowledge of the materials.

The teacher can further build on the answers to his queries by asking students such questions as, "Now that we have talked about the structure of a cell in a plant and a cell in human tissue, would you please show how the two are similar?" Or, "What conclusions can we draw from the many facts relating to France's rejection of Great Britain's application to join the Common Market?" Or, "Now that we've pointed out what occurred in *Hamlet*, what is your interpretation of Prince Hamlet's relationship with Ophelia?" It is with questions like these that the teacher moves beyond mere rehash and recall. Such questions—along with student reactions (upon which the teacher expands, elaborates, and comments)— allow the student to further his learning, in addition to reviewing it. (For more details and suggestions about this type of questioning, see Chapter 14.)

4. Because of the obvious, serious limitations of the recitation method, the teacher ought to use this method sparingly. All of the dangers are exacerbated when the method is used often and for entire class sessions. The teacher should try to blend the recitation with other teaching methods; for example, he might alternate recitation sessions with lectures. He should also allow the recitation to lead into other methods.

5. The teacher should use a variety of sources and devices in making the initial presentation upon which he will base the recitation session. That is, he should use not only a textbook as a basis for his session, but also films, phonograph recordings, videotape and audiotape recordings, television, and radio programs. Such visual and/or aural devices not only add variety but also broaden the scope of available knowledge and better suit the abilities of those students who do not learn well from reading.

6. The teacher should seek to enliven the class by employing such devices as humor. For an extended treatment of this subject see the section on humor in the following chapter.

References

1. Association of Teachers of Social Studies of the City of New York. *Handbook for Social Studies Teachers.* 3d ed. New York: Holt, Rinehart, and Winston, 1967.

2. Dewey, John. *How We Think: A Restatement of the Relation of Reflective Thinking to the Educative Process.* Boston: D. C. Heath, 1933.

3. Kuethe, James L. *The Teaching-Learning Process.* Glenview, Ill.: Scott, Foresman, 1968.

4. Lewenstein, Morris R. *Teaching Social Studies in Junior and Senior High Schools.* Chicago: Rand McNally, 1963.

5. McMurry, Charles A., and Frank M. McMurry. *The Method of the Recitation.* New York: Macmillan, 1926.

6. Page, David P. *Theory and Practice of Teaching: Or, the Motives and Methods of Good School-Keeping.* New York: A. S. Barnes, 1854.

7. Thayer, V. T. *The Passing of the Recitation.* Boston: D. C. Heath, 1928.

IO Lecturing and Interaction

This chapter treats the lecture method of teaching. A clear distinction is intended here between the lecture method of teaching and the simple lecture, in which someone speaks before a large group. The latter situation is not necessarily teaching. The reader is asked to recall the underlying justification for this method, as outlined in Chapter 8.

It is essential that the teacher keep in mind that he is using the lecture method to *teach*. This will help him to avoid the many misuses of this technique; the faults are in the users, not in the method.

Misuses of the method of verbal learning are so well-known that only the following more flagrant practices need be mentioned: premature use of verbal techniques with cognitively immature pupils; arbitrary, cook book presentation of unrelated facts without organizing or explanatory principles; failure to integrate new learning tasks with previously presented materials; and the use of evaluation procedures that merely measure the ability to recognize discrete facts or to reproduce ideas in the same words or in the identical context as originally encountered. Although it is entirely proper to caution teachers against these frequent misuses of verbal learning, it is not legitimate to represent them as inherent in the method itself (2:23–24).

In this chapter, we shall present an illustrative lecture and, through analysis of that lecture, demonstrate how a teacher can fruitfully employ the lecture method.

Example and Analysis

Reprinted below is a lecture that its author, Winslow R. Hatch (11), claims "exploits certain good conditions for learning." The reader is asked to carefully consider the characteristics this lecture manifests. He must remember, obviously, that he is reading what was originally intended to be heard.

LECTURE: THE NATURE OF LIFE*

One of the wisest men I know once told me that after 30 years of teaching and some 6 or 7 years of retirement, he thought he knew why one goes to college. 'One goes to college to learn how to ask questions.' How, then, does one learn something about biology? By asking questions. Now about biology, the science of life, what would you like to know?

"What is life?" [†]

That is a good question, almost too good. While we could engage the subject on a broad front, let us try for something that will be more manageable. Let us separate structure from function and examine these two aspects one at a time.

Were we to do this, our first questions might well be, *Does life have a structure? If it does what is it?* But how does one determine whether life has a structure? To answer these questions one must learn a good deal about the structure of living things. But in doing this, and even in advance, it would expedite our study if we knew what it is in all this structure that is relevant to our problem.

You know the story of the blind men and the elephant. (Here is read the poem "The Blind Men and the Elephant" by John Godfrey Saxe. Six blind men, approaching the elephant from different directions, felt only parts of the animal. One feeling its side described it "as a wall"; one its tusk, "like a spear"; one its trunk, "like a snake"; one its knee, "like a tree"; one its ear, "very like a fan"; one its tail, "very like a rope.") What does this story suggest as to how we might best proceed?

"We have to have ALL the facts."

All the facts there are on morphology, anatomy, histology, and cytology—that is to say, the structure of better than two million species?

"Oh no. Not in a 3-hour course."

Before we conclude that we do not have enough time, that the problem is too big for us, let us state and restate our problem and see if we cannot find some way of determining what structure is relevant to our inquiry. What are we looking for? We will certainly want to know this before we start looking for it.

* By Winslow R. Hatch. Reprinted with permission from *Improving College and University Teaching*, Winter 1958. (Also reprinted in reference 11.)

† Hatch states in a footnote here that "Student responses are quoted in separate, italicized paragraphs."

You say you don't know enough about the structure of living things to do this. You don't know very much, but you know enough. Let us start with some pretty obvious living things—you and me. What is there about us that identifies us as living entities? Do we have something that makes us alive, something that distinguishes us from the steel girder above our heads? Do we have something that that girder lacks? We have appendages, we have arms and legs, we have a head and torso. Yes, and we have organs, stomachs, intestines, hearts, and brains. But how relevant to this study are appendages and organs?

"*Not very, because our analysis must include living things—all of them, not just one or some.*"

Yes, we must keep in mind that there are living things other than ourselves; that there are the other animals and there are the plants. A survey, however, of the animal and plant kingdom, done well, could take a year. Before we abandon our inquiry for lack of time, let us see if we do not have sufficient common knowledge about animals and plants to see us through.

The structure we are looking for must, of necessity, be found not only in the most elaborate of animals, animals like ourselves, but in very small and very different animals. You may not know very much about the protozoa, the smallest animals, but you have at least heard of the *Amoeba*. The *Amoeba* is of microscopic size; is a single cell; is, as we say, unicellular. While you may not recognize it, you have just acquired some useful information. What is it?

"*It is that anything as large and as complex as organs is too large for the purpose of this study.*"

Very good. What about tissues, the component parts of organs? What of the stomach lining, for example? It is not very substantial, to be sure, but it is large enough to be seen by the unaided eye—it is still macroscopic in size. This and other tissues are made up of cells.

Tissues are "out" too, you say, because an amoeba is microscopic and tissues are macroscopic.

The only structures, then, that are common to animals would appear to be—?

"*Microscopic in size, or smaller.*"

Let us examine this suggestion. Let us think about plants and see if we cannot make the little we know work for us. The most elaborate plants have organs: leaves, stems, and roots. These organs are composed of tissues. The epidermis of a leaf, and the pith in stems and roots are tissue. Plant organs are easily seen by the unaided eye. Tissues can be seen, if not as well, without using a microscope. Plant organs and tissues are macroscopic. Plant tissues are typically composed of cells, and these cells are microscopic in size, as they are in animals.

Let us also consider some of the smaller entities in the plant kingdom, for example, the unicellular green alga, *Chlamydomonas*. The name of this organism is not a household word, but it is a common enough plant. This whole plant is microscopic in size. From this we can conclude, without opening a book, that we must look for and at structures and entities of microscopic size or smaller, that is, of cells or of living material no larger than cells. How can we afford to say this?

"*Cells, or structures of this size, are all that all plants and animals have in common.*"

On the basis of *your* facts, it would appear that living things have a cellular organization, for they seem to exist as single cells or aggregates of cells. But what are *the* facts?

There are certain categories of living things which we call slime molds. In most humid forests, if you look closely enough, you will find, scattered over the forest litter, little splotches of yellow or of pink, purple, or pale green material. These splotches are living things. If you were to study them under a microscope, you would find that the thin, wet, and slimy sheets have a structure. They look like old lace with a webbing which is heavier in some places than in others. But look as hard as you will, you will find no compartmentation of the mass. Since some splotches are as large as the palm of your hand, they are large enough to have cells, as we have been using the word—but they don't.

Now, when we find something which does not fit our "scheme of things," what are we going to do about it? Darwin had a good, if jocular, answer—grind it under your feet and forget about it. This is what we have done in biology, more or less, with this type of organism. But we can hardly forget it, because within perhaps 10 feet of the place where the slime mold was found, there may be a little stream. In that stream—growing on old seeds, twigs, or fruits—you might see, if you looked closely, some white, cottony tufts. These plants are water molds. If you were to place one of the white threads under a microscope and were to study it from one end to the other, you would discover that it is not compartmented, but is one long, open tube. It is not cut up into cells, as you would expect.

Finally, let us take a microscopic look at a bit of our own bodies. Even here we are going to make an unusual discovery, for we are going to find that, by weight, less of us is cellular than is noncellular. If you were to take a fiber out of those muscles of yours and were to have a good look at it, you would discover that these so-called striated muscles are made up of long, blunt-ended cylindrical objects not unlike rolled-oats cartons. These cylindrical objects abut on one another. But they are not subdivided into cells. They are large enough to be constructed of cells, but they are not.

If you were to look at heart muscle, you would find that bits of it draw off into fine branches like this (a diagram is drawn on the board) and run into similar branches from other concentrated masses. While these bits of the heart are constricted in these branches, there are no membranes across them. The heart is, apparently, one continuous mass.

When we take all this into account (the structure of the slime molds, water molds, striated and heart muscles), what does it do to the hypothesis we were toying with, that life has a cellular structure? It puts a pretty serious crimp in it. But we have not wasted our time, because we have learned that we not only do not need to study organography, the structure of organs, or histology, the structure of tissues, or even cytology, if by this we mean cellular structures. That structure we are looking for must be found in organs, tissues, and cells, but it must also be found where life shows no cellular organization. What is more, we have discovered the approximate dimensions of our structure. 'It must be—?

" *Microscopic or smaller in size; cellular structure won't do?* "
What might? It's so obvious as to be difficult!

" *That stuff, that content of cells and of noncells. It's the only thing left which is common to all living things and to all parts of all living things.* "

We have a word for it. The "stuff" the living content of living things, is protoplasm.

Now, at least, we know where to look. The structure we are looking for, if there is a structure peculiar to living things, must be found in protoplasm, be it organized in cells or not.

Keeping in mind what we are looking for, that structure associated with living things and all of them, it must be clear that it will not help us at all to study and memorize the structure of a generalized cell. A generalized cell is a biological monstrosity. Generalized animal and plant cells will not, then, advance our study either. Actually, the facts we are looking for cannot be found in any series of types shorter than the one on the board. We need this many illustrations to make certain that the facts are presented in such number and kind that they fairly represent the differences in microscopic structure to be found in living things. We shall, accordingly, have to look at the microscopic structure of man, a vertebrate; the *Amoeba* and *Diplodinium*, protozoans; the apple tree, a flowering plant; *Anthoceros*, a liverwort; the green algae *Chlydomonas*, *Coleochaete*, and *Vaucheria;* a blue-green alga or two; the fungus *Allomyces;* several bacteria; a slime mold; the flagellates; and a virus.

It is also our responsibility to assemble *our* facts, both those you can supply and those that are known to me. Our final responsibility is to order our facts so as to improve our chances of making sound generalizations. I will not make them for you because I want you to know the joy of discovery, a satisfaction we professors do not always share with our students. All we are saying is that even in lectures students can make discoveries.

It is now your move. You have some facts; you can dig out others. We shall assemble and order them in subsequent lectures, examine them in discussions, and test our ideas and methods in the laboratory. This is all being done to help you shape some hypotheses, some tentative conclusions about the structure of living things. *Does life have a struc-*

ture? If so, what is it? You will need to be critical and you had better be explicit and as complete as possible in developing your proofs. *What is the approximate size of the critical elements, their chemical nature, and how are they organized?*

I will throw questions like this at you until the air is blue with them, but I do not propose to answer them because I do not like to steal from my students. Doing your thinking for you is worse than taking your money because it adds insult to injury.

Now that you know *what* you are looking for you can, and should, start looking, and this as soon as possible. Now that you know *how* to look, I should get out of your way. Beginning now, you are about to come of age; you are about to become a student; and you are about to make this a university, so far at least as you are concerned because for you it becomes a "place of inquiry." Good luck and good hunting. Class dismissed.

(The hypothesis ultimately developed by the students is one known to biologists as the Protein Molecular Network hypothesis. Other explanations or hypotheses will, of course, be advanced and found wanting. In the framing of this hypothesis, the students will have closed in on the DNA molecule and the newer research on it, which constitutes a veritable biological breakthrough.)

This lecture manifests several excellent features of the lecture method. (1) The lecturer is acutely aware of the fact that the students must understand the problem before they proceed. Indeed, unless we know what it is we are investigating, we cannot collect data about it. Searching requires us to be clear about the question we seek to answer. How else can we recognize the factors that will help to provide us with an answer? Bayles puts it this way: "Until one has pretty clearly in his mind just what it is that causes perplexity, one is unlikely to be a very good judge of what constitutes a valid solution" (4:81). It is for this reason that the lecturer "states and restates" the problem to see "what structure is relevant." This is in accordance with the idea that "the first stage of inquiry is concerned with the analysis of the problem which initiates inquiry" (16:30).

Working With the Students

(2) This lecture has also served to point up the questions that will face the students in the study of life from a biological point of view. It was intended to be a spur to further study. It was intended to clarify for the students what to look for as they pursue their inquiry. Or, to state it in negative terms, this lecture has not

emphasized the transmission of knowledge, although such transmission was involved in parts. Rather, the teacher has woven the material to be transmitted into the questions and the answers of the students. All of this was intended as an impetus to the students' subsequent work. The lecturer has done these things quite deliberately—and rightly so.

When a lecture serves largely to transmit knowledge from teacher to student, one can legitimately ask, "Why not tape-record the teacher's remarks and allow the students to listen at their own convenience?" It is more convenient and more economical in terms of the teacher's time for the teacher to record his remarks when he chooses. He can then play them back and make corrections. He can also use the tape for future classes and thus save multiple preparations and deliveries. One research project studied two classes, one taught through live lectures and the other through tape-recorded lectures. The researcher concluded that, from performance measured by several criteria, no statistically significant differences between the tape-taught and conventionally taught students were found (19). Then why not use tape recordings? Or films? Or books? Indeed, Hatch, the author of the illustrative lecture, has himself written, "Of the expository lecture one must ask whether its general use is justifiable when teachers are in short supply but books, mimeographed materials, teaching tapes and film can be mass-produced" (11:11).

The answer to these questions lies in the illustrative lecture itself. The lecturer was not simply telling a story to the students that they could hear on tape or read in a book. The lecturer was working *with the students* on a problem in biology. The lecturer had obviously prepared his lesson well; he had clearly outlined for himself the main ideas he wanted to treat, gathered the relevant data, and planned questions that were germane and provocative. In this way the lecturer not only had an identifiable theme with data to transmit to the students, but he also was prepared to build upon and interpret student responses. But perhaps more important is the point that the lecturer opened up the topic of the biology of life. Through his reactions to student responses and his own countering questions, he so shaped the topic that students felt they could tackle it. He thus treated the topic in such a way as to encourage students to pursue their own study. In writing about teaching on the high school level, Heller supports this idea with the claim that the "lecture can challenge the imagination of each student, arouse curiosity, develop his spirit of inquiry, and encourage his creativity" (12:99).

By conducting his talk in this manner, the teacher has shown that it *is* possible to work with students in a lecture. It necessitates careful planning and a willingness to begin the lecture without knowing exactly what you will say. The lecturer must be quick to pick up the meaning of the students' questions and responses—not only the meaning of the words used, but also why the students are questioning and responding in a particular manner. The teacher must be willing to alter his intended course in light of the students' remarks. The lecturer should

take his lead from the students when practicable by beginning his lecture with a carefully framed question. He does this, in part, because he wants to involve his students even in his lecturing. Of the different ways of developing the lecture, the best one is usually the one that the students suggest by their answers. Their responses often have to be rephrased because they concern material too involved for them, or unavailable to them, or they require equipment or skills they do not have (11:12).

Most of all, the lecturer must be willing to leave the topic open. At times he must be willing not to give answers even though he knows them and may be tempted to impress students with his wealth of knowledge—for this might dampen the students' own desire to study the topic. He must not, as this lecturer said, steal from his students. Bane captures the essence of this idea when he says, "It is not inherent in the method that the lecturer should make ex cathedra pronouncements. He may, on the contrary, afford stimulus for thought and manifest a broad perspective for the apprehension of truth" (3:7). This, it seems, is what Dewey meant when he said, ". . . material should be supplied by way of stimulus, not with dogmatic finality and rigidity. When pupils get the notion that any field of study has been definitely surveyed, that knowledge about it is exhaustive and final, they may become docile pupils, but they cease to be students" (8:258).

(3) Also, the lecturer in the illustration has not concentrated on specific facts, but rather has directed the students' attention to the concepts, generalizations, and principles associated with the topic. The lecturer did not dispense minute details about cells and organs and tissues, as he might have done. One does not imagine that the students filled their notebooks with page after page of minutiae about the biology of life. The lecturer has, rather, drawn everyone's attention to such concepts as the "structure of life." He looked for the possibility of generalizing when he introduced biological facts.

The lecturer has done this in accordance with the notion that teaching, if its aim is the student's ultimate independence, must deal with generalizations and principles. Indeed, Hare points out that:

without principles most kinds of teaching are impossible, for what is taught is in most cases a principle ... that to learn to do anything is never to learn to do an individual act; it is always to learn to do acts of a certain kind in a certain kind of situation; and, this is to learn a principle. Thus, in learning to drive, I learn not to change gear *now*, but to change gear when the engine makes a certain kind of noise. If this were not so, instruction would be of no use at all; for if all an instructor could do were to tell us to change gear *now*, he would have to sit beside us for the rest of our lives in order to tell us just when, on each occasion, to change gear (10:60–61).

Student Involvement

(4) The lecturer has clearly involved the students in his lecture. This is in contrast to perhaps the strongest and most common criticism of the lecture method—that students remain passive absorbers of the speaker's message.

The most obvious consequence of this lack of opportunity to talk by students under the lecture method and the necessity of remaining quietly at their seats throughout the lecture is that the students become members of a lecture audience and are reduced to little more than background. The lighting in the lecture-room frequently accentuates this. The lecturer is the one upon whom all eyes and ears are focused. He is the individual with the greatest visibility and the one who is given the most attention. From this viewpoint, a lecture is a clear-cut affair in that the manners, characteristics, and message of a single person are central. It requires little effort for the lecturer to dominate the situation (5:164).

The students, though they spend most of their time listening, can be actively involved in the lecture, as the illustration by Hatch shows. The key disadvantage popularly associated with the lecture, then, "is not inherent in the method itself" (23:474). The lecturer cited above purposely got the students actively involved in the lecture (11:7). He involved the students by asking them questions to which he expected responses—not rhetorical questions that the students might brush aside and forget, but questions to which they had to respond. The students did respond, and their remarks were subsequently woven into the lecturer's presentation. The students helped to develop the lecture; they did not merely absorb it. This is what is meant by active rather than passive participation.

Another technique for actively involving the students in the lecture is to permit, or better, to encourage, the students to ask questions. This allows them to seek immediate clarification of ideas and expansion of points that are of particular interest and relevance. Further, this technique provides constant, continuous feedback to the lecturer. The students' questions indicate how well the lecturer is making his point and how well the students are receiving the message he thinks he is communicating. The danger, of course, is that so many questions will be asked that the lecturer will be forced to digress from his planned remarks. The lecturer, if he does allow and encourage questioning, must be careful that one or two students do not in fact disturb all the others. That is to say, the greatest percentage of students may indeed be able to follow and understand the lecturer, but these students may be thrown off the track by the interference in their listening/following momentum.

Many lecturers thus prefer that students save their questions until the end of the prepared presentation or ask them at a special critique period at a later time. The lecturer must choose between the advantages of immediate clarification, constant feedback, and comprehension by all the students on the one hand and disruption of the class by a small minority of students, digression from prepared remarks, loss of the flow of the lecture, and the possibility of not finishing prepared remarks on the other hand. There is no absolute way to tell each teacher which technique is best for each situation, since every situation is different. Naturally it is possible to combine these two lecture techniques by allowing for questions up to a point and then requesting that students hold them thereafter until the end of the lecture or until the critique period. Or it is possible to plan for questions at the ends of several sections of the lecture, and thus assure a continuous train of thought as well as a natural division of the lecture.

It is entirely possible for students to participate actively in a lecture without asking or responding to questions. It is entirely possible that the students are intellectually stimulated and are pondering the issues raised by the teacher. It is not correct to equate physical passivity with intellectual passivity (12). Yet, it is difficult for students to be involved in this manner over a long period of time, since their attention can and does stray easily.

Furthermore, the teacher has hardly any way of knowing whether the students are involved. Generally speaking, long periods of outward inactivity are signs of passive participation, or non-involvement.

The choices that the lecturer must make depend on the overall context—the number of students, whether or not a critique session is scheduled, the degree of complexity of the topic, the time of day. It is generally best to allow for some student questions and also to plan for sectional question periods. This will provide for active student involvement if the teacher himself does not ask questions that require student responses. It is not wise to assume that students will actively participate if they have remained silent for a long time. By asking several questions or responding to several, the lecturer not only increases the involvement of the student but also builds feedback into his lecture. Thus he can better suit his remarks to his students.

Lecturing without feedback can be diagrammed as a one-way system as follows (17:61):

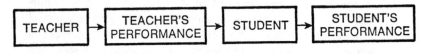

Figure 10–1*

With questions as one instrument for gaining feedback, the teacher, who has the power to alter the communication flow depicted above, can create a loop system diagrammed as follows (17:62):

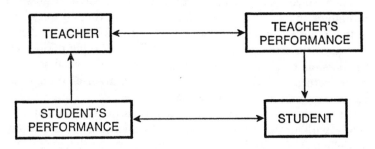

Figure 10–2*

* Reprinted with permission of journal and authors Kyle C. Packer and Toni Packer, from "Cybernetics, Information Theory, and the Educative Process," *Teachers College Record*, December 1959.

It is definitely possible to create a loop system when lecturing in spite of the popular image to the contrary. The advantages of doing so are too numerous and too obvious to detail.

Use of Props

(5) Lastly, the lecturer in the illustration augmented his verbal presentation with at least one pertinent diagram (of heart muscles) on the chalkboard. The use of props, whether they are chalkboard diagrams, overhead transparency projections, demonstrations, scale models, films, slides, maps, or mimeographed handout sheets, is very important. In describing the "secrets of master lecturers" Davis claims that the abundant use of examples is an essential element of an effective lecture (7:150). The lecturer, in addition to giving and soliciting examples, can effectively use the chalkboard to record and categorize the examples given. This also serves the purpose of reviewing examples that may not have been heard the first time.

Even a line drawing of a heart (Figure 10-3) on the chalkboard can be a most useful prop. The lecturer does not necessarily need expensive and elaborate equipment. Chalkboards are always available.

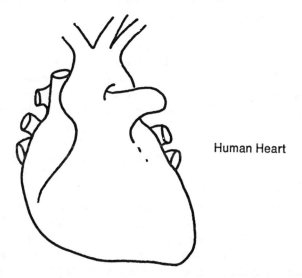

Human Heart

Figure 10-3

Or Figure 10-4 to represent the eastern coast of the United States.

Figure 10–4

An educational prop is not merely a gimmick to attract attention. It is much more than that. First, it serves to focus the attention of the student and the teacher (21:186). In any classroom there are many natural distractions that compete with the teacher for the students' attention. Obviously, the lecturer must seek to remove as many of them as possible. But once he has removed the distractions, he must provide a focus for his students' attention, and a prop is most effective for this (much more effective than the lecturer's voice).

An educational prop also serves as a reference point for subsequent remarks and questions. The lecturer has the opportunity to say, for example, "If you'll recall, these are the heart muscle branches we looked at before." The prop is something tangible—spoken unrecorded words are not—that the students and teacher can always return to and build upon.

An educational prop serves, too, as a respite from the constant talk of the lecturer. After continuously focusing on the lecturer, the student is given some relief and is then better able to pay attention to the lecture.

Most important, an educational prop serves to concretize the abstract nature of a lecture. Though students in secondary school and college have the cognitive maturity to deal with abstractions, they still have the need to visualize, smell, touch, taste, or hear (depending on the prop) empirical referents from time to time.

In short, props are essential and are often the key to the student's grasp and retention of the ideas set forth by the lecturer. Though the student is ready by the secondary school level to learn from oral presentations, since he is no longer developmentally dependent on firsthand experience to give meaning to abstractions or ideas about objects and phenomena, he still needs props, for they supply vicarious firsthand experience. Ausubel asserts that "even though an individual characteristically functions at the abstract level of cognitive development, when he is first introduced to a wholly unfamiliar subject-matter field he tends initially to function at a concrete, intuitive level" (1:271). The props provide the concrete referents the student needs. Bradley reports that a class in general physical science at Michigan State University taught by the lecture-demonstration method did as well as a similar class doing individual laboratory work (6:39). As Ausubel states:

On developmental grounds, he is ready at the secondary school level for a new type of verbal expository teaching that uses concrete-empirical experience primarily for *illustrative* purposes, *i.e.*, to clarify or dramatize truly abstract meanings rather than to generate intuitive meanings (1:272).

The lecture cited above was obviously intended to "kick off" a semester or unit of work. That is to say, the lecturer and student identified problems they would later investigate. The lecture method of teaching can be effectively employed for another pedagogical purpose, for recapitulating or analyzing or synthesizing at the middle or end of a unit of study. One can well imagine that after several weeks of work on the structure of life, the teacher might attempt a quite different type of lecture. He might very well ask his students to spend some of their class sessions taking a critical look at their own work.

The teacher who conducts such a lecture has the task of identifying, in his own preparation and then in the students' contributions during the class session, the key points that have been studied up to that time. That is to say, he must identify the important facts that have been learned in laboratory work and in class readings; he must also draw generalizations about the subject of study from the work that has been done so far. He can then treat the significance of each key point as it relates to the class theme of "What is life?" and he can also show how these points, which may seem disjointed, fit together. This synthesis will point the students to further questions. In this way the teacher can bring some order into what may appear as chaos to some students. Walton has aptly characterized the purpose of the lecture as a "guide through [the] bewildering thickets of information that characterize most fields of study" (22:144).

The teacher in the example being analyzed is indeed teaching, not just speaking before an audience. He is seeking to develop his students' independence by encouraging them to question, to study on their own, and to learn generalizations and principles. There are several additional techniques and pointers for lecturing that a teacher may employ, but which are not necessarily evident in the illustrative lecture.

Other Lecture Techniques

First, one technique for clearly formulating the ideas he wishes to present is for the lecturer to tell himself in all seriousness, "If my students were to learn only one thing from this lecture, I would prefer it to be that ————." Or, to put it another way, "If a student's friend or father asked him what the main thought he learned today was, I would hope he would reply that ————." The lecturer will no doubt wish to make several points. Four or five seem best, for if there are more than that, they tend to lose their individual force. In this case the lecturer would do well to proceed with similar self-questioning to arrive at his key points. This technique will give unity to the lecture. Such unity is most important in maintaining the active participation of the students and in establishing the value of the lecture in the students' minds.

It is generally effective for the lecturer to open his lecture by dramatically stating the key points he wishes to make. This has the positive effect of attracting the students' attention, and it also gives them a clear framework within which they can understand the subsequent development and justification of the lecturer's ideas. It further minimizes the need for note-taking that sometimes proves to be a distraction, instead of an aid. This is the technique employed by Woodrow Wilson in his professional tenure at Princeton University. Wilson, who was known as the outstanding lecturer of his day, was described by Bane as follows: "At the beginning of a lecture he read from manuscript four or five striking generalizations to be taken down verbatim by his students. The remainder of his lecture was but an elaboration of these statements" (3:66).

In thus formulating his lecture, the lecturer serves as the model of a person grappling with the "thickets" of the subject matter. He provides a model for how to analyze and synthesize.

He does what he will expect his students to be able to do. He allows them to witness and participate in his endeavor. The lecturer is, in fact, proclaiming, "Do as I do." This is what Loud, who in general opposes lecturing, refers to in his few positive statements about this method:

> I expect the student to witness a distinctive competence and a distinctive commitment to a particular intellectual undertaking. I want the student to recognize a scrupulous use of technical language and some uniquely significant selection, emphasis, and organization of problem material. I hope that the student—if he is, in fact, successfully led step by step through an analysis—will experience a reassurance that the problems and procedures of this science are, after all, intelligible (14:31).

Second, as was pointed out earlier, the lecturer must strive to stimulate the students intellectually. He should strive to make them active participants. One way of doing this is to ask the students questions. A second way is to respond to the questions the students ask. These are indeed good and useful techniques that quickly come to mind. Another important technique, which is not common, deserves careful consideration, for it serves to point up that, while lecturing is a mass method, learning is individual. *The lecturer must teach in such a way as to stimulate each student.*

This technique, suggested by Gotesky (9), essentially involves teaching the students critical thinking by indirection, that is, through the deliberate insertion of false, misleading, or irrelevant data, or faulty reasoning, into the lecture as supposed supports for the generalizations, conclusions, interpretations, and syntheses that are being made. Obviously, this requires careful planning on the part of the teacher. It requires that the teacher, in all fairness, serve notice of his intentions to the students at the *outset*. Or, he must do so at least the first few times he tries this technique in order to alert and accustom students to the technique. It also requires him to allow students to interrupt when they detect "errors" and to set aside time at the end of the lecture for a critique session. During the critique, the teacher and students should carefully review the steps in the lecture, point out where the errors occurred, and indicate the consequences that resulted from these errors. This is absolutely essential, for without it the point of the technique is lost. Without it, students who did not detect the errors on their own will learn errors. Obviously, this all presupposes that the students already have learned or are now learning some fundamentals of clear thinking, e.g., what constitutes a valid conclusion and what constitutes a good reason.

The lecturer is in essence teaching the students on two levels at the same time—he is teaching the subject matter at hand, e.g., history or physics, and he is teaching the skills of listening and clear thinking. Indeed, one strong justification for employing the lecture method, and this technique in particular, is that listening is a necessary skill for mature adults. "One of the characteristics of an educated person is his ability to listen intelligently. The large group can help the pupil to develop this ability" (12:100). Listening skill here indicates not just the ability to recall what the lecturer has said. It also means the ability to follow remarks. It includes the student's ability to assess the validity of the lecturer's conclusions, the adequacy of his reasons, the relevance of his evidence, and the quality of the basic issues involved in disputes treated. This is a tall order, but, nonetheless, a mature adult needs this ability. Without it he cannot function independently. Gotesky claims that the lecturer must not be concerned with rote learning as it is typically described, but must transform the lecture into an instrument for developing the critical listening skills suggested (9).

The following should illustrate this point. A teacher, before beginning a lecture on the current economic scene of the United States, alerts his students to the fact that he will deliberately contradict himself in his forthcoming analysis. He asks the students not to interrupt him when he makes his mistakes but to jot down the contradiction in their notes (without alerting their classmates). This, he says, will give each student the challenge of catching the lecturer. He announces that he will allow ten minutes after the lecture for the students to point out this deliberate error and its consequences. Such a technique presents an opportunity for the teacher and the students, not only to correct the errors made in the lecture and thus arrive at a better understanding of the subject matter at hand, but also to explore the fundamentals of critical listening and thinking.

The teacher proceeds, and during the course of the lecture he says:

One of the strengths of the American economic system is that it is based on the free choices of the open market. The seller and buyer mutually decide the price of goods and services. If, for example, the seller offers

Christmas cards at one dollar a box, the buyer can decide on his own whether or not to purchase them at that price. If he decides not to, the seller, since he will be left with Christmas cards in January, may decide to store them until the next December, or he may offer them on sale for seventy cents or less, in order to induce buying. The point is that the market is open, and price fluctuates according to competition and supply and demand; in other words, according to the law of supply and demand, which is the basic economic law of our country. . . .

Indeed the government as of late has become interested in the consumer just as it became interested in the laborer earlier. Accordingly it has established various agencies to protect the consumer. These agencies examine the rates of electric power companies, telephone companies, railroads, and airlines. They then set a fair price on their products and services. Actually this is a governmental service to the consumer since the individual himself cannot easily fight the big corporations. In effect there is, for this reason, no price competition in the telephone business or in electricity. The buyer cannot negotiate his price with the big monopolistic corporations. Nor can he go elsewhere to buy electricity and telephone service. He either pays the price or does without the goods, and in today's society he cannot very well do without electricity or a telephone. He has no choice, because there is no open market. So you see, in these important, fundamental industries there is no competition; and these industries set the tone for the entire country. . . .

When he has finished, the teacher opens the floor for a critique period. Here the students will hopefully note the lecturer's contradiction about the open market and the possibility for resolving that conflict. With this technique the teacher sharpens the critical listening skills of the students. The critique period is essential because it is then that the teacher will drive home his lesson in listening, as well as correct any substantive errors, so that the students will not retain false data or conclusions. Errors in the illustration may seem obvious to the reader, but may not be at all evident to a student hearing them in the context of an entire lecture.

As the students become more adept at noting other intentional errors, such as false data, insinuations, invalid conclusions, and irrelevant supporting data, the lecturer can inject more subtle mistakes into the lecture, in order to refine even further the students' listening skills. The point is that the teacher uses these devices to encourage active, and individual, participation by the students; he uses these devices to teach both his substantive topic and the skill of critical listening.

This is a somewhat difficult technique to employ, and the

teacher is cautioned to use it with care. But he is encouraged to use it, nevertheless, for it is, as Gotesky states, a way of transforming the lecture "into an instrument for developing critical thought" rather than keeping it as an "instrument for rote-learning" (9:180).

To use the devices suggested above, a lecturer must know exactly what he is doing. He must know exactly when to use false data, misleading data, or irrelevant conclusions. Moreover—and this is particularly important—he must know exactly how his assignments are logically related to his lecture. For example, he must know exactly where in his lecture and assignments data and conclusions, implicit and explicit, are in conflict. Last, he must employ pedagogic devices that place the student in the position to discover false or misleading information, or irrelevant or implausible conclusions.
This is far from easy (9:187).

Far from easy—but quite useful in making the lecture an effective teaching method.

Third, in order to keep physically inactive students intellectually active, alert, and attentive, the lecturer must present his remarks in a lively, vibrant manner. He must use his voice to good advantage. Indeed the unique characteristic of a live-voice presentation, as opposed to a recording or printing of a lecture, is the potential for employing "aliveness" to make the point. This is, in fact, another justification for the lecture method.

There is, with those few who know how to employ it, a penetrating power of persuasion in the human voice which the secondary hieroglyphics of print cannot match; an intimacy, even with large audiences, not to be challenged as yet—improvable as they are—even by the devices of broadcasting. Politicians know this only too well (20:20).

The lecturer must show, through appropriate modulation and clear enunciation, that he himself is interested in the topic and that what he has to say is important. His presentation must have aliveness and dramatic quality. Otherwise the students might just as well read, as hear, the lecture. He must use his very presence, as well as his voice and gestures, to help him make his points. "Principally, I expect the student to be *affected*. I expect the personality of the lecturer to make an impression that reading the lecture in article form would not make" (14:31).

This all sounds quite obvious—almost too obvious. Yet students are quick to indicate that all too often lecturers are dull and boring. The students' attention may wander so much that they literally do not perceive the words being spoken. Witness the many ingenious, as well as common, games students who sit next to each other play in order to "pass the time": tic-tac-toe, dots and squares, word square, etc. Bloom reports that about 31 percent of the time students' thoughts during a lecture are irrelevant, or not on the matter at hand. This includes (a) thoughts about persons, objects, and events not in the classroom environment and (b) tangential thoughts about words and phrases used (5:166).

Lack of attention on the part of the students is potentially the great limitation of the lecture method. Thus it is wise for the lecturer to use language that the students will not find puzzling and difficult to understand. It is excellent practice for the lecturer to provide comic relief in his talk. This is not to say that the lecturer must be an entertainer. Rather, he must use humor to relieve tension, refocus the attention of students who may be distracted, and create a mutual bond with the students. Laughter is important in teaching because people who laugh together are basically communicating their feelings to one another. Peters, the British philosopher, puts it this way:

The great teachers are those who can conduct such a shared exploration in accordance with canons, and convey, at the same time, the contagion of a shared enterprise in which all are united by a common zeal. That is why humor is such a valuable aid to teachers; for if people can laugh together they step out of the shadows of self-reference cast by age, sex, and position. This creation of a shared experience can act as a catalyst which releases a class to unite in their common enterprise (18:105).

Horace Kallen even connects laughter with democracy and liberation. He goes so far as to call laughter the "secret weapon" of man's expression of his freedom.

Carl Sandburg signalizes it as the spirit of democracy. For laughter shows up the irreverence of the strong for the weak, blows its preponderance down to parity, and lifts the weak's subservience up to liberty. Laughter is the familiar secret weapon of the peaceful war of all against all, lowering the mighty from their seat and exalting those of low degree. Among the patron gods of men who would be free, the God of Laughter has no peer (13:196).

The humor suggested here is not the type that stems from, "I shall precede my remarks with a story about what happened to me today on the way to the classroom. . . ." Humor of this type is tiring and difficult to tolerate on a steady basis. Rather, lecture humor should be spontaneous and should arise from the flow of remarks or events. Such humor is difficult to describe, since its context and timing are so much a part of it; it is ad-libbed and genuine. This is the kind of humor a teacher must use and rely on.

Another good device that the lecturer can employ to promote the effective use of his voice and to capitalize on the ongoing situation is *not* to write out his lecture. In this way he can play it by ear and "feel more or less reliably whether the excitement or clarification he is trying to convey actually reaches the larger portion of the assembled group before him" (14:31). In order to compensate for not knowing exactly how long to spend on each subtopic, which he would know if he were to write out his remarks, the lecturer should carefully outline his lecture and note in the margins the time he wishes to allot for each section. This device will assure him of finishing what he sets out to say.

Fourth, it is essential that a lecturer see to it that his students are adept at note-taking. If the students do not know the proper method of taking notes, then the teacher must teach them the skill. "Early in any course the conscientious teacher will find out what sort of notes his students are taking and adjust himself accordingly. He cannot evade this issue" (3:117). On the one hand, note-taking can help students to pay attention to the lecturer and to listen for key points. It further provides them with physical activity while they sit. Notes are also a personal means of reviewing and "rehearsing" the lecture, which is probably not recorded and might otherwise be forgotten. On the other hand, improper note-taking can distract the student from listening carefully. A student may be so busy jotting down notes or attempting to take down sentences verbatim that he cannot grasp the meaning of the lecture as a whole. He may lose the flow of the lecturer's remarks and miss key points.

The lecturer may find that writing a brief, simple outline on the chalkboard at the outset will help the students to follow his talk and to take clear notes (15:17). Sometimes it is quite helpful to distribute a printed outline or set of notes. This technique will not only increase the likelihood that the students will follow the lecturer's ideas, but it also will give the students tangible aid in reviewing the lecture at a later date. In all cases, what is handed out should be simple. According to Davis, simplicity in lecture design and the abundant use of examples are the important secrets of master lecturers (17:150).

Fifth, the length of the lecture is a critical factor in its effectiveness. The most common length of lectures for adults is about one hour; this is based on the average adult attention span. For younger secondary school students, the lecturer may find that the optimum length ranges from twenty to forty minutes. There is no way of knowing in advance what will suit a particular class, especially one not accustomed to listening to lectures. The secondary school teacher is wise to start with a short (twenty-minute) lecture and then increase the length of subsequent lectures as the students gain in listening skill and attention span.

References

1. Ausubel, David P. "Implications of Preadolescent and Early Adolescent Cognitive Development for Secondary School Teaching." *High School Journal* 45:268–275, April 1962.

2. Ausubel, David P. "In Defense of Verbal Learning." *Educational Theory* 11:15–25, January 1961.

3. Bane, Charles L. *The Lecture in College Teaching*. Boston: Richard G. Badger, 1931.

4. Bayles, Ernest E. *Pragmatism in Education*. New York: Harper and Row, 1966.

5. Bloom, B. S. "Thought-Processes in Lectures and Discussions." *Journal of General Education* 7:160–169, April 1953.

6. Bradley, Robert L. "Lecture Demonstration Versus Individual Laboratory Work in a General Education Science Course." *Journal of Experimental Education* 34:33–42, Fall 1965.

7. Davis, Robert J. "Secrets of Master Lecturers." *Improving College and University Teaching* 13:150–151, Summer 1965.

8. Dewey, John. *How We Think: A Restatement of the Relation of Reflective Thinking to the Educative Process*. Boston: D. C. Heath, 1933.

9. Gotesky, Rubin. "The Lecture and Critical Thinking." *Educational Forum* 30:179–187, January 1966.

10. Hare, R. M. *The Language of Morals*. New York: Oxford University Press, 1952.

11. Hatch, Winslow R. *Approach to Teaching*. Washington, D.C.: U.S. Department of Health, Education, and Welfare, 1966.

12. Heller, Melvin P. "Learning through Lectures." *Clearing House* 37:99–100, October 1962.

13. Kallen, Horace M. "The Comic Spirit in the Freedom of Man." *Teachers College Record* 68:187–196, December 1966.

14. Loud, Oliver S. "Lecture and Discussion in General Education." *Journal of General Education* 8:30–33, October 1954.

15. McKeachie, Wilbert J. *Teaching Tips*. 5th ed. Ann Arbor, Mich.: George Wahr, 1965.

16. Northrop, F. S. C. *The Logic of the Sciences and the Humanities.* New York: Meridian Books, 1959.

17. Packer, C. Kyle, and Toni Packer. "Cybernetics, Information Theory, and the Educative Process." *Teachers College Record* 61:134–142, December 1959. Reprinted in *Teaching: Vantage Points for Study,* edited by Ronald T. Hyman (Philadelphia: J. B. Lippincott, 1968), pp. 58–69.

18. Peters, R. S. "Education as Initiation." In *Philosophical Analysis and Education,* edited by Reginald D. Archambault, pp. 87–111. New York: Humanities Press, 1965.

19. Popham, W. James. *Tape Recorded Lectures in the College Classroom—An Experimental Appraisal.* Pittsburg, Kans.: Kansas State College of Pittsburg, 1960.

20. Quiller-Couch, Arthur. *A Lecture on Lectures.* London: Hogarth Press, 1927.

21. Vavoulis, Alexander. "Lecture vs. Discussion." *Improving College and University Teaching* 12:185–189, Summer 1964.

22. Walton, John. *Toward Better Teaching in the Secondary Schools.* Boston: Allyn and Bacon, 1966.

23. Wesley, Edgar B. *Teaching the Social Studies.* Boston: D. C. Heath, 1942.

4 Role-Playing

II Introduction to Role-Playing

"The games we play
To fill the frittered minutes of a day
Good glasses are to read the spirit through. . . ."*
—*"Dear Friend," Edwin Arlington Robinson*

In the next two chapters, the third major method of teaching, role-playing, will be treated. The role-playing method of teaching is not new by any means, in spite of the attention it is now receiving in all quarters. For many years law students have conducted moot courts, and the general student body has conducted mock political conventions. Nevertheless, simulation techniques are now experiencing their greatest development. We shall treat the underlying justification of simulation games and sociodrama, examples, techniques for employing these methods, and the organization of teachers and students in order to utilize these techniques. First, some definitional distinctions will be made between simulation, game, simulation game, sociodrama, and dramatization, all of which are essentially role-playing methods.

Working Definitions

Simulation is a "general term referring to constructing and operating on a model that replicates behavioral processes" (22:8). "A simulation is an operating imitation of a real process" (3:29). Moot courts and mock political conventions are examples of simulation.

"*A game* may be defined as any contest (play) among adversaries (players) operating under constraints (rules) for an objective (winning, victory, or payoff). . . . [Games] have the characteristics

* Reprinted with permission of Charles Scribner's Sons from Edwin Arlington Robinson's poem, "Dear Friend," in *The Children of the Night*.

of reciprocal actions and reactions among at least partly independent entities having different objectives" (2:5). Checkers and poker are examples.

A game is a learned cultural sequence characterized by six factors:

1. Roles: The game assigns roles to the human beings involved.
2. Rules: A game sets up a set of rules which hold only during the game sequence.
3. Goals: Every game has its goals or purpose. The goal of baseball is to score more runs than the opponents. The goals of the game of psychology are more complex and less explicit but they exist.
4. Rituals: Each game has its conventional behavior pattern not related to the goals or rules but yet quite necessary to comfort and continuance.
5. Language: Each game has its jargon, unrelated to the rules and goals and yet necessary to learn and use.
6. Values: Each game has its standards of excellence or goodness (32:104).

Simulation game refers to a combination of a simulation and a game. In such a game people assume the roles of decision-makers, act as if they were actually involved in real life, and compete for certain objectives (i.e., try to win) according to specified rules. "*Simulation games* are operating models of central features of real or proposed systems or processes. Scenarios are developed, roles are defined in interacting systems, and players are given goals, resources, and rules. They then make the system 'go,' trying out alternative strategies within the system constraints presented" (29). "War or Peace," described in Chapter 12, is a simulation game.

Sociodrama refers to group problem-solving that enables people to explore real-life situations through spontaneous enactments followed by guided discussion (43:9). "A sociodrama is a re-creation of a dilemma in human relations through spontaneous and faithful enactment of the roles with accompanying feelings involved in the situation" (47:7). Compared with simulation games, sociodrama involves more freewheeling by the participants, in that there are few rules, resources, and specific goals (other than to solve the given problem). An example of sociodrama appears in Chapter 13.

Sociodrama should be distinguished from a third form of role-playing: *dramatization*. A dramatization is merely the playing out of roles decided upon in advance—for example, an enactment of the signing of the Declaration of Independence as it occurred in

1776. Dramatization lacks the elements of spontaneity and unknown resolution, features of sociodrama. Nevertheless, this form of role-playing has several advantages and can be used in teaching. For example, in dramatization by students, an historical event can come to life, and the interplay among people involved in the original event can then be better understood. However, sociodrama must not be confused with dramatization.

Many people today do not make clear the distinctions among the terms *simulation, games,* and *simulation games.* In many places these three terms are used interchangeably. Yet, upon close consideration of the definitions offered above, it is clear, for example, that not every simulation involves a game, nor does every game involve a simulation (15; 16). At a time when simulation games are being used increasingly—and these games are now being developed by curriculum projects and commercial publishing houses—it is important for teachers to understand their nature and characteristics. In particular, it is important for them to remember that these games combine the characteristics of games and simulations.

Also, as a sociodrama conforms more to the rules, regulations, setting, and roles of an actual situation (e.g., an angered district attorney examining an innocent murder suspect), it becomes a simulation of a social relation. The distinction between sociodrama and simulation turns out to be a matter of the degree to which the role-playing represents an actual situation. But the essential elements of a sociodrama and a simulation are the same.

The definitions offered above are working definitions. It is very possible that they may be further refined as these methods are more fully developed by social scientists, physical scientists, and teachers.

Underlying Justifications

Those who support simulation games and sociodrama as teaching methods are guided by a point of view in which a few major arguments and many subordinate points are included. *The first of these arguments* claims that teaching by the use of simulation games* is a continuation of the very method students have used

---

* Although only simulation games will be referred to for simplicity's sake in the section on justification, it should be borne in mind that what is said about simulation games almost always applies to sociodrama as well. The important exception concerns the element of competition, which is present in some simulation games but not in sociodrama.

in order to gain knowledge all their lives. That is to say, people learn to act by acting; they learn to live by living; they learn to do things by doing them. And simulation games present this very opportunity, a specifically designed, limited framework in which the teacher teaches about selected aspects of life by having his students actively engage in them.

Children all over engage in mimetic play, in which they practice and learn about life (12). Children play, for example, house, school, doctor and nurse, cowboys and Indians, cops and robbers, and army. By engaging in role-playing they practice the actions they have observed or heard about, and in this way internalize them. This type of play is important as well as enjoyable for the child (12; 28; 30).

Children also learn to play completely fabricated games quite early in life.* They play simple games at first like jacks, hopscotch, tag, red light, and giant steps. Then they move on to more complicated games such as checkers and kickball. Eventually some move on to even more complex games like chess. Since games and play are things all children participate in, supporters of simulation games say, "What could be more natural, then, than to continue the play-learning process in the schools? It would exploit a behavioral mode toward which children are already strongly motivated, and by the use of which they have repeatedly demonstrated impressive learning performances" (2:7).

Lest we think that it is only within the last decade that teachers have recognized the commonness and value of play, let us recall how Dewey in 1899 approvingly summarized one of Froebel's principles from the first half of the nineteenth century:

That the primary root of all educative activity is in the instinctive, impulsive attitudes and activities of the child, and not in the presentation and application of external material, whether through the ideas of others or through the senses; and that, accordingly, numberless spontaneous activities of children, plays, games, mimic efforts, even the apparently meaningless motions of infants—exhibitions previously

---

* It is important to remember that *games* and *play* are not synonymous. Not all play involves contests, an essential element of games. For instance, children playing house are not competing to win. Nor is every game play. Though amateurs may "play at" a game, professional athletes do not. On the other hand, it cannot hurt to remember that many people consider children's playing house a game, since game is used here in a very broad sense.

ignored as trivial, futile, or even condemned as positively evil—are capable of educational use; nay, are the foundation-stones of educational method (24:117).

Socrates himself said something on this matter in Plato's *Republic*, Book VII (38:336):

"The free man must not learn anything coupled with slavery. For bodily labours under compulsion do no harm to the body, but no compulsory learning can remain in the soul."
"True," said he.
"No compulsion, then, my good friend," said I, "in teaching children; train them by a kind of game, and you will be able to see more clearly the natural bent of each."

By using the method of simulation games the teacher builds upon the knowledge and skills the student brings to the teaching situation. The student at home and on the street has learned how to play make-believe and how to compete to win a game. With simulation games the teacher continues what has already been a highly popular and effective mode of activity for the student (20). With simulation games it is indeed possible for a student to learn and have fun at the same time (8:130; 18:109).

Moreover, according to James Coleman, a director of the Johns Hopkins center for developing simulation games, the use of simulation reverses a common situation for the student. Instead of having learning as his primary goal, the student has learning of the material as a secondary motivation, a step necessary to reach his goal—i.e., winning of the simulation game (19:70). In a simulation game, the student "is assimilating the material in order to be able to efficiently carry out actions toward his goal" (19:70). Hence, simulation games encourage the student to learn, since learning is directly pertinent to goal attainment. Thus, this teaching method differs greatly from those in which the teacher sets up learning as the students' primary goal. It is for this reason that its supporters claim that the simulation game represents not merely a new gimmick but a "fundamental change" from the concept of teaching as the transmitting of knowledge (19:75).

Motivation

The second main argument for the simulation game technique centers on the motivations which arise with the use of these games. People, especially young people, like to play games.

"Animals and humans love to explore, to try things out, to be the causes of effects. Games provide this kind of participant pleasure" (1:3). Since a student already has the motivation to play, he will therefore learn, since learning is required in order to play and win. Thus, the teacher has great leverage in harnessing the motivation that the student brings with him to the teaching situation. This is significant because the problem of motivation is one that faces many teachers.

Furthermore, this participant pleasure, active participation rather than spectator participation, spurs the student on to keen study. As an active participant in a confrontation, he can see and sense the issues as they arise. The identification with a particular side compels continued probing. Herman Kahn, who has used simulation games at the highest levels of international policy study, says, "Most people are naturally partisan. Just as lawyers for two litigants are likely to do a better job of raising and investigating the issues involved in a dispute than if they sat as judges, so does the role-playing in a game make for a more intense and thorough investigation. In addition most people trying to understand the reactions of others in a complicated hypothetical situation are more effective if they are forced to identify actively with one of the participants" (31:164–165).

This built-in motivational thrust obtained from simulation games is for many people the "clearest advantage" of using this method (2:22; 40:64). In a study involving students from ages ten to nineteen playing games of logic, Robert W. Allen concludes that motivation increases with games. In regard to this matter he states that "the motivation provided by the games was the most important single factor in the learning situation" (5:79). Similarly, in reviewing the findings of six simulation studies, Cherryholmes concludes that the motivation was high when the teacher employed simulation games (15; 17).

The motivating power of games has long been evident (23; 27; 28). According to Huizinga (30), play lies at the very basis of civilization. Play and games are essential to man, and man has a natural desire to play. Play is an integral part of man. It is not something he has invented in order to avoid work. As much as the term *homo sapiens* is appropriate for man, so is *homo ludens*, man the player. In commenting on Huizinga's claim, Phenix says, "It is clearly evident that play, far from being a trivial and peripheral human activity, has been one of the fundamental factors in the creation of culture. The impulse to play is deeply rooted in human nature, and from it have sprung the most varied flowerings of civilization—in language, law, philosophy, religion, science and the arts. When the play spirit dies, the freshness, joy, and spontaneity of life are quenched, and routine, compulsion, and mechanization supervene" (36:300).

This power to motivate has its strongest impact on those students who are labeled "unmotivated" or, to use a current phrase, on those students who are "turned off." This term most often refers to the slow student or the disadvantaged student who fails to comprehend how he benefits from fully engaging himself in the teaching situation (19:71). Such a student, if he sees a benefit at all, sees it as lying so distant in the future that it fails to excite him. He may be unmotivated because the situation, in his judgment, is not relevant to his present life. It is in this way that motivation and relevance are linked. "The greatest problem, then, appears to be due to a mismatching of time. The child is being taught for a future whose needs have not yet impressed themselves upon him; hence he sees little need to focus his energies upon learning. He is, moreover, being taught for a future that is different from that his familiar adults are presently experiencing. The rapidity of social change induces uncertainty about what skills will be relevant to it" (9:217).

Simulation games provide a means for making the topic at hand relevant in the present. The student needs to gain knowledge in order to win *now*. Hence, the material is relevant to the student's goal of playing to win. "The contents of games are inherently relevant to any participating players, because to achieve their immediate objectives they must know these contents. If students enjoy a game at all, they must be interested in its content. If that content consists of facts, processes, and concepts to be learned, then the players will try to learn these simply to perform well in the game" (1:4).

Also, the student can, within the limited time and space framework of the simulation game, take on the future roles. He can see what the future might demand of him if he chooses to follow certain courses. He can for the moment turn the present into the future and sample that future. Likewise, he can turn the past into the present and can sample the issues that faced others who lived before him. He can, in effect, act in the past and thus better understand it. In being able to manipulate time and space, the student has the opportunity to participate in events that otherwise might be irrelevant to him because of their distance from him.

This ability to transform the present into the future is particularly important for those students who find the time interval between learning and its application too long (41:8).

Students must believe, and believe correctly, that what they learn will be useful to them as adults. Utility here should be defined broadly, to include not only practical career guidance and training, but also the appreciation of general intellectual and social values. Students should have reason to believe that what they learn will help them to understand, predict, and control to a socially acceptable degree their own future environment, as well as their own actions in it (1:10).

Through simulation games the student can eliminate the interval between learning and applying. He can learn and apply soon thereafter. He can see how and what knowledge helps him to deal with his future and his past. He can thereby tie the present, the future, skills, values, and knowledge all together to make the ongoing situation relevant and meaningful to him.

Students who are slow or disadvantaged or unmotivated receive simulation games positively, for it is primarily they who have difficulty in merging the aspiration of the present with preparations for the future. Disadvantaged students have little motivation "even for such a basic skill as reading, since the lives of their family and friends include little reading" (9:217). But the problem is not theirs alone. Students from all economic levels find little motivation for the present in studying advanced subjects that are particularly geared to the distant future. By manipulating time, simulation games afford these students the opportunity of dealing with the future while enjoying the present.

Education conceived within the framework of play will be increasingly necessary as a preparation for living in an age of growing leisure. If leisure is to be anything more than the absence of work—and what a dreary conception that is—if it is to be a kind of activity in which genuinely humane qualities may grow and prosper, then there must be a preparation for this creative sort of living through education conducted in the spirit of play (36:307–308).

Simulation games have the ability to stretch the attention span of students by giving them an added motivation. This is true of all students, since attention span is closely connected with motivation. Simulation games provide not only initial motivation but also continuing motivation since the interaction among the players serves to keep the goal before the student at all times (33:32). The pleasure of playing, the active participation, and the suspense about outcome all combine to lengthen the time a student will attend to the ongoing activity. Furthermore, as the student continues to play, his comprehension of the interrelationships among key elements of the game increases, and this serves to sustain his interest. He begins to see that variables do not stand alone as he strategically maneuvers toward his goal. "The purpose of the game is to be suggestive and illustrative—to stimulate and provoke the players and to increase their understanding of situations involving the interaction of a large number of more or less independent forces and to give examples, i.e., scenarios" (31:165). This leads to the next main argument.

Thinking and Learning Involved

The third argument for simulation games concerns the types of thinking that this method encourages and gets the student to practice. Simulation games motivate and reward critical thinking in that they involve analyzing possible moves and probable consequences of those moves. This is particularly true since winning necessitates not only careful planning of one's own moves but also analysis of the moves of opponents. Thus the game, in the playing, demonstrates to the student the value of analysis, rational planning, and countering moves. Indeed, simulation games are basically devices for critical "if A, then B" type thinking (31:166).

In addition to critical thinking, simulation games also encourage intuitive thinking. A player can benefit from intuition if it leads him to his goal, short-range or long-range, "because results rather than methods are stressed" (1:5). Though intuitive solutions are risky because of the complexities of strategy planning (10:89), even if the student fails, his penalty will be limited to the game—he is taking no real risk. The student can therefore come to see that sometimes intuitive thinking is preferable over critical analysis, which, though less risky, is slower. The results of intuitive thinking and critical thinking are there for the player to assess (and to recall later when deciding whether to rely on his intuitive judgment or critical analysis).

Moreover, simulation games also can demonstrate that life is not always affected by logical plans or even intuitive solutions. Indeed, chance has a significant effect on the life of every man. No man can completely control his life. Unpredictable natural disasters and so-called "acts of God" do affect our lives all the time. Remote, unpredictable activities of other men, even on another continent, can also affect us deeply. For this reason, in part,* designers have deliberately included a chance variable in the simulation game (26:80). For example, in the Life Career game designed by the Johns Hopkins group "a chance or luck factor is built into the game by the use of spinners and dice" (8:108). The player, through playing, comes to understand to some degree the effect of chance. The interaction between planned moves (decided upon either through critical or intuitive thinking) and chance moves is evident to the student as he participates in the activity.

The chance element in simulation games has another function also. As students deal with chance, they come to realize the value of rules. Only when all the players observe the rules can a player win even in games of chance. "With games of chance, the potential win is the same for all players, and this truth encourages the child to learn to obey and respect the rules" (7:11).

The fourth main argument for this type of teaching concerns the actual playing of the simulation game. According to Clark C. Abt, a leading designer (and proponent) of simulation games, the student is learning on three levels while participating—he is: "(1) learning *facts* expressed in the game context and dynamics; (2) learning *processes* simulated by the game; and (3) learning the relative costs and benefits, risks and potential rewards of *alternative strategies* of decision-making" (2:19). That is to say, the student learns a combination of facts, processes, and strategies as the simulation game proceeds. Furthermore, in a multistudent simulation game, students differ as to which level they are on at any given time. Thus, by using a simulation game the teacher can teach on three levels simultaneously.

It is levels two and three, processes and alternative strategies of decision-making that are particularly noteworthy. Decision-making processes are quite complex and therefore difficult to talk about and understand. It is possible to teach these complex processes through the simulation-game technique because each student will be facing concrete examples of the processes. Simulation games

present *concrete* problems in a simplified but dramatic form that mediates between abstraction and confusion, between dry theory and

---

* See also the ninth argument: on suitability for a wide range of student abilities.

multi-variable reality. . . . Games present simultaneously progressing multiple interactions that can first be examined one at a time, and then gradually together with increasing comprehensibility (2:20).

People learn to make decisions by engaging in, not talking about, decision-making. Moreover, a person can witness the consequences of a decision he makes in a simulation game. The effects of a decision will be felt without any belaboring of the point. The results of a particular decision are fed back rapidly and concretely. They are felt before the student can forget the factors that led to the decision. Assessment for future decision-making is both facilitated and made necessary. "In a simulated situation students get a sense of the reality of decision-making. They learn that it's not as simple as it seems in textbooks" (14:64).

The same pertains to the development of alternative strategies. The very workings of a simulation game lead the student to the recognition that he must develop a strategy in order to succeed. As he becomes more alert to the play within the game, he starts developing alternative strategies. He can assess the value of strategy development by carefully observing the consequences of his strategy as play continues. "While games may teach *more* than winning strategies, the learning of strategies has in a sense priority over other possible learning. It is the most direct outcome of playing a game and thus, I would conjecture, the point where the game is likely to have the strongest impact" (42:151).

It is this characteristic of complex alternative strategies that appeals to bright students in particular. Whereas simulation games serve as a motivation technique for slow or disadvantaged students, they provide a vehicle for bright students to develop alternative strategies; such students enjoy developing, manipulating, and altering strategies. Simulation games offer the opportunity to continually think of new variations of strategy. However, the range of students who can play the game productively is great; "the same game may be played successfully—usually at a less sophisticated level, but not always—by children who perform poorly in school" (21:70).

Social Values

Fifth, simulation games provide a vehicle for teaching certain social values (see 25:159–163 and 32:13–108). Outstanding among these are competition, cooperation, and empathy. By virtue of the fact that they are playing a game, the students compete to win. But in contrast with competition they engage in elsewhere, they know exactly what the rules are. They know whom they are competing against, and they know what constitutes winning. They learn that to compete is acceptable and enjoyable. They learn, through introspection and retrospection, in what way they can better compete. In short, such competition is presented as an acceptable value in our society.

At the same time, however, teachers can teach students the advantages of cooperating. Many current simulation games, e.g., Seal Hunting (developed by Abt) and Disaster (developed at Johns Hopkins), clearly indicate that players have to cooperate in order to play and win. The need to cooperate with other players, as opposed to merely competing against them, is built into such games. By cooperating on problems that affect the attainment of their goals, students come to understand the social value of co-operation.

Through simulation games students can take on the roles of others. They often become very involved in these roles. To the extent that the student identifies with the person he is portraying, he becomes sensitive to the feelings of that person. Indeed, for George Mead, the very process of socialization involves being able to take on the roles of other people and also to see oneself as if one were another person. When the student plays a game,

each one of his own acts is determined by his assumption of the action of the others who are playing the game. What he does is controlled by his being everyone else on that team, at least in so far as those attitudes affect his own particular response.... He must also, in the same way that he takes the attitudes of other individuals toward one another, take their attitudes toward the various phases or aspects of the common social activity (34:154–155).

If he plays a legislator, for example, and fully identifies, the student will come to feel as a legislator. By taking on the role of another person, the student often emphasizes—and sometimes sympathizes—with that person. The teacher can show the students how a legislator feels when confronted by the conflicts inherent in democratic legislature, by engaging students in the particular roles. "Frequently they [the students] reported that after representing a small country, they 'understood' how small nations' representatives see the world" (39:112).

The teachers can inspire students to empathize and to be sensitive to the feelings of others (43; 47).

The role-playing group may come to a generalization: behavior often exacts a toll of feelings, and if these feelings are painful, the consequences of questionable behavior may be far too costly. When such a generalization is arrived at through an interchange of opinion among peers, it carries far more weight and is far more likely to influence future choices of behavior than if it comes as a moral or directive from an adult exhorting a group "to be good" (43:106).

Control of Environment

The sixth argument for this technique concerns the importance of practicing control over one's future. Indeed, as detailed earlier, a significant aspect of the concept of teaching involves independence and self-determination. "If one believes he cannot control his future, he collapses into numbing ennui" (44:140).

In the report to the U.S. Office of Education on a national survey of American elementary and secondary schools [*], one of the most powerful predictors of school success is feeling that one's share of the rewards of the school system is not controlled by luck or other forces beyond one's control, but that one's own efforts will be rewarded. While feelings of efficacy have also been found to be related to other characteristics such as family status and the quality of school attended, Campbell and Coleman find the relationship between efficacy indicants and school performance holds even when these other factors are held constant. The implication is that if a way can be found to imbue students with the feeling that it is possible to control their environment and that it is therefore worth making an effort to understand it, the level of student performance can be raised, regardless of the other features of the school and its student body (8:127).

By participating in simulation games the player gets to make decisions and (because of rapid feedback) sees the consequences of his decisions. He soon realizes that by changing his strategy, or game plan, he can alter the consequences. Even with some luck factors involved—no current simulation game is based exclusively on luck—the player realizes that his own actions count. His actions affect him and the other players. He realizes that though chance events do affect him, he still can maintain control over his environment by carefully planning for and reacting to chance happenings.

* Boocock here cites Ernest Campbell, James S. Coleman, and Alexander Mood, *Equality of Educational Opportunity* (Report to U.S. Office of Education, 1966 [known as *The Coleman Report*]); see also reference 13.

The very working of the simulation game demonstrates to the student that skill based on deliberate moves is the major component that promotes control of one's environment and one's future.

By playing in this way the student develops a sense that he can affect his future not only in the simulation game but in real life as well. "By a careful structuring for reality and security, boys and girls may be led slowly along a continuum of simulations providing at once increasingly greater and more realistic control over their own destinies" (44:140).

Consider a player in the game of Legislature who has promised another player to vote in favor of a certain issue; the other player may already have kept *his* part of the agreement. Our player may suddenly be tempted by a third player to vote *against*; in terms of his own interest it may be clearly profitable to break the original promise. The rules of the game explicitly permit the violation of promises, and no immediate punishment is suffered by the violator. But if the player breaks his promise, he will, in the next round of the game, realize that the player who was cheated will be rather less inclined to make any agreements with him. Also other players who witnessed the event may hesitate to enter into agreements with him. And if other players are not prepared to make agreements and form coalitions with a certain player, his chances of winning are not great. Thus, the player learns to accept certain values, not because of any conviction of their intrinsic rightness, but because of the realization that in the long run it is expedient to behave this way. He learns to discriminate between short-range self-interest and long-range expediency. He may realize that much sermonizing actually refers to behaviors which are clearly expedient—in the long run. The rapid feedback which is so characteristic of the simulated environments pushes the players into long-range considerations (41:13–14).

This feeling of being able to control one's own environment is an outstanding aspect of simulation games. It results not only from rapid feedback but also, and more importantly, from the opportunity to make mistakes, assess consequences, and make corrections. Students "cannot learn that they have made mistakes unless they can make them" (2:3). Thus, simulation games provide the student with an excellent opportunity to learn from his successes and from his failures. Moreover, the student receives his penalties not from an authority figure but from the rules of the game from his own peers. The student learns that to err is indeed human and that often, though not always, he will have opportunities to correct the consequences of his mistakes.

It is because of such aspects that simulation games are self-disciplining. The student realizes that to win he must correct his errors. He must plan, act, assess, adjust his plans, act, etc. To do so he must discipline himself. But the players must also discipline each other if the simulation game is to proceed. There is no game unless the players obey the rules. Hence discipline is internal (9:219); in short, the activity takes care of itself.

Relationships Encouraged

Seventh, the use of simulation games brings about a desirable situation between teacher and student. The teacher is no longer the judge of the student's activity; he does not enforce appropriate conduct; and he does not pass sentence on violations committed by the student. In a simulation game the rules of the game direct the student in his activity. And what the rules do not or cannot do is accomplished by the student's fellow player. Other competing players surely make an offending student tow the line, and other players on the team, if teams are involved, surely cheer the student on to do his best.

When he is not judge and jury, the teacher can focus his attention on the act of teaching rather than on evaluation of the student, whether in terms of reward or punishment. The atmosphere is thus more relaxed, since the student does not have to keep one eye on the teacher for fear of punishment or low grades (which could have some significant effect on his life). By eliminating or greatly deemphasizing the teacher as judge, the student is much less likely to "develop attitudes toward the teacher that can interfere greatly with learning: hostility, servility, alienation, and other reactions to an authority figure" (9:217–218).

The very structure of the simulation game provides evaluation of the student's activity. The teacher is free to concentrate his efforts on providing the knowledge and skills the student will need in order to win or get a high score. Obviously a simulation game for teaching must be so designed that winning or scoring high is facilitated by the knowledge and skills the teacher helps the student gain before and during the play (9:218; 19:70; 35:29; 41:8). Yount and Dekock depict the teacher's task in this way:

The teacher no longer tells or dictates knowledge; he simply provides an organizational structure allowing the student to discover knowledge. The teacher no longer demands that the student learn; he simply provides a stimulating environment where learning has immediate impact. Finally, the teacher no longer dominates, standing over his students as though he were their lord and master; he simply starts them on their way, steps to the periphery of the action, and there arbitrates disputes when necessary, gives tutorial help to the floundering, acts as a resource for the fast, and, in general, merely facilitates learning (46:32).

The eighth argument for the technique concerns the fact that simulation games also encourage the student to communicate frequently with his fellow players. To win, the student must interact with other players to a high degree. This is so both in games in which one player competes against another player or players and in games involving teams of players competing against one another. If there are teams, then there is both inter- and intra-communication. "The children are encouraged (indeed, required) to talk to their fellow students instead of the usual rule of silence being enforced. This not only helps to relieve boredom but also gives the children the idea that their conversation may be of some value when it is addressed to other children" (45:5). This student-to-student interaction is both an effect and a cause of the teacher's special role in reference to the game. It is desirable since it leads the student away from dependence on the teacher. But, in turn, the teacher becomes an aid and support to the students.

Simulation games require this student-to-student communication because they are *strategy* rather than *showdown* games (2:6, 16). In the strategy game, a player or team directly interferes with the play of another player or team. The player must then work out with his competitor a means of mutual advancement. In the showdown game, each player or team plays his best without interference from his opponents. This distinction in types is particularly important to the teacher as he designs his own simulation game or selects from available ones designed by others. The degree to which inter- and intra-team communication is required or encouraged is one salient criterion for choosing to play a particular simulation game.

The use of simulation games also leads to a high degree of student physical mobility. Students who play cannot be restricted to their seats. They move from area to area as they confer with other players and as they conduct the various types of activities involved in the simulation game. There are home areas, large meeting areas, caucus areas, and equipment areas. Movement from one area to another is essential. This further leads to the independence of the student since it is he, not the teacher, who decides where to go within the space boundaries of the game. It further deemphasizes the teacher, since the student can generally move away from the teacher at will. In a simulation game, in contrast to other activities, the student can absent himself from the teacher (46:26).

Range of Student Abilities

Ninth, in teaching with this method the teacher can work with a wide range of student capabilities at the same time. That is to say, the same simulation game can be played by many students with different levels of knowledge and varying values and skills. For the teacher facing many students at the same time the problem of individual differences is one that must be seriously attended to. Simulation games offer a solution because there are so many aspects to them, some of which are appropriate to each of the various student levels.

In a given simulation game involving more than one player, the motivating power of play may attract the slow or disadvantaged student, while the development of alternative strategies may appeal to the bright student. In addition, "the slower students also learn from the faster ones sometimes better than from teachers" (2:19). This occurs because all the players get to observe the moves of the brighter students. A slower student can benefit from observing a better one. "Observers of graduate education have commented on the fact that graduate students appear to teach each other far more than professsors teach students. The graduate student subculture is peculiarly organized to provide student-to-student feedback. Simulation and games appear to introduce something of this process into high school and college courses" (6:66). In commenting on the simulation games he has designed and employed, Layman E. Allen makes this significant observation: "Everyone else in these games learns from the best player. His strategies are developed openly so that all others may learn to adopt them. In effect, the best players act as teachers, although they are not formally assigned this role by the rules of the games" (4:499). Furthermore, while one student may be learning new facts about the topic at hand, another student, who already knows these facts, may be developing alternative strategies based on them. It is in this way that there is something for a broad range of learning abilities in a single simulation game.

Moreover, the combination of the skill element and the chance element in a simulation game appeals to students of different abilities and outlooks. The chance component may, on the one hand, appeal to those who lack certain skills and knowledge, by allowing them to play with those who are more skilled; on the other hand, the chance component has a general appeal to everyone. There is a fascination in acquiring great gains all at once, and without effort. The "seductive mirage" of sudden winnings attracts all players alike (12:145). Still, the skill component appeals to those who possess certain skills and knowledge, as good moves based on special abilities are rewarded. This encourages and furthers the development of pertinent skills. Thus again, the very design of a simulation game provides the means of working with many different types of students at the same time.

Organizing for Simulations and Sociodrama

The key to organizing teachers and students for simulation games and sociodrama is flexibility and imagination. These two teaching methods necessitate flexible groupings of students, as well as actual fluidity of movement within classroom and building. The methods require the rearranging of classroom furniture as well as the imaginative use of that furniture. In some simulation games, students may need private places and extra time allotted in which to carry out confidential, classified negotiations. For example, rearranged desks could become borders between countries or insurmountable mountains that establish the territory of a particular state (11). Or, an open area created by the rearrangement of the furniture could easily become the principal's office (as in the illustrative sociodrama), the family living room, or a public square. It is most important that the students not be deskbound when involved in role-playing.

Students and teachers will also need easy access to other facilities such as the library and the mimeograph room. They must have the freedom of movement to carry out the various decisions they make. The teacher may have to arrange for tapes or audiovisual equipment. However, the significant thrust in the organization both of sociodrama and simulation games is to be imaginative—players and leaders alike.

References

1. Abt, Clark C. "Education Is Child's Play." Paper presented at the Lake Arrowhead Conference on Innovation Education, December 1965.

2. Abt, Clark C. "Games for Learning." Occasional Paper No. 7, The Social Studies Curriculum Program. Cambridge, Mass.: Educational Services Inc., 1966.

3. Abt, Clark C. "War Gaming." *International Science and Technology* 32:29–37, August 1964.

4. Allen, Layman E., and others. "The ALL Project (Accelerated Learning of Logic)." *American Mathematical Monthly* 68:497–500, May 1961.

5. Allen, Robert W. "The Fourth R." *California Journal of Educational Research* 16:75–79, March 1965.

6. Anderson, Lee F., and others. *A Comparison of Simulation, Case Studies, and Problem Papers in Teaching Decision-Making.* Project No. 1568, Cooperative Research Program of the Office of Education, U.S. Department of Health, Education, and Welfare. Evanston, Ill.: Northwestern University, 1964.

7. Bettelheim, Bruno. "Play and Education." *School Review* 81:1–13, November 1972.

8. Boocock, Sarane S. "An Experimental Study of the Learning Effects of Two Games with Simulated Environments." In *Simulation Games in Learning*, edited by Sarane S. Boocock and E. O. Schild, pp. 107–133. Beverly Hills, Calif.: Sage Publications, 1968.

9. Boocock, Sarane S., and James S. Coleman. "Games with Simulated Environments in Learning." *Sociology of Education* 39:215–236, Summer 1966.

10. Bruner, Jerome S., Jacqueline J. Goodnow, and George A. Austin. *A Study of Thinking.* New York: Science Editions, 1962.

11. Burgess, Philip M., Lawrence E. Peterson, and Carl D. Frantz. "Organizing Simulated Environments." *Social Education* 33:185–192, February 1969.

12. Caillois, Roger. *Man, Play, and Games.* New York: Free Press, 1961.

13. Campbell, Ernest, James S. Coleman, and Alexander Mood. *Equality of Educational Opportunity.* Washington, D.C.: Department of Health, Education, and Welfare, U.S. Office of Education, 1966.

14. Carlson, Elliot. "Games in the Classroom." *Saturday Review*, April 15, 1967, pp. 62–64, 82–83.

15. Cherryholmes, Cleo. "Developments in Simulation of International Relations in High School Teaching." *Phi Delta Kappan* 46:227–231, January 1965.

16. Cherryholmes, Cleo. "Simulating Inter-Nation Relations in the Classroom." *International Dimensions in the Social Studies*, Thirty-eighth Yearbook of the National Council for the Social Studies, edited by James M. Becker and Howard D. Mehlinger, pp. 173–190. Washington, D.C.: National Council for the Social Studies, 1968.

17. Cherryholmes, Cleo. "Some Current Research on Effectiveness

of Educational Simulations: Implications for Alternative Strategies."
American Behavioral Scientist 10:4–7, October 1966.

18. Christine, Charles, and Dorothy Christine. "Four Simulation Games That Teach." *Grade Teacher* 85:109–120, October 1967.

19. Coleman, James S. "Academic Games and Learning." In *Proceedings of the 1967 Invitational Conference on Testing Problems,* Benjamin S. Bloom, Chairman, pp. 67–75. Princeton: Educational Testing Service, 1968.

20. Coleman, James S. "Introduction: In Defense of Games." *American Behavioral Scientist* 10:3–4, October 1966.

21. Coleman, James S. "Learning through Games." *NEA Journal* 56:69–70, January 1967.

22. Dawson, Richard E. "Simulation in the Social Sciences." In *Simulation in Social Science: Readings,* edited by Harold Guetzkow, pp. 1–15. Englewood Cliffs, N.J.: Prentice-Hall, 1962.

23. De Grazia, Sebastian. *Of Time, Work, and Leisure.* Garden City, N.Y.: Doubleday, 1964.

24. Dewey, John. *The Child and the Curriculum* and *The School and Society* (combined edition). Chicago: University of Chicago Press.

25. Dewey, John. *Human Nature and Conduct: An Introduction to Social Psychology.* New York: Henry Holt, 1922.

26. Giffin, Sidney F. *The Crisis Game: Simulating International Conflict.* Garden City, N.Y.: Doubleday, 1965.

27. Goffman, Erving. *Encounters: Two Studies in the Sociology of Interaction.* Indianapolis: Bobbs-Merrill, 1961.

28. Green, Thomas F. *Work, Leisure, and the American Schools.* New York: Random House, 1968.

29. Greenblat, Cathy S. "Gaming as Applied Sociology." In *Sociology in Action,* edited by Arthur Shostak. New York: Wiley and Sons, 1973.

30. Huizinga, Johan. *Homo Ludens: A Study of the Play-Element in Culture.* Boston: Beacon Press, 1955.

31. Kahn, Herman. *Thinking about the Unthinkable.* New York: Avon, 1962.

32. Leary, Timothy. "How to Change Behavior." In *LSD: The Consciousness-Expanding Drug,* edited by David Solomon, pp. 103–118. New York: Berkeley Medallion, 1966.

33. McKenney, James L., and William R. Dill. "Influences on Learning in Simulation Games." *American Behavioral Scientist* 10:28–32, October 1966.

34. Mead, George H. *Mind, Self, and Society.* Chicago: University of Chicago Press, 1934.

35. Nesbitt, William A. *Simulation Games for the Social Studies Classroom.* New York: Foreign Policy Association, 1968.

36. Phenix, Philip H. "The Play Element in Education." *Educational Forum* 29:297–306, March 1965. Reprinted in *Teaching: Vantage*

Points for Study, edited by Ronald T. Hyman (Philadelphia: J. B. Lippincott, 1968), pp. 299–308.

37. Piaget, Jean. *The Moral Judgment of the Child*. Translated by Marjorie Gabain. New York: Collier Books, 1962.

38. Plato. *Great Dialogues of Plato*. Translated by W. H. D. Rouse. New York: Mentor, 1956.

39. Robinson, James A. "Simulation and Games." In *The New Media and Education*, edited by Peter H. Rossi and Bruce J. Biddle, pp. 93–135. Garden City, N.Y.: Anchor Books, 1966.

40. Robinson, James A., and others. "Teaching with Inter-Nation Simulation and Case Studies." *American Political Science Review* 60:53–66, March 1966.

41. Schild, E. O. "Learning in Simulated Environments." Address at the Rider College School of Education Conference on *New Approaches to Social Studies*. Trenton: Rider College, 1966.

42. Schild, E. O. "The Shaping of Strategies." In *Simulation Games in Learning*, edited by Sarane S. Boocock and E. O. Schild, pp. 143–154. Beverly Hills, Calif.: Sage Publications, 1968.

43. Shaftel, Fannie R., and George Shaftel. *Role Playing for Social Values*. Englewood Cliffs, N. J.: Prentice-Hall, 1967.

44. Taylor, Charlotte P. "Games—and the Ghetto." *Educational Leadership* 26:139–142, November 1968.

45. Wolff, Peter. "The Game of Empire." Occasional Paper No. 9, The Social Studies Curriculum Program. Cambridge, Mass.: Educational Services Inc., 1966.

46. Yount, David, and Paul DeKock. "Simulations and the Social Studies." In *Innovation in the Social Studies*, edited by Dale L. Brubaker, pp. 25–40. New York: Thomas Y. Crowell, 1968.

47. Zeleny, Leslie D. "How to Use Sociodrama." In *How to Do It Series, No. 20*. Washington, D.C.: National Council for the Social Studies, 1960.

12 Simulation Games

What, then, should a teacher do in order to teach using the simulation-games method? Note that the word used is *teach*, not *play*. It might indeed be possible to "play" a simulation game, even one specifically designed for teachers; but the concern here is with teaching via the simulation games, and this goes beyond playing.

Example and Analysis

Reprinted below is *War or Peace: A Simulation Game* by John D. Gearon (9). The reader is asked to keep in mind that this simulation game is intended as a *simple*, teacher-produced example.* This is, in its simplicity and the brevity of its playing time and instructions, in contrast to most of the simulation games now available from commercial firms and foundation institutes. Nevertheless, it is a completely adequate example of a simulation game. It is not necessary to present a long, complex example here. *War or Peace* and the activities it projects will serve as a springboard for subsequent comment. The reader is asked to read the description of *War or Peace* carefully and to picture it being played. In this example—in contrast to the illustrative lecture, discussions, and sociodrama—it is not the ongoing activity that is being presented (for that is impossible to do), but rather a description of the rules and the projected performance. To present the ongoing activity we need a video recording rather than a book. Also, a strategy for conducting a simulation game follows.

* Note that the sample simulation game and sample sociodrama that follow were both made up by teachers. This type of example is used here deliberately to show that execution of the role-playing methods of teaching is very much within the power of the individual teacher. The teacher does not have to rely on outside experts in order to use these methods. It is hoped that these examples will encourage other teachers to create their own material to fit their particular needs.

War or Peace: A Simulation Game*

This is a simple international relations game that can be played by ninth-grade classes in world history. Aside from the enjoyment students derive from playing the game, the activity is designed to provide a genuine learning experience. It may be used to introduce or to strengthen several valuable historical insights.

As a model of international relations, for example, the game can be effectively used to point out the condition of international anarchy that has been an important part of the affairs of people and nations throughout history. A fundamental pattern of international relations, the concept of balance of power, may also emerge clearly as a discovery of the students during their playing of the game. Too, international relations terms come to be better understood in classroom action—such terms as foreign policy, crisis, alliance, diplomacy, treaty, neutrality, and peace conference.

The classroom becomes during the game an imaginary world made up of a continent and an island—the arena of interaction of seven sovereign nations. A map of this little world (Figure 1) and a chart showing the relative war powers of the nations (Figure 2) are all the

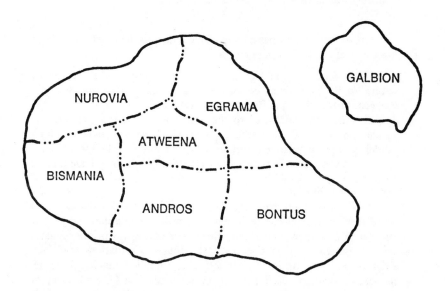

Figure 1: The Continent and the Island*

* Reprinted with permission of the author, John D. Gearon, and the National Council for the Social Studies. From *Social Education* 30:521–522, November 1966.

materials a student needs to play the game. These may be duplicated and given to the students, or they may be drawn on the chalkboard and copied by each student.

The numbers presented in Figure 2 for army and navy do not correspond to numbers of men, regiments, divisions, or ships of war. They are relative figures that express the comparative war powers of the nations. "NMF" stands for National Morale Factor. All nations are equal in NMF, and these NMF points cannot be taken away from the students who make up the original nations.

Nation	Army	Navy	NMF	Total
Andros	700	600	240	1540
Atweena	1000	0	240	1240
Bismania	800	700	240	1740
Bontus	460	400	240	1100
Egrama	520	400	240	1160
Galbion	500	1000	240	1740
Nurovia	500	500	240	1240

Figure 2: Relative War Powers of the Nations*

Once each student has a copy of the map and the chart, three steps are necessary to set up the game:

1. Students may be divided into small groups for the game by counting off by sevens. Number 1's are Androsians; number 2's, Atweenans; number 3's, Bismanians; and so on.

2. The map is oriented to the classroom ... as it appears to the teacher in front of the class ... [and, with this top view in mind, students] find the relative positions of their nations in the room. [They are aided by nation name-cards on the tables.] Once they have located their respective countries, they may form small circles of chairs as their national headquarters.

3. Their first job, when settled, is to pick a ruler for the nation to serve as chairman of the team and to speak out internationally. The ruler may be either a king or a queen—or perhaps a prime minister or a president. The teacher calls the roll of the nations and each ruler responds, introducing himself in a dignified manner by title, name, and country: 'King Alfred of Bismania!' or 'Queen Mary of Atweena!'" No suggestion is to be given by the teacher as to the ruler's power. Decision making within the nations is to be left entirely to the students who make up the nation-teams.

*Reprinted with permission of the author, John D. Gearon, and the National Council for the Social Studies. From *Social Education*, November 1966.

Before the game begins the students are given some ideas as to the realities of the international power situation as it exists according to the map and the chart. Atweena, a landlocked nation, has no navy, but it does have the most powerful army. Galbion, an island nation, has the largest navy. The two most powerful nations are Bismania and Galbion. The two weakest are Bontus and Egrama. It is a competitive and hostile world and each nation is faced with a different problem in maintaining its power, security, and independence.

The basic rules and pattern of the game should now be explained. In any war the more powerful nation, or alliance of nations, always wins and dictates the terms of the peace settlement. In a war a defeated nation can lose some or all of the power of its army, navy, and its territory on the map to the victorious nation or nations.

Students who belong to a nation that has been wiped out of existence in war and its power and territory lost can continue as a part of the game with their NMF points. They may stay together as a group without nation status to negotiate for the restoration of their independence in return for the use of their NMF points in another war. As a group, they may join another nation with their NMF points. Or, they may go as individual refugees to join other nations, each taking along his equal share of the NMF points.

The game is played in cycles of well-defined phases, and each cycle begins with an international crisis. The basic four phases for the first cycle are: (1) planning foreign policy; (2) negotiations; (3) international declarations; and (4) peace conference. In later cycles additional phases of planning foreign policy, negotiations, or special international conferences may be called for on the request of the rulers of two or more nations.

CRISIS. The game begins in the first cycle with a predetermined international crisis. A state of war exists between Nurovia and Atweena. It must be emphasized to the students that neither side is to be considered the aggressor; there is no right or wrong that can be attached to either; and all possibilities for peace have been thoroughly exhausted. The peace and security of every other nation is threatened. Atweena will conquer Nurovia unless Nurovia is able to bargain successfully to bring other nations into the war on her side. Atweena is, therefore, forced to seek allies. Every nation is faced with the decision to enter the war or remain neutral, on whose side to fight, and what kind of bargain to make for joining one side or the other.

PLANNING FOREIGN POLICY. This first phase of the first cycle should last about five minutes. Each nation goes into secret conference to decide what to do in the crisis, what its long term foreign policy ought to be, and what nations its ambassadors should visit for negotiations. No communication with other nations is permitted during this phase.

NEGOTIATIONS. In this phase, lasting about ten minutes, rulers are not allowed to leave their countries. National objectives are to be carried out by sending diplomats to confer secretly—and quietly—with the rulers of other nations. Rulers should generally receive only one diplomat at a time, and they have the right to refuse to confer with any nation's diplomats.

INTERNATIONAL DECLARATIONS. Diplomats return to their own countries. Rulers stand. The five nations not originally concerned in the war are asked, in order, to declare themselves. The teacher's question is "War or peace?" If the answer is for war the nation must state whether it is joining Atweena or Nurovia. Nothing else can be stated by the rulers. [The rulers read their declarations from slips they prepare before the teacher begins the questioning.] The teacher totals the powers of the belligerents and announces the results of the war.

PEACE CONFERENCE. If more than the original two nations were involved in the war, the victorious rulers go to a peace conference to decide what is to be done with the defeated. At the end of a period of from five to ten minutes they must announce whether the defeated are to be wiped out of existence or merely weakened and left alive. The victor, or victors, may revise the map of the world on a chalkboard for all to see, but the changes of national strength need not be given to any nation not involved in the war. Thus ends the first cycle of the game.

The game continues with an intermediate cycle of three phases. The nations meet for planning their postwar foreign policy, and this action is followed by a phase of negotiations. The rulers then stand for international declarations. They are called in alphabetical order and the question is still "War or peace?" The answer can be "Peace." Or any nation may declare war on any other nation. No nation can commit any other nation in its declaration.

The first declaration of war precipitates a crisis. When this happens the declarations stop and the game goes into a new cycle of phases the same as in the first cycle. This is the pattern of the game from then on.

The game can come to an abrupt end during any time of international declarations if all nations declare for peace. Unfortunately this has never happened in the experience of the writer. If it does happen, perhaps there is real hope for the future of mankind.

Analysis

War or Peace contains some of the general features that promote effective teaching through simulation games. These points deserve comment.

1. This simulation game clearly focuses on the concepts and processes selected by the teacher-designer as the ones that students are to consider. The teacher, since he is involved in the field of social studies,* has selected two basic concepts of social science, balance of power and international anarchy, and the processes involved in balancing power and avoiding anarchy, as the backbone of this simulation game. In this way *War or Peace* has a clear teaching purpose. The selection of and focusing upon concepts and processes to be simulated is the first necessary step in using a simulation game for teaching purposes (6:14).

This initial feature is not to be underestimated. It is precisely this beginning that distinguishes a simulation game from a game played for entertainment. It is the grounding of the simulation game in fundamental concepts and processes that makes it a suitable activity for teaching purposes. The selection and designation of processes are necessary for a game in which people can interact as they follow through on the decisions they have made. Once this feature is designed into the game, the other essential features can follow. If this step is omitted or left vague, the other features lose cohesiveness.

2. The game involves the players in a simulation of the critical elements of the selected social processes. The designer has obviously analyzed the decision-making process involved in balancing power and avoiding anarchy when the threat of war arises. Then, he has constructed a model of it. He has specified the key people or groups involved, the operations each can perform, the interrelationships among them, and the rules for reacting to other people's actions. He has specified, for example, that, on the basis of their army and navy power, nations must at least decide for war or peace, that a ruler must announce his nation's decision, that ambassadors must negotiate with other nations, and that victorious rulers must decide on the fate of the vanquished. This second step in the design of a simulation game thus involves a systemic analysis and model formation (1:11).

This is a crucial feature, because the value of a simulation game depends on the validity of the model formulated; the simulation must essentially represent reality. Hence, the creation of an

---

* Most available simulation games are currently in the field of the social studies. This seems to be due to the common interest in social processes shared by those studying the social sciences and those proposing the use of simulation games. There are, however, simulation games in other fields, such as English, science, mathematics, business, and language.

adequate model is a central problem in the design of a simulation game. "If the simulation does not validly model the necessary attributes of the real system, the results found in solving problems in the simulated environment cannot successfully indicate the behavior of the real system" (5:14). The question, then, for all simulation games is, "How valid is the model that is at the core of the activity?" Before that question can be answered for *War or Peace*, another point should be mentioned.

The game is built on only the essential elements of the decision model for war or peace. The use of only the essential elements is necessary in order to make the simulation game playable. If a very complex decision model is used, it will most likely confuse the student (remember that this simulation game was designed for ninth-graders) or take too long (1:12).

Care should be exercised to insure that only the essential elements of the situation are built into the model. If extraneous elements are utilized, they may obscure the process sufficiently so that the student will not be able to recognize the actions taking place and the reason for those actions. The inclusion of unnecessary elements also makes the construction of the model a more complicated process (6:15).

3. *War or Peace* has further combined its simplified—but essential—analytical decision model with the dramatic qualities of a game. This is needed in order to evoke the student's interest and thereby convey to him an understanding of the decision model for balancing power.

To communicate effectively with the student the model must be translated into a social drama that involves the student's interest and enables him to experiment actively with the consequences of various "moves," or changes in the system under study. This remains the case whether the "system" is a psychological one, as in the conventional drama, a sociopolitical one, as in most historical crises, or a socio-economic one, as in most situations of technological innovation and social change (1:12).

Furthermore, according to Yount and DeKock, two teachers who have designed and marketed several of their own simulation games, the element of competition in games is the key to vibrant interaction among the students (14:29). Indeed, *War or Peace* does engage the students in competition in order to win. This includes the totaling of earned points to determine the winner.

In this way there is not only competition but also a qualification of each nation's war power, another excellent characteristic. In a simulation game, quantification is desirable, since it is "useful to have some way by which the players may measure with some precision the amount of power which each actor possesses. This is desirable because the students do not possess adequate information concerning the relative power of the elements in the simulation model, and they are able to operate more effectively if some means is provided for gauging the relative power of the respective elements" (6:15). Along with competition and quantification, other game characteristics are woven together with the analytical model, such as rules,* teams, and moves. The use of only the essential elements of the decision model is further justified by the fact that the analytical model merges with the game feature. It is virtually impossible to dramatize a complicated analytical model in a game. Hence, there must be a balancing between the validity of the model and its playability. Selection must be made regarding both the elements of the model and the elements of the game. Thus, there are "compromises or 'tradeoffs' between the competing objectives of comprehensive realism and simplification for the sake of playability (a form of experimental manipulability)" (1:12).

In short, both for the sake of clarity (in order not to obscure the process and thereby confuse the student) and for ease in translating the model into a dramatic game, only the essential—and sometimes even only some of the essential—elements of the analytical model are utilized in a simulation game. For this reason certain elements actually present in the process of balancing power are absent in *War or Peace*. For example, no one dies as a result of waging war. Also, the victor pays no cost for going to war. The

---

* Coleman treats five types of rules (4:32–35): "*Procedural rules* describe how the game is put into play, and the general order in which play proceeds." Subordinate to procedural rules are *mediation rules*. These specify "how an impasse in play is resolved or a conflict of paths resolved." *Behavior constraint rules* "specify what the player must do and what he cannot do . . . they represent the role specifications for each type of player." *Goal rules* specify the goals and the means of achieving the goals. *Environment response rules* "specify how the environment would behave if it were present as part of the game." For example, a ground-rule double in baseball results from a situation where a ball bounces into the center-field bleachers and is not retrievable. *Police rules* specify "the consequences to a player of breaking one of the game's rules." For a teacher designing his own simulation game, it is most helpful to keep these five types in mind.

elimination of these otherwise present elements is the result of a compromise made by the designer. It is in this light that the question, "How valid is the model?" must be answered.

4. This simulation game begins with an explicitly prepared scenario (and playing directives) in order to warm up the players and lead them into the activity. Inbar reports in his study of the varied effects of a simulation game upon players that this initial warm-up period is critical to the use of the method.

Thus a careful handling of the players before the session starts might be all that is needed to induce those predispositions which seem to produce desired results in the playing session. In this respect, and recalling our previous finding on the unexpected importance of the first few minutes which precede the beginning of the play, one cannot avoid reaching the general conclusion that the person in charge of the session is of tremendous importance, at least for games which are not really self-taught and/or self-administered (11:26).

The starting scenario is obviously essential. It is of "prime importance in that it sets the stage for the entire play, which thereafter will be largely extemporized by the players" (10:73). In *War or Peace* the starting scenario is quite short and simple, in keeping with the entire simulation game. Therefore, it is printed in Figures 1 and 2 (pages 255, 256) and also set forth orally. If this were a more complex simulation game, more of the scenario might be in the form of a "fact book" covering other matters (such as facts of economics, geography, or history) that had a bearing on the conflict. But whether delivered orally or in writing, game-significant data must be given at the beginning, in order to assure a common understanding and to provide a springboard (10:75).

5. The game involves each player—whether merely as a member of a nation or as ruler or ambassador—in the decision-making process, and further requires each player to live with the results of his decision. Decision-making is required in the starting scenario. There is a predetermined crisis: "A state of war exists between Nurovia and Atweena." Each nation must then make a decision "to enter the war or remain neutral, on whose side to fight, and what kind of bargain to make for joining one side or the other." With the initial decisions made, the activity of the simulation game begins.

As important as the requirement to make a decision is the requirement to deal with the consequences of one's own decision.

This simulation game gives the student fast feedback, so he can see the results of the decision he has made; then it requires him to make further decisions on the basis of these results. Built-in cycles of deciding, declaring, assessing, and negotiating follow one another. This action-reaction pattern is critically important in the simulation game, as the game is geared to teach students the decision-making process.

6. In playing this game, the students are required to assume general rather than specific roles. That is, a student becomes a ruler or ambassador or citizen; he is not President John F. Kennedy or Ambassador Adlai E. Stevenson. This is important, for it is simply too difficult for any student (even a college student) to portray accurately a real person. Impersonation requires that students improvise the people being portrayed and therefore increases the danger of conveying false information or impressions.

Robinson, who has worked with simulation games on the college level, states this point clearly in the question below. He further claims another advantage—personal insight—for the generic role as opposed to the specific role. This is to be underscored in using simulation games for teaching. Note that what Robinson says about college students is all the more valid for students at lower levels.

For one thing, college students are simply not qualified to play Kosygin or Johnson. Although, when they are given such an assignment, they may read up on the person they are to play, still one runs the risk that they will "boot-leg" as much inaccurate or irrelevant motivation as correct motivation into their performance of a world dignitary's role. Although playing an anonymous role may not encourage the student to extend his knowledge to the biographies of current leaders and their policies, it also may not lead him astray as he plays out the roles in the simulation. In fact, he will be challenged to play the role as he personally would play it, gaining some insight into his own performance and considering which model of diplomacy and negotiation he would like to adopt for himself (12:100–101).

7. *War or Peace* is designed to start quickly and to last a relatively short period of time. Its designer, Gearon, states in another article that *War or Peace* can start after ten minutes of explanation and organization and "is meant to occupy two, three, or at most, four periods of class time" in a typical school setting (7:386). Thus, not much time and effort has to be expended in preparing for the game. Nor does the game drag on endlessly,

boring the students. Also, the game does not become the sole method of teaching: because it is short, it can easily be combined with other methods of teaching about balance of power and avoidance of anarchy.

This is significant because the simulation game is just one method of teaching and should rightfully be supplemented by other methods. Just as the lecture, recitation, Socratic dialogue, and discovery methods have limitations that can be partially remedied in combination with other methods, so too must this method be used along with others. This method is most easily mixed with other methods when the game is short. A long simulation game is very likely to leave both the teacher and the students unwilling to tackle the same topic by another method. Furthermore, a long, drawn-out simulation tends to dull the students' critical perspective (10:177) and becomes somewhat self-defeating.

8. The game is so designed as to keep the teacher's own preferences from influencing the play. The students do not know— and do not have to know—whether the teacher wants war or peace, or which country the teacher prefers. The teacher is outside the game, as he should be, and his personal preferences do not count. Furthermore, the quality of the play is not influenced by any statement by the teacher that those who play well and win will receive high grades as rewards. The simulation derives its thrust from the student's motivation and energy, rather than from the teacher's power to assign grades.

Other Possible Game Features

In this short presentation of *War or Peace* it is obvious that the teacher-designer focused on the playing and did not mention several additional activities that might be incorporated into the game. Listed below are other features of simulation games that the teacher who employs the method would do well to include.

First, the simulation game must be followed up with a critique, or debriefing period in which both teacher and students carefully analyze the play. "The best strategy for capitalizing on the learning potential of games is in the postgame discussion wherein students can inductively arrive at a consensus of ideas gleaned from the simulation experience" (8:275). In this critique session, which, in essence, is similar to the session suggested in the chapters on the discovery method, the teacher has the opportunity to direct the students' critical attention to the concepts and processes simulated. Students deeply engaged in a game are not always aware of the meaning of the simulation design. Playing dulls a student's critical sense because of the emotional involvement in a tense situation (10:177). (See the strategy suggestions following.)

This dulling of the senses may at first appear to be a limitation of using the simulation game. However, it is something for the teacher to stress in the critique session. While treating the substance of the simulation game, the teacher could stress that a person intensely involved in a conflict situation may indeed lose his critical sense. On this matter simulation games "may reflect at least one characteristic of life" (10:178). Thus, this apparent defect can serve as the springboard for teaching an important point.

In the critique session, the teacher must discuss the adequacy of the game's model of the selected social processes. Since a simulation game necessarily involves simplification, comparison of the simplified model with a more complex model is essential lest the students conceive of the social processes only as represented in the simulation game. By comparing, the teacher can offset and correct those limitations of the simulation game that result from oversimplification. For example, the teacher using *War or Peace* would do well to treat the point that the effective strength of the seven hypothetical nations is calculated strictly in military terms (army and navy power) because the National Morale Factor is the same for all seven. In the debriefing, students should, in contrast, become aware of the multiplicity of factors that in reality contribute to the war power of any country.

Furthermore, since the simulation game involves role-playing, the events of a particular session may not be in accord with theory or actual events (if the simulation is based on an historical event). Here the teacher has the obligation to differentiate between the events of the game and expected or actual events.

It is an essential part of the simulation technique that the teacher uses periods subsequent to each simulation period as a time in which to compare the simulation activities with the appropriate theory, and to indicate to the students how and when actions violated theory or failed to indicate good judgment or the application of all known information to the solution of the problem; and conversely, the teacher should carefully call the attention of the students to those instances in which events were in accord with theory or in which good judgment was applied (6:13).

Second, in light of the points mentioned above, the teacher would do well to supplement simulation games with other teaching sessions. The teacher could lecture and conduct discussions on the topic at hand. He could request that students prepare their own research assignments pertinent to the topic (2:231). Yount and DeKock, certainly strong proponents of the simulation-game method, state the following in contemplating their use of simulation games.

Freedom, interaction-involvement, competition—all these principles are fine, but we wanted our students to grasp history as well as appreciate how human beings encounter one another in groups. To insure knowledge of history, we organized the simulation so that each student performed a number of *basic* assignments. If the student accomplished each satisfactorily, he then had the opportunity to do *depth* assignments involving individual research (14:30).

This use of a cluster of methods to supplement the simulation game offers the teacher the opportunity to handle the same topic in several ways. The points that remain fuzzy after the simulation game is played can and should be clarified through other teaching methods. It is the task of the teacher to "highlight the lessons to be learned," lest the entertainment value of the activity gain the ascendancy, resulting in little teaching benefit from the game (6:13).

It is for this reason that simulation games are often integrated into a unit of study. The designers of the games plan them with this in mind. In this way, the simulation-game method complements, and is complemented by, other teaching methods.

Third, the teacher would do well, as students become comfortable in playing, to encourage students to add refinements to the game. For example, in *War or Peace*, the students might add an element of luck or chance to the game. (The chance element is indeed missing from the game as it now stands, and the attempt by students to incorporate it would be worthwhile in itself whether or not it was successful. For example, the teacher or leader of the game might unexpectedly announce the assassination of one of the country's rulers.) Or with help the students might design their own simulation game. This would put them in the position of social scientists attempting to formulate the relationships among the elements being studied. This is quite different from accepting the relationships and rules designed by someone else. Though designing a simulation game might be difficult and time-consuming, the challenge could offer the students a unique opportunity to deal with selected social processes (3:7). "Perhaps the greatest learning occurs when students build their own simulations" (13:21).

Fourth, the teacher might vary the type of simulation games he uses. For example, since *War or Peace* deals with a hypothetical situation, the teacher might next use a game that deals with an actual past historical event or process. He might use a simulation game dealing with the Korean War (such as *Dangerous Parallel*, sponsored by the Foreign Policy Association and available from Scott Foresman and Company of Glenview, Illinois) or the Articles of Confederation (such as *Disunia*, available from Interact of Lakeside, California). Such models might more easily integrate, for the student, the playing of the simulation game with the study of history.

Or, the teacher might use a more complex simulation game than *War or Peace*, in order to tactfully lead the students into consideration of the intricacies of decision-making when many elements are involved in a situation. All communication might have to be done in writing in such a complex situation. This in itself would be a learning experience for the students. Or, the teacher might use a simulation game based on real events that are projected into the future. This variation is essentially the crisis-game method, developed by Giffin (10). For example, the students in 1973 might be asked to play out the ongoing crisis between Israel and the Arab neighbors or the ongoing crisis between French-Canadian secessionists and English-Canadian loyalists. By using a variety of types of simulation games, the teacher and students will come to see the great potential of this teaching method.

Strategy

Below are some steps for conducting a simulation game based on the activity from *War or Peace*. The reader can use these steps to play other simulation games, adapting these steps where appropriate.

Step 1. Warm up the group with a brief introduction to the game.

Step 2. Divide the group into smaller groups to become the seven nations.

Step 3. Present the situation involved in the scenario. Distribute sheets with map and table as in Figures 1 and 2. Go over sheet to clarify the scenario for everyone.

Step 4. Explain the rules and pattern of play. Do not get bogged down here. Be clear and move on. Clarity will come as the activity progresses.

Step 5. Engage the group in the game. Follow the manual's instructions for the leader of the game. The leader should try to be as unobtrusive as possible.

Step 6. Introduce refinements into the game as appropriate. For example, the teacher can unexpectedly announce the assassination of one of the nation's rulers in order to introduce the element of chance into *War or Peace*.

Step 7. Halt the game when play ceases or when time runs out, but leave enough time for debriefing. To bridge from the activity part to the debriefing part say, "Now let's talk about what happened during the past half-hour or so."

Step 8. Debrief.

A. It is best to begin debriefing by encouraging students to talk simply about what happened. That is, ask such questions as: What happened when Atweena sought allies? What were the line-ups in regard to power? What led you to do this? Who declared for neutrality? Why? Did you as a ruler find it difficult to stay at home? How did you choose your ambassadors? How did the assassination affect your plans? This will review the activity and provide a foundation of data from which to draw in analyzing the scenario's conceptual model. It will loosen up the group and get them talking, since it is easy to talk on this concrete, non-threatening level.

B. Encourage students to talk about their beliefs and feelings during the simulation game. Ask such questions as: How did you feel when war broke out and you lost and were divided up? How did you feel when you declared for war in the second cycle? What feelings did you think other players held? What values does *War or Peace* attempt to teach? In what ways did feelings and beliefs affect the activity of the simulation game? What is peace?

C. Encourage students to talk about the similarity of the game to the world's reality. That is, in what ways is the activity of the game's participants similar to the activity of people in general in the world. Ask such questions as: In what ways is the picture or view of the world in *War or Peace* similar to the real world?

What was missing in the game that is important in the real world? What assumptions are built into this game? What are the key concepts this game teaches us? How much depends on chance factors?

D. Encourage students to talk about future activities that can build upon their experience with this simulation game. This includes refining or redesigning the game, doing independent or small-group projects, and playing other, related simulation games. Ask such questions as: Since this game necessarily presents a fairly simple view of the world for us to begin with, what suggestions do you have for changing the game for others or ourselves if we play it again? What aspect of war, peace, balance of power, and international anarchy as key concepts of this game would you like to pursue in depth? In what ways ought we to change our classroom activity as a result of what we have learned from playing this simulation game? How can we alter this game to make it more congruent with the real world?

Step 9. Summarize, generalize, and conclude. At various spots, but especially at the end, there is a great need for summarizing, generalizing, and concluding. The generalizations and conclusions constitute the message which arises from the simulation game. The teacher can do this task himself if he chooses. Better yet, he should request the students to list first some key, specific ideas that have come forth during the discussion, then to offer some generalizations based on these ideas, and finally to draw some conclusions. This latter approach is more effective in that the generalizations and conclusions will be more meaningful to the students since they come from the students themselves.

Step 10. Move forward. Before leaving the simulation activity behind, structure the situation so that you launch yourself into new activities built upon the game. In this way the leader bridges current activity with future activity while interest is high.

References

1. Abt, Clark C. "Games for Learning." Occasional Paper No. 7, The Social Studies Curriculum Program. Cambridge, Mass.: Educational Services Inc., 1966.

2. Cherryholmes, Cleo. "Developments in Simulation of International Relations in High School Teaching." *Phi Delta Kappan* 46:227–231, January 1965.

3. Cherryholmes, Cleo. "Some Current Research on Effectiveness of Educational Simulations: Implications for Alternative Strategies." *American Behavioral Scientist* 10:4–7, October 1966.

4. Coleman, James S. "Social Processes and Social Simulation Games." In *Simulation Games in Learning*, edited by Sarane S. Boocock and E. O. Schild, pp. 29–51. Beverly Hills, Calif.: Sage Publications, 1968.

5. Dawson, Richard E. "Simulation in the Social Sciences." In *Simulation in Social Science: Readings*, edited by Harold Guetzkow, pp. 1–15. Englewood Cliffs, N.J.: Prentice-Hall, 1962.

6. Garvey, Dale M. "Simulation, Role-Playing, and Sociodrama in the Social Studies." *Emporia State Research Studies* 16:5–21, December 1957.

7. Gearon, John D. "Response to the Kaplan-Gordon Critique." *Social Education* 31:385–387, May 1967.

8. Gearon, John D. "Simulation and Stimulation: Teaching Politics and Government in High School Social Studies." *Social Education* 32:273–278, 281, March 1968.

9. Gearon, John D. "War or Peace: A Simulation Game." *Social Education* 30:521–522, November 1966.

10. Giffin, Sidney F. *The Crisis Game: Simulating International Conflict*. Garden City, N.Y.: Doubleday, 1965.

11. Inbar, Michael. "The Differential Impact of a Game Simulating a Community Disaster." *American Behavioral Scientist* 10:18–27, October 1966.

12. Robinson, James A. "Simulation and Games." In *The New Media and Education*, edited by Peter H. Rossi and Bruce J. Biddle, pp. 93–135. Garden City, N.Y.: Anchor Books, 1966.

13. Sprague, Hall T., and R. Garry Shirts. "Exploring Classroom Uses of Simulations." Mimeographed. La Jolla, Calif.: Western Behavioral Sciences Institute, 1966.

14. Yount, David, and Paul DeKock. "Simulations and the Social Studies." In *Innovation in the Social Studies*, edited by Dale L. Brubaker, pp. 25–40. New York: Thomas Y. Crowell, 1968.

13 Sociodrama

Sociodrama is the most highly developed form of spontaneous role-playing except for the simulation game. Although the term has many other applications, sociodrama will be discussed here as a teaching method. However, many teachers who are aware of this method of teaching do not necessarily employ it—perhaps because of the openness it requires in facing problem situations. When not retreated from and when used correctly, the technique can become an excellent device for allowing students to gain empathic awareness of situations involving conflict. The reader is asked to recall that the underlying justifications presented in the introductory section apply to sociodrama as well as simulation games.

Example and Analysis

Presented below is a tapescript of a session of sociodrama conducted in a senior class in high school. The drama was later modified by the teacher in an interesting and useful way. Analysis will follow as well as suggestions for use with other levels of students.

Teacher: Class, in light of our previous lessons these past few weeks, I'd like to read you a description of a situation (about five to six lines). The description is not finished but is wide open. I'd like you to listen carefully and think about how you'd like to finish it. Let me read it:

Jack Vander was sent to the principal's office by his teacher with the complaint that Jack's hair was too long. Jack has refused to cut his hair, so Mr. Sewell, the principal, has asked Jack's father to come to school to discuss this situation with him. The three of them, Mr. Sewell, Mr. Vander, and Jack Vander are seated together. Mr. Vander opens the conversation with, "_____."

That's the situation. It isn't finished, but perhaps we can finish it. Let's do it by acting it out, since that will help, I'm sure. Let's get the players. Who'll play Mr. Sewell, the principal?—Okay, Alice, you'll be Mr. Sewell. Mr. Vander?—Okay, Jim. And Jack Vander?—Fine, Joan, you'll be Jack.

Joan: Just call me Jackie.

Teacher: Yes, Jackie—now that's fine since Jackie's in the news these days. Some of us have all the luck! (Class laughs.) [Note: Jackie Kennedy Onassis was married a few days before this lesson was taped.]

Well, you three gather your thoughts a bit about this situation. The rest of you—I'd like to ask to listen carefully to what they're saying, so when they've finished we can talk about it. Not about dramatic quality but about how they're working out the situation. (The three, with the teacher, set up a table with three chairs around it as the stage prop.)

Okay. Let me read the story again to give you your cue and you continue right on. Let's get everyone straight. Alice, you're Mr. Sewell; Jim, you're Mr. Vander; and Joan, you're Jack Vander.

Joan: I'm Jackie. (Class laughs.)

Teacher: Well, at this point we better stick with "Jack." Here we go. (Teacher reads story again.)

Mr. Vander: Well, why does the administration think that my son's hair has to be a certain length?

Mr. Sewell: The administration doesn't put any restrictions on the length of your son's hair. But there are school rules about the limit that Jack's hair can be.

Mr. Vander: Why should there be a limit at all? Jack is a very good student, and I don't see where his hair has anything to do with the way he's acting in class. Why should he have to cut it?

Mr. Sewell: We feel his hair looks ratty and that he should get it cut because it has a bad influence on the rest of the school. He gives us a bad name. He gives the picture that all our students are like him, and they aren't.

Jack: But my hair hasn't influenced my grades any. My hair hasn't had a bad effect on the school. School isn't a fashion show; it's for learning. So why should I get it cut?

Mr. Vander: Why have him conform to a rule that has no bearing on the school itself, just on appearance and what you think?

Jack: Do you think everyone should follow along like sheep if a few people get short haircuts. Just because your hair is short, I shouldn't have to have mine cut short.

Mr. Sewell: We're not asking you to cut it short but to cut it to a decent length where it looks presentable.

Jack: It's my hair. I don't tell you when to cut your hair. Besides, who are you to say what's decent and what isn't?

Mr. Sewell: I think I have that right.

Mr. Vander: I think you ought to take this up with the administration again and then call us back; then we'll talk again about what you all have decided.

Mr. Sewell: What different angle do you want us to talk about? We don't want to simply repeat.

Mr. Vander: Give us a better reason than just because it's too long and you don't like it that way.

Mr. Sewell: You mean . . .

Mr. Vander: Give a reason like—it's disrupting the class or it's bothering the teacher or something like that—more than that you don't like it long.

Mr. Sewell: It is bothering the teacher.

Mr. Vander: In what way?

Mr. Sewell: It looks awful; it's dirty and long; and it has bugs in it, and it's greasy.

Jack: I beg your pardon! I wash my hair.

Mr. Sewell: Maybe you should wash it more often.

Jack: Do I tell you how often to wash your hair? Do I tell you how often to take a bath?

Mr. Sewell: I was only advising.

Mr. Vander: I see, then you're just *advising* us to have Jack's hair cut.

Teacher: Could we stop right here.

Mr. Sewell: Let's! (Class laughs.)

Teacher: Quote of the day: "Let's!" (More class laughter.) (To the class as the three students return to their seats) How did it go? Was the solution one you could accept?

Helen: I thought it was a bit odd that the father sided with the son. Usually the father sides with the administration.

Bob: They all had good points.

Teacher: Bob, do you agree with Helen that the father usually sides with the administration and that she's surprised to hear it the other way around?

Bob: (Bob shakes his head no.)

Shirley: I think that's a broad generalization. You can't say for sure how any person is going to act—you can't say for sure that the father is going to side with the administration this time, and that's it, because he's a member of the older generation.

Jeff: I agree that the father would side with the principal, but I would want him to take the side of his son.

Teacher: What do you think would have happened had the father gone the other way—taken the side of the administration? Yes?

Judy: Probably the son would have gotten his hair cut right away. The father would have pressured him into it.

Teacher: Yes, go ahead.

Allen: I disagree. I think it would only have confirmed the adamancy of the student. I think he would have become even more stubborn had he seen his parent side with the administration, and he wouldn't have gotten his hair cut.

Teacher: Suppose we try this again. Can we get three other people but just change one thing around as suggested here by Helen—to have the father take the other part instead of the one he did. Let's get three people—including you three from before—who want to play it out that way.—Okay, there's Allen's hand. What part do you want?

Allen: I'll play Mr. Vander.

Teacher: Okay. (Anita's hand goes up.) Do you want to take the part of Jack?

Anita: (Nods yes.)

Teacher: Okay. Now we need a principal. Anyone for the principal?

Allen: Come on, Bob! (Bob reluctantly gets up.)

Teacher: You don't have to if you don't want to. (Bob sits down.) There we go. Hilda will be principal. This time will you three just think it through yourselves without talking it over. Just think about your own part and what you want to do.

Allen: Do I have to open?

Teacher: Yes, same situation as before. I'll read the same story to give you a cue, and you just continue right on. We'll change only one thing, as suggested by Helen—that Mr. Vander take the side of Mr. Sewell. You all set? Okay, here we go. (Reads story again.)

Mr. Vander 2: Mr. Sewell, perhaps you could tell me a little more about why the administration objects to Jack's hair.

Mr. Sewell 2: Well, if he could keep it a little neater it wouldn't be so bad. But he comes to school, and it's down to his shoulders.

He just wears it tossed all over his head, and it's always greasy and not very clean. The teachers and the administration are afraid that if he keeps it the way it is and doesn't do anything to improve it, then certainly bugs and insects will be crawling around in it. And if they were to get too bad, it would spread throughout the school.

Mr. Vander 2: I'd like to hear from Jack. We're here to discuss so discuss. Jack, we're willing to hear your point of view.

Jack 2: I have nothing to say except I'm not going to get my hair cut, and that's that. Just lay off me!

Mr. Vander 2: Mr. Sewell, I'm glad you finally brought my son in, because this is the problem I've experienced so often myself at home. I've suggested many times that . . .

Jack 2: "Suggested," huh?!

Mr. Vander 2: . . . Jack get it cut. I've harped on it repeatedly but I haven't been able to get through to him. I hope that between the two of us. . . .

Mr. Sewell 2: Yes, between the two of us—I'll need your help, too, because a student should start his learning and manners at home. So with your help we can get Jack's hair cut to a moderate length.

Mr. Vander 2: We need a specific suggestion here because of Jack's adamancy, which is so evident. Now I'd like to know the consequences along with Jack, so we'll all know what will happen if he doesn't get it cut. I don't want to threaten Jack but . . .

Jack 2: What can you do anyway? Take the car away?!

Mr. Vander 2: Jack, I'd like to hear from Mr. Sewell first.

Mr. Sewell 2: Well, we could keep him out of school till he does get it cut and cleaned up.

Jack 2: Great, I've got lots of things to do.

Mr. Sewell 2: And if that doesn't work, we'll give him a two- or three-day period and since this is a vocational high school and we do have a beautician and barber department, we could ask the student barbers to do a little job on him.

Mr. Vander 2: That's an excellent suggestion.

Jack 2: How do you think I should have it styled, huh?

Mr. Sewell 2: Well, you don't have to get a butch or anything but . . .

Jack 2: How 'bout me wearin' ribbons in my hair, huh!

Mr. Sewell 2: If you want to wear it long like a girl, you might *want* to wear ribbons in it.

Mr. Vander 2: I think, Jack, we've been reasonable about this, but if you maintain your defiance, we're going to have to put our foot down. You're a seventeen-year-old boy, and you have a responsibility to your school, your school rules, and Mr. Sewell.

Jack 2: I come first. I have a responsibility to myself first.

Mr. Vander 2: You don't come first. You have a responsibility to yourself and you have a responsibility to others. You have to maintain that responsibility to both. And if you don't comply voluntarily, we'll have to see to it that you do comply.

Teacher: Can we cut it here.

Jack 2: Please!

Teacher: Well, we now have two quotes of the day: "Let's!" and "Please!" (Class laughs.) Well, how did it go this time? Let's concentrate first on Jack.

Jerry: I thought Jack played it right, because if he felt that his hair was important, he'd play it that way.

Teacher: Yes?

Marilyn: Well, I think that the only situation like this is in the movies or some problem school, but this isn't typical at all.

Chris: No, that's not so. I've read about stuff just like this in the newspaper. I remember one in Boston and one here in New Jersey.

Marilyn: I wasn't generalizing to all schools but . . .

Chris: But it has been in the papers.

Shirley: Boys in this school have long hair.

Teacher: The question here is whether the situation is real or not. Let me interject that there was indeed a case just like this before the New Jersey Supreme Court last year—the valedictorian of Edison High School. So, assume this situation is real, and make your comments on this basis.

Helen: I thought this father was more realistic than the first. Also, I liked the way Mr. Sewell gave a two- to three-day period to get the hair cut. It's good to give the boy a chance.

Bob: I was going to say something about Jack. I think he didn't play it right. If he wants to combat reason—and his father and the principal were trying to give reasons—then he has to give better reasons. If he wants to combat emotions, then he can be more emotional. But he should have given better reasons for keeping his hair long.

Jack 2: But I played it the way I thought a teenager would play it.

Bob: I'm sure that fellow in Edison used reason, if he went to the Supreme Court.

Teacher: Okay, let's pursue this a bit. Were the objections offered by Mr. Vander and Mr. Sewell—the first and second times—acceptable to you? Were they valid?

Gordon: Well, Mr. Sewell said there were bugs in the hair. For hygiene, this is okay, but Jack claimed that he did wash his hair. So if he did, then the bugs idea wasn't so good.

John: The principal seems to be asking for regimentation and conformity. He wants everybody to look alike. He might as well ask us to dress alike like they do in some parochial schools. But this is a public school, and everybody has a right to wear his hair the way he wants. The long hair has nothing to do with school itself.

Mary: I wanted to say that I thought the father was too reasonable. I think that a father in that situation would be real mad, and Allen didn't play Mr. Vander mad enough.

Teacher: Marilyn? You'll be last since we have just a few minutes left.

Marilyn: Well, I thought they should have worked to a compromise, but they didn't. The way they played it, Jack will only resent it more because he felt so strongly. And they didn't give him a reason he could accept, and he just was adamant. So they aren't going any place that way—a compromise might be better.

Teacher: Okay. Let me take a minute to make some observations and raise some questions for further thought. Both sets of actors and the students who commented raised some excellent points that we'll have to consider at length as we move ahead. I noticed that no one made specific mention of the Constitution (which we've been studying)—I carefully avoided mentioning it at the start of the lesson. Perhaps you got caught up in the acting and drama. But you might consider tonight if and where the Constitution has anything to say on this matter. Keep in mind what John said about Jack's *right* to wear his hair the way he wants. Does a boy have a right to do so? Further, what would be *good* reasons—valid or acceptable reasons—to plead in the Supreme Court. Bob was right about needing good reasons in court. What arguments could you give on both sides of this long-hair issue? And one last question, though there are at least a hundred more we could ask; why do you think Mr. Sewell introduced such words as *ratty* and *bugs?* That is, is there anything behind the hygiene argument? Well, those are some questions that we'll pick up tomorrow, so please give them your consideration, especially in light of our sessions on the first ten amendments. There goes the bell.

Analysis

At the outset it should be noted that this sociodrama took place in a single typical high school session. There is much "written" talk simply because it involves the transcription of rapid conversation, especially during the two enactments of the situation. Also, it should be noted that this enactment is a good working example of a sociodrama at any level. Five of the most significant features of this sociodrama will now be discussed. The reader should bear in mind the comments made about *War or Peace* in the previous chapter.

1. This sociodrama is based on a problem story that invites completion, is relevant to today's youth, and is open-ended as to how the three people act as the situation unfolds. Such a feature is absolutely fundamental to the sociodrama. There must be a problem or conflict in the situation that the actors seek to resolve through their interaction. What the problem is about is clear to the students, because it is relevant to them. Only one student, Marilyn, says that the situation does not seem real. The others do not feel that way, as evidenced from the enactment as well as the quick refutation of Marilyn's remark. As witnessed in the general eagerness to act out the situation, and especially the eagerness to react to the enactments, it is clear that the situation is appealing to the students.

Moreover, and highly important, the story is so constructed as to encourage the actors to play their roles as they themselves choose. This is especially true for Mr. Vander, for it is he who opens the sociodrama. The student who volunteers to be Mr. Vander must decide on his own whether to back his son, whether to back the teacher, or whether to take some sort of middle position. The story itself does not indicate to Mr. Vander the way to play his role. The other two roles are open, too, although they are significantly modified by Mr. Vander's opening remarks. It is for this reason that it is important that the beginning line not be predetermined by the story. Thus, the very construction of the story impels the sociodrama forward.

2. The teacher in the illustration is clear about the framework within which he wishes to deal with the problem situation. He wishes to treat the long-hair conflict primarily from the viewpoint

of political science. This is evident from his allusions to the Constitution and his asking for reasons that would be acceptable to the Supreme Court. Yet he has not specified the exact nature of the issue to the students. That is to say, it is within the framework of political philosophy that the class is to decide about the specific issue involved in the situation. There are many different issues the students might focus on within this framework.

It is most important for a teacher to have his particular framework clearly in mind. If he does not, it would be easy for him to start considering extraneous matters such as the dramatic qualities of the role-playing. Also, without a framework clearly in mind there is the great danger that the teacher will get involved in the psychotherapeutic elements of role-playing. This is so because of the close relationship between sociodrama and psychodrama as developed by Moreno (3). The reader is asked to keep in mind that sociodrama is being presented here as a teaching method and not as a device for practicing psychotherapy.

This is not to say that sociodrama as a teaching method should be restricted to a political science framework. It is equally suitable for dealing with issues in ethics—ethical problems involving honesty and fair play, for example. Sociodrama can also be useful for dealing with such economic issues as labor strikes and such sociological issues as problems involving the elderly. In short, the sociodrama method of teaching is suitable for a variety of frameworks dealing with personal and group issues.

3. The story that touches off this sociodrama leaves open to the actors and reacting students the decision on the nature of the conflict involved. Granted that the students recognize that the conflict revolves around Jack's refusal to cut his hair. Granted that the teacher has directed the students to use the framework of political science. Yet the very essence of this sociodrama demands that the students decide, for example, if the conflict is one involving Jack's personal rights, or one involving due process, and so on. Unless this matter is clarified, it is impossible to decide what evidence to bring forward as acceptable. That is, in order to know what constitutes a good reason (and note that Mr. Vander 1 requests a "better" reason from Mr. Sewell 1), it is necessary to decide what the issue at hand is. If the issue is one of personal rights, for example, then remarks about decency and fashion are inappropriate. It is up to the students, then, to decide what this precise issue is. The teacher wisely recognizes this point and does not make the decision for the students in introducing the socio-

drama. Even at the end of the lesson he only raises questions in connection with the class's previous study of the Constitution. It is possible that this teacher sees the issue as one centering on personal rights, but he only hints at it by raising a question. He directs the students to the Constitutional amendments but does not specify which ones are related to the case of Jack Vander. There is still a great deal of room left for the students to decide for themselves the nature of the conflict.

4. Procedurally there are several interrelated steps. The teacher in the illustration got the students quickly involved in their role-playing, without a long introduction that might have overshadowed, impeded, or influenced the enactment of the problem situation itself. If he did otherwise, spontaneity would suffer, and in a sociodrama it is the teacher's function to facilitate and "release spontaneous action" (5:1). The teacher moved right into the heart of the lesson with only a short warmup, so there was ample time left for the spontaneous enactments and subsequent class discussions.

The teacher is careful to let only volunteers play the roles, since he is interested in open, spontaneous enactments. He thus allows Bob to remain in the audience even though Allen pressures Bob to play Mr. Sewell 2. He allows the actors a minute or so to give some thought to their roles. He uses this time to alert the audience to listen carefully, in preparation for the critical discussion that is to follow. He carefully points out that the students are to focus on the content of the enactment and not the dramatic quality, for indeed sociodrama is not a practice ground for stage actors. This step also has the effect of indicating that the actors should be as relaxed as possible and not get stage fright.

This teacher moves from the enactment to the critique period by raising some question that permits the students to react in their own terms. In other words, the floor is wide open, and the teacher keeps it wide open at all times by not taking a position. He does this in spite of the fact that the students will not always respond directly to his question. Nevertheless, this encourages the expression of varying viewpoints.

Since the students open with a reaction to the way Jim played Mr. Vander 1, the teacher moves to a second enactment on the basis of the class's suggestion. That is, the second enactment comes in response to the reactions of the audience. It is not forced. At least one reenactment is essential in a sociodrama, since it gives the class another opportunity to solve the problem on the basis of critical comments, and it also clearly demonstrates to the students that there is not only one way to approach a social problem. If a teacher and students feel it appropriate, there may be three or even more enactments of the same situation.

In recognition of these points this teacher moves quickly to the second enactment, while the class still has the first one clearly in mind. Also, when there is a second performance soon after the first, a lengthy discussion period can follow, based on at least two enactments. Such a discussion has more material to deal with and hence has more potential for being fruitful than only a single critique period or a short second one. The reader should note that this teacher deliberately read the capsule situation before each performance, not only to aid the actors but also to keep the openings of the sociodrama similar.

The teacher in the example given recognizes that it is vital to the sociodrama method to have a critique discussion after the enactment. Actual role-playing should be followed by an analysis of the solution to the conflict. Such a discussion gives each student the opportunity to present his thoughts on the problem. "While research has indicated that the actual taking of roles may have greatest influence on attitudinal change, it is in the give-and-take of discussion that problem-solving procedures are refined and learned" (4:79). It is for this reason that the teacher in the example given encourages the free flow of discourse among all participants. (The critique period following a sociodrama is similar to that following a simulation game.)

The teacher in question closes the session with some personal observations that relate the sociodrama to previous class sessions. He also raises some questions for further consideration. These further questions are to serve as a springboard for future lessons and also as guides to the students' thoughts about the problem outside of the classroom. (If the sociodrama has been effective, students may very likely raise the problem later with friends and relatives.) The teacher thus gives the students a basis for pursuing the problem further.

5. This teacher makes good use of spontaneous humor both in the warm-up for role-playing and in moving from the enactments to the critique periods. Humor is particularly useful in sociodrama because tension builds up in the enactments. (This tension tends to arise from the student efforts to resolve conflicts and to properly assume as assigned role.) What was said earlier

about humor, in Chapter 6 (pp. 119–149), is especially pertinent here, and the reader is urged to recall it at this point.

Other Possibilities with This Sociodrama on Long Hair

The reader is probably aware that there are other things the teacher and students could have done in a sociodrama about long hair. Obviously it is impossible to do everything in a single session. However, there are four steps the teacher might well take in the future. (These points are similar to points raised in the section on simulation games.)

First, the teacher might well direct the students' attention to the decision-making process itself. Even a short sociodrama enactment lasting three to five minutes is entirely sufficient to illustrate to the students the complexities of making a decision for the purpose of resolving a conflict. On the basis of a concrete problem, such as Jack Vander's refusal to cut his hair, the teacher could well teach some of the skills involved in decision-making. The need for teaching those skills is particularly evident with younger students (ages ten to fourteen) who might participate in sociodrama. But, the reader will notice, even this class of high school seniors had some difficulty in working toward a solution in the first enactment. The class could discuss how two people arrive at a compromise when they have opposing beliefs. The class might also explore the conditions under which a person should maintain his original position and refuse to compromise. In short, the teacher might well use the sociodrama method to focus explicitly on the decision-making skills necessary for solving social problems.

Second, the teacher might also specify to the players whether they should act as they think things are or as they would like things to be. For example, the teacher could ask a student to play Mr. Vander as he would like to see a father act and, for the same performance, ask another student to play Jack Vander as he thinks Jack would in fact act. This sort of combination, or even a performance with each student acting "the way you would like it to be," would add a fruitful dimension to the sociodrama. This could bring to the floor, for example, the students' concepts of the ideal father. The audience, in reacting to such role-playing, would get involved in comparing their own ideals with those of the role-players. The critique discussion would be most enlightening to the students and the teacher.

Third, the teacher, in later class sessions, might encourage his students to create their own sociodramatic situations. This would assure a problem relevant and meaningful to the students. It would not only give the students the added opportunity to identify problems, but also the opportunity to decide by themselves which framework to use in approaching the problem. Students need practice in such matters. For a person to be independent he must identify problems himself and carry through their solutions on his own initiative. In preparation for this more difficult task the teacher might well discuss with the students the problems confronting them. Furthermore, he could take one particular problem as an example and explore with the students which of the alternative frameworks or solutions seems appropriate, relevant, and fruitful. Crystal, in reflecting on her use of sociodrama with "disadvantaged" students, whom she had create their own problem stories, comments: "When children are removed from the emotionally charged context in which conflicts usually occur, they are likely to come to an intellectual understanding of what is going on. . . . The time to reach disadvantaged children is now. Role-playing offers some hope" (2:179).

Fourth, to increase the number of students actively playing roles, the teacher could have many simultaneous enactments of a particular situation. This would quickly involve many students in direct use of decision-making skills. It might also involve some students who might otherwise be too shy to engage in role-playing before an entire class. The overall critique period could then initially be devoted to a comparison of how the various enactments turned out. Possibly this could be preceded by student-led discussions of each separate enactment. Such a procedure would demonstrate quite readily that there are various ways to approach a problem (1:42).

Sociodrama and Pictures

Sociodrama is an especially good method for young students. However, some young students find it difficult to engage in role-playing based on a story script as presented here in the situation involving long hair. A superb way to involve these students is to use pictures depicting problem or conflict situations. The observation of the picture, preferably featuring students of the students' own age, serves to evoke verbal and dramatic responses. For example, a photograph or drawing of a short five-year-old trying to mail a letter but unable to reach the handle to pull down the slot will serve to get youngsters talking and acting out a solution.

Or, a picture of an eleven-year-old bully taunting several eight-year-olds will serve to get youngsters of these ages to talk, dramatize, and solve such a situation.

In short, it is possible to launch a sociodrama from a picture as well as a story script. A teacher could also use a section of a film or even the retelling of an event. The essential point is to have a scenario that presents a problem for the students to solve in a dramatic role-playing situation. Once the problem is presented and understood, the method of teaching via sociodrama is the same whether the teacher uses a story script, a picture, a film, a photograph, or an oral report.

Strategy

Below are some steps for conducting a sociodrama based on the activity from *Jack Vander's Hair*. The reader can use these steps to conduct other sociodramas, whether he uses a story script or picture to present the situation. The teacher should adapt these steps to fit the age of the students. The reader should see the analysis for details on this sociodrama scenario.

Step 1. Warm up the group with brief introduction to the sociodrama. Get into the sociodrama quickly.

Step 2. Present the problem situation. Read the scenario or present the picture, film, photograph, or report.

Step 3. Be sure that students understand the situation. To check, especially when using pictures with young students, the teacher should ask, "What's happening here?" If the teacher feels that students need some help in getting ideas for role-playing, he can ask, "What do you think will happen next?" This will help evoke further responses from the students.

Step 4. Select volunteers to act out the situation. The key to spontaneity and openness is that the players are volunteers.

Step 5. Enact the situation. Review the situation quickly, and let the students enact the situation freely.

Step 6. Halt the enacting. Stop the enacting when students request it, when the acting bogs down, ends, or when the situation gets to a point leading to fruitful discussion.

Step 7. Debrief. Discuss the enactment. The teacher can begin by asking such questions as, What happened in their short act? How did it go? Was the solution of the actors one that really could happen? Was the solution one you could accept? This debriefing should be short, just enough to lead to a second enacting.

Step 8. Suggest that the students re-enact the problem situation based on an *alternative* possibility as raised by the students' reactions.

Step 9. Select volunteers for the second enactment.

Step 10. Enact the situation again.

Step 11. Halt the enacting. See Step 6 above.

Step 12. Debrief again. Debriefing a sociodrama is similar to debriefing a simulation game as presented in the previous chapter. Begin as before with a simple, concrete question to get the discussion going. The teacher can then focus on the acceptability and workability of the solution presented by the actors. The teacher should also include discussion of feelings and attitudes evoked in the students. For more details and suggestions for specific questions, see Step 8 in the strategy presented for conducting a simulation game.

Step 13. Summarize, generalize, and conclude. The teacher and students should summarize, generalize, and conclude as suggested in Step 9 in the strategy for conducting a simulation game.

Step 14. Move forward. The teacher should launch new topics and activities before leaving the sociodrama behind. In this way the teacher bridges current activity with future activity while interest is high.

References

1. Chesler, Mark, and Robert Fox. *Role-Playing Methods in the Classroom.* Chicago: Science Research Associates, 1966.

2. Crystal, Josie. "Role-Playing in a Troubled Class." *Elementary School Journal* 69:169–179, January 1969.

3. Moreno, Jacob L. *Who Shall Survive?* Beacon, N.Y.: Beacon House, 1953.

4. Shaftel, Fannie R., and George Shaftel. *Role Playing for Social Values.* Englewood Cliffs, N.J.: Prentice-Hall, 1967.

5. Zeleny, Leslie D. "How to Use Sociodrama." *How to Do It Series, No. 20.* Washington, D.C.: National Council for the Social Studies, 1960.

5 Questioning—
Observing—
Evaluating

14 The Art of Questioning

In any discussion method of teaching—Socratic dialogue, valuative discovery, or nonvaluative discovery—questioning is a central, critical element. This is true also in role-playing when the teacher conducts the debriefing session, and in the recitation session as well. The teacher questions the students as a means of treating the topic at hand. The students question the teacher and each other about the topic. Questions both prompt thinking and direct thinking into selected areas. In a discussion, topics are formulated as questions because "a question sets the mind working, as the announcement of a general subject does not" (20:4). According to research, questions constitute about one-third of classroom discourse and teachers ask about 86 percent of the questions (4). Because questioning is so essential in the classroom, special attention will be given to it here.

Basic Terms

In order to treat questions, specific terms must be designated to serve as the basis for a language of questioning. The word *question* will be used to refer to the eliciting of a verbal response. The question may take any grammatical form—declarative, interrogative, or imperative. Grammatical form is unimportant in questioning since it is intent that is central. *Response* will refer to the fulfillment of the expectation of a question—an answer. Questions and responses are reciprocal; questions elicit responses, and responses arise directly and only from questions. *Reaction* will refer to the modifying (by clarifying, synthesizing, or expanding) and rating (positively or negatively) of what was said previously. A reaction may follow a question, a response, or another reaction. Whereas a response is directly elicited by a question, a reaction may be occasioned by a question, response, or another reaction. For example:

> *Question:* How was the Grand Canyon formed?
> *Response:* It was formed by a river cutting through the rock.
> *Reaction:* Very good, Ruth (Reaction to Response 1).

> *Question:* Tell me where Jonathan's room is.
> *Response:* Upstairs.
> *Reaction:* No, downstairs and to the left (Reaction to Response 2).

> *Question:* The president of the United States, please.
> *Reaction:* That question is too easy (Reaction to Question 3).
> *Reaction:* I don't think it's too easy (Reaction to Reaction 3).
> *Response:* Nixon, I believe.

> *Question:* Do you like Shakespeare's poetry?
> *Response:* Sometimes.

These three terms—questions, responses, reactions—will be key words in this chapter. New terms will be added as they are needed.

The Cognitive Vantage Point

To talk about questions we must be able to describe and analyze them. There are many ways to do this. The most common, and still the most fruitful, is to describe questions in terms of purpose rather than grammatical form or length. That is to say, questions are asked in order to accomplish something. Thus a teacher may ask a question in order to:

1. Get a particular student to participate.
2. Check on the student's comprehension.
3. Attract a student's attention.
4. Test a student's knowledge of the topic.
5. Diagnose a student's weaknesses.
6. Break the ice and get a discussion going.
7. Allow a student to shine before his classmates.
8. Establish an explanation for a problem.
9. Review work for yesterday's absentees.

10. Build up a student's security when the teacher is quite sure the student will respond correctly.

11. Learn about a student's personal activities (which affect his classroom performance).

12. Attack issue A rather than B.

Questions based on these purposes are found to arise at one point or another in teaching. Furthermore, the list could be expanded fivefold. But the issue is already obvious—there are many vantage points from which to talk about the purpose of a question. The question's purpose could, for example, be described in terms of social climate, or emotional climate, or student management, or assessment and evaluation of the student, or influencing thinking processes, or changing the content of the topic. A particular vantage point must be chosen in order to deal with the subject.

In this chapter, questions will be treated, for the most part, in terms of the *cognitive, or intellectual, processes* that they would effect in the respondent. That is, questions shall be considered in regard to what the questioner asks the respondent to do with the topic under study. This is the most fundamental way of looking at questions, for every question must have a cognitive base. The cognitive purpose of questions will serve as the focus in this section and as the springboard for venturing into other purposes that questions can have, such as affecting emotional climate. All other purposes are built on the cognitive.

Consideration primarily of the cognitive effects of questions is in accordance with the usual manner of dealing with questions. Consider the admittedly naive and inadequate popular dichotomy of *memory* questions versus *thought* questions. This dichotomy stems from the cognitive vantage point. Even people who emphasize the emotional and psychological aspects of the teacher's activity most often employ a cognitive perspective in treating questions.

Even within the cognitive vantage point we need a way to describe questions, since we wish to offer suggestions on the art of questioning. Obviously certain types of questions elicit certain responses; certain questions suit particular situations and strategies. With knowledge of the various types and their effects, the teacher can talk about questions and strategically plan for their use.

Every system for categorizing questions has certain advantages. Each highlights a particular way of viewing questions and calls our attention to specific features. On the other hand, each system limits our view. For this reason we shall present three cognitive vantage points with the belief that among them the limitations of any one set will be eliminated. At the same time we shall be offering three helpful spotlights. These three complementary approaches—verification, productive thinking, and cognitive function—and some suggestions for their use follow.

Verification

According to John Wilson (29:51), verification* is "not only the best method of distinguishing one type of statement from another but also throws light upon each individual type." Verification is the determination of whether or not a statement† is true. Although a question is not in itself a statement, questions are described in terms of the responses (the statements) that they elicit. Verification is thus a guide to the meaning of statements and a guide to determining their truthfulness. Hence verification becomes a powerful means of describing questions and responses in teaching, since teaching centers on the intellectual meaning communicated between teacher and students.

This approach may be stated in slightly different terms. When describing questions we must do so in terms of the kind of evidence that would be appropriate to the particular question. According to this notion, "the key question that we must ask as a preliminary to any sort of problem-solving is this: What kind of evidence would have a bearing on this question?" (18:31). In other words, the questioner, if he is asking a genuine question, must have some idea of the terms he wishes in the response. Questions are thus described according to the type of evidence appropriate to their solutions.

ANALYTIC QUESTIONS. In regard to questions in teaching there are four main classifications that will be treated here.‡ First, there are analytic questions, i.e., questions that elicit responses that are

* This approach is essentially the one used by Smith and others (17; 25; 26) and Bellack and others (2; 3; 4) in their research on classroom language.

† In this treatment of questions, *statement* will be used in a technical sense. Following Henderson (15:50), the term will be defined as follows: "A statement is one kind of sentence. It is a sentence which asserts that something is the case; it makes a truth claim." A sentence may or may not be complete in terms of grammatical construction.

‡ This section will draw heavily on Wilson (29).

analytic statements. Analytic statements are "necessarily true. By this I mean that they are true by virtue of the meaning of the words of which they are composed" (15:52). Analytic questions may be about words, terms, symbols, phrases, or sentences. A few examples will be helpful here. The reader should note that the examples given here and in following sections serve to represent the various subtypes of each classification. The reader should also bear in mind that many questions, responses, and reactions are elliptical; that is, they are not complete grammatically, and the speaker assumes that the listener understands the parts omitted. These are classified, nevertheless, according to their type, which becomes more obvious when they are completed.

1. *Question:* What is a sitar?

Response: An Indian instrument something like a guitar—but longer with more strings.

2. *Question:* What does "We Shall Overcome" mean?
Response: It means that in the long run we will win.

3. *Question:* What is the square root of 256?
Response: Sixteen.

If we wish to verify the three responses above, we would not go for evidence to the world of our sense experience. We would look rather to the various sets of rules men have established. A particular Indian instrument is called a sitar simply because men have agreed to call it that. Questions seeking definitions of terms, translations, or meanings of phrases or statements are all analytic. The square root of 256 is 16 because it follows from an agreed-upon symbolic system—mathematics. Sixteen times 16 must be 256; it cannot be otherwise, given the common system of numbers. In short, these sample questions are all analytical, because the responses to them are verified by examining the way we use language or some other system of symbols that has been established by agreement.

EMPIRICAL QUESTIONS. Empirical questions are questions that elicit responses that are empirical statements. We verify an empirical statement by gathering evidence from the world of our sense experience. "In other words, we make observations in the world and decide whether the statement is true or false" (29:59).

Empirical questions may elicit facts, explanations of empirical situations, comparisons, and if-then inferences of empirical conditions.

1. *Question:* If you put a cold bottle of water from the refrigerator onto the table, will it sweat or remain dry?
Response: It'll sweat.

2. *Question:* Did the minor scales develop from the Greek modes?
Response: Yes.

3. *Question:* When will the United States send a man to Mars?
Response: I predict by 1974.

4. *Question:* Why did he become deaf?
Response: Because someone shot off a firecracker very near his ear.

Even though the United States has not yet sent a man to Mars, the statement in Response 3 is still empirical, since the criterion for judging is the empirical verification procedure—an empirical question may refer to past, present, or future matters. Also, empirical statements are to be judged in context, in order not to be confused with analytical ones. For example, a teacher may say in introducing a unit on magnetism, "This is a magnet. A magnet is an object that attracts iron filings." Later in the unit he may say that a magnet hanging freely will point to the north. In its context, the first statement is analytical, since it is used to define the word *magnet*, whereas the second one is empirical, since it tells us something new about magnets once we know what they are (15:53). It is possible, of course, to reverse these two statements about magnets and have the second serve as the definition.

VALUATIVE QUESTIONS. Valuative (or value or evaluative) questions are questions which elicit responses that are value statements by the respondent. Value statements praise, blame, commend, criticize, or rate something. To verify a valuative statement it is necessary to know the criteria being used by the respondent. For example, to verify the statement "Truman was a great president," it is necessary to know the criteria for being considered a great president. One person may be able to describe, i.e., make empirical statements about, Truman's acts as a president and have another person agree with him completely. But unless both share common criteria for what constitutes a great president, no amount of facts or accurate descriptions will provide a basis for assessing the evaluation. If we do not know what the appropriate criteria are, then we cannot verify a valuative statement. Valuative questions may elicit opinions and/or the justification of opinions.

1. *Question:* Who is your favorite president and why?
Response: I guess it sounds silly, but I like Coolidge, because he was the strong, silent type. That's my type of man.

2. *Question:* Which do you believe to be a better drama, *King Lear* or *Hamlet*?
Response: Hamlet.

3. *Question:* Is it okay for mathematicians to use their math knowledge to play the odds at the racetrack and at the dice table?
Response: Sure, someone's got to win, so it might as well be a mathematician.

METAPHYSICAL QUESTIONS. Metaphysical questions elicit responses that are metaphysical statements. Such questions and responses are rare in public schools and are found in only a few teaching situations. Many metaphysical questions deal in some way with God, and as yet there is little agreement as to the verification method to be employed in response to them. That is to say, there is no common agreement, for example, on how to verify the statement, "God exists." What evidence or criteria will help a person to decide if the statement is true or false? Some people deny that any verification is possible or necessary since the statement is true by faith—either you believe it or you do not. In any case, such statements involving God remain unsettled by empirical evidence, though there is agreement about the element of faith.

1. *Question:* Where do the righteous go when they die?
Response: To heaven.

2. *Question:* Did God punish Hitler for his cruel behavior?
Response: Yes.

3. *Question:* Who created the beautiful trees and the other beautiful parts of this world?
Response: God.

Productive Thinking

The concept of productive thinking was initially applied to the verbal interaction between teacher and student by Aschner and Gallagher in their research with gifted children (11; 12). They drew on the research of Guilford, in which he developed a theoretical model of the structure of the intellect (13). Part of Guilford's model deals with the operations of the intellect. "The operations consist in those activities of intelligence by means of which the organism deals with information. And 'information' is defined in this theory as 'that which the organism discriminates'" (1:57).

The four classifications developed by Aschner and Gallagher are an adaptation of the part of Guilford's model dealing with the operations of the intellect. Productive thinking is defined as "consisting in those divergent, convergent, and evaluative operations whereby the individual draws upon available past and present acts, ideas, associations, and observations in order to bring forth *new* facts, ideas, and conclusions. Productive thinking, so defined, includes both the creative and critical-analytic dimensions of reasoning" (12:120).

Four main types of questions in teaching will be treated here.* The reader will note that there is some overlap among these and the four types of questions classified according to the verification method. Nevertheless, he should keep in mind that each set arises from a different basic concept. The four types of questions outlined below complement the four discussed previously.

COGNITIVE-MEMORY QUESTIONS. Cognitive-memory questions are questions that elicit responses requiring cognitive-memory operations. These cognitive-memory operations represent nonproductive thinking operations (11:24). "Cognitive-memory operations represent the simple reproductions of facts, formulae, or other items of remembered content through the use of such processes as recognition, rote memory, and selective recall" (11:24).

1. *Question:* How do you spell *thyme* (the spice)?
Response: T-h-y-m-e.

---

* The following discussion, which draws heavily on the work of Aschner and Gallagher (1; 11; 12), will encompass, in the examples, the main types of cognitive educational objectives as set forth in Bloom's *Taxonomy of Educational Objectives* (6) and as applied by Sanders (23).

2. *Question:* Does anybody remember what we said yesterday about why President Johnson decided not to run again in 1968?
Response: One reason was because he wanted to bring peace in Korea.

3. *Question:* Do you mean Korea or Vietnam?
Response: Oh, boy, I guess I mean Vietnam.

4. *Question:* Who was the sixteenth president of the United States?
Response: Lincoln.

Note that even though Question 2 elicits as a response possible reasons why Johnson decided to retire (this position would be classified as an empirical explanation under the verification vantage point), it is here classified as cognitive-memory or nonproductive thinking. The respondent has only to recall what was said yesterday, and not to produce his own explanation now. Had the student been required to produce the explanation response, it would be classified differently. This point is important: in order to classify a question it is necessary to know what preceded the question. A "Why?" or "How?" is not sufficient to classify a question. Many people have a fallacious "belief that a 'why' or 'how' question necessarily demands more than memory" (23:9). However, the decision to classify a question as cognitive-memory is based on the context of previous sessions (1:62).

CONVERGENT QUESTIONS.   Convergent questions elicit responses requiring convergent thinking operations, which involve the merging of diverse data. "Convergent thinking represents the analysis and integration of given or remembered data. It leads to one expected end-result or answer because of the tightly structured framework through which the individual must respond" (11:25; 12:122, 131). These operations are considered productive thinking since they require that the respondent reason in order to arrive at his response. More is involved in the response than mere memory.

1. *Question:* Can you think of another, perhaps a 1970s way of saying, "A rose by any other name would smell as sweet"?
Response: Even if you changed the Mets' name to *Cardinals* they'd still play like Mets.

2. *Question:* Compare King David with King Solomon.
Response: Well, King David was primarily a warrior, but King Solomon was perhaps more of a scholar as well.

3. *Question:* "Can you sum up in one sentence what you think was the main idea of Paton's novel, *Cry the Beloved Country?*"
Response: "That the problem of the blacks and the whites in Africa can only be solved by brotherly love; there is no other way" (11:25).*

4. *Question:* Explain why Jonathan's room is so bright.
Response: Because his walls are white.

A convergent question asks for one of the following: a comparison, a contrast, the drawing of a conclusion, a summary, a generalization based on prior data, the translation of material from one form to another, or an explanation (generalization-specific instance, purpose or function, or sequential). Once again, the respondent must produce the explanation, rather than recall, for example, what the text said, in order that the response be classified as convergent thinking. The context of the situation is the basis for classifying the question as convergent. "The manner of the response itself sometimes provides a cue, as also does the phrasing of the question soliciting the response" (1:62).

DIVERGENT QUESTIONS.   Divergent questions elicit responses requiring divergent thinking operations. "Divergent thinking represents intellectual operations wherein the individual is free to generate independently his own ideas within a data-poor situation, or to take a new direction or perspective on a given topic" (11:25). Divergent questions encourage the elaboration of previous ideas, the drawing of implications, the generation of new data and ideas, as well as spontaneity, originality, flexibility, and initiative (1:63–64). These questions often ask about contrary-to-fact situations in order to provide freedom in response.

1. *Question:* Say more about your idea of phases in Picasso's works.
Response: Well, I mean that his work—well, you can see that

* In this section, as throughout the chapter, sources of examples, when not this author, have been cited. However, examples have been set up in this author's format, as in *Question, Response* (above) or *Question, Response, Question.*

he tried to be a Cubist, and a Realist, and then he had a Blue Period and others, too, more than most painters.

2. *Question:* "What comes to mind when you think of Plymouth Colony?"

Response: "Well, the only thing I can think of is it seemed like every time you turned around, all of a sudden there was a war" (1:64).

3. *Question:* What would have happened if Jefferson had not purchased the Louisiana Territory?

Response: Maybe our South would be more like Montreal than Toronto is, and I'd be answering in French, not English.

4. *Question:* What comes to mind when you think of television-telephones?

Response: Let's just think simply of what it would be like if we could control the phone we have now, like being able to decide who should be able to call us and when.

These questions ask the respondent to come up with responses unknown beforehand. They ask the respondent to generate a variety of ideas within a framework which is data-poor. Question 4 somehow got the respondent to take off on his own in an open situation. The respondent changed the direction of the question toward an entirely new problem. This is self-initiated and surely unexpected by the questioner. Nevertheless, it is relevant to the ongoing general topic.

It is appropriate here to mention that in his eulogy of his brother, Senator Robert F. Kennedy, Senator Edward M. Kennedy virtually noted his brother's self-characterization as a divergent-thinking man. He ended the eulogy with this quotation from Robert F. Kennedy, which, without using the exact term, describes divergent thinking quite well: "Some men see things as they are and say why. I dream things that never were and say, why not" (16:56).

EVALUATIVE QUESTIONS. Evaluative questions elicit responses requiring evaluative thinking operations. "Evaluative thinking deals with matters of judgment, value, and choice, and is characterized by its judgmental quality" (11:26). These questions ask the respondent to express his personal opinion about some person, event, or policy; to estimate on the basis of his own assessment of a situation or policy what probably will occur; and to offer a judgment based on a judgment previously offered.

1. *Question:* What do you think of Mike Nichols as a film director [*The Graduate*]?

Response: He's clever, and he really understands the audience he's aiming his film at—he sure knows how to make an impact.

2. *Question:* Do you think Arthur Miller will be considered a major playwright in fifty years?

Response: No, because even though he's timely, and topical —and that's why people like him now—his stuff isn't for all time, and people will see this in fifty years.

3. *Reaction:* Okay, that'll get us started.

Question: Would you comment on Suzanne's estimation of Arthur Miller, Joyce.

Response: Well, I think his fame will last, just because he was so much of his time. As a matter of fact, he's really a key to understanding America today.

4. *Question:* Do you think there will be more riots this summer?

Response: Yes, since nothing has really changed since last summer—the mood's the same.

Cognitive Function

Questions may also serve particular cognitive functions within the immediate interplay of the discourse. For example, a teacher or student may ask a question that calls for an explanation or divergent thinking in order to accomplish something else as well. This is a most important point to note. A question may have the function of focusing the discourse or clarifying a response. Function here refers to a specific purpose within verbal interaction rather than to broad teacher goals, such as "stimulating thinking." Indeed, every question serves to stimulate thinking on some level.

It is always possible to claim that a divergent-thinking question, for example, has the function of giving the respondent the opportunity to perform a divergent-thinking operation. The questioner, that is to say, asks the question just because it is a divergent-thinking question. Such a claim as to the function of a question, however, though it may sometimes be valid, is not always helpful, because many questions are clearly not limited to such a function. Yet, it is wise to remember that this goal of stimulating thinking ought to lie behind most questions.

To decide which cognitive function a question performs, it is absolutely necessary to view the question in the context of the ongoing interaction. Context is more important in classifying the function of the question than it is in classifying the productive thinking elicited by a question. Furthermore, it is possible for a question to have more than one function simultaneously. Thus a question may fit into more than one of the types presented below.

FOCUSING QUESTIONS.   In regard to questions in teaching, five main types will be treated.* First, there are focusing questions, questions whose function it is to provide the topic of a discourse. Focusing questions serve to introduce a topic and thereby indicate to the participants the intended direction of the discourse. These questions may also serve to refocus or sharpen a discussion that has strayed somewhat from its original course. They also may serve to change the subtopic of the discourse. That is, while studying the topic of the factors of production in economics, a question may have the function of switching the conversation from the subtopic of labor to that of land or capital. Or, a focusing question may serve to switch the discourse from its intended direction. Such a question may induce the participants in the discussion to deviate from the previously indicated topic.

1. *Reaction:* Okay. We have treated the effects of water on fire.
Question (same speaker): Now, please explain how running water affects rocks and mountains.

2. *Question:* What are the various types of tariff, and how do they inhibit trade? That's the question for today, in view of our discussion on free trade yesterday. What types of tariff are there, and in what ways do they hinder trade?

3. *Question:* Would you try to characterize Kandinsky as an artist?
Response: He painted around the turn of the twentieth century and . . .
Reaction: Yes, that's his life but . . .
Question (same speaker): . . . Would you characterize him regarding his painting and what he did, rather than by his biography?

* The following draws on the work of Taba (references 27; 28).

4. *Question:* Would you think of as many combinations of instruments as you can that you think would make a desirable musical quartet.

Response: Let's see, the clarinet, the piano, the guitar, and the bass . . .

Question (third speaker)*:* How come the guitar has gotten popular lately?

Focusing questions are attempts to set the discourse in an intended direction as in the first three examples above. Or, as in the fourth example, such a question can serve to deliberately switch the discourse from one direction to another, causing a deviation from the previous intention. In any case, focusing questions deal with the direction of the discourse as a whole.

FOUNDATION QUESTIONS. Foundation questions are questions whose function it is to elicit responses that will serve as the basis of a more complex question or discussion. They might request, for example, connecting evidence or criteria for an explanation schema, a valuative judgment schema, or a divergent-thinking operation. The questioner asks the question in such a way as to bring out the evidence of criteria to be used in a more complex thought operation. The question may seek its information through a review of a previous session, a recapitulation of the ongoing discourse, or the presentation of new information not yet offered.

1. *Question:* Will you review for us the main products grown in Latin America.

Response: Coffee, sugar cane, and bananas.

Question: Now, why do we trade with Latin America?

2. *Question:* How much has the volume of stocks and bonds trading been?

Response: Ten million a day.

Question: What's the capacity of the brokers in handling trading?

Response: About eight or nine million a day.

Question: So?

3. *Question:* Will you now sum up the points we've made so far about a rhombus, so we'll be ready to compare it with a triangle.

These questions serve to build up the case, so to speak. They evince statements that the participants will need and use as they advance in the topic at hand and into more complex ideas. These questions occur most often as the participants gather the data relevant to the overall problem before them.

EXTENDING QUESTIONS. Extending questions are questions that clarify or elaborate upon the statements already made. An elaboration, or probe, may be requested in order to help the respondent and listeners to realize what else is implied in (or will result from) the previous statements. A person may ask a clarifying question either because he as a listener did not understand a previous remark, or because he feels that the speaker himself is unclear about the meaning of his own remark.

1. *Reaction:* Yes, what you said about what happens if the president dies is fine.
Question (same speaker): Now tell us what you mean when you say "incapacitated."

2. *Reaction:* I don't understand you at all.
Question (same speaker): Please explain again how the heart gets its fresh blood, and that'll help me, maybe.

3. *Question:* Tell us more about the sonata form.

Extending questions keep the discourse on the same level of thought, whatever that is at the time. They seek only to make points more explicit or complete. This may be contrasted with the next type of function.

LIFTING QUESTIONS. Lifting questions have the function of eliciting from the respondent a level of thought higher or more complex than what has already been established for the ongoing discourse. For example, the response elicited may be an explanation of the facts previously offered, or a justification of a valuative opinion, or a prediction of the likelihood that an event already cited will occur, or a general label for grouping items previously identified.

1. *Response:* "They carried things in baskets on their heads."
Question: "Explain why."
Response: "I suppose they can carry more things that way" (28:205).

2. *Question:* Which modern novelist do you like best?
Response: Faulkner.
Question: Why?

3. *Question:* When did we get to the moon?
Response: July, 1969.
Question: How soon do you think men might land on Mars? Venus?

4. *Response:* Computers, autos, television sets . . .
Reaction: That's right.
Question (same speaker): Now what do these items have in common? What can they all be called?

Only the context will indicate if a question serves to extend or lift the level of thought in the discourse. For example, a request for an explanation may lift the level of thought to an explanation at one point, but at another only extend an explanation already given. An illustration will be helpful here.

Response: "They were working fast on the house."
Question: "Why?"
Response: "They wanted to get the house done before the rain came."
Question: "Why?"
Response: "Because unless it is finished the rain will destroy it" (28:204).

The first question attempts to elicit an explanation based on fact. It lifts the level of thought. The second question only seeks to extend (elaborate or complete) the explanation established in the second response. It does not lift the level of thought.

PROMOTING QUESTIONS. Promoting questions have the function of elicting responses that promote the flow of the discourse. Such questions clear up impasses in the discussion; as, for example, when participants are seeking to establish a sequence explanation and cannot get the sequence correct. Or, these questions elicit responses which will fill in missing parts in an explanation schema or valuative judgment schema. Promoting questions also might prompt participants to draw explanatory conclusions or value judgments, and thereby keep the discourse from bogging down.

This tends to occur when a participant, though he has sufficient evidence, fails to employ it.

1. *Question:* Considering your available data and your criteria, rate the candidates. Then we'll be able to rank and order them.

2. *Response:* I know water wears away the rocks, and rocks fall from the slopes.
Reaction (same speaker): But that doesn't add up to much, so I'm stuck.
Question: What's the one thing he's missing about the Grand Canyon?
Response: That there was, by some means, an uplift of the rock to about six thousand feet.
Reaction: Right.

3. *Question:* What are we missing?
Response: I have it—the color of his walls.
Question: Well, what color are they?
Response: White.
Reaction: All right.

These promoting questions prompt the participants to keep the discourse moving. Such questions, asked at the appropriate times, keep the participants from being overwhelmed by the complexity of the problems being studied. Often they will ask the participants to look at what they have been saying for clues as to what else has to be discussed.

Comments and Suggested Applications

With these three cognitive vantage points in mind, it is possible to make several comments and applications.

1. The teacher must keep the differences between questions clearly in mind, just as he must be clear about the various schemas of explanation and justification presented earlier. Many a discussion has failed to end successfully because the participants were confused about the type of question before them and thus did not know what would be an appropriate response. For example, unless people agree as to the appropriate verification method for a particular response, they cannot assess that response. It is fruitless to treat a response as an empirical statement and demand further evidence when it is offered as an analytic statement.

An illustration: When the teacher asks, as in the valuative discussion about teenage lawbreakers, "What is a juvenile delinquent?", both he and his students must know the type of response expected (see page 120). In the context of that illustrative discussion the teacher sought a definition and clearly indicated so by using the phrase, "What do you mean by . . . ?" An appropriate response was offered; i.e., a definition was sought, and a definition was obtained. Had a student reacted to the response with, "That's not what a juvenile delinquent is—I know one when I see one, and you're wrong," then the teacher, if he was familiar with the four types of verification, could easily have handled the confusion. For, in these terms, the student who had reacted negatively had understood the response as an empirical statement, and an incorrect one. The respondent had made, rather, an analytic statement in which he proposed the common usage of a term.

In that valuative discussion the teacher clearly realized that he had sought and obtained an analytic statement about juvenile delinquents. He emphasized this several times by using such phrases as "definition," "let's all stick with this notion," and "if we use it this way." Consider now the question "What is life?" offered by a student in the illustrative lecture in Chapter 10. Was the student seeking a definition? Was the student seeking an empirical response? A valuative response? Indeed it is difficult to determine what the student was seeking, especially in light of the teacher's evaluative reaction ("That is a good question") and subsequent change of direction. It may well be that the student sought a clarifying definition but the teacher mistakenly took the question to be an empirical one.

2. The teacher must teach his students, too, that various types of questions elicit different responses. The teacher may directly explain the differences among questions. Or, he may comment on the various questions and responses as they are raised, pointing out how to *verify* the response, offer the correct type of *productive thinking*, or perform the appropriate *function*. This indirect approach will keep the focus on the topic, while at the same time it will sensitize the students to the various verification methods. This is just the approach taken in the illustrative discussion on jailing teenage lawbreakers, for the teacher there comments as part of the discussion that the group needs a way of deciding who is right. Whether or not this teacher has ever treated the various types of questions directly we cannot know from just the illustration presented. In any case, the need for a

student to be alert to this matter of verification is obvious if he is to become independent. If the student is not alert to the different types of questions, he is subject to self-misdirection.

3. The teacher, since he strives to lead the student to independence, has the obligation to vary the types of questions he asks. Students require practice in handling the various types of verification, productive thinking, and cognitive function questions. They need practice in responding to the various questions themselves as well as practice in reacting, silently and verbally, to others' responses.

It is wise for a teacher to vary the types of questions he asks. In the research reported by Gallagher, using the productive thinking vantage point, the teachers (junior and senior high school in English, science, and social studies) devoted about 60 percent of their questions to cognitive-memory, about 30 percent to convergent thinking, 6 percent to evaluative thinking, and 4 percent to divergent thinking. The report does not give information on the teaching methods employed by the teachers. Whatever the methods, however, it is clear that the teachers limited their questions to two main types. In regard to verification, current research shows that teachers predominantly ask empirical questions. In research dealing with the topic of world trade, over 80 percent of the questions were empirical (4:112). Smith and Meux also report that empirical categories predominate in the secondary school classrooms they studied in mathematics, science, social studies, English, and Core (a variable but generally integrated curriculum (26:116–117).

If the teacher wants his students to develop whatever creative talents they may have, he must make it his business to vary his questions. The divergent questions, in particular, tap and develop the student's creative dimension. The teacher must ask these questions with the realization that the students' performance is closely related to his own. That is to say, students answer the questions that the teacher asks of them.

Figure 14–1 illustrates the relationship between the teacher's questions and the thinking of the students. The figure is based on data from one social studies class of gifted children studied over five consecutive fifty-six-minute sessions. The profile of divergent thinking production for both boys and girls follows the teacher's divergent questions as the percentage shifts from session to session. However, a slight increase in the percentage of teacher divergent thinking questions yields a large increase in divergent production by students. "This results from the fact that a single question, such as, 'What would happen if the United States were colonized from the West Coast to the East instead of vice versa?', can bring forth as many as fifteen or twenty responses, each related to divergent production on the part of these gifted students" (12:127).

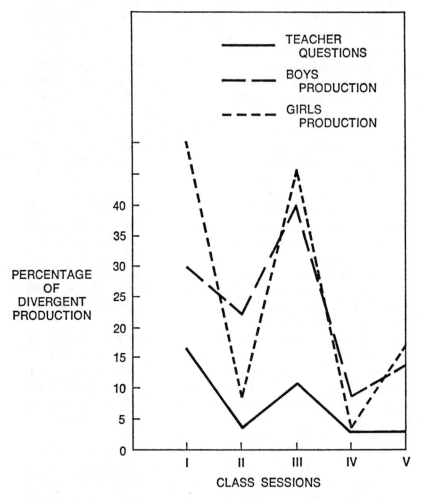

Figure 14–1: Relation of Teacher Questions to Student Divergent Thinking Production*

* Reprinted with permission of senior author and publisher, from James J. Gallagher and Mary Jane Aschner, "A Preliminary Report on Classroom Interaction," *Merrill-Palmer Quarterly of Behavior and Development*, July 1963.

As with questions classified according to the verification method, no research evidence as yet exists on the desirable percentage for each type of productive thinking question. Each teacher must decide on his own for each particular group of students. This decision should take into account the nature of the topic being studied, the level of the students' understanding, and what was done in prior sessions. There probably should be more divergent thinking and evaluative thinking questions, but it is impossible at this time to specify how much more.

4. The productive thinking vantage point clearly exposes a myth that has misled teachers for a long time, namely, that those questions that begin with *why*, by their very construction, are thought questions. On the contrary, a question is not a memory question or a thought question in and of itself. Rather, only by knowing the context of the lesson can questions be classified. A teacher cannot ask a thought question on Monday and then ask the same question on Tuesday in review as a thought question. A teacher who accepts the myth finds it difficult to understand the workings of his class on Tuesday, for on that day he has only asked a cognitive-memory question. A question that stimulated students on Monday may fail to do so on Tuesday.

5. For many years people who have had the courage to advise teachers have implied or explicitly said that memory questions are inferior to thought questions. That is to say, good teachers ask thought questions, while poor teachers ask memory questions. Yet it is evident that there is an interdependency among questions. The four types of productive thinking questions are not unrelated to one another. This interdependency can best be shown as in Figure 14–2 (11:39).

It can be seen from Figure 14–2 that it is not adequate to conceive of the three productive thinking types as independent and yet all supported by cognitive-memory. Rather, while all three rely on cognitive-memory, so does evaluative thinking rely on convergent and divergent thinking. This means that if a teacher wants to ask some evaluative questions, for example, he may feel it necessary to ask some cognitive-memory, convergent, and divergent questions to prepare the way. In this sense it seems pointless to say that memory questions are bad and thought questions are good.

Once sensitive to the differences among questions and the desirability of varying their questions, teachers would do well to take steps to reexamine their own verbal activity. Some teachers

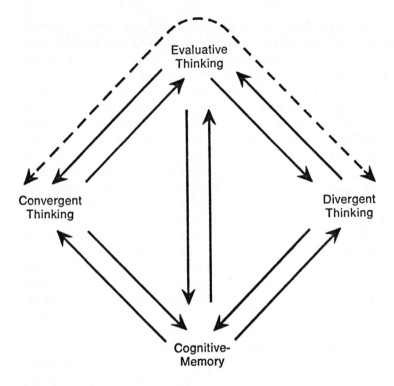

Figure 14–2: (Based on Gallagher)*

will decide to alter the types of questions they usually ask and the ways that they react to the student's responses. This does not mean that they must artificially inject, for example, definitional questions simply to increase the frequency of analytic questions. Rather, it means that the teacher will be ready to ask for a definition of a key term and to point out its appropriateness to the flow of the discourse.

On the other hand, some topics do not seem to encourage certain questions. For instance, it would be unwise in a mathematics lesson on parallelograms or in an economics lesson on the history of the Federal Reserve System to bend over backwards to ask a metaphysical question. Nor does it seem appropriate to ask some evaluative questions about the honesty of mathematicians

* Reprinted with permission of author, James J. Gallagher, from *Productive Thinking of Gifted Children*, Cooperative Research Project No. 965, U.S. Department of Health, Education, and Welfare. Urbana, Ill.: Institute for Research on Exceptional Children, 1965.

or government officials every few minutes. But at some time or another, especially in mathematics and science—which are popularly conceived to be value-free—the teacher can appropriately ask valuative questions. In other words, it is unwise for a teacher to restrict his questions in a particular field of study to only one or two types of questions. It is unwise and misleading for students to be deprived of opportunities to question, respond, and react valuatively with their physical science, natural science, and mathematics teachers.

Similarly, students should have many opportunities in the areas of language arts, social studies, and mathematics to ask divergent questions as well as respond to them. Teachers in certain fields ought not to restrict themselves to a narrow range. They ought to utilize a mixed bag of questions so as to provide a rich experience for their students.

6. Many people advise teachers to ask *why* questions because such questions are said to elicit a high level of "thought" from students. Yet, as shown earlier, within the context of a teaching situation not all *why* questions are "thought" questions. Moreover, even those *why* questions which are thought questions are not all alike, and therefore the teacher must carefully consider his use of them.

A *why* question requests reasons from the respondent. Yet the side effects of that question are different when it deals with physical phenomena from when it deals with personal feelings. For example, "Why did the mountain erode?" can have a quite different effect on the respondent from "Why do you distrust me?" though both questions apparently request reasons only. The first question may provoke some personal challenge, but not a great one since the challenge is essentially a cognitive one. The second question, however, may provoke a great challenge and threaten the respondent since it challenges not only his cognitive position but also his personal feelings. The student respondent must face up to the teacher questioner and defend himself. Thus, the effect of a request for reasons through a *why* question is different depending on whether the question is an empirical one or a valuative one. Furthermore, even within the valuative mode there is a difference in questions. The defense of personal feelings elicited by "Why do you distrust me?" is much more threatening to the student respondent than the defense of a policy position elicited by "Why do you support high tariffs on imported silverware?"

On this basis the teacher must monitor his *why* questions and consider the side effects of the *why* question he asks. In regard to personal feelings a *why* question often implies, "Now we'll get down to the truth," and puts the respondent in an unpleasant and unfortunate defensive position (24:165). If the teacher is dealing with policy issues and especially personal feelings, he may well avoid *why* questions in favor of *what* questions and *how* questions. These questions are not nearly as threatening and therefore facilitate interaction rather than inhibit it. For example, if the teacher wishes to treat the matter of distrust, then questions such as "What am I doing?", "What are you doing?", and "How are we doing this?" are much more likely to promote meaningful, honest interactions than a *why* question. The teacher must look not only at the cognitive level of the question but also the affective effect a question has on the respondent as he teaches. Contrary to a popular notion, a decrease in the number of *why* questions in favor of *what* and *how* questions may well improve the interaction between teacher and student.

7. Discourse in teaching flows quickly. For this reason, perhaps more than any other, a question designed to serve a particular function must be asked at the appropriate time. If not, the question may not serve the intended function at all. Timing is most important in regard to cognitive function, much less so in regard to verification method. A teacher can improve his chances of asking the appropriate question at the proper time by careful lesson planning. He can list possible lifting and extending questions, for example, that might follow unexpected responses or reactions. The teacher can and should review his plans before his lesson and refer to them during his lesson so as to improve his ability to ask certain types of questions at the correct time.

8. By keeping in mind these various types of questions, as well as the many points previously made about the discussion method, the teacher has a definite criterion for assessing responses to questions. He may indeed point out that a response that is incongruent—as when the teacher's questions call for an explanation but the student responds with an evaluation—should be corrected. Furthermore, an incongruent response is powerful feedback to the teacher, and it deserves diagnosis. This is particularly so since incongruence of the sort just described is somewhat rare. In the research on the language of the classroom using the verification vantage point, it occurred in about 1 percent of the responses (4:126).

Information Process Activity

There is another way of looking at questions that goes hand in hand with the entire cognitive vantage point as seen in verification method, productive thinking, and cognitive function. Here the concept of *information process activity* will be used (4:90). Information process activity refers to the operation the questioner intends for the respondent to perform. Every question, by its very nature, indicates to the respondent the information process activity expected. This is understood from the way that questions are phrased. Sometimes the question explicitly indicates to the respondent what the information process activity is. But even if it is not that explicit, it can be known by the respondent simply from his understanding of the language of the question.

YES/NO QUESTIONS.   Three main types and three variations of these types of questions will be treated in this section.* Yes/no questions indicate that the respondent is to respond with simple affirmation or denial. The respondent may answer yes or no; he may use a verbal equivalent such as "sure," "absolutely," or "mm hm" for yes, or he may use a verbal equivalent such as "certainly not," "not at all," or "uh uh" for no; he may say a complete sentence that implies yes or no; or he may combine a yes or no with a complete sentence. Response in any of these four ways is appropriate.

1. *Question:* Was Lincoln the sixteenth president?
Response: Yes.

2. *Question:* Do you think we will have an inflation in the economy?
Response: Certainly not.

3. *Question:* If it rains, will the river overflow?
Response: If it rains, the river will overflow.

4. *Question:* Did Shakespeare write *Macbeth?*
Response: Sure, Shakespeare wrote *Macbeth.*

* This section draws heavily on research of the author and his colleagues at Teachers College, Columbia University. The study was supported by a grant from the Cooperative Research Program of the U.S. Office of Education. It was reported in *The Language of the Classroom* (reference 4; see also 2; 3).

The short response of "yes" in the first example is the equivalent of saying, "It is the case that Lincoln was the sixteenth president." Each of the other three responses can also be similarly rephrased to fit a complete schema. This is not necessary, however, for an understanding of the use of yes and no comes with a knowledge of everyday speech.

It is also appropriate to say "I don't know" to this type of question and to any other. This indicates, not that the respondent has failed to understand which information process activity was indicated, but that he cannot supply an answer without guessing. Also, in cases involving probability and judgment it is appropriate to respond with such phrases as "maybe," "somewhat," or "sometimes," which indicate that there is a range of possibilities involved rather than a yes/no dichotomy.

What if the first question had been, "Was Washington the sixteenth president?" It would be appropriate to respond: (1) "No"; (2) "Washington wasn't the sixteenth president"; (3) "No, Washington wasn't the sixteenth president"; and even (4) "Yes," though this last response would be incorrect. But it would also be appropriate to answer: (5) "Lincoln was"; or (6) "No, Lincoln." Answer 5 contains an implied no, whereas 6 states it explicitly. Both are short for "No, it is the case that Washington was not the sixteenth president. It is the case that Lincoln was the sixteenth president." In other words, Responses 5 and 6 go beyond the requirement of the question. Simply responding no will not reveal who the sixteenth president was. By supplying the added information the respondent fills in the gap left by the negative response.

SELECTION QUESTIONS. Selection questions indicate that the respondent is to respond by selecting from stated alternatives. Though any number of alternatives may be offered, only two or three are usually given, since it is difficult to keep more than this number in mind.

1. *Question:* Was Lincoln, Jefferson, or Garfield the sixteenth president?
Response: Lincoln.

2. *Question:* Do you think we'll have an inflation or deflation in the economy?
Response: Deflation, within six months.

3. *Question:* Did Poe or Sophocles write *Macbeth*?
Response: Neither.

4. *Question:* Did Poe or Sophocles write *Macbeth*?
Response: Shakespeare.

Here, again, short responses stand for complete ones. The first response is short for, "It is the case that Lincoln was the sixteenth president." The second response is in shortened form, but adds new information. (This goes beyond the question, which merely requires selection between the stated alternatives, inflation and deflation.) In the third example no stated alternative will yield a correct response. Therefore, "neither" is appropriate. Note that this response, too, is short for the complete statement that could be constructed. In the fourth example, the response implies "neither," and then supplies the correct answer. The single word *Shakespeare* in the fourth response implies a great deal. In any case it is appropriate and comprehensible. In all of these four responses the respondent indicates that he understands the expected information process activity.

CONSTRUCTION QUESTIONS. Construction questions indicate that the respondent is to construct his own response based on information provided in the question. The question itself does not give a clue as to the correct response—the respondent must supply it himself.

1. *Question:* Who was the sixteenth president?
Response: Lincoln.

2. *Question:* What will happen if it rains?
Response: The river will overflow.

3. *Question:* Why is Jonathan's room so bright?
Response: Because his walls are white.

4. *Question:* What would have happened if Jefferson had not purchased the Louisiana Territory?
Response: Maybe our South would be more like Montreal than Toronto is, and I'd be answering in French, not English.

Once again, in the first example the single word *Lincoln* stands for the complete sentence, "It is the case that Lincoln was the sixteenth president." The respondent assumes that there was a sixteenth president and then tells who that president was. The question itself gives no clue to the president's identity, as did the yes/no and selection questions. In the three other examples as well, the respondent must make up the terms of his response himself.

On the basis of these three main types it is possible to set forth three variations as the fourth, fifth, and sixth types.

CONSTRUCTION—YES/NO QUESTIONS. Construction—yes/no questions indicate that the respondent should respond yes or no and at the same time construct his own response. This type is ambiguous, as it sometimes is not clear to the respondent that he is to construct his own response in addition to supplying a yes or no.

1. *Question:* Does anyone know who the sixteenth president was?

Response: Yes, I do. It was Lincoln.

2. *Question:* Does anyone know what will happen if it rains?
Response: The river will overflow.

3. *Question:* Does anyone know why Jonathan's room is so bright?

Response: Yes.

All these three responses are appropriate. The first respondent says yes and supplies the answer, too. In the second question, yes is implied by the response. In the third the respondent says only yes and thereby technically satisfies the form of the question. However, he obviously does not infer that he is also expected to construct a response. If the questioner did indeed desire the respondent to construct a response explaining why Jonathan's room is so bright, he would then have to ask a straight construction-type question. If he did so desire, it is not clear why he chose this fourth type of question rather than, "Why is Jonathan's room so bright?"

SELECTION—YES/NO QUESTIONS. Selection—yes/no questions are ambiguous in that they indicate that the respondent may select from the stated alternatives or may respond yes or no. That is, it is not clear exactly what information process activity is expected.

1. *Question:* If it rains, will the river overflow or flow rapidly?
Response A: Yes.
Response B: Overflow.

2. *Question:* Did Shakespeare or Morley write *Hamlet*?
Response A: Yes.
Response B: Shakespeare.

In these examples, both Response A and Response B are appropriate. This is due to the ambiguity arising from the word *or* in the question. In English *or* has two related but distinguishable meanings. The first, the inclusive sense, indicates that *either, possibly both* alternatives are correct. Thus, in the second example, Response A would mean, "Yes it is true that either Shakespeare or Morley wrote *Hamlet*—one of the two or possibly both of them." The second sense of *or*, the exclusive sense, indicates that *at least one and at most one* alternative is correct (8:240). That is, Response B in the second example means, "It was Shakespeare, not Morley, who wrote *Hamlet*."

Respondents A in these two examples understood *or* in its inclusive sense, while Respondents B understood it in its exclusive sense. To these respondents it was not clear which sense of *or* was intended by the questioner. For more precision the questioner should use *and/or* if he intends the inclusive sense and should use *but not both* if he intends the exclusive sense. Most of the time, however, the sense of *or* intended is made clear by the tone of the questioner's voice and the context.

SELECTION-CONSTRUCTION   QUESTIONS.   Selection-construction questions indicate that the respondent may select the one stated possibility or construct his own response. This question is a cross between the selection and construction types.

1. *Question:* Was Lincoln the sixteenth president, or who was?
Response: Lincoln.

2. *Question:* If it rains, will the river overflow, or what will happen?
Response: The river will simply carry away the excess rapidly by widening a bit.

3. *Question:* Do you approve of jailing teenagers, or what do you feel about it?
Response: Well, I'd jail only the murderers and drug addicts— the others I'd fine or send to reform school.

Comments and Suggested Applications

With these six types of questions in mind it is possible to make several points. First, a myth is now prevalent regarding the undesirability of yes/no questions. This myth claims that yes/no questions require little thought, and hence should be avoided "like poison," as one books puts it (7:221). Another author states it this way: "The teacher should not ask questions which yield a simple yes or no answer. Very little information or thought is required to answer yes or no. The student has a fifty-fifty chance of guessing the right answer even if he has no idea of the nature of the question" (19:255). Numerous other references could be cited.

However, no available research evidence shows that all yes/no questions elicit "very little" thought. On the contrary, it is possible to phrase all types of verification-method questions—analytic, empirical, and valuative—in a yes or no form. Surely, for example, questions such as, "Well, do you support the president's policy in Vietnam?" (valuative) and "In light of your study would you claim that the moon's craters were formed by impact from meteorites?" (empirical explanation) involve complex schemata. And, thus, to answer yes or no about Vietnam or the moon's craters demands that the respondent consider and weigh a great deal of evidence before offering his conclusion. Similarly, it is possible to phrase convergent-thinking and evaluative-thinking questions in a yes/no form, and these require more than low-level thought operations. Then why did the myth arise that yes/no questions require very little thought on the part of the respondent?

This myth derived from the fact that all too often people ask yes/no questions that have only one right answer. Indeed, it is possible in these cases to guess on such matters with a fifty-fifty probability of being correct. But, if this is the basis of the myth, then it rests on three false assumptions: (1) *Yes/no questions can be asked only where there is one correct answer to a question.* That this assumption is false is demonstrated in the two examples given in the above paragraph; there is no one right answer about Vietnam or, in light of present knowledge, about the moon's craters. (2) *If there is one right answer, the respondent will flippantly respond with a yes or no rather than think about the answer to the question.* Indeed, it is easier to guess when responding to a yes/no question than to a construction* question. However, though this assumption about guessing may be true of some people, it surely is not true for everyone at every time. Some people will not guess;

---

* In a selection question with only two stated alternatives, guessing is as easy as with a yes/no question. This is so because a selection question with only two alternatives is, in effect, a yes/no question. If alternative A is wrong, then B must be right.

they will say, "I don't know," or they will not respond rathc. than give a quick yes or no that is not a result of serious thought. (3) *There are few, if any, appropriate times for asking questions with only one right answer* (such as, "So, then, was Lincoln the sixteenth president?"). Obviously, the appropriateness of such questions cannot be decided ahead of time, because it depends on the context of the discourse, the respondent, and considerations over and above cognitive processes (e.g., supporting a shy student in order to make it easy for him to participate in verbal interaction at the outset). There may well be appropriate times to ask yes or no questions in teaching, but that must be decided by each teacher after assessing the total teaching situation.

The task of the teacher may well be to work with the students even more than with himself if he wishes to deemphasize questions that encourage guessing. If there is to be a variety of questions or an avoidance of yes/no questions, then the students as well as the teacher must vary their questions. In the study of teacher-student interaction in fifteen high school economics classes, the following distribution was found (4:114):

	Percent of Teachers' Questions	*Percent of Students' Questions*
Yes/No	12.5	60.5
Selection	2.0	4.3
Construction	79.2	33.9
Construction–Yes/No	6.3	1.3
Selection–Yes/No	0.0	0.0
* Total	100.0	100.0

These data show that in the observed classes the students predominantly asked yes/no questions. About four out of every five of the teachers' questions required the students to construct their own responses, whereas about one-eighth required them to respond yes or no. Thus a teacher must take steps to encourage students to ask other types of questions. One method is for the teacher to reduce his own use of guessing questions in order to set an example. Another way is to request students to rephrase

* Reprinted with the permission of the publisher from Arno Bellack, Herbert Kliebard, Ronald Hyman, and Frank Smith, *Language of the Classroom* (New York: Teachers College Press), copyright 1966. Selection-construction type was not included in this study.

their questions. This is possible after the teacher has treated the various types of questions according to information process activity.

Also, although it is not apparent why the students in this study preferred yes/no questions, it is possible to suggest an explanation. According to O'Connor yes/no questions and selection questions with two stated alternatives are the most precise types of questions. As the number of alternatives increases, the question becomes less precise. The larger the number of alternatives, the more general the question (18:32). In addition, children tend to look at people and events in black and white terms rather than in grays. Young people simply are not mature enough to handle the very wide gray area between the two extremes of a dichotomy (5:35). Thus, it may well be that yes/no questions provide precise responses which students (particularly young students) can handle.

If this is so, then yes/no questions surely are appropriate in some cases and ought not to be avoided "like poison." However, the teacher should show his students that people and their activities can be classified as more than only good and bad, black and white. He should work more and more with the gray area as the students mature, in order to help his students mature in their outlook on people and events. The teacher's task somehow should be to balance the frequency of yes/no questions with other types—too many yes/no questions may well encourage guessing and the continuation of thinking in terms of black and white, while too few yes/no questions may well create an uneasy situation for the students.

Lastly, the construction–yes/no, selection–yes/no, and selection-construction types of questions are, by their very nature, ambiguous types. Though they can be helpful, the teacher should be careful in using them.

Response Clues

In addition to the several ways, already presented, in which to characterize questions, it is also possible to do so in terms of the clues to the appropriate response within the question. For example, in the question, "Who was the sixteenth president?", the word *who* gives a clue that the answer involves a person. Several types of clues given to the respondent will be considered below. These clues will primarily be found in construction-type questions.

Yes/no and selection questions by their very design have built-in clues. Construction questions, however, may or may not contain clues. Therefore, attention will be devoted primarily to this type of question. Note in the examples used that construction questions may contain more than one type of clue.

"WH" CLUES. In the following section five main types of questions will be treated in relation to the clues they give.* Questions with WH clues give the respondent clues based on such words as who, where, when, why, which, what, whose, and whom, as well as how and how much. These WH clues derive their meaning from the content of the discourse. For example, *what* varies in meaning in: What are whales?, For what reasons did McNamara resign as Secretary of Defense?, and In what place did the Civil War start? By understanding the meaning of the WH word in the question, the respondent can get a clue as to the appropriate type of answer. From the "what place" clue above, the respondent knows that the appropriate response involves space in some manner. From a "when" clue, the respondent knows that the response is a date of some sort or involves some relationship between events.

1. *Question:* When was World War II?

2. *Question:* Why is Jonathan's room so bright?

3. *Question:* Who wrote *Hamlet*, Shakespeare or Morley?

4. *Question:* How was the Grand Canyon formed?

PARALLEL TERMS CLUES. Questions that give clues in parallel terms give the respondent clues by indicating that the appropriate response is like some other information given previously in the discourse. The clue usually involves "some other," "another," or "something else."

1. *Question:* Who was in George Washington's cabinet?
Response: Thomas Jefferson.
Question: Who else?
Response: Hamilton.

* This section also draws heavily on the research of the author and his colleagues at Teachers College, Columbia University. For further details see footnote, page 313.

2. *Question:* Give me an element.
Response: Hydrogen.
Question: And another?
Response: Carbon.

The clue "else" in the first example not only serves to provoke an additional response but also guides the response to the same level as the first response. If the first response had been "the secretary of state" (which is an appropriate response) rather than "Thomas Jefferson," the clue would have served to elicit something like "the secretary of the treasury" rather than "Hamilton."

EXCLUDED-TERMS CLUES. Questions with excluded terms give the respondent clues as to what not to use in his response. In some cases the excluded terms serve also to set the level of the terms to be used in the response, even though the terms themselves are not identified.

1. *Question:* Aside from Lincoln and Kennedy, which presidents were assassinated?

2. *Question:* What country has the most oil deposits—with the exception of the Arab countries?

CITED-TERMS CLUES. Questions with cited terms give the respondent clues as to the terms in which he should phrase his response. These terms may be general categories that should be further specified, or they may indicate the framework of the response.

1. *Question:* In terms of countries and not persons, who are the leaders in jazz today?

2. *Question:* Explain how the Grand Canyon was formed, in terms of process.

LEADING-QUESTION CLUES. Leading questions give the respondent strong clues as to what specifically is expected in response. Leading questions are phrased as yes/no questions. The clue usually involves, "It is, isn't it?" or some variation of this. For example, the expression "It is, isn't it?" provokes the respondent to respond "Yes."

1. *Question:* The formula for water is H_2O, isn't it?
Response: Yes.

2. *Question:* Don't you think that Beethoven was a great composer?
Response: Yes.

3. *Question:* Whales aren't fish, are they?
Response: Right, whales aren't fish.

In effect, the leading question makes a statement and then asks the respondent to accept it or agree with it. Thus the third example may be rephrased as, "Whales are not fish. Is this correct?" This question suggests its own response. It can be used by the questioner to ask a question and at the same time indicate his own viewpoint on the matter. In this respect a leading question lies between a statement and other types of questions.

Comments and Suggested Applications

With these five types of questions in mind, it is possible to make several points. First, the teacher can use these various types of clues to clarify for his students how the expected response should be phrased. This is one way that he can guide the discourse in specified directions. A question with several clues will not be vague to the respondent. The respondent, by knowing what is expected of him, can meaningfully continue in the direction already established.

Second, the teacher can use these clues to support weak or shy students. For example, a shy student may not participate in a discussion for fear of responding incorrectly. The teacher may encourage the student to participate by making it easier for him by asking questions with several clues. After the student has experienced successful participation in the discourse, the teacher may slowly shift to questions with fewer and weaker clues. Gradually, the teacher will be asking that student the same types of questions he asks other students. It is possible, then, to use selected questions and clues as one way of encouraging certain students to participate verbally in the discussion.

Third, with younger students or beginning students in a new field of study the teacher may find it wise to use questions with specific clues. This technique will aid the beginner in feeling comfortable with the new topic and may well ease the task of responding to subsequent questions. When he is at ease, the student may very likely begin to ask questions of his own.

Overall Suggestions and Applications

Teaching involves questioning. It is virtually impossible to think of teaching (over a period of time) that does not involve questioning. Indeed, questioning is the teacher's chief means of directing or channeling discourse. No doubt the teacher will ask fewer questions in a discussion than in a recitation. However, precisely for this reason he must be aware of the various types of questions. He must deliberately frame the questions appropriate to the context of the discourse and the students involved. By varying his questions the teacher can elicit a wide range of responses, thereby developing in the students a broad set of cognitive skills. (See the three sections on comments and applications following the cognitive vantage point, page 305; information process activity, page 317; and response clues, page 323.)

The reader has probably noticed that I am not presenting an overall strategy for asking questions. The reason for this is simple. A strategy built on questions only is indeed not consonant with the kinds of teaching advocated in this book and the research data on teacher verbal behavior. First, a 100 percent questioning strategy (i.e., deciding precisely which question to ask first, which second, which third, and so forth) necessitates the asking of only certain types of questions, those whose correct answers the teacher already knows beforehand. Because the teacher knows the precise correct answer, he knows what to expect from his students. Thus, he knows which question will follow after the expected answer, can plan for it, and then ask it upon receiving that expected answer.

However, in general, the type of teaching I am advocating, as shown in the various ways of teaching presented in this book, is not congruent with asking only "know-the-answer-beforehand questions." I am suggesting that, *in addition* to questions where the teacher knows the answers, the teacher should ask many questions for which he does not have the answers. There are three such types of questions if we examine the vantage points listed in this chapter: (1) those dealing with policy issues (valuative questions) such as, "Should Congress legalize the use of marijuana?"; (2) those dealing with contrary-to-fact situations (divergent questions) such as, "If our country had no laws, how would our lives be affected?"; and (3) those dealing with explanations that the teacher does not yet know but possibly could someday learn such as, "Why are some people allergic to chocolate?" (explaining questions). Since the teacher does not know the correct answer nor exactly what to·expect from his students when asking such questions, he cannot know precisely which question to ask following the students' responses.

Furthermore, and this point is most important because it is all too often forgotten by those proposing a questioning strategy, the teacher does more than ask questions in his interaction with students. He also makes reacting and structuring moves. That is, he summarizes, elaborates, shapes, and focuses the discourse. For example, in the illustrative discussion on juvenile delinquency (see page 119), the teacher carefully directed the discourse. His questions, structurings, and reactions to the elicited responses were quite different from those of the teachers involved in the illustrative lecture (see page 208) and recitation (see page 199). First of all, the teacher leading a discussion does more than question the students. He summarizes and also sharpens the responses and reactions by rephrasing them. He spotlights the essential points made by the students. Second, he plays discussion "traffic cop" in that he calls on students who wish to speak and requests others to comment on previous remarks. This is an essential discussion technique. Third, he does not always expect "correct" answers to his questions. He also encourages multiple responses and recitations. Because he does more than question, he does not rely only on questioning to bring ideas to the floor. Ideas come forth in student responses and in his own remarks. Therefore, he cannot know ahead of time just what question will be his next one.

The most a teacher can do in advance, then, is to study the topic deeply, determine what particular ideas (concepts, generalizations, explanations, inferences) will probably suit the class, and plan some varied, key questions. While he teaches, he must attend to remarks of the students. He can draw on his advance planning, but the decision as to which question follows which he will make as he teaches based on his ongoing assessment of the interaction. There may be no need to ask certain planned questions in light of some student responses and reactions. He probably will also have to formulate new questions to precisely fit the situation.

The reason for asking questions for which the teacher has yet no correct answers is to eliminate the pointless game wherein the student tries to guess what is in the teacher's mind. Moreover, these questions put the teacher and the student in the role of co-inquirers. For the student, this means stimulation. For the teacher, this means that he is taking on the role of acting as guide to the student and as a model of an adult inquirer exploring new ground.

This proposal stands in almost direct contrast to the popular "discovery" approach which all too often turns out to be deception. As often practiced, the teacher knows what is to be discovered and by subtle manipulation of materials and questions leads the students, frequently painstakingly, to the present goal. This is not to deny all validity to discovery projects. Rather I am advocating here that the asking of questions for which the teacher does not have the "right" answers will enliven the teaching situation and foster the critical and creative thinking teachers seek to develop in students.

To deal with questions in this way the teacher obviously needs practice. He also, no doubt, should modify his activity in light of his own reflections or the suggestions of a colleague. He should establish a procedure through which he will be in a position to reconsider his own questions—he might arrange for a colleague to observe him and to confer with him about the observation, or he might arrange to tape-record some sessions and later listen to them critically.

A teacher, especially a novice, may find it difficult to formulate certain types of questions—e.g., divergent-thinking questions—while in the act of teaching. Also, he may not be able to formulate, while engaged in the act of teaching, a *variety* of questions within the five categories presented: verification method, productive thinking, cognitive function, information process activity, and response clues. This is so because the flow of the discourse in teaching is quite rapid and complex, and makes on-the-spot assessment difficult.

In short, to provide the needed variety, the teacher, novice and veteran alike, should formulate key questions in advance and set them down in his plans. In a less hectic planning period, the teacher will be much freer to formulate pertinent questions of many types. He will not be able to plan every question, nor should he try to, for that would effectively eliminate the spontaneity and flexibility essential to discussion. Nevertheless, he can and should formulate the key, pivotal questions that will serve as his basic guide. He should concentrate on those few "pivotal questions upon which the development of the lesson turns" (10:43). If he plans in this way, the teacher will often be able to ask those varied and key questions that he considers important in his teaching.

The teacher must remember that his questions may at times prove confusing or difficult to understand. A confusing situation will arise, for example, when the teacher asks two or more questions at the same time. The student may not know which question to respond to. Even a single question that is long and composed of several distinct parts may lead to confusion. Therefore it is preferable to ask uncomplicated questions, one at a time, as a means of obviating confusion.

Elliptical questions may also lead to confusion. The student may not understand what the missing part of the question is. If the teacher perceives a puzzled, confused expression after asking an elliptical question, he would do well to restate the question in its complete form in order to help the student to respond. Similarly, the student will often be confused by and not know how to respond to questions that are vaguely phrased, such as, What about Vietnam? or, What about Einstein's theory? Hence such "what about" questions should be used cautiously, if at all.

Perhaps the greatest task facing the teacher in regard to questioning is to encourage the students to question—to question both the teacher and each other. Obviously the student must learn to question as well as to respond if he is to become independent of the teacher. This is precisely the rationale supporting the Inquiry Training Program established by the University of Illinois (see pages 79, 181). Despite its many excellent characteristics it is good to note two negative points of that program so as to obviate them in the future. In that program the student asked questions (1) instead of the teacher and (2) to the teacher alone and not to other students. But if teaching is to involve significant interaction between teacher and students, then the teacher must get the students to ask questions while he himself continues to do so. It seems unwise to buy student questions at the price of teacher restraint when it is possible to do otherwise. Surely there are situations in which a well-phrased question by a teacher can generate a multitude of questions from students.

The task of getting students to ask questions is underscored by research on current classroom interaction. In the research on high school classrooms cited above, it was found that students asked about 14 percent of all the questions (4:112). In a study of social studies lessons in fourteen elementary school classrooms (grades two to six in two San Francisco Peninsula school districts),

Dodl found that student questions took up slightly less than 2 percent of the time. "But for this sample, it is quite clear that pupil questions arise very infrequently during social studies instructional situations. Of a total of 43,531 behavior incidents recorded during this study only 728 were pupil questions" (9:173–174).

Naturally, the teacher must directly invite student questions. More than that, however, he must establish such a tone in the discourse that the students feel at ease in asking questions (14). The questions that students ask should arise from a desire to understand both the topic at hand and the position taken by the other participants. This is in contrast to asking questions in order to gain the teacher's favor. Also, the student must not feel obligated to remain silent lest he be resented by the other students.

The simplest technique for encouraging student questions is for the teacher to establish himself as a model that the student might do well to emulate. As such, the teacher must take care to ask many types of questions and to respect the many questions he hears. As he responds or reacts in other ways to questions, the teacher has an opportunity to show his respect for the students' questions, to commend the questioner, and to show how unclear or off-target questions can be reformulated.

The virtue of patience will aid the teacher in questioning. When a teacher asks a question that demands complex thinking operations, the students may remain silent for a while. None of the students may be eager to respond even though the question is clearly understood. The teacher would do well in this case to admit that the question is difficult, and to deliver a quick response. Or, if the teacher waits respectfully, thereby acknowledging that students are not yet prepared to speak, he will most often get a meaningful response. The teacher can also amend a fuzzy response in his later comments. With appropriate clues he can then continue to ask other questions along the same lines, if he wishes. On the other hand, if the students are not able to respond to questions the teacher may wish to halt the discussion temporarily to allow for further independent or small-group study. It is often wise to be patient rather than jump to another question.

The research data on questions completely support this position. On the average teachers allowed children only one second to start to answer a question. If students did not begin a response within one second, teachers usually either repeated the question or called on other students to respond. Also, when students responded, teachers usually waited slightly less than a second before reacting to the response, or asking another question, or launching a new topic. When teachers increased their wait-time to three to five seconds under training, the following significant results occurred:

(1) The length of student responses increased.

(2) The number of unsolicited but appropriate responses increased.

(3) Failure to respond decreased.

(4) Confidence as reflected in fewer inflected responses increased, i.e., fewer responses had the tone of "Is that what you want?"

(5) The incidence of speculative thinking increased.

(6) Teacher-centered show and tell decreased, and student-student comparing increased.

(7) More evidence followed by or preceded by inference statements occurred.

(8) The number of questions asked by students increased, and the number of [science] experiments they proposed increased.

(9) The number of responses from "slow" students increased so that there was a greater variety of students participating in the class (21;22).

All these nine student results occurred simply because the teacher was more patient. There was also an effect of patience on the teachers. As a result of an increased wait-time:

(1) Teachers became more flexible in their discourse.

(2) Teachers asked fewer questions.

(3) Teachers increased the variety of their questions.

(4) Teachers improved their expectations of performance of "slow" students (21;22).

All this occurred by increasing wait-time to three to five seconds. That patience is a virtue in teaching cannot be overemphasized here.

In closing, it may well be remarked that questioning is essential in teaching and that the teacher who can ask the right question at the right time has gotten to the core of his task. It may indeed be difficult to ask the right questions, but it is an end worthy of the effort it takes.

References

1. Aschner, Mary Jane McCue. "The Analysis of Verbal Interaction in the Classroom." In *Theory and Research in Teaching*, edited by Arno A. Bellack, pp. 53–78. New York: Bureau of Publications, Teachers College, Columbia University, 1963.

2. Bellack, Arno A., in collaboration with Ronald T. Hyman, Frank L. Smith, Jr., and Herbert M. Kliebard. *The Language of the Classroom: Meanings Communicated in High School Teaching, Part Two.* Cooperative Research Project No. 2023, U.S. Department of Health, Education, and Welfare, Office of Education. New York: Institute of Psychological Research, Teachers College, Columbia University, 1965.

3. Bellack, Arno A., and Joel R. Davitz, in collaboration with Herbert M. Kliebard and Ronald T. Hyman. *The Language of the Classroom: Meanings Communicated in High School Teaching.* Cooperative Research Project No. 1497, U.S. Department of Health, Education, and Welfare, Office of Education. New York: Institute of Psychological Research, Teachers College, Columbia University, 1963.

4. Bellack, Arno A., Herbert M. Kliebard, Ronald T. Hyman, and Frank L. Smith. *The Language of the Classroom.* New York: Teachers College Press, 1966.

5. Bettelheim, Bruno. "Their Country, Right or Wrong." *Ladies' Home Journal* 85:35–38, June 1968.

6. Bloom, Benjamin S., ed. *Taxonomy of Educational Objectives. The Classification of Educational Goals. Handbook I: Cognitive Domain.* New York: David McKay, 1956.

7. Clark, Leonard H., and Irving S. Starr. *Secondary School Teaching Methods.* New York: Macmillan, 1967.

8. Copi, Irving M. *Introduction to Logic.* 2d ed. New York: Macmillan, 1961. Chaps. 2, 4.

9. Dodl, Norman R. "Questioning Behavior of Elementary Classroom Groups." *California Journal of Instructional Improvement* 9:167–179, October 1966.

10. Douglass, Harl R. *Modern Methods in High School Teaching.* Boston: Houghton Mifflin, 1926.

11. Gallagher, James J. *Productive Thinking of Gifted Children.* Cooperative Research Project No. 965, U.S. Department of Health, Education, and Welfare, Office of Education. Urbana, Ill.: Institute for Research on Exceptional Children, College of Education, University of Illinois, 1965.

12. Gallagher, James J., and Mary Jane Aschner. "A Preliminary Report on Classroom Interaction." *Merrill-Palmer Quarterly of Behavior and Development* 9:183–194, July 1963. Reprinted in *Teaching: Vantage Points for Study*, edited by Ronald T. Hyman (Philadelphia: J. B. Lippincott, 1968), pp. 118–133.

13. Guilford, J. P. "The Structure of Intellect." *Psychological Bulletin* 53:267–293, July 1956.

14. Hallman, Ralph J. "Techniques of Creative Teaching." *Journal of Creative Behavior* 1:325–330, Summer 1967.

15. Henderson, Kenneth B. "Uses of 'Subject Matter.'" In *Language and Concepts in Education*, edited by B. Othanel Smith and Robert H. Ennis, pp. 43–58. Chicago: Rand McNally, 1961.

16. Kennedy, Edward M. "Eulogy of Robert F. Kennedy." *New York Times*, June 9, 1968, p. 56.

17. Meux, Milton, and B. Othanel Smith. "Logical Dimensions of Teaching Behavior." In *Contemporary Research on Teacher Effectiveness*, edited by Bruce J. Biddle and William J. Ellena, pp. 127–164. New York: Holt, Rinehart, and Winston, 1964.

18. O'Connor, D. J. *An Introduction to the Philosophy of Education.* London: Routledge and Kegan Paul, 1957.

19. Oliva, Peter F. *The Secondary School Today.* Cleveland: World Publishing, 1967.

20. Passmore, John. *Talking Things Over.* Melbourne, Australia: Melbourne University Press, 1963.

21. Rowe, Mary Budd. "Science, Silence, and Sanctions." *Science and Children* 6:11–13, March 1969.

22. Rowe, Mary Budd. "Wait-Time and Rewards as Instructional Variables: Their Influence on Language, Logic, and Fate Control." Paper delivered at the National Association for Research in Science Teaching, April 1972.

23. Sanders, Norris M. *Classroom Questions: What Kinds?* New York: Harper and Row, 1966.

24. Shedd, Mark R., Norman A. Newberg, and Richard H. de Leone. "Yesterday's Curriculum—Today's World: Time to Reinvent the Wheel." In *The Curriculum: Retrospect and Prospect*, Seventieth Yearbook, Part 1, of the National Society for the Study of Education, edited by Robert M. McClure, pp. 153–180. Chicago: National Society for the Study of Education, 1971.

25. Smith, B. Othanel, and others. *A Study of the Strategies of Teaching.* Cooperative Research Project No. 1640, U.S. Department of Health, Education, and Welfare, Office of Education. Urbana, Ill.: Bureau of Educational Research, College of Education, University of Illinois, 1967.

26. Smith, B. Othanel, and Milton Meux. "A Study of the Logic of Teaching." In *Teaching: Vantage Points for Study*, edited by Ronald T. Hyman, pp. 101–117. Philadelphia: J. B. Lippincott, 1968.

27. Taba, Hilda, and Freeman F. Elzey. "Teaching Strategies and Thought Processes." *Teachers College Record* 65:524–534, March 1964. Reprinted in *Teaching: Vantage Points for Study*, edited by Ronald T. Hyman (Philadelphia: J. B. Lippincott, 1968), pp. 441–458.

28. Taba, Hilda, Samuel Levine, and Freeman F. Elzey. *Thinking in Elementary School Children.* Cooperative Research Project No. 1574, U.S. Department of Health, Education, and Welfare, Office of Education. San Francisco: San Francisco State College, 1964.

29. Wilson, John. *Language and the Pursuit of Truth.* Cambridge: Cambridge University Press, 1958.

15 Observing and Evaluating Teaching

This final chapter demands a disclaimer and perhaps an apology at the outset. In spite of the fact that people have been teaching for thousands of years, the development of procedures and instruments for observing teaching is relatively new and, to say the least, incomplete. The same holds true for the evaluation of teaching, an area which is further complicated by a lack of agreement as to what constitutes good teaching. Yet, even though the field is not as advanced as educators would like it to be, there is definitely a strong need for a means of observing and evaluating teaching. Therefore, this chapter is included, but is presented with a special humility.

Two critical questions will be considered here: How does one properly observe teaching? and, How should one evaluate teaching? Because the teacher is engaged in an activity that involves influencing other people, there is an obligation to assess and evaluate his work. Furthermore, if the teacher wants to improve his performance, it is helpful for him to have data about it and an evaluation of it (10; 18; 41). Therefore, the problems of how to observe and how to evaluate teaching are an essential part of any attempt to deal with overall teaching performance.

This chapter will begin with some basic definitions, followed by an extensive treatment of the issues of observing and evaluating.

Working Definitions

Observing involves the intentional and methodical viewing of some object or activity. Observing is more than mere seeing; it entails planned, careful, focused, active attention by the observer.

Measuring is the assigning of numbers (quantitative values) to a set of people, objects, or activities, according to some established rules (33:2). Measuring is a descriptive activity that expresses quantitatively the degree or type of characteristic possessed by a person, object, or activity.

Evaluating is the judging or rating of persons, objects, or activities to be good or bad, right or wrong, worthy or unworthy, desirable or undesirable, etc. Evaluating is not, like measuring, a descriptive activity; it is the "systematic process of judging the worth, desirability, effectiveness, or adequacy of something according to definite criteria and purposes. The judgment is based upon a careful comparison of observation data with criteria standards" (24:95).

Assessing involves comparison between given measurements, to determine to what degree the measurements meet given objectives or criteria. Assessing does not involve value judgments, since the objectives or criteria of comparison are simply accepted as given.

These four terms are obviously related to one another in that observing becomes one aspect of measuring, and measuring, in turn, is often involved in evaluating. Measuring does not necessarily lead to evaluating or assessing, though it is often used to obtain data upon which value judgments are based.

Observing Teaching

Observing serves several important functions in teaching. First and foremost, it provides the teacher with feedback about his teaching. To begin with, the teacher himself must look at his class with the eye of an observer. Kohl, in *36 Children*, a reflective chronicle of teaching in an urban slum school, states this strongly.

I am convinced that the teacher must be an observer of his class as well as a member of it. He must look at the children, discover how they relate to each other and the room around them. There must be enough free time and activity for the teacher to discover the children's human preferences. Observing children at play and mischief is an invaluable source of knowledge about them—about leaders and groups, fear, courage, warmth, isolation. Teachers consider the children's gym or free time their free time, too, and usually turn their backs on the children when they have most to learn from them (27:23).

But the teacher needs more than he can glean from his own impressions and those of his students. The impressions of students are helpful indeed, yet they lack the perspective that the observations of someone not at all directly involved in the teaching situation can offer. The teacher definitely needs feedback from an outside observer to supplement his own impressions. "It is my belief that such self-analysis will not be fully valid and useful until teachers receive a rather complete feedback of the nature of their own performance and of their pupils' response such as can be supplied through . . . objective observation procedures and functional classification system[s]'' (36:52).

Second, whether the teacher desires it or not, people do evaluate a teacher on his teaching. Principals and parents, for example, evaluate teachers. Such evaluating will continue to go on. Given this situation, it is, no doubt, best that those who evaluate teaching base their evaluations on significant data gained from competent observation of teaching.

Third, observing provides an opportunity for teachers, both during pre-service and in-service preparation, to further their own understanding of teaching. Teachers can observe their colleagues using various teaching methods. They can observe how other teachers deliver their material, how they use equipment and props, and how they organize their students. They can observe the intellectual and social interaction of the teaching situation. The value of observing teaching was recognized as long ago as 1904 by Dewey:

> The first observation of instruction given by model—or critic—teachers should not be too definitely practical in aim. The student should not be observing to find out how the good teacher does it, in order to accumulate a store of methods by which he also may teach successfully. He should rather observe with reference to seeing the interaction of mind, to see how teacher and pupils react upon each other—how mind answers to mind. Observation should at first be conducted from the psychological rather than the "practical" standpoint. If the latter is emphasized before the student has an independent command of the former, the principle of imitation is almost sure to play an exaggerated part in the observer's future teaching, and hence at the expense of personal insight and initiative. What the student needs most at this stage of growth is ability to see what is going on in the minds of a group of persons who are in intellectual contact with one another. He needs to learn to observe psychologically—a very different thing from simply observing how a teacher gets "good results" in presenting any particular subject (17:18–19).

Nature of Observing

These are the purposes of observing. But what exactly is observing? For example, what constitutes a formal observation: "Each observer or recorder is restricted to some fragment of what is going on. The best we attain is some indication of what is outwardly visible from a single point of view for a limited time," says the philosopher Morris Cohen in his comments on the historian's formidable task (16:24). But it is not only historians who must select when they observe. Whoever wishes to observe any complex activity (and surely teaching qualifies as complex) must select the aspect he wishes to focus on. It is necessary for every observer to recognize this fact. Those who receive an observational report should recognize, on the other hand, that the report is not a complete account but rather a treatment of some selected aspect of the observed person, object, or activity.

VIEWPOINT.   There is yet more to Cohen's comment. Not only is observing selective, but it also must be done from a particular point of view. Gerbner suggests that when we observe, "we perceive in terms of prior *assumptions*, . . . we fit perceptions into a *context* of our own, and . . . we can only perceive (or conceive of) something from where we are—from a *point of view*" (22:23). Thus, every observer chooses a point of view that fits in with his past experience and present expectations. It is also the case that the notions of viewpoint and selection are interrelated. Depending on what segment of teaching we wish to focus our attention on, we choose what appears to be an appropriate point of view. This also happens in reverse.

Because a teacher is a concrete human being, the most complex entity we know, and because teaching is a syndrome that involves many such human entities, it lends itself to any analysis you please. Some look at it as a set of interactions between a teacher and one or more pupils. Some interactions are interpreted psychologically as ways of controlling responses; some are broken down into types of discourse between pupil and teacher. Some regard the teaching act as an encounter between persons in which a drama is played out between forces of dominance and submission, strong and weak selves. Some regard teaching as analogous to an artistic performance, to be judged as a critic would judge a work of art; some think of teaching as an input-output-feedback flow of information.

There is little point in asking which of these ways of looking at the teaching act is right or wrong—about as little point as asking whether it is more right to compare life itself to a race, or a drama, or a dream, or a comedy, or a tragedy. These are figures of speech, analogies, models, not scientific theories. There is no limit to the number of relevant aspects; any one aspect is as apt and as limited as the other. Nor is there any harm in talking about teaching in figures of speech or comparing it to operations found in other areas of life, provided one remembers what one is doing and does not get illusions of scientific grandeur (11:32).

Moreover, the taking of a point of view serves two inter-dependent purposes. First, individual events are meaningless unless they can somehow be fitted together. Such events can be fitted together meaningfully within a particular framework (8:61). Second, the point of view taken is a necessary guide in the collection of data. We do not know what data to gather unless we get guidance from a framework consisting of certain accepted concepts. Schwab has written on this matter in regard to observing in the biological sciences. He tells about the study of small aquatic animals at the turn of the century. The biologist's knowledge of the dartings, play, and other movements of tadpoles and small fish was meager indeed. Even when a biologist wanted to know more, he did not know exactly what to observe—what to enquire about, as Schwab would put it. This frustration disappeared when biologists accepted the framework of a simple machine. "This idea of a simple machine was applied to the study of behavior by supposing that every movement through space of an animal was a response to some single, specific, stimulating factor in the environment" (37:26). Later, biologists discarded this conception as naïve, but at the time it did give them a framework within which they could make meaningful observations.

The importance of a point of view—a framework—cannot be overestimated. The observer's viewpoint consists of some set of concepts that causes him to view things in a particular way. To understand the observations made, one must be aware of that framework. As Susanne K. Langer writes:

The formulation of experience which is contained within the intellectual horizon of an age and a society is determined, I believe, not so much by events and desires, as by the *basic concepts* at people's disposal for analyzing and describing their adventures to their own understanding. Of course, such concepts arise as they are needed to deal with political or domestic experience; but the same experiences could be seen in many different lights, so the light in which they do appear depends on the genius of a people as well as on the demands of the external occasion. Different minds will take the same events in very different ways (30:3).

INFORMAL AND FORMAL OBSERVING/THE OBSERVATIONAL INSTRUMENT. Teaching can be viewed without being measured. An observer of a teaching situation could employ, for example, a psychological point of view consisting of such concepts as security, anxiety, acceptance, and rejection. Yet he would not be measuring teaching if he had not established rules for assigning quantitative values to the various aspects of teaching. Such viewing (without measuring) might be labeled informal observing. Informal observing can only yield general statements, the value of which depends greatly on the sensitivity of the observer and on his purpose.

Formal observing, however, involves measuring. Here the observer uses an *observational instrument* or guide to guarantee systematic observing and obtaining of data. The observer records what he sees according to established rules. In this way he observes and measures without distinguishing between the two activities. The basis for formal observing, the observational instrument, consists of "*procedures which use systematic observations of classroom behavior to obtain reliable and valid measurements of differences in the typical behaviors which occur in different classrooms, or in different situations in the same classroom*" (34:250). The observer who wishes to employ an observational instrument will obviously require preparation in its use. It is such observing—observing with an observational instrument—that is used in empirical research on teaching.

Feedback to the teacher based on data from observing with an observational instrument can be most helpful. For example, it can help the teacher with the specific parts of his teaching. A global statement such as, "Your questions today were mostly of the same type, and somehow the students didn't seem to be involved in them," would not be very helpful to the teacher who wished to change his approach. With data obtained from an observational instrument, however, an observer might say, "Today you asked fifteen empirical questions—fourteen to elicit facts and one to elicit an explanation—but you asked only two valuative questions." Such a comment is useful in that it not only points out to the teacher the type of question he asks, but it also gives him a quantitative picture of his teaching. With such specific data in mind this teacher, for example, would be better able to change the proportion of question types in his teaching, if he believed that this would lead to desirable results.

This type of observing is preferable to informal observing, not only because it yields valid and reliable measurements but also because it yields specific data that are useful to both observer and observed teacher. However, the development of observational instruments has not advanced to the stage where there is a wide range and diversity available. Unless an observer wishes to create his own observational instrument—and to do so requires a great effort, time, money, and cooperation from others—he may have to observe a number of teaching situations without a tested instrument. Also, even if there is a suitable instrument available, an observer may not be properly prepared for using it at a given time.

Yet the choice is not between the two extremes of observing with an instrument or not observing at all. Observing is not a casual activity; a guide of some sort is necessary to focus the observer's attention, to assure that he notes aspects of teaching he might otherwise overlook. If he cannot use an observational instrument, the observer can always prepare a guide for himself, based on his preferred point of view.

Three Observational Instruments

Three observational instruments representing three different frameworks will now be presented. It would be pointless, if not impossible, to present all the available instruments of observation in this book. The intention here is not to prepare the reader to be a certified observer, but rather to illustrate what an observational instrument is and how such an instrument manifests the framework employed by its designers. The three selected instruments may also serve as sources of ideas for those who wish to design their own observational guides (22) or instruments.*

The reader should note that the three observational instruments treated below are used to observe teacher-student verbal interaction. They direct the observer to particular dimensions of the total verbal interaction occurring between the teacher and his students.

The first instrument is designed to focus on the communications among teacher and students. This instrument, designed by Lewis, Newell, and Withall (32), is based on a definition and some assumptions and concepts concerning communication (31).†

---

* Those who are interested in other frameworks and other instruments will wish to see the anthology *Teaching: Vantage Points for Study* (26); the six volumes edited by Simon and Boyer, *Mirrors for Behavior* (39); *Handbook of Research on Teaching*, edited by Gage (21); and Chapter 14 of this book.

† The following material is from Wilbert W. Lewis, "Selected Concepts of Communication as a Basis for Studying Mental Health in the Classroom," *Journal of Communication* (September 1961). Reprinted with permission of the International Communication Association.

Definition: *Communication* "is a process by which a person reduces the uncertainty about some state of affairs by detection of cues which seem to him to be relevant to that state of affairs" (31:44).

Assumption 1: "The continuous flow of experience to which every individual is subjected is not inherently structured or meaningful, but is given meaning by the person who experiences it" (31:44).

Assumption 2: "Beliefs are constantly being tested by the stimuli an individual receives from the events in which he is a participant" (31:45).

Concept 1: *Receptiveness* "is the willingness to find out what another person thinks about a topic of mutual interest. A working knowledge of language and intact audio-perceptual mechanisms for both children and teachers are assumed. . . . Receptiveness includes behaviors that convey to another person the information, 'Lines of communication are open between us; I am interested in hearing what you have to say'" (31:45–46).

Concept 2: *Accuracy* of received communication "refers to how the receiver uses information relative to a sender's meaning. The receiver may believe he understands the arrangement of events in a concept used by the sender, but the criterion of accuracy requires that understanding be validated through 'correct' predictions of additional verbalizations or other behavior of the sender" (31:46).

Concept 3: *Mobility* "refers to the tendency of a sender to move up and down the abstraction ladder in his attempts at communication. If a teacher speaks of both courtesy and such specific acts as opening the door for another person, she is demonstrating mobility in her communication. On the other hand, if she relates 'courtesy' to 'kindness' and other abstractions, or if she refers only to behaviors, 'Jimmy, open the door for Sally,' etc., she is nonmobile, although at different levels of abstraction" (31:47).

Concept 4: *Responsiveness* "is the sender's 'taking audience reaction into consideration.' The information concept of feedback is relevant here. Both speaker and listener are involved, for responsiveness designates both the corrective information which the receiver of the message emits and the sender's adjustments to that information. . . . Responsiveness thus pertains to modifications in the pattern of the sender's behavior which reflect his detection of changing interests, feelings, abilities, etc., in the receiver" (31:47–48).

Based on the above definition, assumptions, and concepts, the following thirteen categories were developed for observing (32:50–53).*

1. *Asks for Information*

An act having as its major intent the eliciting of a response which presumably may be evaluated for accuracy, either by objective operation, general acceptance, or reference to an authority (such as the teacher or a text book).

Examples.—Asks question about content of lesson; asks for report; asks for confirmation of response previously given; asks for repetition of what has been said; offers incomplete statement with the expectation that another will finish it; asks any question in a way as to imply that there is a "right" answer; asks name of an object; asks for definition; asks for enumeration.

2. *Seeks or Accepts Direction*

An act implying willingness to consider suggestion or direction from another, or if suggestion or direction has already been offered, an act or statement indicating compliance.

Examples.—Asks how to begin an assigned task; asks what to do next; asks which procedure to follow; asks for volunteers; follows directions of another; agrees with suggestion or direction; indicates that direction will be followed at some future time; asks for permission for a specific act.

3. *Asks for Opinion or Analysis*

An act intended to elicit problem-structuring statements from others, either affective-evaluative or cognitive-interpretive.

Examples.—Asks for opinion, wish, feeling, belief, or preference, asks for evaluation of behavior; requests for interpretation or explanation of some phenomena without implying that there is one "correct' answer; requests for elaboration or examples of a concept; requests for statement of relationships between concepts; non-directive leads or questions to facilitate self-exploration by others; reflection of feeling or alternate meaning of what another has said for purposes of clarifying meaning; asks for interpretation of another's personal experience (as distinguished from asking for a report of experience).

* Reprinted with permission of authors and publisher: Lewis, W. W., Newell, J. M., and Withall, J. An analysis of classroom patterns of communication. *Psychological Reports*, 1961, 9, 211–219. (Item 1, page 212, through item 13, page 214, only.)

4. Listens

Five seconds or more out of any ten-second interval where an individual is listening or attending to another individual is given a listening score (less than five seconds is not scored).

5. Gives Information

An act intended to convey, confirm, or infer "facts" which may be evaluated by objective operation, general acceptance, or reference to an authority.

Examples.—Giving data such as names, dates, speed, capacity, etc., relevant to a topic under discussion; attempting to provide information requested by another; confirming the accuracy of others' responses; denying the accuracy of others' responses; gives report on what one has seen, heard, read, etc.; gives repetition of what has been said; names object; gives definition; gives enumeration.

6. Gives Suggestion

An act intended to structure action or indicate alternatives for others which, at the same time, implies autonomy for others by providing more than one alternative or allowing for refusal.

Examples.—Offering a procedure in a tentative way; offering two or more procedures; leaving choice to others; stating a preferred behavior without indicating that the preference holds for others; volunteers own services.

7. Gives Direction

An act intended to structure some action of another in which compliance seems to be taken for granted, or in which non-compliance would probably elicit some form of disapproval.

Examples.—Calling class to attention; calling attention to some detail; getting attention of another by calling his name; routine administrative directions or orders; stating expectation of behavior to be followed; setting limits on behavior; stating consequences of behavior; granting a request; denying a request.

8. Gives Opinion

An act intended to structure or give direction to a topic under discussion by use of speaker's internal, private, or unstated criteria.

Examples.—States opinions, wish, feeling, belief, or preference; makes a statement or asks a question reflecting a personal point of view; verbalizes introspective processes; gives criticism or evaluation of a behavior or concept; agrees or disagrees with opinion voiced by another.

9. Gives Analysis

An act intended to structure or give direction to a topic under discussion by reference to a frame of reference or a criterion that is explicitly stated and external to speaker's personal point of view.

Examples.—Gives interpretation or explanation of some phenomena without implying that it is the only "correct" way of looking at it; elaborates or gives examples of a concept; points out relationships between examples and concepts or between two or more concepts; points out discrepancies between concept and examples; proposes hypothetical example or case to illustrate a point or raise a question.

10. *Shows Positive Feeling*
An act which implies positive evaluation of some behavior or interaction in the observational field, regardless of whether the referent is the self or some other person.
Examples.—Any friendly act or overture, such as greeting or responding to a greeting; praising, approving, encouraging, rewarding, or showing active attention to others; sharing or sympathizing with others, expressions of satisfaction, enjoyment, or relief; joking or laughing "with" others.

11. *Inhibits Communication*
An act which implies unwillingness or inability to engage in the ongoing process of communication, regardless or whether the act stems from negative evaluation, internal tension, or disinterest.
Examples.—Does not respond when response would ordinarily be expected; is cool, aloof, or disinterested in what is going on; is inattentive to or ignores a question or request; does not comply with a request; shows tension by blocking, "fright," etc.; accepts criticism or rebuff without reply.

12. *Shows Negative Feeling*
An act which implies active negative evaluation of some behavior or interaction in the observational field, regardless of whether the referent is the self or some other person.
Examples.—Disapproving, disparaging, threatening, discouraging another's behaviors; lowering another's status; defending or asserting self; poking fun, belittling, or laughing "at" others; expressing fear, rage, hostility, disappointment, discouragement, displeasure, unhappiness, etc.

13. *No Communication*[1]
The behavior occurring in the classroom is not relevant to teacher-pupil communication during a ten-second interval.

The observer may use these categories in a live situation or with tape recordings. Every ten seconds* the observer categorizes the interaction according to what he perceives to be the main

---

[1] Since the completion of this study, an additional category, 14, Perfunctory Agreement or Disagreement, has been added.

* In one research study using these same categories a five-second time unit was employed (42:324).

intent of the communicator during that time interval. The observer uses verbal and nonverbal cues (if detectable), as he assumes the role of the intended receiver of the communication.

The second observational instrument to be treated was designed to focus on the social and emotional climate created in the interaction of the teacher and the students. Though there have been several modifications (2; 25) of this instrument as designed by Flanders (20) in 1959, it is presented below in its original form because of its simplicity and use as a basis for other instruments.

"The term 'classroom climate' refers to generalized attitudes toward the teacher and the class that the pupils share in common despite individual differences. The development of these attitudes is an outgrowth of classroom social interaction." It is from this definition that the Interaction Analysis instrument develops. It is further based on the concepts of direct influence by the teacher (which restricts the student's freedom of action) and the indirect influence of the teacher (which expands a student's freedom of action by encouraging his verbal participation and initiative) (20:251).

Based on these concepts, ten categories (Figure 15–1) were developed for observing in Ned Flanders' monograph, "Teacher Influence, Pupil Attitudes, and Achievement" (20:259).

The observer may use these categories in a live situation or with tape recordings. At the end of every three-second period the observer decides which of the ten categories best represents the interaction just completed. He writes the numbers of the categories in columns on his paper in order to preserve the sequence of the interaction.*

The third observational instrument as developed by Bellack, Davitz, Kliebard, Hyman, and Smith (4; 5; 6; 7) is designed to focus on the pedagogical significance of the verbal interaction among the teacher and the students and the content of that communication. That is to say, this instrument focuses on what the speaker does pedagogically with his words (e.g., launches a new topic, asks a question, or responds to a question) and on the content of the speaker's communication in terms of the substantive topics at hand, the cognitive processes used in verifying†

---

* Techniques for analyzing the interaction can be found in more detailed sources, such as the article by Chapline (15) and the text edited by Amidon and Hough (1).

† See the section on verification in Chapter 14. That section was based in part on this instrument.

TEACHER TALK	**INDIRECT INFLUENCE**	1.* ACCEPTS FEELING: accepts and clarifies the tone of feeling of the students in an unthreatening manner. Feelings may be positive or negative. Predicting or recalling feelings are included.
		2.* PRAISES OR ENCOURAGES: praises or encourages student action or behavior. Jokes that release tension, but not at the expense of another individual, nodding head or saying "um hm?" or "go on" are included.
		3.* ACCEPTS OR USES IDEAS OF STUDENT: clarifying, building, or developing ideas suggested by a student. As teacher brings more of his own ideas into play, shift to category 5.
		4.* ASKS QUESTIONS: asking a question about content or procedure with the intent that a student answer.
	DIRECT INFLUENCE	5.* LECTURING: giving facts or opinons about content or procedure; expressing his own ideas, asking rhetorical questions.
		6.* GIVING DIRECTIONS: directions, commands, or orders which students are expected to comply with.
		7.* CRITICIZING OR JUSTIFYING AUTHORITY: statements intended to change student behavior from unacceptable to acceptable pattern; bawling someone out; stating why the teacher is doing what he is doing; extreme self-reference.
STUDENT TALK		8.* STUDENT TALK—RESPONSE: talk by students in response to teacher. Teacher initiates the contact or solicits student statement.
		9.* STUDENT TALK—INITIATION: talk initiated by students. If "calling on" student is only to indicate who may talk next, observer must decide whether student wanted to talk.
SILENCE		10.* SILENCE OR CONFUSION: pauses, short periods of silence and periods of confusion in which communication cannot be understood by the observer.

Figure 15–1: Categories for Interaction Analysis

   * There is NO scale implied by these numbers. Each number is classificatory, designating a particular kind of communication event. To write these numbers down during observation is merely to identify and enumerate communication events, not to judge them.

what is said about these topics, and the social and managerial aspects of the teacher-student interaction. The simultaneous interest in these several dimensions of teacher-student verbal interaction arises from the conviction that both the "stuff" being talked about in a teacher-student situation and the functions of the various utterances are essential aspects to describe.

For this reason, data are assorted simultaneously into six categories. This is done because it is quite evident that in a single utterance a teacher can accomplish many things. He can, for example, launch a new topic in economics by clarifying the concepts of market and money, and at the same time give the students guidelines for reading the textbook material related to these concepts. Such an utterance would be difficult for an observer to categorize in a live situation. Hence, this instrument, which involves up to six simultaneous categories, has so far been formally used solely with typescripts of verbal interaction. (However, individual observers informally report that they can use one or two sets of categories in a live situation or with tape recordings.)

The six sets of categories are:*

1. Speaker, i.e., source of the utterance.
2. Pedagogical Move, i.e., function of the verbal interaction.
3. Substantive Meaning, i.e., subject matter being studied.
4. Substantive-Logical Meaning, i.e., verification process used with 3 above.
5. Instructional Meaning, i.e., the social and managerial aspects of teacher-student interaction.
6. Instructional-Logical Meaning, i.e., verification process used with 5 above.

Obviously, it is the specific items within each category that are important. These are outlined below (6:88–91):

1. Speaker
   A. Teacher
   B. Pupil
   C. Audiovisual devices
2. Pedagogical Move

* The following description of this third observational instrument is drawn entirely from the work of Arno A. Bellack et al., *The Language of the Classroom* (see references 4, 5, 6, and 7).

   A. *Structuring* moves "serve the pedagogical function of setting the context for subsequent behavior by launching or halting-excluding interaction between pupils and teachers and by indicating the nature of the interaction" (6:86–7).

   B. *Soliciting* moves "are designed to elicit a verbal response, encourage persons addressed to attend to something, or elicit a physical response. All questions are solicitations, as are commands, imperatives, and requests" (6:87).

   C. *Responding* moves "bear a reciprocal relationship to soliciting moves and occur only in relation to them. Their pedagogical function is to fulfill the expectation of soliciting moves" (6:87).

   D. *Reacting* moves "are occasioned by a structuring, soliciting, responding, or another reacting move, but are not directly elicited by them. Pedagogically, these moves serve to modify (by clarifying, synthesizing, or expanding) and/or to rate (positively or negatively) what has been said previously" (6:87).

   E. *Not Codable*—function uncertain because interaction inaudible (on tape).

3. Substantive Meaning—when this instrument was designed, the lessons were based on a unit concerned with world trade (economics). The items thus included such topics as factors of production, imports/exports tariffs, and free trade. These topics change as the unit of study changes.

4. Substantive-Logical Meaning* (reference to cognitive process used in dealing with subject matter)

   A. Analytic Process
     (1) Defining
     (2) Interpreting

   B. Empirical Process
     (1) Fact-stating
     (2) Explaining

   C. Evaluative Process
     (1) Opining
     (2) Justifying

   D. Logical Process Not Clear

5. Instructional Meaning (factors related to classroom management)

---

  * In the section on verification in Chapter 14, these items were used solely with questions. However, their use here includes all four pedagogical moves. See that section for definitions of these items.

    A. Assignment
    B. Material
    C. Person
    D. Procedure
    E. Statement
    F. Logical Process
    G. Action—General
    H. Action—Vocal
    I. Action—Physical
    J. Action—Cognitive
    K. Action—Emotional
    L. Language Mechanics

6. Instructional—Logical Meaning (cognitive processes related to teacher's didactic verbal moves)
    A. Analytic Process
        (1) Defining
        (2) Interpreting
    B. Empirical Process
        (1) Fact-stating
        (2) Explaining
    C. Evaluative Process
        (1) Opining
        (2) Justifying
        (3) Rating
            a. Positive
            b. Admitting
            c. Repeating
            d. Qualifying
            e. Not Admitting
            f. Negative
            g. Positive/Negative
            h. Admitting/Not Admitting
    D. Extralogical Process (when physical response is elicited, or logic of verbal response cannot be determined)
        (1) Performing
        (2) Directing
        (3) Extralogical Process Not Clear

    The observer listens to a tape recording and reads a typescript. He categorizes the verbal interaction in each of the six categories every time there is a change of speaker and/or pedagogical move. He writes down the chosen categories on the side of the typescript along with the number of typed lines used in transcribing the interaction. The number of typed lines is divided appropriately to account for how much is used with category 4 and how much is used with category 6. In this way there is a quantitative measure as well as a functional measure of verbal interaction.

This third observational instrument is complex. This is due to the simultaneous categorizing within six sets of categories as opposed to the single set used in the other two illustrative instruments. The instrument is indeed more difficult to employ than the other two, but, on the other hand, it yields data in more than one dimension.

These three instruments differ in several other significant ways. First and foremost, they stem from different frameworks— the communications viewpoint, the social-emotional viewpoint, and the pedagogical and substantive-meaning viewpoint. The illustrative instruments are not the only ones that can possibly represent these three viewpoints. Each instrument is merely one way to observe within a particular framework. Second, while the first two instruments use a time interval to determine when to categorize (i.e., every ten or three seconds), the third instrument uses a natural, functional unit (i.e., the pedagogical move and/or the speaker). Third, the first two instruments can be used live in a teacher-student situation. The third instrument to this point has proved largely effective when used with a tape recording and typescript. Perhaps some observers will soon devise a method of using this third instrument or a modification reliably in a live situation.

These three illustrative instruments are used to categorize the total verbal interaction among teacher and students. However, an observer can modify this if he chooses. For example, whatever his observational viewpoint, an observer may choose to focus only on the teacher, or only on the students, or on questions raised or responses given. The observer could also choose to sample the interaction by categorizing it only during alternating time periods.

These three illustrative instruments focus on *verbal* interaction, as do most observational instruments. This in no way implies that verbal interaction is the only aspect of teaching worthy of observation. Nonverbal interaction is certainly an important aspect of teaching. It can be and should be observed, too, no matter what the observational point of view. Nonverbal interaction is particularly important when observing the teacher-student situation in terms of skills and values.

Constructing An Observational Instrument

There are no step-by-step guides to follow in constructing an observational instrument or personal observational guide. At this point in the development of techniques of observing, it is possible only to offer guidelines in the form of basic questions to answer. The designer of an observational instrument should carefully consider the answers to the following questions if he wishes to construct a category system (the most common type of instrument) similar to the three illustrative instruments. (For a guide to another type of instrument, the sign system, the reader is referred to Medley and Mitzel [34:301].)

1. Do the categories chosen clearly represent the selected framework of observation? Do the categories reflect the concepts basic to the viewpoint?

2. Are the categories all-inclusive? That is, do all instances of the observed activity fit into one of the categories? (If it is not possible to categorize a specific instance, then the set of categories is incomplete and requires further expansion.)

3. Are the categories mutually exclusive? That is, are the categories so precisely defined that each is distinct from the others? (If this is so, each instance of behavior will fit into one and only one category.)

4. Are observations with this set of categories reliable? That is, will trained observers generally agree on which category to use in a given instance?

5. Is the instrument usable and useful? "Somewhere between too many and too few categories is an optimum number" (19:197). If there are too many categories, so much skill will be required of the observer that the usability of the instrument is doubtful. On the other hand, if there are too few categories, observations based on them will not have much significance since they will not separate various aspects of the activity from one another. If there must be a choice between too few and too many, it is best to err in excess. Several categories can later be combined into one so as to reduce the overall number (34:300).

6. How does the observer determine when to categorize? What is the unit of categorization? Does this unit (time unit, natural functional unit, etc.) fit well with the categories and the purposes of the observing?

7. In summary, does the total instrument offer the observer

a tool with which to observe and measure what he wishes to investigate in the complex interaction occurring in the teacher-student situation.

Evaluating Teaching

To observe is one thing; to evaluate, another. The definitional distinction between observing and evaluating deserves repetition at this point because lack of clarity about the differences between these two terms is disastrous. Observing involves viewing methodically. To use an observational instrument or guide is to observe and measure. Both observing and measuring are descriptive activities. Evaluating is not descriptive; it involves description but goes beyond it. Evaluating also involves judging or rating. It is at this point that observing and measuring differ significantly from evaluating. To evaluate teaching, one must also observe and measure it, but this does not necessarily work in reverse.

One must not only observe teaching in order to improve it. One must evaluate performance measures up to a well-defined concept of teaching and teaching responsibilities. To evaluate teaching is as necessary as to decide which teaching method to employ.

As a judging or rating activity, evaluating is composed of several parts. What follows is just one way of stating what an evaluator must do to evaluate teaching (12:147; 23; 38; 40). It will be readily seen that in actual practice there is no special sequence for steps 1, 2, and 3 below. As a matter of fact there is interplay among these three aspects of evaluating, and each influences the other two. But steps 4 and 5 must follow the others.

1. The evaluator must decide what he will evaluate. Since teaching is most complex, the evaluator will be unable to evaluate all its many facets at any given time. What he selects to evaluate will be determined by the priorities he establishes. For example, the evaluator may decide to focus on the teaching of word-attack skills in a remedial reading situation rather than on the teaching of values, since in that situation skills are the raison d'être of the class. Stake puts it this way: "In the matter of selection of variables for evaluation, the evaluator must make a subjective decision. Obviously, he must limit the elements to be studied. He cannot look at all of them. The ones he rules out will be those that he assumes would not contribute to an understanding of the educational activity" (40:532).

Tied in with the selection of the aspects of teaching to be evaluated is the necessity of deciding on the purpose of the evaluation. For example, does the evaluator intend to compare the teaching of Teacher A with that of Teacher B to see which is better? If so, then he must answer, "Better for what?" The evaluator must select those elements common to the teaching of both, or else he cannot make a comparison. Or, does the evaluator intend to determine the stability of the teaching of Teacher A for Student A? If so, the investigator will focus on only those aspects of Teacher A's teaching that relate to Student A. If the evaluator does not select and focus, the evaluating activity will become so complex, time-consuming, and hence outdated (because of continual teacher and student changes), that the results will lose their usefulness. In short, the evaluator must be clear about why he is evaluating teaching as he selects what to evaluate.

2. The evaluator must establish criteria as to what constitutes good (or desirable, or effective, or worthwhile) teaching. The criteria should be established so as to reflect the elements crucial to teaching, as well as the purposes of evaluation. Without such criteria there can be no evaluation.

Criteria are not empirical facts about good teaching. Rather, they represent the preferences of the individual or group that establishes them. Criteria are agreed upon; they are not empirically correct or incorrect, or true or false. Therefore, criteria chosen should be open to continual inspection and emendation. For example, to say that six problems answered correctly out of ten is a demonstration of successful learning—and hence successful teaching—is a matter of judgment and not fact. Someone else who accepts successful learning as a manifestation of successful teaching might draw the line at five or four, or perhaps seven, correct answers.

Successful teaching, for the purposes of this book, involves the development of mutual respect, trust, dignity, and independence between the teacher and the student, as well as the acquisition or learning of the intended skills, values, and knowledge. There is no hard and fast rule for weighing these criteria, however, for much depends on the particular teaching situation. Each evaluator must make his own decision on how to weight the criteria according to the circumstances he confronts.

3. The evaluator must gather data about teaching. It is in light of his decisions about what aspects to evaluate that the evaluator must collect relevant data. He will use these data in

part 4, below. First, the evaluator must formally observe the ongoing teaching he wishes to evaluate. The evaluator must choose his observational framework and instrument to fit his criteria and purposes. Second, the evaluator must also gather data about the results of various instances of teaching, particularly learning. Teaching is intentional in regard to learning, and the evaluator has the task of determining what type of learning and how much learning has taken place. There will be no attempt in this book to delve into the specific procedures for constructing and interpreting tests. These constitute a special, technical area, and there is no reason to merely repeat or condense any of the available books on this topic. There is already a library of volumes to which the reader can easily refer.*

If the evaluator is eventually to render a judgment about good teaching, then he will have to collect data on learning and provide answers to such questions as (13; 14; 28; 29):

A. What constitutes learning in respect to the teaching situation under consideration?

B. When and how often should learning be observed and measured?

C. By what means should learning be observed and measured?

D. How much has the student learned prior to this teaching situation? That is, the evaluator must know the antecedents relevant to what is being evaluated in order to evaluate the student's learning in a particular teaching situation (40:528).

4. The evaluator must compare the data collected with his criteria; that is, the evaluator must match "what is" with "what ought to be." The need for carefully recorded data and clearly defined criteria becomes evident in this part of the evaluating activity. The data and the criteria cannot be compared unless they are clear and designed to lend themselves to such comparisons.

5. The evaluator must make a judgment about the teaching under consideration. The judgment—in terms of goodness, worth, desirability, or effectiveness—is a conclusion that follows from the first four steps above. The evaluator must take care that he does not inadvertently take additional data or criteria into account at this point. The conclusion drawn is the considered evaluation.

* One short, recommended book that treats teacher-made tests and other instruments used to measure student growth is *Educational Measurement*, by Lindeman (33).

If someone disagrees with the evaluation offered, then he must reexamine the data and the criteria. If he accepts the data and the comparison of data with criteria as valid, then obviously he must give further consideration to the acceptance of the criteria themselves.

Problems In Evaluating Teaching

In spite of the apparent coherence of the five aspects of evaluating presented above, there are many problems encountered in any attempt to evaluate teaching. Some of the more salient issues will be presented here, not with the intention of solving the problems involved, but rather with the intention of alerting the reader to those problems. Seven specific issues will be considered on the following pages.

The first significant issue that the evaluator confronts is the one commented on most often, namely, the problem of *measuring the outcomes of teaching*. The problems involved here loom especially large for evaluators who wish to determine the success of teaching in terms of the student's achievement. Several points are of concern here.

It is evident from the treatment of teaching presented so far that it is not valid to determine the success of teaching solely in terms of learning achieved. Teaching can be considered an intentional act of the teacher with the student. Therefore, if the success of teaching is to be determined, what must be described are the intentions, the interaction during teaching, and results. The learning is only one result, and results constitute only one aspect of teaching. There is no adequate justification for measuring learning to the exclusion of intentions, transactions, and other results. It was precisely in consideration of this point that the detailed treatment of observation was included in this book. This position is in direct opposition to that of many teachers, who only measure learning as they evaluate their work with students. Intentions, too, must be taken into account; they must be stated clearly by the teacher to form part of the overall data of observing and evaluating.

Furthermore, it is also unreasonable to use learning achievements of the student as the sole data upon which to evaluate the teacher's accomplishment. The teacher inevitably teaches, but it is the student who must learn. If the student does not cooperate or expend the necessary effort (for example, he might be extremely tired due to lack of sleep) and hence does not learn what the teacher intends for him to learn, it is unfair to fault the teaching (rather than the student's physical state). That is, it seems unjustified to evaluate teaching according to the performance of someone other than the teacher when certain factors affecting that person's performance may be completely beyond the teacher's control. In evaluating teaching the evaluator must consider many types of data other than learning achieved by the student.

Another problem involved in using student achievement as the sole or even key measurement concerns *the element of time.* When should the student's achievement be measured? Often student achievement is measured immediately after a lesson or series of lessons. This indeed is the most practical time to do so. But with this as the sole measurement there are no data about what has been achieved in the long run. "Some growth which is immediately measurable will rapidly disappear" (35:217), and hence the measurement obtained immediately after a lesson may be misleading. However, even if measuring of student achievement is delayed, some point in time must be chosen as optimum. Should it be delayed a week? A month? A year? There can be no absolute answer to this, for much depends on varying factors in teaching situations—intentions, subject matter, students, and administrative requirements, among others. Yet this is a crucial point in evaluating teaching, especially the teaching of values and skills (e.g., voting in a democratic election).

When the teaching situation involves one teacher and more than one student, as is most often the case, the problem of *student achievement* further complicates the evaluating activity. What if one student learns the intended subject matter or skills and one does not? Obviously the general labels of "good teaching" and "successful teaching" are not adequate in the situation where there is success with one student but not with another. Nor is teaching necessarily equally successful with various students. Therefore, for example, an arithmetic average is meaningless in determining the degree of achievement in a class situation.

Finally, although teaching is intentional in regard to learning, there is no way to specify the exact relationship between teaching and student achievement. This is especially true when measurement is delayed, but is true even when it is not. Additional factors enter the situation and may affect the achievement positively. For example, we do not yet know how much of a student's achievement can be attributed to teaching, how much to self-study, and how much to extra, tutorial aid. Thus, even if other issues are resolved, the problem of the relationship between teaching and learning still exists.

Related to the previous issues is the problem of *how to measure the results of teaching*. It is entirely possible that, for a given teaching situation, no adequate measuring instrument may exist or be created in a reasonable time. For example, with what instrument can the outcomes of teaching the value of democratic action be measured? It is also clear that even if certain results can be measured, these results may not necessarily be the most important ones to measure. We cannot assume that what we can measure is indeed the most important aspect of teaching or even that it is a representative sample of all the results.

Indeed, this issue plagues the people involved in evaluating today's current reform projects in teaching. Atkin, an educator involved with reform in the area of science teaching, writes as follows on this point.

It is difficult to resist the assumption that those attributes which we can measure are the elements which we consider most important. . . . The behavioral analyst seems to assume that for an objective to be worthwhile, we must have methods of observing progress. But worthwhile goals come first, not our methods for assessing progress toward these goals. Goals are derived from our needs and from our philosophies. They are not and should not be derived primarily from our measures. It borders on the irresponsible for those who exhort us to state objectives in behavorial terms to avoid the issue of determining worth. Inevitably there is an implication of worth behind any act of measurement. What the educational community poorly realizes at the moment is that behavioral goals may or may not be worthwhile. They are articulated from among the vast library of goals because they are stated relatively easily. Again, let's not assume that what we can presently measure necessarily represents our most important activity (3:30).

Another major issue that the evaluator must face is *the problem of criteria*. The evaluator must inevitably be able to say how much of a particular quality a teaching situation must possess in order to merit the label of good, fair, excellent, or superior. It is here that the evaluator must determine how well a person must perform a skill in order to deserve the label of success, or to what extent people must manifest a value in order to be termed successful at it (for example, mutual respect, dignity, trust, independence, or democratic action). The answers to these questions are not facts; they are matters of judgment and become criteria. Once again, there is no single set of answers for all teaching situations.

It is therefore clear that one must make judgments that are definitional in character. These judgments are not made on the basis of empirical data. They are, rather, matters of agreement. (For guidance the evaluator can turn to the definitional concept of teaching in the book's introduction.) But is it the evaluator's task both to establish criteria and to collect data? If so, then there is considerable danger of mutual influence between the data and the criteria. This is similar to Atkin's position, above, and is Brown's point when he notes that the evaluating activity usually "dictates" the way the teacher works (13:185). However, if it is the task of the teacher to decide on specific criteria, then there is a danger that the criteria will reflect the ongoing practical situation rather than preferences about good teaching. But if not the evaluator or the teacher, who else is qualified to establish reasonable criteria of judgment? The answer to this question is critical, but is not easily obtainable.

Another issue faces the evaluator. He might decide to evaluate exclusively in terms of how well the teaching achieves its goals. But use of this approach may cause teaching which has very limited, immediate goals to be labeled good in spite of the obvious limitations in its scope. More ambitious teaching would probably suffer. On the other hand, it is possible to evaluate teaching on *the worth of the goals and criteria* as well as the achievement of the goals. If the goals and criteria of a particular teaching situation are judged unacceptable, then no matter how well the teaching meets its goals, it cannot be rated good. However, we must ask if it is fair or valid to evaluate someone's teaching according to goals he did not choose. Many would answer this question in the negative. The evaluator must decide whether to evaluate in terms of the goals set by the teacher or according to external goals. Or, he can formulate a middle position on this issue, balancing one approach with the other (38:52).

Finally, the evaluator must face up to the fact that the research literature on teaching is confusing and inconclusive. "Few, if any facts are now deemed established about teacher effectiveness, and many former 'findings' have been repudiated" (9:vi). This is so because of *the difficulties of doing research on evaluation* of teaching. One main source of the difficulty is the complexity of exercising the necessary experimental controls. Teaching is a complicated family of activities, and, precisely because it involves multiple interactions, it is quite difficult—if not impossible—to exercise control over all the variables involved.

If we are to show relationships between teacher behavior and pupil behaviors, our experimental procedures must be free from sources of contamination. But pupil behavior is obviously determined by a large number of variables, and it is virtually impossible to control them all. To isolate and assess the influence of the teacher independent of other influences (parents, relations, past teachers, friends, self, books, etc.) requires specialized techniques which cannot easily be applied to the classroom situation (35:217).

Concluding Remarks

This final chapter will end with the humble acknowledgment with which it began. Evaluation of teaching, though necessary in the total schema of teaching, is indeed most difficult to accomplish. There is not an adequate technology available in terms of observational instruments, and such a technology is essential for purposes of gathering data. Also, it is difficult to define operationally (and therefore to observe) the manifestations of such concepts as trust and dignity that are often used as the criteria of good teaching. The evaluator must proceed as best he can with whatever is available to him. This may mean that at times he will have to rely on his personal, professional judgment, without support from an observational instrument or precise and weighted criteria established by colleagues. However, the evaluating of teaching does not have to be a trap that impedes teaching, if both the teacher and evaluator keep in mind the larger perspective of evaluation, as suggested in this chapter. In conclusion, even if we cannot yet to our satisfaction observe, measure, and evaluate teaching, teaching itself merits our strongest commitment.

References

1. Amidon, Edmund J., and John B. Hough, eds. *Interaction Analysis: Theory, Research, and Application.* Reading, Mass.: Addison-Wesley, 1967.
2. Amidon, Edmund, and Elizabeth Hunter. *Improving Teaching: The Analysis of Classroom Verbal Interaction.* New York: Holt, Rinehart, and Winston, 1966.
3. Atkin, J. Myron. "Behavioral Objectives in Curriculum Design." *Science Teacher* 35:27–30, May 1968.
4. Bellack, Arno A., and Joel R. Davitz, in collaboration with Herbert M. Kliebard and Ronald T. Hyman. *The Language of the Classroom: Meanings Communicated in High School Teaching.* Coopera-

tive Research Project No. 1497, U.S. Department of Health, Education, and Welfare, Office of Education. New York: Institute of Psychological Research, Teachers College, Columbia University, 1963.

5. Bellack, Arno A., in collaboration with Ronald T. Hyman, Frank L. Smith, Jr., and Herbert M. Kliebard. *The Language of the Classroom: Meanings Communicated in High School Teaching, Part Two.* Cooperative Research Project No. 2023, U.S. Department of Health, Education, and Welfare, Office of Education. New York: Institute of Psychological Research, Teachers College, Columbia University, 1965.

6. Bellack, Arno A., and Joel R. Davitz, in collaboration with Herbert M. Kliebard, Ronald T. Hyman, and Frank L. Smith, Jr. "The Language of the Classroom." In *Teaching: Vantage Points for Study*, edited by Ronald T. Hyman, pp. 84–97. Philadelphia: J. B. Lippincott, 1968.

7. Bellack, Arno A., Herbert M. Kliebard, Ronald T. Hyman, and Frank L. Smith, Jr. *The Language of the Classroom.* New York: Teachers College Press, 1966.

8. Belth, Marc. *Education as a Discipline.* Boston: Allyn and Bacon, 1965.

9. Biddle, Bruce J., and William J. Ellena, Preface to *Contemporary Research on Teacher Effectiveness*, edited by Bruce J. Biddle and William J. Ellena, pp. v–vii. New York: Holt, Rinehart, and Winston, 1964.

10. Bloom, Benjamin S. "Some Theoretical Issues Relating to Educational Evaluation." In *Educational Evaluation: New Roles, New Means*, Sixty-eighth Yearbook of the National Society for the Study of Education, Part II, edited by Ralph W. Tyler, pp. 26–50. Chicago: National Society for the Study of Education, 1969.

11. Broudy, Harry S. "The Continuing Search for Criteria." In *Changing Dimensions in Teacher Education*, Twentieth Yearbook of the American Association of Colleges for Teacher Education, pp. 30–39. Washington, D.C.: American Association of Colleges for Teacher Education, 1967.

12. Broudy, Harry S., B. Othanel Smith, and Joe R. Burnett. *Democracy and Excellence in American Secondary Education.* Chicago: Rand McNally, 1964.

13. Brown, Marcus. "The Importance of a Theory of Knowing for a Theory of Learning." In *Psychological Concepts in Education*, edited by B. Paul Komisar and C. B. J. Macmillan, pp. 167–192. Chicago: Rand McNally, 1967.

14. Castell, Alburey. "Pedagogy Follows Learning Theory." In *Psychological Concepts in Education*, edited by B. Paul Komisar and C. B. J. Macmillan, pp. 158–166. Chicago: Rand McNally, 1967.

15. Chapline, Elaine B. "A Case Study in Interaction Analysis Matrix Interpretation." In *Teaching: Vantage Points for Study*, edited by Ronald T. Hyman, pp. 265–271. Philadelphia: J. B. Lippincott, 1968.

16. Cohen, Morris R. *The Meaning of Human History*. LaSalle, Ill.: Open Court Publishing Co., 1947.

17. Dewey, John. "The Relation of Theory to Practice in Education." In *The Relation of Theory to Practice in the Education of Teachers*, Third Yearbook of the National Society for the Scientific Study of Education, Part I, pp. 9–30. Chicago: University of Chicago Press, 1904.

18. Dressel, Paul L. "The Role of Evaluation in Teaching and Learning." In *Evaluation in Social Studies*, Thirty-fifth Yearbook of the National Council for the Social Studies, edited by Harry D. Berg, pp. 1–20. Washington, D.C.: National Council for the Social Studies, 1965.

19. Flanders, Ned. "Some Relationships among Teacher Influence, Pupil Attitudes, and Achievement." In *Contemporary Research on Teacher Effectiveness*, edited by Bruce J. Biddle and William J. Ellena, pp. 196–231. New York: Holt, Rinehart, and Winston, 1964.

20. Flanders, Ned A. *Teacher Influence, Pupil Attitudes, and Achievement*. Cooperative Research Monograph No. 12, U.S. Department of Health, Education, and Welfare, Office of Education. Washington, D.C., 1965. Reprinted in *Teaching: Vantage Points for Study*, edited by Ronald T. Hyman (Philadelphia: J. B. Lippincott, 1968), pp. 251–265.

21. Gage, N. L., ed. *Handbook of Research on Teaching*. Chicago: Rand McNally, 1963.

22. Gerbner, George. "A Theory of Communication and Its Implications for Teaching." In *The Nature of Teaching*, edited by Louise M. Berman. Milwaukee: University of Wisconsin–Milwaukee, 1963. Reprinted in *Teaching: Vantage Points for Study*, edited by Ronald T. Hyman (Philadelphia: J. B. Lippincott, 1968), pp. 18–31.

23. Harris, Ben H. *Supervisory Behavior in Education*. Englewood Cliffs, N.J.: Prentice-Hall, 1963.

24. Harris, Wilbur. "The Nature and Function of Educational Evaluation." *Peabody Journal of Education* 46:95–99, September 1968.

25. Honigman, Fred K. *Multidimensional Analysis of Classroom Interaction (MACI)*. Villanova, Pa.: Villanova University Press, 1967.

26. Hyman, Ronald T., ed. *Teaching: Vantage Points for Study*. Philadelphia: J. B. Lippincott, 1968.

27. Kohl, Herbert. *36 Children*. New York: Signet Books, 1967.

28. Komisar, B. Paul. "More on the Concept of Learning." In *Psychological Concepts in Education*, edited by B. Paul Komisar and C. B. J. Macmillan, pp. 211–223. Chicago: Rand McNally, 1967.

29. Komisar, B. Paul. "The Non-Science of Learning." *School Review* 74:249–264, Autumn 1966.

30. Langer, Susanne K. *Philosophy in a New Key*. New York: Mentor, 1942.

31. Lewis, Wilbert W. "Selected Concepts of Communication

as a Basis for Studying Mental Health in the Classroom." *Journal of Communication* 11:157–162, September 1961. Reprinted in *Teaching: Vantage Points for Study*, edited by Ronald T. Hyman (Philadelphia: J. B. Lippincott, 1968), pp. 43–48.

32. Lewis, W. W., John M. Newell, and John Withall. "An Analysis of Classroom Patterns of Communication." *Psychological Report* 9:211–219, October 1961. Reprinted in *Teaching: Vantage Points for Study*, edited by Ronald T. Hyman (Philadelphia: J. B. Lippincott, 1968), pp. 48–58.

33. Lindeman, Richard H. *Educational Measurement.* Glenview, Ill.: Scott, Foresman, 1967.

34. Medley, Donald M., and Harold E. Mitzel. "Measuring Classroom Behavior by Systematic Observation." In *Handbook of Research on Teaching*, edited by N. L. Gage, pp. 247–328. Chicago: Rand McNally, 1963.

35. Rabinowitz, W., and R. M. W. Travers. "Problems of Defining and Assessing Teacher Effectiveness." *Educational Theory* 3:212–219, July 1953.

36. Rose, Gale W. "Performance Evaluation and Growth in Teaching." *Phi Delta Kappan* 45:48–53, October 1963.

37. Schwab, Joseph J. "Structure of the Disciplines: Meanings and Significances." In *The Structure of Knowledge and the Curriculum*, edited by G. W. Ford and Lawrence Pugno, pp. 6–30. Chicago: Rand McNally, 1964.

38. Scriven, Michael. "The Methodology of Evaluation." In *Perspectives of Curriculum Evaluation*, essays by Ralph W. Tyler, Robert M. Gagne, and Michael Scriven, pp. 39–83. Chicago: Rand McNally, 1967.

39. Simon, Anita, and E. Gil Boyer, eds. *Mirrors for Behavior.* 6 vols. Philadelphia: Research for Better Schools, Inc., 1968.

40. Stake, Robert E. "The Countenance of Educational Evaluation." *Teachers College Record* 68:523–540, April 1967.

41. Wilhelms, Fred T. "Evaluation as Feedback." In *Evaluation as Feedback and Guide*, 1967 Yearbook of the Association for Supervision and Curriculum Development, edited by Fred T. Wilhelms, pp. 2–17. Washington, D.C.: Association for Supervision and Curriculum Development, 1967.

42. Withall, John. "Mental Health—Teacher Education Research Project." *Journal of Teacher Education* 14:318–325, September 1963.

Index

Printer and Binder: R. R. Donnelley & Sons Company
82 83 84 10 9 8 7